**Publisher:** José A. Blanco

**President:** Janet Dracksdorf

**Vice President, Editorial Director:** Amy Baron

**Senior National Language Consultant:** Norah Lulich Jones

**Executive Editor:** Sharla Zwirek

**Editorial Development:** Diego García, Erica Solari

**Project Management:** Maria Rosa Alcaraz, Sharon Inglis, Adriana Lavergne, Elvira Ortiz

**Technology Editorial:** Lauren Krolick, Paola Ríos Schaaf

**Design and Production Director:** Marta Kimball

**Senior Creative Designer, Print & Web/Interactive:** Susan Prentiss

**Production Manager:** Oscar Díez

**Design and Production Team:** Liliana Bobadilla, María Eugenia Castaño, Michelle Groper, Mauricio Henao, Andrés Vanegas, Nick Ventullo

Printed in Canada.

DESCUBRE Level 1B Student Edition ISBN: 978-1-61857-202-8

Library of Congress Control Number: 2012945953

2 3 4 5 6 7 8 9   TC   17 16 15 14 13

# DESCUBRE | 1B

## Lengua y cultura del mundo hispánico

**SECOND EDITION**

# Table of Contents

## hola, ¿qué tal?

## en la clase

### Lección preliminar

## contextos

## fotonovela

### Lección 5
### Las vacaciones

### Lección 6
### ¡De compras!

## cultura

## la familia

## los pasatiempos

## cultura

## estructura

## adelante

# Table of Contents

| | contextos | fotonovela |
|---|---|---|
| **Lección 7**<br>**La rutina diaria**<br> | Daily routine . . . . . . . . . . . . . 226<br>Personal hygiene . . . . . . . . . 226<br>Time expressions . . . . . . . . . 226 | **¡Necesito arreglarme!** . . . . . . 230<br>**Pronunciación**<br>The consonant **r** . . . . . . . . . 233 |
| **Lección 8**<br>**La comida**<br> | Food . . . . . . . . . . . . . . . . . . . 262<br>Food descriptions . . . . . . . . . 262<br>Meals . . . . . . . . . . . . . . . . . . 264 | **Una cena... romántica** . . . . . . 268<br>**Pronunciación**<br>**ll, ñ, c,** and **z** . . . . . . . . . . . 271 |
| **Lección 9**<br>**Las fiestas**<br> | Parties and celebrations . . . . 300<br>Personal relationships. . . . . . 301<br>Stages of life . . . . . . . . . . . . 302 | **El Día de Muertos** . . . . . . . . . 304<br>**Pronunciación**<br>**h, j,** and **g** . . . . . . . . . . . . . . 307 |

## Consulta

| cultura | estructura | adelante |
|---------|------------|----------|

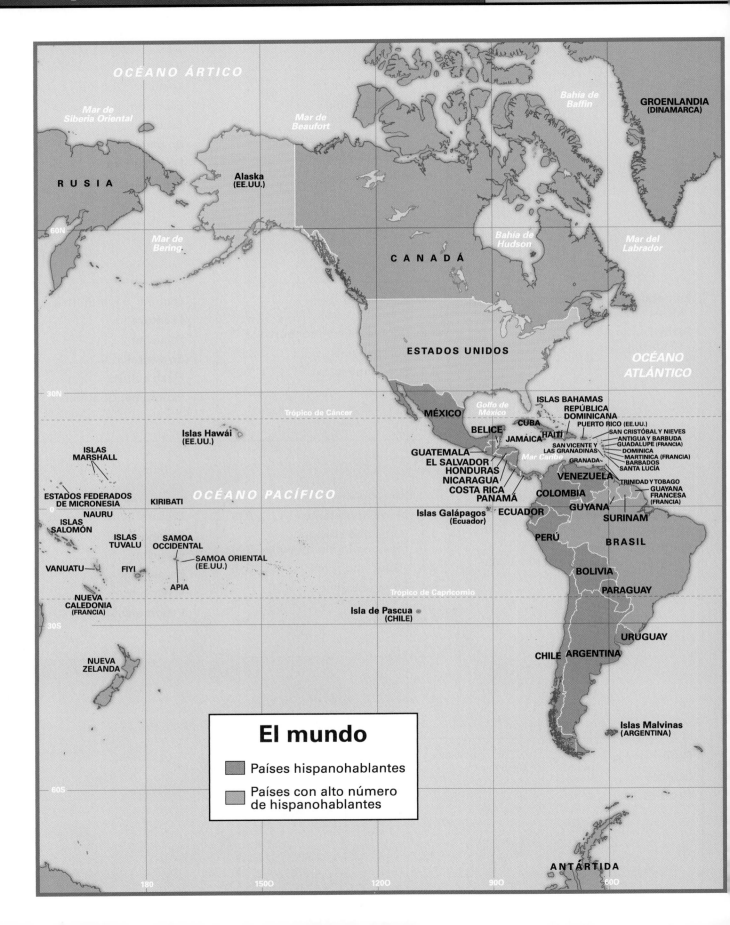

OCÉANO ÁRTICO

Mar de Siberia Oriental

Mar de Beaufort

Bahía de Baffin

GROENLANDIA (DINAMARCA)

RUSIA

Alaska (EE.UU.)

60N

Mar de Bering

Bahía de Hudson

CANADÁ

Mar del Labrador

ESTADOS UNIDOS

OCÉANO ATLÁNTICO

30N

Trópico de Cáncer

MÉXICO

Golfo de México

ISLAS BAHAMAS
REPÚBLICA DOMINICANA
PUERTO RICO (EE.UU.)

Islas Hawái (EE.UU.)

CUBA

BELICE

HAITÍ

ISLAS MARSHALL

GUATEMALA
EL SALVADOR

JAMAICA

SAN CRISTÓBAL Y NIEVES
ANTIGUA Y BARBUDA
GUADALUPE (FRANCIA)
DOMINICA
MARTINICA (FRANCIA)
BARBADOS
SANTA LUCÍA

SAN VICENTE Y LAS GRANADINAS

GRANADA

ESTADOS FEDERADOS DE MICRONESIA

OCÉANO PACÍFICO

HONDURAS
NICARAGUA
COSTA RICA
PANAMÁ

Mar Caribe

VENEZUELA

TRINIDAD Y TOBAGO
GUAYANA FRANCESA (FRANCIA)

KIRIBATI

COLOMBIA

0

NAURU

ECUADOR

GUYANA

ISLAS SALOMÓN

Islas Galápagos (Ecuador)

SURINAM

ISLAS TUVALU

SAMOA OCCIDENTAL

PERÚ

BRASIL

VANUATU

FIYI

SAMOA ORIENTAL (EE.UU.)

BOLIVIA

APIA

Trópico de Capricornio

PARAGUAY

NUEVA CALEDONIA (FRANCIA)

Isla de Pascua (CHILE)

30S

URUGUAY

NUEVA ZELANDA

CHILE ARGENTINA

Islas Malvinas (ARGENTINA)

## El mundo

Países hispanohablantes

Países con alto número de hispanohablantes

60S

ANTÁRTIDA

180  150O  120O  90O  60O

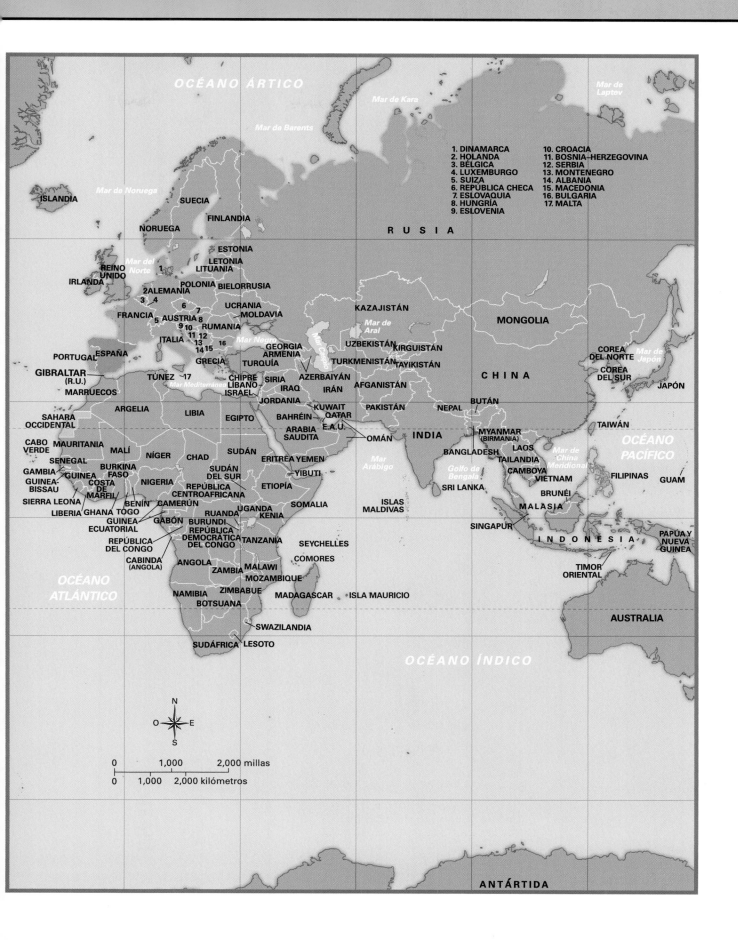

OCÉANO ÁRTICO

Mar de Kara

Mar de Laptev

Mar de Barents

1. DINAMARCA        10. CROACIA
2. HOLANDA          11. BOSNIA–HERZEGOVINA
3. BÉLGICA          12. SERBIA
4. LUXEMBURGO       13. MONTENEGRO
5. SUIZA            14. ALBANIA
6. REPÚBLICA CHECA  15. MACEDONIA
7. ESLOVAQUIA       16. BULGARIA
8. HUNGRÍA          17. MALTA
9. ESLOVENIA

Mar de Noruega

ISLANDIA

SUECIA

FINLANDIA

NORUEGA

RUSIA

ESTONIA
Mar del Norte    LETONIA
REINO           LITUANIA
UNIDO    1
IRLANDA         POLONIA    BIELORRUSIA
        2 ALEMANIA
    3  4
        6    7    UCRANIA
FRANCIA  5 AUSTRIA  8    MOLDAVIA
    9 10  RUMANIA
ITALIA   11 12
        13  15   16    Mar Negro
        14        GEORGIA    Mar Caspio
PORTUGAL  ESPAÑA        ARMENIA
        GRECIA  TURQUÍA
GIBRALTAR            CHIPRE  SIRIA  AZERBAIYÁN
(R.U.)   TÚNEZ  17        LÍBANO    IRÁN
        Mar Mediterráneo  ISRAEL  IRAK
MARRUECOS                JORDANIA

KAZAJISTÁN

Mar de Aral

MONGOLIA

UZBEKISTÁN    KIRGUISTÁN
TURKMENISTÁN   TAYIKISTÁN

COREA DEL NORTE    Mar de Japón
CHINA            COREA DEL SUR
                JAPÓN

AFGANISTÁN

ARGELIA    LIBIA    EGIPTO    KUWAIT  QATAR    PAKISTÁN    NEPAL    BUTÁN
SAHARA                        BAHRÉIN            TAIWÁN
OCCIDENTAL                    E.A.U.
                ARABIA    OMÁN    INDIA    MYANMAR
CABO   MAURITANIA   MALÍ   NÍGER   CHAD   SUDÁN   SAUDITA            (BIRMANIA)    OCÉANO
VERDE                                        BANGLADESH   LAOS    PACÍFICO
SENEGAL                    ERITREA  YEMEN                TAILANDIA  Mar de China
GAMBIA   BURKINA          SUDÁN            Mar Arábigo   Golfo de   CAMBOYA  Meridional
GUINEA   FASO            DEL SUR   YIBUTI            Bengala            FILIPINAS   GUAM
GUINEA-  COSTA   NIGERIA   REPÚBLICA  ETIOPÍA        SRI LANKA   VIETNAM
BISSAU   DE                CENTROAFRICANA                    BRUNÉI
SIERRA LEONA  MARFIL              SOMALIA    ISLAS
LIBERIA  GHANA  TOGO  CAMERÚN   UGANDA            MALDIVAS       MALASIA
GUINEA              RUANDA  KENIA
ECUATORIAL   GABÓN  BURUNDI                            SINGAPUR
REPÚBLICA    REPÚBLICA                                    INDONESIA
DEL CONGO    DEMOCRÁTICA  TANZANIA    SEYCHELLES                PAPÚA Y
CABINDA      DEL CONGO                                        NUEVA
(ANGOLA)                COMORES                            GUINEA
        ANGOLA                                        TIMOR
            ZAMBIA   MALAWI                            ORIENTAL
OCÉANO              MOZAMBIQUE
ATLÁNTICO   NAMIBIA   ZIMBABUE                AUSTRALIA
        BOTSUANA    MADAGASCAR   ISLA MAURICIO

SWAZILANDIA

SUDÁFRICA  LESOTO

OCÉANO ÍNDICO

N
O    E
S

0        1,000        2,000 millas
0    1,000    2,000 kilómetros

ANTÁRTIDA

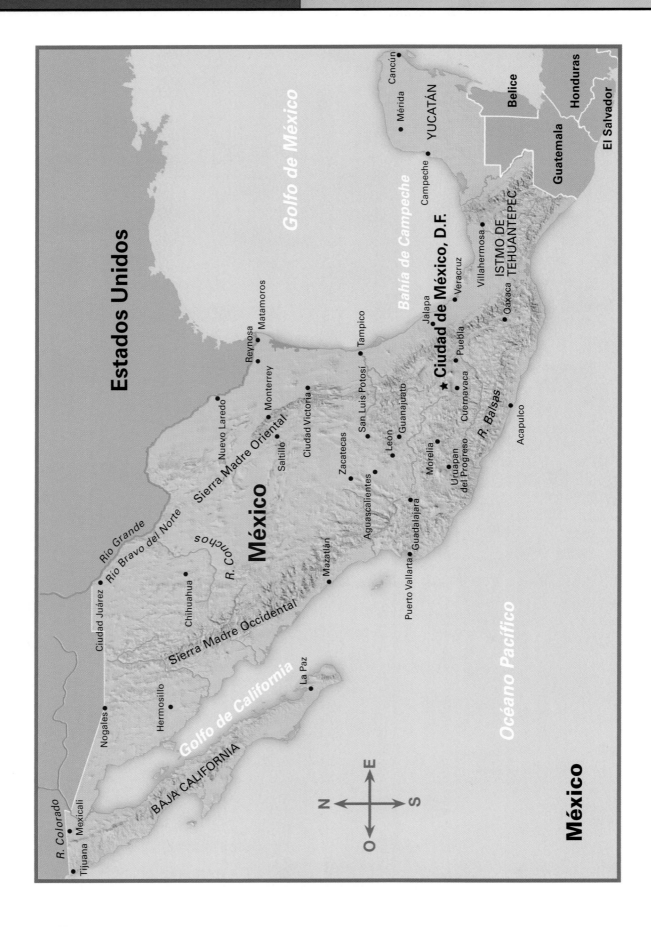

**México**

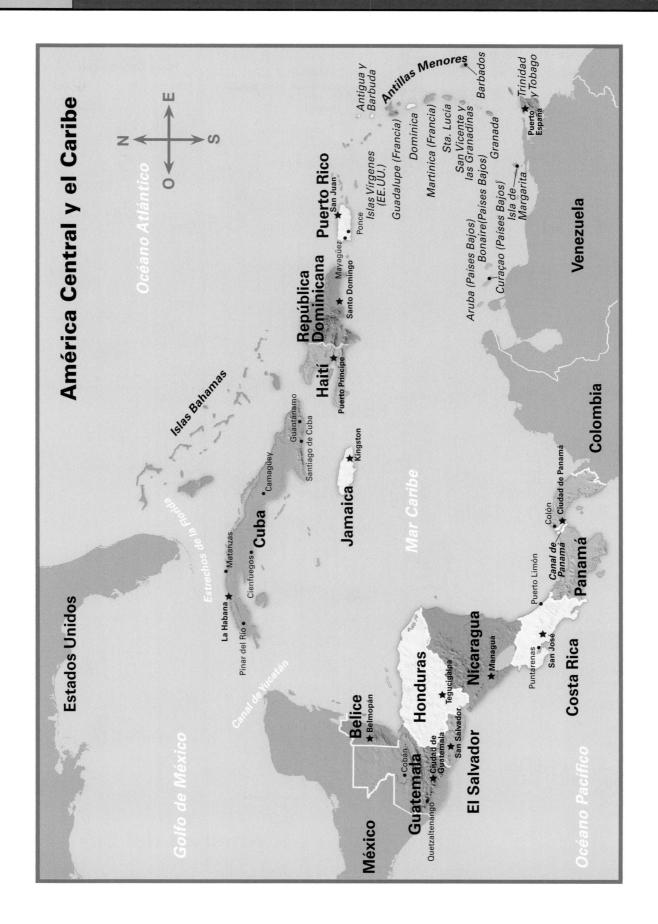

## América Central y el Caribe

N
E
S
O

Océano Atlántico

Estados Unidos

Golfo de México

Islas Bahamas

Estrechos de la Florida

Canal de Yucatán

La Habana
Matanzas
Pinar del Río
Cienfuegos
Cuba
Camagüey
Santiago de Cuba
Guantánamo

Jamaica
Kingston

Mar Caribe

Haití
Puerto Príncipe

República Dominicana
Santo Domingo
Mayagüez

Puerto Rico
San Juan
Ponce

Islas Vírgenes (EE.UU.)

Antigua y Barbuda

Antillas Menores

Guadalupe (Francia)

Dominica

Martinica (Francia)

Sta. Lucía

San Vicente y las Granadinas

Barbados

Granada

Trinidad y Tobago
Puerto España

Aruba (Países Bajos)
Bonaire (Países Bajos)
Curaçao (Países Bajos)
Isla de Margarita

Venezuela

Colombia

México
Belice
Belmopán
Cobán
Guatemala
Ciudad de Guatemala
Quetzaltenango
El Salvador
San Salvador
Honduras
Tegucigalpa
Nicaragua
Managua
Costa Rica
Puntarenas
San José
Panamá
Puerto Limón
Colón
Ciudad de Panamá
Canal de Panamá

Océano Pacífico

**Mar Caribe**

Barranquilla
Maracaibo
Caracas
Puerto España
**Trinidad y Tobago**

**Venezuela**

Medellín
**Colombia**
Bogotá
Cali

Georgetown
**Guyana**
Paramaribo
**Surinam**
Cayena
**Guayana Francesa**

*R. Orinoco*

Pasto
**Ecuador**
Quito
Guayaquil

*R. Negro*
*R. Amazonas*
Belém
Manaus

Iquitos
**Perú**

*R. Madeira*

Recife

Lima
Cuzco
*Lago Titicaca*
Arequipa
La Paz
**Bolivia**
Sucre

**Brasil**
Brasilia

Salvador

*Océano Pacífico*

Arica
Iquique

Antofagasta

*R. Paraguay*
*R. Paraná*

Belo Horizonte
São Paulo
Rio de Janeiro
Santos

**Paraguay**
Asunción

**Chile**

Salta

Córdoba
Mendoza
Valparaíso
Santiago

*R. Paraná*
*R. Uruguay*
Pôrto Alegre

Rosario
Buenos Aires
**Uruguay**
Montevideo

*Océano Atlántico*

**Argentina**
Concepción
Bahía Blanca

*Cordillera de los Andes*

Puerto Montt

N
O — E
S

*Estrecho de Magallanes*
Punta Arenas
*Islas Malvinas*

*Tierra del Fuego*

**América del Sur**

**Islas Galápagos**

*Océano Pacífico*

Isla Pinta
Isla Marchena
Isla Genovesa
Isla Isabela
*Línea ecuatorial*
Volcán Darwin
Isla Santiago (San Salvador)
Isla Fernandina
Puerto Ayora
Isla San Cristóbal
Isla Santa Cruz
Santo Tomás
Puerto Baquerizo Moreno
Isla Santa María
Isla Española

*Cordillera de los Andes*

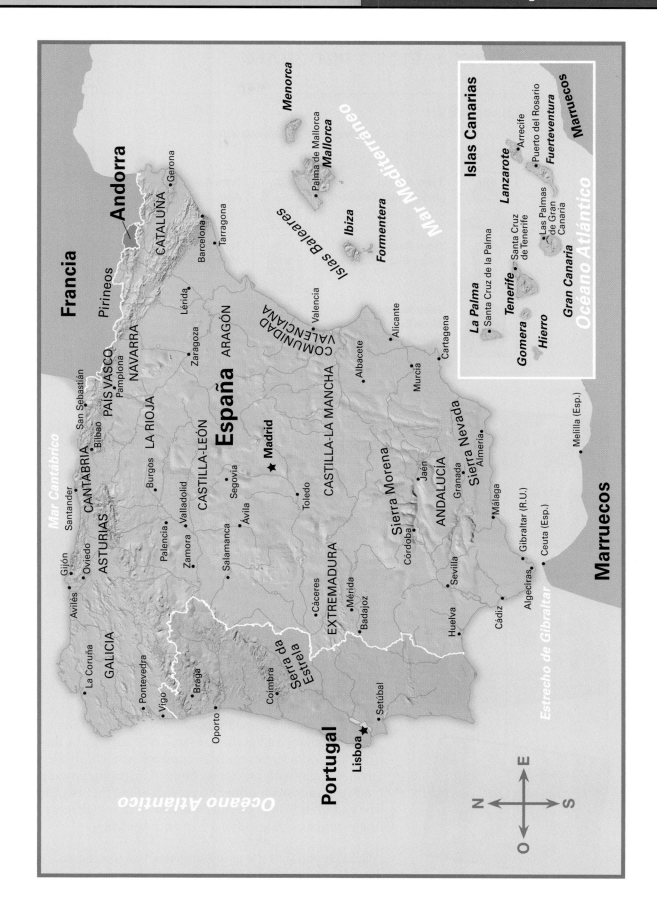

Francia

Andorra

CATALUÑA

Pirineos

Gerona

Tarragona

Barcelona

Lérida

Zaragoza

ARAGÓN

NAVARRA

Pamplona

San Sebastián

PAÍS VASCO

Bilbao

LA RIOJA

Burgos

CASTILLA-LEÓN

Valladolid

Palencia

Zamora

Salamanca

Segovia

Ávila

Toledo

España

★ Madrid

CASTILLA-LA MANCHA

COMUNIDAD VALENCIANA

Valencia

Albacete

Alicante

Murcia

Cartagena

Sierra Morena

Córdoba

Jaén

ANDALUCÍA

Granada

Sierra Nevada

Almería

Málaga

Sevilla

Huelva

Cádiz

Algeciras

Gibraltar (R.U.)

Ceuta (Esp.)

Estrecho de Gibraltar

EXTREMADURA

Cáceres

Mérida

Badajoz

Serra da Estrela

Coimbra

Braga

Oporto

Vigo

Pontevedra

GALICIA

La Coruña

Gijón

Aviles

Oviedo

ASTURIAS

Santander

CANTABRIA

Mar Cantábrico

Océano Atlántico

Portugal

Lisboa ★

Setúbal

Marruecos

Melilla (Esp.)

Menorca

Palma de Mallorca

Mallorca

Islas Baleares

Ibiza

Formentera

Mar Mediterráneo

Islas Canarias

Marruecos

Lanzarote

Arrecife

Puerto del Rosario

Fuerteventura

La Palma

Santa Cruz de la Palma

Tenerife

Santa Cruz de Tenerife

Las Palmas de Gran Canaria

Gran Canaria

Gomera

Hierro

Océano Atlántico

N    E
O    S

## *FOTONOVELA* VIDEO PROGRAM

### The cast NEW!

Here are the main characters you will meet in the **Fotonovela** Video:

 From Mexico,
**Jimena Díaz Velázquez**

 From Argentina,
**Juan Carlos Rossi**

 From Mexico,
**Felipe Díaz Velázquez**

 From the U.S.,
**Marissa Wagner**

 From Mexico,
**María Eugenia (Maru) Castaño Ricaurte**

 From Spain,
**Miguel Ángel Lagasca Martínez**

Brand-new and fully integrated with your text, the **DESCUBRE 2/e Fotonovela** Video is a dynamic and contemporary window into the Spanish language. The new video centers around the Díaz family, whose household includes two college-aged children and a visiting student from the U.S. Over the course of an academic year, Jimena, Felipe, Marissa, and their friends explore **el D.F.** and other parts of Mexico as they make plans for their futures. Their adventures take them through some of the greatest natural and cultural treasures of the Spanish-speaking world, as well as the highs and lows of everyday life.

The **Fotonovela** section in each textbook lesson is actually an abbreviated version of the dramatic episode featured in the video. Therefore, each **Fotonovela** section can be done before you see the corresponding video episode, after it, or as a section that stands alone.

In each dramatic segment, the characters interact using the vocabulary and grammar you are studying. As the storyline unfolds, the episodes combine new vocabulary and grammar with previously taught language, exposing you to a variety of authentic accents along the way. At the end of each episode, the **Resumen** section highlights the grammar and vocabulary you are studying.

We hope you find the new **Fotonovela** Video to be an engaging and useful tool for learning Spanish!

## *EN PANTALLA*
## VIDEO PROGRAM

The **DESCUBRE** Supersite features an authentic video clip for each lesson. Clip formats include commercials and newscasts. These clips, many **NEW!** to the Second Edition, have been carefully chosen to be comprehensible for students learning Spanish, and are accompanied by activities and vocabulary lists to facilitate understanding. More importantly, though, these clips are a fun and motivating way to improve your Spanish!

Here are the countries represented in each lesson in **En pantalla:**

Lesson 5 Mexico

Lesson 6 Spain

Lesson 7 Argentina

Lesson 8 Colombia

Lesson 9 Chile

## *FLASH CULTURA*
## VIDEO PROGRAM

In the dynamic **Flash cultura** Video, young people from all over the Spanish-speaking world share aspects of life in their countries with you. The similarities and differences among Spanish-speaking countries that come up through their adventures will challenge you to think about your own cultural practices and values. The segments provide valuable cultural insights as well as linguistic input; the episodes will introduce you to a variety of accents and vocabulary as they gradually move into Spanish.

## *PANORAMA CULTURAL*
## VIDEO PROGRAM

The **Panorama cultural** Video is integrated with the **Panorama** section in each lesson. Each segment is 2–3 minutes long and consists of documentary footage from each of the countries featured. The images were specially chosen for interest level and visual appeal, while the all-Spanish narrations were carefully written to reflect the vocabulary and grammar covered in the textbook.

Each section of your textbook comes with resources and activities on the DESCUBRE Supersite. You can access them from any computer with an Internet connection. Visit vhlcentral.com to get started.

**Audio: Vocabulary Tutorials, Games**

### CONTEXTOS

Listen to audio of the **Vocabulary**, watch dynamic **Presentations** and **Tutorials**, and practice using Flashcards, **Games**, and activities that give you immediate feedback.

**Video: *Fotonovela* Record and Compare**

### FOTONOVELA

Travel with Marissa to Mexico and meet her host family. Watch the **Video** again at home to see the characters use the vocabulary in a real context.

**Audio: Explanation Record and Compare**

### PRONUNCIACIÓN

Improve your accent by listening to native speakers, then **recording** your voice and **comparing** it to the samples provided.

**Reading, Additional Reading**

### CULTURA

Explore cultural topics through the *Conexión Internet* activity or **reading** the *Más cultura* selection.

**Explanation Tutorial**

### ESTRUCTURA

Review the **Explanation** or watch an animated **Tutorial**, and then play the games to make sure you got it.

**Audio: Synched Reading Additional Reading**

**Video: TV Clip**

**Video: *Flash cultura***

**Interactive Map Video: *Panorama cultural***

### ADELANTE

Listen along with the **Audio-Synched Reading**. Watch the *En pantalla*, *Flash cultura*, and *Panorama cultural* **Videos** again outside of class so that you can pause and repeat to really understand what you hear. Use the **Interactive Map** to explore the places you might want to visit. There's lots of additional practice, including Internet searches and auto-graded activities.

**Audio: Vocabulary Flashcards**

**Diagnostics Remediation Activities**

### VOCABULARIO - RECAPITULACIÓN

Just what you need to get ready for the test! Review the **vocabulary** with **audio**. Complete the Diagnostic *Recapitulación* to see what you might still need to study. Get additional **Remediation Activities**.

# Icons

Familiarize yourself with these icons that appear throughout **DESCUBRE**.

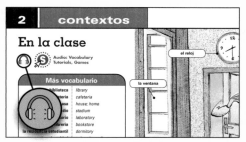

### Listening

The Listening icon indicates that audio is available. You will see it in the lesson's **Contextos**, **Pronunciación**, **Escuchar**, and **Vocabulario** sections, as well as with all activities that require audio.

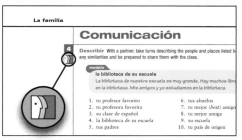

### Pair/Group Activities

Two faces indicate a pair activity, and three indicate a group activity.

### Handout

The activities marked with this icon require handouts that your teacher will give you to help you complete the activity.

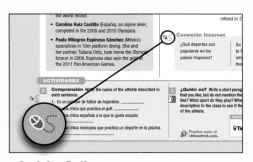

### Activity Online

The mouse icon indicates when an activity is also available on the Supersite.

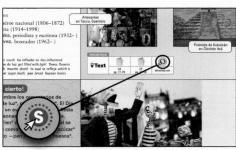

### Supersite

Additional practice on the Supersite, not included in the textbook, is indicated with this icon.

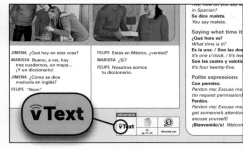

### vText

Material is also available in the interactive online textbook.

# Recursos

**Recursos** boxes let you know exactly which print and technology ancillaries you can use to reinforce and expand on every section of the lessons in your textbook. They even include page numbers when applicable.

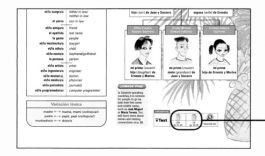

**Cuaderno de práctica y actividades comunicativas**

CPA
pp. 61–63

**Cuaderno para hispanohablantes**

CH
pp. 33–34

# The Spanish-Speaking World

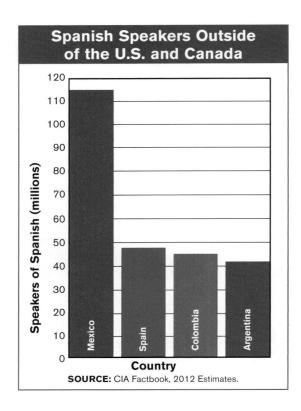

### Spanish Speakers Outside of the U.S. and Canada

Speakers of Spanish (millions)

120
110
100
90
80
70
60
50
40
30
20
10
0

Mexico • Spain • Colombia • Argentina

**Country**

**SOURCE:** CIA Factbook, 2012 Estimates.

Do you know someone whose first language is Spanish? Chances are you do! More than approximately forty million people living in the U.S. speak Spanish; after English, it is the second most commonly spoken language in this country. It is the official language of twenty-two countries and an official language of the European Union and United Nations.

## The Growth of Spanish

Have you ever heard of a language called Castilian? It's Spanish! The Spanish language as we know it today has its origins in a dialect called Castilian (**castellano** in Spanish). Castilian developed in the 9th century in north-central Spain, in a historic provincial region known as Old Castile. Castilian gradually spread towards the central region of New Castile, where it was adopted as the main language of commerce. By the 16th century, Spanish had become the official language of Spain and eventually, the country's role in exploration, colonization, and overseas trade led to its spread across Central and South America, North America, the Caribbean, parts of North Africa, the Canary Islands, and the Philippines.

## Spanish in the United States

## 1500    1600    1700

**16th Century**
Spanish is the official language of Spain.

**1565**
The Spanish arrive in Florida and found St. Augustine.

PEDRO MENENDEZ DE AVILES.

**1610**
The Spanish found Santa Fe, today's capital of New Mexico, the state with the most Spanish speakers in the U.S.

# Spanish in the United States

Spanish came to North America in the 16th century with the Spanish who settled in St. Augustine, Florida. Spanish-speaking communities flourished in several parts of the continent over the next few centuries. Then, in 1848, in the aftermath of the Mexican-American War, Mexico lost almost half its land to the United States, including portions of modern-day Texas, New Mexico, Arizona, Colorado, California, Wyoming, Nevada, and Utah. Overnight, hundreds of thousands of Mexicans became citizens of the United States, bringing with them their rich history, language, and traditions.

This heritage, combined with that of the other Hispanic populations that have immigrated to the United States over the years, has led to the remarkable growth of Spanish around the country. After English, it is the most commonly spoken language in 43 states. More than 12 million people in California alone claim Spanish as their first or "home" language.

You've made a popular choice by choosing to take Spanish in school. Not only is Spanish found and heard almost everywhere in the United States, but it is the most commonly taught foreign language in classrooms throughout the country! Have you heard people speaking Spanish in your community? Chances are that you've come across an advertisement, menu, or magazine that is in Spanish. If you look around, you'll find that Spanish can be found in some pretty common places. For example, most ATMs respond to users in both English and Spanish. News agencies and television stations such as CNN and **Telemundo** provide Spanish-language broadcasts. When you listen to the radio or download music from the Internet, some of the most popular choices are Latino artists who perform in Spanish. Federal government agencies such as the Internal Revenue Service and the Department of State provide services in both languages. Even the White House has an official Spanish-language webpage! Learning Spanish can create opportunities within your everyday life.

## 1800 — 1900 — 2010

**1848**
Mexicans who choose to stay in the U.S. after the Mexican-American War become U.S. citizens.

**1959**
After the Cuban Revolution, thousands of Cubans emigrate to the U.S.

**2010**
Spanish is the 2nd most commonly spoken language in the U.S., with more than approximately 40 million speakers.

# Why Study Spanish?

## Learn an International Language

There are many reasons to learn Spanish, a language that has spread to many parts of the world and has along the way embraced words and sounds of languages as diverse as Latin, Arabic, and Nahuatl. Spanish has evolved from a medieval dialect of north-central Spain into the fourth most commonly spoken language in the world. It is the second language of choice among the majority of people in North America.

## Understand the World Around You

Knowing Spanish can also open doors to communities within the United States, and it can broaden your understanding of the nation's history and geography. The very names Colorado, Montana, Nevada, and Florida are Spanish in origin. Just knowing their meanings can give you some insight into, of all things, the landscapes for which the states are renowned. Colorado means "colored red;" Montana means "mountain;" Nevada is derived from "snow-capped mountain;" and Florida means "flowered." You've already been speaking Spanish whenever you talk about some of these states!

| State Name | Meaning in Spanish |
|:---:|:---:|
| Colorado | "colored red" |
| Florida | "flowered" |
| Montana | "mountain" |
| Nevada | "snow-capped mountain" |

## Connect with the World

Learning Spanish can change how you view the world. While you learn Spanish, you will also explore and learn about the origins, customs, art, music, and literature of people in close to two dozen countries. When you travel to a Spanish-speaking country, you'll be able to converse freely with the people you meet. And whether in the U.S., Canada, or abroad, you'll find that speaking to people in their native language is the best way to bridge any culture gap.

# Why Study Spanish?

## Expand Your Skills

Studying a foreign language can improve your ability to analyze and interpret information and help you succeed in many other subject areas. When you first begin learning Spanish, your studies will focus mainly on reading, writing, grammar, listening, and speaking skills. You'll be amazed at how the skills involved with learning how a language works can help you succeed in other areas of study. Many people who study a foreign language claim that they gained a better understanding of English. Spanish can even help you understand the origins of many English words and expand your own vocabulary in English. Knowing Spanish can also help you pick up other related languages, such as Italian, Portuguese, and French. Spanish can really open doors for learning many other skills in your school career.

## Explore Your Future

How many of you are already planning your future careers? Employers in today's global economy look for workers who know different languages and understand other cultures. Your knowledge of Spanish will make you a valuable candidate for careers abroad as well as in the United States or Canada. Doctors, nurses, social workers, hotel managers, journalists, businessmen, pilots, flight attendants, and many other professionals need to know Spanish or another foreign language to do their jobs well.

# How to Learn Spanish

## Start with the Basics

As with anything you want to learn, start with the basics and remember that learning takes time! The basics are vocabulary, grammar, and culture.

**Vocabulary** Every new word you learn in Spanish will expand your vocabulary and ability to communicate. The more words you know, the better you can express yourself. Focus on sounds and think about ways to remember words. Use your knowledge of English and other languages to figure out the meaning of and memorize words like **conversación, teléfono, oficina, clase,** and **música**.

**Grammar** Grammar helps you put your new vocabulary together. By learning the rules of grammar, you can use new words correctly and speak in complete sentences. As you learn verbs and tenses, you will be able to speak about the past, present, or future, express yourself with clarity, and be able to persuade others with your opinions. Pay attention to structures and use your knowledge of English grammar to make connections with Spanish grammar.

**Culture** Culture provides you with a framework for what you may say or do. As you learn about the culture of Spanish-speaking communities, you'll improve your knowledge of Spanish. Think about a word like **salsa**, and how it connects to both food and music. Think about and explore customs observed on **Nochevieja** (New Year's Eve) or at a **fiesta de quince años** (a girl's fifteenth birthday party). Watch people greet each other or say good-bye. Listen for idioms and sayings that capture the spirit of what you want to communicate!

Teenagers celebrating at a **fiesta de quince años.**

# Listen, Speak, Read, and Write

**Listening** Listen for sounds and for words you can recognize. Listen for inflections and watch for key words that signal a question such as **cómo** (*how*), **dónde** (*where*), or **qué** (*what*). Get used to the sound of Spanish. Play Spanish pop songs or watch Spanish movies. Borrow books on CD from your local library, or try to visit places in your community where Spanish is spoken. Don't worry if you don't understand every single word. If you focus on key words and phrases, you'll get the main idea. The more you listen, the more you'll understand!

**Speaking** Practice speaking Spanish as often as you can. As you talk, work on your pronunciation, and read aloud texts so that words and sentences flow more easily. Don't worry if you don't sound like a native speaker, or if you make some mistakes. Time and practice will help you get there. Participate actively in Spanish class. Try to speak Spanish with classmates, especially native speakers (if you know any), as often as you can.

**Reading** Pick up a Spanish-language newspaper or a pamphlet on your way to school, read the lyrics of a song as you listen to it, or read books you've already read in English translated into Spanish. Use reading strategies that you know to understand the meaning of a text that looks unfamiliar. Look for cognates, or words that are related in English and Spanish, to guess the meaning of some words. Read as often as you can, and remember to read for fun!

**Writing** It's easy to write in Spanish if you put your mind to it. And remember that Spanish spelling is phonetic, which means that once you learn the basic rules of how letters and sounds are related, you can probably become an expert speller in Spanish! Write for fun—make up poems or songs, write e-mails or instant messages to friends, or start a journal or blog in Spanish.

# Tips for Learning Spanish

- **Listen** to Spanish radio shows. Write down words that you can't recognize or don't know and look up the meaning.

- **Watch** Spanish TV shows or movies. Read subtitles to help you grasp the content.

- **Read** Spanish-language newspapers, magazines, or blogs.

- **Listen** to Spanish songs that you like —anything from Shakira to a traditional mariachi melody. Sing along and concentrate on your pronunciation.

- **Seek** out Spanish speakers. Look for neighborhoods, markets, or cultural centers where Spanish might be spoken in your community. Greet people, ask for directions, or order from a menu at a Mexican restaurant in Spanish.

- **Pursue** language exchange opportunities (**intercambio cultural**) in your school or community. Try to join language clubs or cultural societies, and explore opportunities for studying abroad or hosting a student from a Spanish-speaking country in your home or school.

- **Connect** your learning to everyday experiences. Think about naming the ingredients of your favorite dish in Spanish. Think about the origins of Spanish place names in the U.S., like Cape Canaveral and Sacramento, or of common English words like *adobe, chocolate, mustang, tornado,* and *patio*.

- **Use** mnemonics, or a memorizing device, to help you remember words. Make up a saying in English to remember the order of the days of the week in Spanish (L, M, M, J, V, S, D).

- **Visualize** words. Try to associate words with images to help you remember meanings. For example, think of a **paella** as you learn the names of different types of seafood or meat. Imagine a national park and create mental pictures of the landscape as you learn names of animals, plants, and habitats.

- **Enjoy** yourself! Try to have as much fun as you can learning Spanish. Take your knowledge beyond the classroom and find ways to make the learning experience your very own.

# Useful Spanish Expressions

The following expressions will be very useful in getting you started learning Spanish. You can use them in class to check your understanding or to ask and answer questions about the lessons. Read **En las instrucciones** ahead of time to help you understand direction lines in Spanish, as well as your teacher's instructions. Remember to practice your Spanish as often as you can!

## Expresiones útiles  *Useful expressions*

| | |
|---|---|
| ¿Cómo se dice _____ en español? | How do you say _____ in Spanish? |
| ¿Cómo se escribe _____? | How do you spell _____? |
| ¿Comprende(n)? | Do you understand? |
| Con permiso. | Excuse me. |
| De acuerdo. | Okay. |
| De nada. | You're welcome. |
| ¿De veras? | Really? |
| ¿En qué página estamos? | What page are we on? |
| Enseguida. | Right away. |
| Más despacio, por favor. | Slower, please. |
| Muchas gracias. | Thanks a lot. |
| No entiendo. | I don't understand. |
| No sé. | I don't know. |
| Perdone. | Excuse me. |
| Pista | Clue |
| Por favor. | Please. |
| Por supuesto. | Of course. |
| ¿Qué significa _____? | What does _____ mean? |
| Repite, por favor. | Please repeat. |
| Tengo una pregunta. | I have a question. |
| ¿Tiene(n) alguna pregunta? | Do you have questions? |
| Vaya(n) a la página dos. | Go to page 2. |

## En las instrucciones  *In direction lines*

| | |
|---|---|
| Cierto o falso | True or false |
| Completa las oraciones de una manera lógica. | Complete the sentences logically. |
| Con un(a) compañero/a... | With a classmate... |
| Contesta las preguntas. | Answer the questions. |
| Corrige la información falsa. | Correct the false information. |
| Di/Digan... | Say... |
| En grupos... | In groups... |
| En parejas... | In pairs... |
| Entrevista... | Interview... |
| Forma oraciones completas. | Create/Make complete sentences. |
| Háganse preguntas. | Ask each other questions. |
| Haz el papel de... | Play the role of... |
| Haz los cambios necesarios. | Make the necessary changes. |
| Indica/Indiquen si las oraciones... | Indicate if the sentences... |
| Lee/Lean en voz alta. | Read aloud. |
| ...que mejor completa... | ...that best completes... |
| Toma nota... | Take note... |
| Tomen apuntes. | Take notes. |
| Túrnense... | Take turns... |

# Common Names

Get started learning Spanish by using a Spanish name in class. You can choose from the lists on these pages, or you can find one yourself. How about learning the Spanish equivalent of your name? The most popular Spanish female names are Ana, Isabel, Elena, Sara, and María. The most popular male names in Spanish are Alejandro, Jorge, Juan, José, and Pedro. Is your name, or that of someone you know, in the Spanish top five?

| Más nombres masculinos | Más nombres femeninos |
| --- | --- |
| Alfonso | Alicia |
| Antonio (Toni) | Beatriz (Bea, Beti, Biata) |
| Carlos | Blanca |
| César | Carolina (Carol) |
| Diego | Claudia |
| Ernesto | Diana |
| Felipe | Emilia |
| Francisco (Paco) | Irene |
| Guillermo | Julia |
| Ignacio (Nacho) | Laura |
| Javier (Javi) | Leonor |
| Leonardo | Lourdes |
| Luis | Lucía |
| Manolo | Margarita (Marga) |
| Marcos | Marta |
| Oscar (Óscar) | Noelia |
| Rafael (Rafa) | Paula |
| Sergio | Rocío |
| Vicente | Verónica |

| Los 5 nombres masculinos más populares | Los 5 nombres femeninos más populares |
| --- | --- |
| Alejandro | Ana |
| Jorge | Elena |
| José (Pepe) | Isabel |
| Juan | María |
| Pedro | Sara |

# Acknowledgments

On behalf of its authors and editors, Vista Higher Learning expresses its sincere appreciation to the many instructors and teachers across the U.S. and Canada who contributed their ideas and suggestions. Their insights and detailed comments were invaluable to us as we created **DESCUBRE**.

## In-depth reviewers

Patrick Brady
Tidewater Community College, VA

Christine DeGrado
Chestnut Hill College, PA

Martha L. Hughes
Georgia Southern University, GA

Aida Ramos-Sellman
Goucher College, MD

## Reviewers

Kathleen Aguilar
Fort Lewis College, CO

Aleta Anderson
Grand Rapids Community College, MI

Gunnar Anderson
SUNY Potsdam, NY

Nona Anderson
Ouachita Baptist University, AR

Ken Arant
Darton College, GA

Vicki Baggia
Phillips Exeter Academy, NH

Jorge V. Bajo
Oracle Charter School, NY

Ana Basoa-McMillan
Columbia State Community College, TN

Timothy Benson
Lake Superior College, MN

Georgia Betcher
Fayetteville Technical Community College, NC

Teresa Borden
Columbia College, CA

Courtney Bradley
The Principia, MO

Vonna Breeze-Marti
Columbia College, CA

Christa Bucklin
University of Hartford, CT

Mary Cantu
South Texas College, TX

Christa Chatrnuch
University of Hartford, CT

Tina Christodouleas
SUNY Cortland, NY

Edwin Clark
SUNY Potsdam, NY

Donald Clymer
Eastern Mennonite University, VA

Ann Costanzi
Chestnut Hill College, PA

Patricia Crespo-Martin
Foothill College, CA

Miryam Criado
Hanover College, KY

Thomas Curtis
Madison Area Technical College, WI

Patricia S. Davis
Darton College, GA

Danion Doman
Truman State University, MO

Deborah Dubiner
Carnegie Mellon University, PA

Benjamin Earwicker
Northwest Nazarene University, ID

Deborah Edson
Tidewater Community College, VA

Matthew T. Fleming
Grand Rapids Community College, MI

Ruston Ford
Indian Hills Community College, IA

Marianne Franco
Modesto Junior College, CA

Elena García
Muskegon Community College, MI

María D. García
Fayetteville Technical Community College, NC

Lauren Gates
East Mississippi Community College, MS

Marta M. Gómez
Gateway Academy, MO

Danielle Gosselin
Bishop Brady High School, NH

Charlene Grant
Skidmore College, NY

Betsy Hance
Kennesaw State University, GA

Marti Hardy
Laurel School, OH

Dennis Harrod
Syracuse University, NY

Fanning Hearon
Brunswick School, CT

Richard Heath
Kirkwood Community College, IA

Óscar Hernández
South Texas College, TX

Yolanda Hernández
Community College of Southern Nevada, North Las Vegas, NV

Martha L. Hughes
Georgia Southern University, GA

Martha Ince
Cushing Academy, MA

# Acknowledgments

## Reviewers

Stacy Jazan
Glendale Community College, CA

María Jiménez Smith
Tarrant County College, TX

Emory Kinder
Columbia Prep School, NY

Marina Kozanova
Crafton Hills College, CA

Tamara Kunkel
Alice Lloyd College, KY

Anna Major
The Westminster Schools, GA

Armando Maldonado
Morgan Community College, CO

Molly Marostica Smith
Canterbury School of Florida, FL

Jesús G. Martínez
Fresno City College, CA

Laura Martínez
Centralia College, WA

Daniel Millis
Verde Valley School, AZ

Deborah Mistron
Middle Tennessee State
University, TN

Mechteld Mitchin
Village Academy, OH

Anna Montoya
Florida Institute of Technology, FL

Robert P. Moore
Loyola Blakefield Jesuit School, MD

S. Moshir
St. Bernard High School, CA

Javier Muñoz-Basols
Trinity School, NY

William Nichols
Grand Rapids Community College, MI

Bernice Nuhfer-Halten
Southern Polytechnic State
University, GA

Amanda Papanikolas
Drew School, CA

Elizabeth M. Parr
Darton College, GA

Julia E. Patiño
Dillard University, LA

Martha Pérez
Kirkwood Community College, IA

Teresa Pérez-Gamboa
University of Georgia, GA

Marion Perry
The Thacher School, CA

Molly Perry
The Thacher School, CA

Melissa Pytlak
The Canterbury School, CT

Ana F. Sache
Emporia State University, KS

Celia S. Samaniego
Cosumnes River College, CA

Virginia Sánchez-Bernardy
San Diego Mesa College, CA

Frank P. Sanfilippo
Columbia College, CA

Piedad Schor
South Kent School, CT

David Schuettler
The College of St. Scholastica, MN

Romina Self
Ankeny Christian Academy, IA

David A. Short
Indian Hills Community College, IA

Carol Snell-Feikema
South Dakota State University, SD

Matias Stebbings
Columbia Grammar
& Prep School, NY

Mary Studer Shea
Napa Valley College, CA

Cathy Swain
University of Maine, Machias, ME

Cristina Szterensus
Rock Valley College, IL

John Tavernakis
College of San Mateo, CA

David E. Tipton
Circleville Bible College, OH

Larry Thornton
Trinity College School, ON

Linda Tracy
Santa Rosa Junior College, CA

Beverly Turner
Truckee Meadows Community
College, OK

Christine Tyma DeGrado
Chestnut Hill College, PA

Fanny Vera de Viacava
Canterbury School, CT

Luis Viacava
Canterbury School, CT

María Villalobos-Buehner
Grand Valley State University, MI

Hector Villarreal
South Texas College, TX

Juanita Villena-Álvarez
University of South Carolina, Beaufort,
SC

Marcella Anne Wendzikowski
Villa Maria College of Buffalo, NY

Doug West
Sage Hill School, CA

Paula Whittaker
Bishop Brady High School, NH

Mary Zold-Herrera
Glenbrook North High School, IL

## About the Authors

**José A. Blanco** founded Vista Higher Learning in 1998. A native of Barranquilla, Colombia, Mr. Blanco holds degrees in Literature and Hispanic Studies from Brown University and the University of California, Santa Cruz. He has worked as a writer, editor, and translator for Houghton Mifflin and D.C. Heath and Company, and has taught Spanish at the secondary and university levels. Mr. Blanco is also the co-author of several other Vista Higher Learning programs: **Vistas, Panorama, Aventuras,** and **¡Viva!** at the introductory level; **Ventanas, Facetas, Enfoques, Imagina,** and **Sueña** at the intermediate level; and **Revista** at the advanced conversation level.

**Philip Redwine Donley** received his M.A. in Hispanic Literature from the University of Texas at Austin in 1986 and his Ph.D. in Foreign Language Education from the University of Texas at Austin in 1997. Dr. Donley taught Spanish at Austin Community College, Southwestern University, and the University of Texas at Austin. He published articles and conducted workshops about language anxiety management and the development of critical thinking skills, and was involved in research about teaching languages to the visually impaired. Dr. Donley was also the co-author of **Vistas, Aventuras,** and **Panorama,** three introductory college Spanish textbook programs published by Vista Higher Learning. Dr. Donley passed away in 2003.

## About the Illustrators

**Yayo,** an internationally acclaimed illustrator, was born in Colombia. He has illustrated children's books, newspapers, and magazines, and has been exhibited around the world. He currently lives in Montreal, Canada.

**Pere Virgili** lives and works in Barcelona, Spain. His illustrations have appeared in textbooks, newspapers, and magazines throughout Spain and Europe.

Born in Caracas, Venezuela, **Hermann Mejía** studied illustration at the *Instituto de Diseño de Caracas.* Hermann currently lives and works in the United States.

# Lección preliminar

**Communicative Goals**

*I will be able to:*
- **Identify myself and others**
- **Talk about the time of day**
- **Discuss everyday activities**
- **Describe people and things**
- **Make plans and invitations**

VOICE BOARD

## 1 Completar Complete the charts according to the models.

| Masculino | Femenino |
|---|---|
| el chico | la chica |
|  | la profesora |
|  | la amiga |
| el señor |  |
|  | la pasajera |
| el estudiante |  |
|  | la turista |
| el joven |  |

| Singular | Plural |
|---|---|
| una cosa | unas cosas |
| un libro |  |
|  | unas clases |
| una lección |  |
| un conductor |  |
|  | unos países |
|  | unos lápices |
| un problema |  |

## 2 ¿Cuántos hay? Tell how many people and/or things there are in each drawing.

1. _____

2. _____

3. _____

4. _____

5. _____

6. _____

## 3 El verbo *ser* Complete the sentences with the correct form of the verb **ser**.

1. El diccionario _____ del profesor.
2. Nosotras _____ amigas
3. Yo _____ de Costa Rica.
4. Ustedes _____ estudiantes.
5. ¿De dónde _____ Valeria?
6. Tú _____ Ricardo, ¿no?

---

## 1.1 Nouns and articles

### Gender of nouns

#### Nouns that refer to living things

|  | Masculine |  | Feminine |
|---|---|---|---|
| -o | el chico | -a | la chica |
| -or | el profesor | -ora | la profesora |
| -ista | el turista | -ista | la turista |

#### Nouns that refer to non-living things

|  | Masculine |  | Feminine |
|---|---|---|---|
| -o | el libro | -a | la cosa |
| -ma | el programa | -ción | la lección |
| -s | el autobús | -dad | la nacionalidad |

### Plural of nouns

► For nouns ending in a vowel: add **-s**
la cosa → las cosas

► For nouns ending in a consonant: add **-es**
el señor → los señores

► For nouns ending in **-z**: **z** changes to **c**; add **-es**
el lápiz → los lápices

### Articles

► Articles tell the gender and number of the nouns they precede.

#### Definite articles (*the*)

| Masculine |  | Feminine |  |
|---|---|---|---|
| Singular | Plural | Singular | Plural |
| el amigo | los amigos | la palabra | las palabras |

#### Indefinite articles (*a, an, some*)

| Masculine |  | Feminine |  |
|---|---|---|---|
| Singular | Plural | Singular | Plural |
| un amigo | unos amigos | una palabra | unas palabras |

## 1.2 Numbers 0–30

| | | | | | |
|---|---|---|---|---|---|
| 0 | cero | 8 | ocho | 16 | dieciséis |
| 1 | uno | 9 | nueve | 17 | diecisiete |
| 2 | dos | 10 | diez | 18 | dieciocho |
| 3 | tres | 11 | once | 19 | diecinueve |
| 4 | cuatro | 12 | doce | 20 | veinte |
| 5 | cinco | 13 | trece | 21 | veintiuno |
| 6 | seis | 14 | catorce | 22 | veintidós |
| 7 | siete | 15 | quince | 30 | treinta |

▶ Before masculine nouns, **uno** (and all numbers ending in -**uno**) shortens to **un**; before feminine nouns, **uno** changes to **una**.

| | |
|---|---|
| **un** chico | **una** chica |
| veintiún chicos | veintiuna chicas |

▶ Use **hay** to express *there is/are*. Use **no hay** to express *there is/are not*.

### 1.3 Present tense of **ser**

¿De dónde es usted?

Yo soy de Cuba.

▶ Uses of **ser**: identity, profession or occupation, origin, possession

### 1.4 Telling time

¿Qué hora es?

Son las cuatro menos diez.

| | |
|---|---|
| Es la **una**. | It's 1:00. |
| Son las **dos**. | It's 2:00. |
| Son las **tres** y diez. | It's 3:10. |
| **Es la una** y cuarto/quince. | It's 1:15. |
| **Son las siete** y media/treinta. | It's 7:30. |
| **Es la una** menos cuarto/quince. | It's 12:45. |
| **Son las once** menos veinte. | It's 10:40. |
| **Es el mediodía.** | It's noon. |
| **Es la medianoche.** | It's midnight. |

▶ To ask what time it is, use **¿Qué hora es?**

▶ To ask at what time an event takes place, use **¿A qué hora (…)?** To state at what time an event takes place, use **a la(s)** + *time.*

---

**4** **Conversaciones** Complete the mini-conversations by choosing the correct word for each blank.

1. —¿De quién _____ (es/hay) la maleta?
   —Es _____ (de/del) señor Rosales.

2. —¿Cuántos estudiantes _____ (eres/son) de España?
   —Dos _____ (son/soy) de España y uno _____ (cuánto/es) de México.

3. —¿_____ (Cuántos/Cuántas) pasajeros hay en el tour?
   —Hmm… hay _____ (veintiuno/veintiuna) [*21*] personas en el autobús ahora.

4. —¿_____ (De dónde/Qué) son ustedes?
   — _____ (Somos/Son) de los Estados Unidos.

**5** **La hora** Write out these times in Spanish. Follow the model.

> **modelo**
> 7:10 a.m.
> *Son las siete y diez de la mañana.*

1. 6:15 p.m. _____
2. 8:40 a.m. _____
3. 1:07 p.m. _____
4. 3:22 p.m. _____
5. 11:30 a.m. _____
6. 12:55 a.m. _____
7. 4:00 p.m. _____
8. 12:00 p.m. _____

**6** **Preguntas** Jot down your answers to these questions. Then, circulate around the room and try to find another student with the same answers. Ask follow-up questions. Be prepared to report back to the class.

> **modelo**
> **Estudiante 1:** ¿Es tu madre o padre de otro estado o país?
> **Estudiante 2:** Sí, mi madre es de otro estado.
> **Estudiante 1:** ¿De dónde es ella?
> **Estudiante 2:** Es de Michigan.

1. ¿Es tu madre/padre de otro estado (*another state*) o país?
2. ¿A qué hora es tu programa de televisión favorito?
3. ¿Cuántas computadoras hay en tu casa?

**7** **Descripción** Write a brief description of yourself and your Spanish class. Include your name, where you are from, who your Spanish teacher is and where he/she is from, what time the class is held, and how many students are in the class.

 Practice more at **vhlcentral.com.**

## 1 Completar

**Completar** Complete the sentences with the correct forms of the verbs in parentheses.

1. Los profesores _____ (explicar) las lecciones.

2. Nosotras _____ (cenar) a las ocho.

3. Tú _____ (desayunar) en la cafetería.

4. ¿_____ (Trabajar) usted los viernes?

5. Me _____ (gustar) cantar y bailar.

6. Yo no _____ (desear) tomar café ahora.

7. Los chicos _____ (dibujar) con tiza.

8. Julio y yo _____ (escuchar) música rock.

9. ¿Te _____ (gustar) las lenguas extranjeras?

10. Ustedes esperan _____ (viajar) a Perú.

## 2 Gustar

**Gustar** Luis studies science. For each item, write what Luis would say about his preferences, according to the cue. Follow the model.

> **modelo**
>
> trabajar en el laboratorio
> *No me gusta trabajar en el laboratorio.*

1. las ciencias marinas 😊

2. los exámenes de física 🙁

3. escuchar la radio cuando estudio 😊

4. trabajar y conversar con los profesores 😊

5. la tarea de química 🙁

6. la clase de biología 😊

## 3 Preguntas

**Preguntas** Write the questions for these answers.

1. —¿_____ la profesora Castillo?
   —Enseña los martes y jueves.

2. —¿_____?
   —Los chicos descansan en la casa.

3. —¿_____ (ustedes)?
   —Deseamos cenar pizza.

4. —¿_____ (tú)?
   — Tomo cinco clases.

5. —¿_____?
   —Trabajo porque necesito dinero (*money*).

6. —¿_____ los cuadernos?
   —Son de Beatriz.

7. —¿_____ la clase de literatura?
   — Es a la una de la tarde.

## 2.1 Present tense of -ar verbs

Juan Carlos estudia ciencias ambientales.

▶ To conjugate most regular **-ar** verbs in the present tense, drop the **-ar** and add the appropriate endings that correspond to the different subject pronouns.

| estudiar | |
|---|---|
| estudi**o** | estudi**amos** |
| estudi**as** | estudi**áis** |
| estudi**a** | estudi**an** |

▶ When two verbs are used together without a change in subject, the second verb is in the infinitive. To make the sentence negative, put no before the conjugated verb.

Necesito comprar **un libro.**     No **deseo viajar hoy.**

**The verb *gustar***

▶ To express your likes and dislikes, use:

**(no) me gusta + el/la +** [*singular noun*] No me gust**a** el horario.
**(no) me gustan + los/las +** [*plural noun*] Me gust**an** las ciencias.

▶ To say what you like and do not like to do, use:

**(no) me gusta +** [*infinitive(s)*] Me gust**a** leer **y** escribir.

▶ To ask a classmate about likes and dislikes, use **te.**

¿Te **gusta la clase?**

## 2.2 Forming questions in Spanish

¿Hablas con tu mamá?

▶ There are three ways to form questions in Spanish: by raising the pitch of your voice at the end of a declarative statement; by inverting the subject and verb in a statement; or by adding tag questions (**¿verdad?** or **¿no?**) to a declarative statement.

¿**Ustedes trabajan** los sábados?

¿**Trabajan ustedes** los sábados?

**Ustedes trabajan** los sábados, ¿verdad?/¿no?

### Interrogative words

| | | |
|---|---|---|
| ¿Adónde? | ¿Cuánto/a? | ¿Por qué? |
| ¿Cómo? | ¿Cuántos/as? | ¿Qué? |
| ¿Cuál(es)? | ¿De dónde? | ¿Quién(es)? |
| ¿Cuándo? | ¿Dónde? | |

**2.3** **Present tense of estar**

### estar

| | |
|---|---|
| estoy | estamos |
| estás | estáis |
| está | están |

▸ Uses of estar: location, health, well-being

### Prepositions often used with estar

| | |
|---|---|
| a la derecha de | delante de |
| a la izquierda de | detrás de |
| al lado de | en |
| allá | encima de |
| allí | entre |
| cerca de | lejos de |
| con | sin |
| debajo de | sobre |

**2.4** **Numbers 31 and higher**

Hay cuarenta y siete estudiantes en la clase de geografía.

| 31 | treinta y uno | 101 | ciento uno |
|---|---|---|---|
| 32 | treinta y dos | 200 | doscientos/as |
| | (and so on) | 500 | quinientos/as |
| 40 | cuarenta | 700 | setecientos/as |
| 50 | cincuenta | 900 | novecientos/as |
| 60 | sesenta | 1.000 | mil |
| 70 | setenta | 2.000 | dos mil |
| 80 | ochenta | 5.100 | cinco mil cien |
| 90 | noventa | 100.000 | cien mil |
| 100 | cien, ciento | 1.000.000 | un millón (de) |

▸ The numbers 200 through 999 agree in gender with the nouns they modify.

**324 plum**as          **trescient**as **veinticuatro plum**as

**4** **En la escuela** There is a substitute teacher in Clara's class today. Complete the conversation with the correct forms of **estar**.

**SR. GARCÍA**  Buenos días. ¿Cómo (1) _____ ?

**CLARA**  Bien, gracias. ¿Cómo (2) _____ usted?

**SR. GARCÍA**  (3) _____ muy bien. Soy el señor García. Y tú eres Clara Rivas, ¿verdad?

**CLARA**  Sí. Perdón, señor García, pero ¿dónde (4) _____ el señor Duque?

**SR. GARCÍA**  (5) _____ en una conferencia, pero regresa mañana. Clara, ¿en qué parte del libro (6) _____ ustedes?

**CLARA**  (Nosotros) (7) _____ en la lección 4.

**SR. GARCÍA**  Y los borradores, ¿dónde (8) _____ ?

**CLARA**  Allí, al lado de la mesa.

**5** **Buscar** Imagine that you are in a school supply store and can't find various items. Ask the clerk (your partner) about the location of five items in the drawing. Then switch roles.

> **modelo**
>
> **Estudiante 1:** ¿Dónde están los diccionarios?
> **Estudiante 2:** Los diccionarios están debajo de los libros de literatura.

**6** **Números** Write these numbers in Spanish.

1. 751 _____
2. 99 _____
3. 4.010 _____
4. 844 _____
5. 738.266 _____
6. 23.110.680 _____
7. 1.033 _____
8. 1.500.307 _____

**7** **Un estudiante español** Complete the paragraph with the appropriate forms of the verbs in the word list. Not all the verbs will be used. Some may be used more than once.

| | | | | |
|---|---|---|---|---|
| bailar | desayunar | estar | gustar | necesitar |
| caminar | esperar | estudiar | hablar | tomar |

Hola, soy Víctor. Soy de Madrid, España. (Yo) (1) _____ en una escuela secundaria. (2) _____ clases de ciencias, matemáticas, arte e inglés. Los días de semana, mis padres y yo (3) _____ juntos (*together*) en casa. Luego mis padres (4) _____ el autobús; sus oficinas (5) _____ lejos de la casa. Yo no (6) _____ tomar el autobús para llegar a la escuela. Afortunadamente (*Luckily*), (7) _____ cerca de mi casa. A veces (*Sometimes*) mi amigo Alberto y yo (8) _____ juntos a la escuela. (9) _____ de deportes, como el tenis o el fútbol. ¿Y tú? ¿(10) _____ en una escuela cerca de tu casa? ¿Qué clases (11) _____ ? ¿A ti te (12) _____ los deportes?

**8** **Describir** With a partner, choose verbs from the list to ask and answer questions about what you see in each drawing.

| | | |
|---|---|---|
| buscar | dibujar | llevar |
| caminar | escuchar | tomar |
| cantar | estudiar | viajar |
| descansar | hablar | |

> **modelo**
>
> enseñar, explicar, hablar
> **Estudiante 1:** ¿Qué enseña la profesora?
> **Estudiante 2:** Enseña química.
> **Estudiante 1:** ¿Explica la lección?
> **Estudiante 2:** Sí, explica la lección.

1.

2.

3.

4.

**9**

**Contestar** Answer these questions.

1. ¿Cuántas clases tomas? ¿Cuál es tu clase favorita?

2. ¿Dónde estudias, en la biblioteca o en casa? ¿Escuchas música cuando estudias?

3. ¿A qué hora llegas a la escuela? ¿A qué hora regresas a casa?

4. ¿Con quién(es) cenas normalmente? ¿Quién prepara la comida (*food*)?

5. ¿Miras mucha televisión? ¿Qué programas te gustan?

6. ¿Te gusta viajar? ¿Qué países o culturas te gustan?

7. ¿Qué música escuchan tus amigos/as y tú? ¿Bailan ustedes? ¿Cantan?

8. ¿Qué te gusta hacer los fines de semana? ¿Descansas, preparas la tarea o pasas tiempo con tu familia?

**10**

**Actividades** With a partner, take turns asking each other if you do these activities. Also ask follow-up questions. Jot down your partner's answers and make note of which activities you both do.

> **modelo**
>
> desayunar en casa
> **Estudiante 1:** ¿Desayunas en casa?
> **Estudiante 2:** Sí, desayuno en casa.
> **Estudiante 1:** ¿A qué hora desayunas los días de semana?
> **Estudiante 2:** Desayuno a las siete de la mañana.
> **Estudiante 1:** ¿Con quién desayunas?
> **Estudiante 2:** Desayuno con mis padres.

> bailar bien
> comprar música en iTunes
> estudiar geografía
> mirar la televisión
> practicar deportes
> tomar clases aparte de la escuela
> trabajar como voluntario(a)
> viajar por el país
> visitar museos de arte

**11**

**Escribir** Write an e-mail to a new friend. Introduce yourself, describe what classes you take, your studying habits, and what you do on school days and weekends. Talk about your likes and dislikes, and ask about your friend's.

> **modelo**
>
> Hola, Andrés:
> Me llamo David y soy de Miami, Florida. Soy estudiante en una escuela secundaria. Tomo clases de historia, arte...

 Practice more at **vhlcentral.com**.

**Reading, Additional Reading**

# El español en Latinoamérica

**As a Spanish language learner, you are on your way** to being able to communicate with a vast number of people from diverse regions, backgrounds, and cultures. There are about 500 million Spanish-speakers in the world, but less than 600 years ago, Spanish was used only in the northern and central regions of the Iberian Peninsula. In 1492, the **Reyes Católicos°** unified Spain under Christian rule and the Spanish language. In that same year, they commissioned **Cristóbal Colón°** to search for a new trade route to India, on which he carried the Spanish language to the Americas.

Although Columbus initially sought to explore and establish trade routes, a principal goal of the Spaniards in the Americas quickly became conquest and evangelism—spreading the Catholic faith. The Spanish encountered millions of indigenous people who spoke a vast number of languages and dialects. The Spanish **conquistadores** used various indigenous languages to communicate their religious message, and several were preserved this way throughout colonial times. For example, **quechua** was the main means of communication in the central Andean region between the Spaniards and the indigenous population. Over time, the geographic reach of quechua continued to expand, and words from many different indigenous languages were incorporated into Spanish. **Papa°** and **jaguar°** are just two examples.

Over the following few centuries of colonial rule, descendants of the Spanish and majority **mestizo°** population perpetuated the use of Spanish. After the wars of independence, most nations opted to have Spanish as their official language. However, millions of Latin Americans continue to speak a multitude of indigenous languages, especially in rural areas. And in several Latin American countries, indigenous languages have co-official status: Bolivia (**quechua, aimará**), Ecuador (**quechua, aimará**), Paraguay (**guaraní**), and Peru (**quechua, aimará**).

| Otras° lenguas indígenas | | |
|---|---|---|
| **Lengua** | **Donde se habla** | **Más información** |
| náhuatl | México | lengua de los aztecas |
| chibcha | (lengua extinta) | lengua dominante en Colombia y Panamá en tiempos precolombinos° |
| maya | Guatemala, México, Honduras | en tiempos precolombinos usan un sistema jeroglífico° |
| taíno | (lengua extinta) | lengua más dominante en la región del Caribe en tiempos precolombinos |
| mapuche | Chile | no tiene relación con otras lenguas indígenas |

**Reyes Católicos** *the Catholic King Fernando de Aragón and Queen Isabel of Castilla* **Cristóbal Colón** *Christopher Columbus* **Papa** *Potato (from Quechua)* **jaguar** *jaguar (from Guaraní)* **mestizo** *mixed Spanish and indigenous ancestry* **Otras** *Other* **precolombinos** *pre-Columbian* **jeroglífico** *hieroglyphic*

---

**ACTIVIDADES**

1 **Cierto o falso?** Indicate whether each statement is **cierto** or **falso**. Correct the false statements.

1. About 500,000 people speak Spanish worldwide.
2. The Spanish **conquistadores** often communicated Catholic teachings in indigenous languages.
3. Indigenous languages did not survive the Spanish conquest.
4. **Quechua** originated in the Caribbean.
5. Many Spanish words have indigenous origins.
6. Today, indigenous languages are not widely spoken in Latin America.
7. **Aimará** is spoken in Paraguay.
8. **Taíno** and **chibcha** are extinct languages.
9. The Aztecs spoke **maya**.
10. **Mapuche** and **quechua** belong to the same linguistic family.

## ASÍ SE DICE

### Palabras de origen indígena

| | |
|---|---|
| el aguacate (náhuatl) | *avocado* |
| la barbacoa (taíno) | *barbecue* |
| la cancha (quechua) | *field, court* |
| el chile (náhuatl) | *chili (pepper)* |
| el coyote (náhuatl) | *coyote* |
| el huracán (taíno) | *hurricane* |
| la maraca (guaraní) | *maraca* |
| la palta (quechua) | *avocado* |
| el puma (quechua) | *puma* |

## EL MUNDO HISPANO

### Civilizaciones precolombinas

**La civilización maya** This civilization is known for its art, architecture, mathematics, and astronomy. The Mayas developed a counting system based on 20 and the concept of zero. Remains of Mayan temples, such as **Tikal** in Guatemala and **Chichén Itzá** on the Yucatan Peninsula, are now popular tourist attractions.

**El imperio azteca** This civilization, based in Mexico's central valley, greatly expanded its domain through military conquest and alliances. The Aztecs founded their capital, **Tenochtitlán**, in 1325; by the time the Spanish arrived in 1519, it was one of the largest cities in the world.

**El imperio incaico** The Incas developed an innovative agricultural system of terraces and constructed a vast network of roads with the capital, Cusco, at its center. One of the most famous legacies of the Incan Empire is the mountaintop ruins of **Machu Picchu**.

## PERFIL

# Día de la Independencia

During the early morning hours of September 16, 1810, a Mexican priest rang his church bell in the town of Dolores and gave a rousing call for a free, independent Mexico: ¡**Viva° la Independencia! ¡Muera el mal gobierno°!** After 11 years of war, Mexico won its independence from Spain, which it commemorates on the 16th of September. Although Mexico's **Día de la Independencia** is officially September 16th, the celebrations begin the night before. Father Miguel Hidalgo's act, now known as **el Grito° de Dolores**, is reenacted every year in **zócalos°** across Mexico, accompanied by fireworks, music, and revelers dressed in the colors of the Mexican flag.

Beginning in 1811, similar movements for freedom ignited all over Central America. Finally, on September 15, 1821, Costa Rica, El Salvador, Guatemala, Honduras, and Nicaragua signed the **Acta de Independencia de Centroamérica**, thus proclaiming their autonomy from Spain. These five countries all celebrate their independence on September 15th.

**Viva** *Long live* **Muera el mal gobierno** *Down with bad government* **Grito** *Shout* **zócalos** *plazas*

 **Conexión Internet**

| | |
|---|---|
| ¿Qué es y qué hace la Real Academia Española? | Go to **vhlcentral.com** to find more cultural information related to this **Cultura** section. |

## ACTIVIDADES

**2** **Comprensión** Complete these sentences.

1. Mexicans reenact _____ as part of Independence Day.
2. The capital of the _____ Empire was one of the largest cities in the world.
3. **Palta** and _____ both mean avocado.
4. Honduras and Nicaragua celebrate their independence on _____.
5. _____ is a Nahuatl word referring to an animal.

**3** **Los indígenas** Have students work in pairs. Ask them to research more about one of the indigenous groups mentioned on these pages, or another pre-Columbian civilization in Latin America. Have students prepare a brief oral presentation about the group's culture, language, customs, and place in history.

 Practice more at **vhlcentral.com.**

**1** **Opuestos** For each adjective, give an adjective that is opposite in meaning. Keep the gender and number the same.

1. tonto
2. baja
3. gordo
4. viejos
5. simpáticas
6. bonito
7. difíciles
8. morena
9. malas
10. blanco

**2** **Completar** Ernesto is talking about life at his new school. Complete the paragraph with the correct form of the adjectives from the list. Use each adjective only once. One adjective will not be used.

| | |
|---|---|
| bueno | mismo |
| difícil | mucho |
| feo | simpático |
| inteligente | tonto |
| interesante | tres |

En la escuela donde estudio tengo (1) _____ amigos: Ignacio, Carlos y Tomás. Son personas muy (2) _____; hablamos de todo. Ellos son (3) _____; reciben A en todos los exámenes. Yo no soy (4) _____, pero no tengo las (5) _____ notas. Las materias son (6) _____ y los profesores son (7) _____, pero en la clase de matemáticas hay (8) _____ tarea y la clase de química es (9) _____. Deseo tomar más clases de historia y de arte.

**3** **Posesivos** Write the correct form of each possessive adjective.

1. _____ (*Your*, fam.) sobrino es muy joven.
2. _____ (*Her*) profesores son estrictos.
3. Olivia es _____ (*my*) hermana.
4. _____ (*Our*) casa es azul.
5. ¿Juliana es _____ (*your*, form.) esposa?
6. _____ (*His*) familia es pequeña.
7. Los libros viejos son de _____ (*our*) abuelos.
8. _____ (*My*) tíos son argentinos.

**4** **Verbos** Complete the chart with the correct verb forms.

| Infinitive | yo | nosotros/as | ustedes |
|---|---|---|---|
| | asisto | | |
| deber | | debemos | |
| | | | leen |
| venir | | | |
| | bebo | | |
| describir | | | describen |

**3.1** Descriptive adjectives

Felipe es gordo, antipático y muy feo.

► Adjectives are words that describe nouns. In Spanish, adjectives agree in both gender and number with the nouns they modify.

**Forms and agreement of adjectives**

| Masculine | | Feminine | |
|---|---|---|---|
| Singular | Plural | Singular | Plural |
| alto | altos | alta | altas |
| inteligente | inteligentes | inteligente | inteligentes |
| trabajador | trabajadores | trabajadora | trabajadoras |

► Descriptive adjectives, color words, and adjectives of nationality follow the noun:

**el chico rubio, las sillas rojas, la mujer española**

► Adjectives of quantity precede the noun:

**muchos libros, dos turistas**

**Note:** When placed before a singular masculine noun, these adjectives are shortened:

**bueno → buen; malo → mal**

**un buen día, un mal hombre**

When placed before a singular noun, **grande** is shortened to **gran**, and the meaning changes to *great*.

**una gran escuela**

**3.2** Possessive adjectives

| Singular | | Plural | |
|---|---|---|---|
| mi | nuestro/a | mis | nuestros/as |
| tu | vuestro/a | tus | vuestros/as |
| su | su | sus | sus |

► Possessive adjectives always precede the nouns they modify:

**nuestros amigos, mi madre**

## 3.3 Present tense of -er and -ir verbs

Jimena lee.

▶ To create the present-tense forms of most regular verbs, drop the infinitive ending (**-er**, **-ir**) and add the appropriate endings that correspond to the different subject pronouns.

| com**er** | | escrib**ir** | |
|---|---|---|---|
| com**o** | com**emos** | escrib**o** | escrib**imos** |
| com**es** | com**éis** | escrib**es** | escrib**ís** |
| com**e** | com**en** | escrib**e** | escrib**en** |

## 3.4 Present tense of **tener** and **venir**

Tengo una familia pequeña.

| tener | | venir | |
|---|---|---|---|
| ten**go** | ten**emos** | ven**go** | ven**imos** |
| tien**es** | ten**éis** | vien**es** | ven**ís** |
| tien**e** | tien**en** | vien**e** | vien**en** |

▶ **Tener** is used in many common phrases expressing feelings and age.

| | |
|---|---|
| tener... años | to be... years old |
| tener calor | to be hot |
| tener frío | to be cold |
| tener ganas de + inf. | to feel like (doing something) |
| tener hambre | to be hungry |
| tener prisa | to be in a hurry |
| tener razón | to be right |
| tener sed | to be thirsty |
| tener sueño | to be sleepy |
| tener que + inf. | to have to (do something) |

**5** **Situaciones** Read these situations. For each one, write a logical sentence using a **tener** expression. Follow the model.

> **modelo**
>
> Mi primo Rubén tiene un examen mañana. Rubén _tiene que estudiar_.

1. Es la medianoche y escribes la tarea. Tú _____.
2. Es la hora de cenar. Yo _____.
3. Buscamos agua. Nosotros _____.
4. Son las 8:50 y José está en casa. La clase es a las 9. José _____.
5. Tus amigos y tú buscan un libro interesante. Ustedes _____.
6. Enrique dice que estamos en el año 2010. Él no _____.

**6** **Oraciones** Arrange each set of words in the correct order to form a complete, logical sentence. **¡Ojo!** Remember to conjugate the verbs according to the subject.

1. las / media / venir / a / yo / escuela / a / siete / y / la

   _____

2. sus / compartir / usted / amigos / con / ¿ / ?

   _____

3. profesor / un / nosotros / buen / tener

   _____

4. interesantes / aprender / sobrinos / libros / leer / mis / a

   _____

**7** **Conversación** Complete the conversation with the correct form of the appropriate verb. Then, act it out with a partner.

—Hola, Raquel. ¿Qué (1) _____ (escribir/comprender) en el teléfono?

—Hola, Simón. (2) _____ (Comer/Escribir) un mensaje de texto (*text message*) para mi amiga Inés.

—¿Inés? Ella (3) _____ (abrir/vivir) cerca del parque, ¿verdad?

—Sí, exactamente. Por las tardes ella y yo (4) _____ (correr/decidir) en el parque.

—¡Qué bien! A mí también me gusta (5) _____ (correr/leer).

—¿Ah, sí? ¿Por qué no (6) _____ (tener/venir) con nosotras? Después (7) _____ (compartir/aprender) un batido de col (*kale smoothie*) en un café.

—¿Ustedes (8) _____ (beber/creer) batidos de col? Em... no, gracias. (9) _____ (Recibir/Tener) que terminar la tarea y a las cinco (10) _____ (describir/asistir) a una lección de piano.

—Ay, Simón. De verdad (11) _____ (deber/compartir) practicar más deportes.

⚙ Practice more at **vhlcentral.com.**

**1** **El verbo *ir*** Complete the sentences with the correct form of the verb **ir** and **a**, **al**, or **a la**.

1. Los jóvenes _____ _____ plaza.
2. ¿Ustedes _____ _____ jugar al golf?
3. Mi abuela _____ _____ iglesia.
4. Tú _____ _____ restaurante.
5. Yo _____ _____ esquiar.
6. Fernanda y yo _____ _____ cine.

**2** **¿Adónde?** With a partner, take turns asking and answering questions about where these people are going and what they are going to do there.

**modelo**

> **Estudiante 1:** ¿Adónde va Estela?
> **Estudiante 2:** Va a la Librería Sol.
> ¿Qué va a comprar allí?
> **Estudiante 1:** Va a comprar un libro.

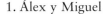

Estela

1. Álex y Miguel

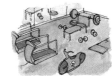

2. mi amigo

3. tú

4. los estudiantes

5. la profesora Torres

6. ustedes

**3** **Verbos** Complete the chart with the correct verb forms.

| Infinitive | yo | nosotros/as | ellos/as |
|---|---|---|---|
| contar | | | |
| | juego | | |
| | cierro | cerramos | |
| traer | | | traen |
| | | | siguen |
| oír | | oímos | |

---

**4.1** **Present tense of *ir***

Ella va al cine y a los museos.

| ir | | | |
|---|---|---|---|
| yo | voy | nosotros/as | vamos |
| tú | vas | vosotros/as | vais |
| Ud./él/ella | va | Uds./ellos/ellas | van |

▶ **Ir** is often used with the preposition **a**; if **a** is followed by the definite article **el**, they form a contraction: **a + el = al.**

▶ **Ir** has many everyday uses, including expressing future plans:

**ir a** + [*infinitivo*] = *to be going to* + [*infinitive*]
**vamos a** + [*infinitivo*] = *let's do something*

**4.2** **Stem-changing verbs e:ie, o:ue, u:ue**

Los chicos empiezan a hablar del cenote.

| | empezar | volver | jugar |
|---|---|---|---|
| yo | empiezo | vuelvo | juego |
| tú | empiezas | vuelves | juegas |
| Ud./él/ella | empieza | vuelve | juega |
| nosotros/as | empezamos | volvemos | jugamos |
| vosotros/as | empezáis | volvéis | jugáis |
| Uds./ellos/ellas | empiezan | vuelven | juegan |

▶ Other e:ie verbs: **cerrar, comenzar, entender, pensar, perder, preferir, querer**

▶ Other o:ue verbs: **almorzar, contar, dormir, encontrar, mostrar, poder, recordar**

## 4.3 Stem-changing verbs e:i

| pedir | | | |
|---|---|---|---|
| yo | pido | nosotros/as | pedimos |
| tú | pides | vosotros/as | pedís |
| Ud./él/ella | pide | Uds./ellos/ellas | piden |

▶ As with other stem-changing verbs you have learned, there is no stem change in the **nosotros/as** or **vosotros/as** forms in the present tense.

▶ Other e:i verbs: **conseguir** (consigo), **decir** (digo), **repetir**, **seguir** (sigo)

## 4.4 Verbs with irregular yo forms

▶ In Spanish, several verbs have irregular **yo** forms in the present tense.

Yo no salgo, yo hago la tarea y veo películas en la televisión.

| hacer | poner | salir | suponer | traer |
|---|---|---|---|---|
| hago | pongo | salgo | supongo | traigo |

▶ The verbs **ver** and **oír**

| ver | | | |
|---|---|---|---|
| yo | veo | nosotros/as | vemos |
| tú | ves | vosotros/as | veis |
| Ud./él/ella | ve | Uds./ellos/ellas | ven |

| oír | | | |
|---|---|---|---|
| yo | oigo | nosotros/as | oímos |
| tú | oyes | vosotros/as | oís |
| Ud./él/ella | oye | Uds./ellos/ellas | oyen |

**4** **Completar** Complete each sentence with the correct form of the verb.

1. Daniela _____ (mostrar) las fotos de su excursión.
2. ¿Cuándo _____ (poder) pasear tú y yo?
3. Tus clases _____ (comenzar) mañana, ¿verdad?
4. Mi familia y yo _____ (oír) música salsa en casa.
5. ¿(Tú) _____ (ver) programas de *reality* en la televisión?
6. Mateo _____ (decir) que hay un problema.
7. (Yo) _____ (suponer) que hay una solución.
8. Tus amigos y tú _____ (jugar) al fútbol los domingos.

**5** **El cine** Complete the paragraph by choosing the appropriate verb and conjugating it in the correct form. **¡Ojo!** Not all verbs have stem changes.

Mis amigas y yo (1) _____ (repetir, ir, ver) al cine el sábado. Pilar y Lucía (2) _____ (volver, abrir, querer) ver una película romántica, pero Teresa, Elena y yo (3) _____ (preferir, traer, ir) una comedia. Entonces (*So*), este sábado nosotras (4) _____ (cerrar, llevar, pensar) comprar entradas (*tickets*) para ver una película cómica. La película (5) _____ (tener, hacer, empezar) a las ocho y (6) _____ (contar, terminar, comenzar) a las 9:45 de la noche; entonces mis amigas y yo (7) _____ (salir, creer, oír) del cine y (8) _____ (viajar, poder, nadar) ir a cenar. Aquí los restaurantes (9) _____ (cerrar, querer, vivir) tarde, más o menos a la medianoche. Normalmente (yo) (10) _____ (perder, conseguir, decidir) las entradas por Internet. Y tú, ¿cómo (11) _____ (poner, contar, comprar) las entradas del cine? ¿(12) _____ (Preferir, Comprender, Salir) películas románticas o cómicas?

**6** **Oraciones** Arrange each set of words in the correct order to form a complete, logical sentence. **¡Ojo!** Make all necessary changes.

1. mi / clase / calculadora / yo / a / rojo / traer

   _____

2. gimnasio / el / ir / a / (tú) / ¿ / ?

   _____

3. en / mis / no / el / radio / la / amigos / programa / oír

   _____

4. tacos / Lucas y yo / mucho / mexicano / en / restaurante / pedir / el

   _____

5. excursión / el / querer / una / quién / viernes / hacer / ¿ / ?

   _____

**7**

**Describir** In pairs, take turns describing what these people are doing, using the verbs from the list. Use each verb only once. One verb will not be used.

| | |
|---|---|
| hacer | salir |
| oír | traer |
| perder | ver |
| poner | |

1. Fernán          2. los aficionados          3. yo

4. nosotros          5. la señora Vargas          6. el estudiante

**8**

**Combinar** Combine elements from the columns to create complete sentences. Add any necessary words.

| A | B | C |
|---|---|---|
| usted | traer | una pizza |
| mis amigos y yo | dormir | viajar |
| tú | empezar | la tarea |
| las clases | pedir | una siesta |
| ustedes | hacer | bailar merengue |
| los profesores | querer | ¿? |
| mi madre | poder | |

**9**

**Situaciones** In pairs, take turns saying where you and your friends go in these situations.

1. Cuando deseo descansar…
2. Cuando mi mejor amigo/a tiene que estudiar…
3. Si mis compañeros de clase necesitan practicar el español…
4. Si deseo hablar con mis amigos…
5. Cuando tengo dinero (*money*)…
6. Cuando mis amigos y yo tenemos hambre…
7. En mis ratos libres…
8. Cuando mis amigos desean esquiar…
9. Si estoy de vacaciones…
10. Si tengo ganas de leer…

**10** **Preguntas personales** Answer these questions.

1. ¿A qué hora sales de la casa los lunes? ¿A qué hora vuelves a casa? ¿Y tus padres?
2. ¿Te gustan tus clases? ¿Qué materias prefieres? ¿Por qué?
3. ¿Haces mucha tarea? ¿Dónde prefieres estudiar?
4. ¿Pones música cuando estudias? ¿Oyes música cuando caminas a la escuela o cuando tomas el autobús? ¿Tus padres escuchan música cuando cenan?
5. Cuando no estás en la escuela, ¿qué haces? ¿Juegas deportes? ¿Juegas en la computadora? ¿Lees? ¿Escribes poemas?
6. ¿Miras la televisión? ¿Qué programas ves?
7. ¿Qué vas a hacer el fin de semana? ¿Tienes ganas de ir al cine? ¿Qué películas te gustan?

**11** **La verdad** Write five sentences about yourself, using the verbs from the list or others that you know. Three of the sentences should be true and two should be false. Then, in small groups, take turns reading your statements aloud. Your classmates will try to determine which ones are true.

| | | | | | |
|---|---|---|---|---|---|
| almorzar | hablar | jugar | salir | tener | vivir |
| dormir | ir | querer | ser | trabajar | ¿? |

**12** **Encuesta** First, read through the items; under **Yo**, write **Sí** if you do the activity and **No** if you do not. Then, under the second column, place one check mark if you do the activity once a month **(una vez al mes)**, two check marks if you do it a few times a week **(varias veces a la semana)**, or three check marks if you do it every day **(todos los días)**.

| | Yo | Frecuencia | Mi compañero/a | Frecuencia |
|---|---|---|---|---|
| 1. almorzar en la cafetería | sí | ✔ ✔ ✔ | Lisa | ✔ ✔ |
| 2. tomar café por la mañana | | | | |
| 3. ir a restaurantes elegantes | | | | |
| 4. dormir ocho horas | | | | |
| 5. jugar a deportes | | | | |
| 6. ver deportes en la televisión | | | | |
| 7. recordar a tus amigos/as de la infancia | | | | |
| 8. escuchar música | | | | |
| 9. salir con amigos/as | | | | |

Now circulate around the room and try to find classmate that does each activity with the same frequency as you. When someone answers yes, write down their name and the corresponding check marks.

**modelo**

almorzar en la cafetería

**Tú:** ¿Almuerzas en la cafetería?

**Lisa:** Sí, almuerzo en la cafetería varias veces a la semana.

**13**

**Situación** Imagine that you are speaking with a member of your family or your best friend. With a partner, prepare a conversation using these cues.

| **Estudiante 1** | **Estudiante 2** |
|---|---|
| Ask your partner what he or she is doing. → | Tell your partner that you are watching TV. |
| Say what you suppose he or she is watching. → | Say that you like the show _____. Ask if he or she wants to watch. |
| Say no, because you are going out with friends and tell where you are going. → | Say you think it's a good idea, and ask what your partner and his or her friends are doing there. |
| Say what you are going to do, and ask your partner whether he or she wants to come along. → | Say no and tell your partner what you prefer to do. |

**14**

**Escribir** Write a journal entry about what you do and various family members do on a typical Saturday. Then talk about what you and your friends are going to do together this weekend. Use at least eight verbs from pages 12–13 to talk about your typical day and **ir a** + [*infinitive/place*] to talk about your plans.

> # Un sábado típico
>
> Generalmente los sábados
> yo...

**15**

**Adivinanza** Complete the rhyme with the appropriate forms of the correct verbs from the list.

| | |
|---|---|
| contar | poder |
| oír | suponer |

**❝** Si no _____ dormir
 y el sueño deseas,
 lo vas a conseguir
 si _____ ovejas°. **❞**

ovejas *sheep*

# Las vacaciones

5

**Communicative Goals**

*I will be able to:*
- **Discuss and plan a vacation**
- **Describe a hotel**
- **Talk about how I feel**
- **Talk about the seasons and the weather**

VOICE BOARD

## A PRIMERA VISTA
- ¿Dónde están ellos: en la playa o en una ciudad?
- ¿Son viejos o jóvenes?
- ¿Toman el sol o nadan?
- ¿Es posible andar en patineta en este lugar?

# Las vacaciones

  **Audio: Vocabulary Tutorials, Games**

## Más vocabulario

| | |
|---|---|
| la cama | bed |
| la habitación individual, doble | single, double room |
| el piso | floor (of a building) |
| la planta baja | ground floor |
| el campo | countryside |
| el paisaje | landscape |
| el equipaje | luggage |
| la estación de autobuses, del metro, de tren | bus, subway, train station |
| la llegada | arrival |
| el pasaje (de ida y vuelta) | (round-trip) ticket |
| la salida | departure; exit |
| la tabla de (wind)surf | surfboard/sailboard |
| acampar | to camp |
| estar de vacaciones | to be on vacation |
| hacer las maletas | to pack (one's suitcases) |
| hacer un viaje | to take a trip |
| hacer (wind)surf | to (wind)surf |
| ir de compras | to go shopping |
| ir de vacaciones | to go on vacation |
| ir en autobús (m.), auto(móvil) (m.), motocicleta (f.), taxi (m.) | to go by bus, car, motorcycle, taxi |

## Variación léxica

automóvil ⟷ coche (*Esp.*), carro (*Amér. L.*)
autobús ⟷ camión (*Méx.*), guagua (*Caribe*)
motocicleta ⟷ moto (*coloquial*)

la agente de viajes

el pasaporte

Confirma una reservación. (confirmar)

**En la agencia de viajes**

la habitación

el ascensor

el empleado

la llave

el botones

el huésped

la huésped

**En el hotel**

**Saca/Toma fotos.**
(sacar, tomar)

BIENVENIDOS

**el avión**

**el viajero**

**la inspectora
de aduanas**

## En el aeropuerto

**Pesca.**
(pescar)

**Monta a caballo.**
(montar)

**Va en barco.**
(ir)

**el mar**

**Juegan a las
cartas. (jugar)**

**la playa**

## En la playa

# Práctica

**1** **Escuchar** Indicate who would probably make each statement you hear. Each answer is used twice.

a. el agente de viajes  1. _____  4. _____

b. la inspectora de aduanas  2. _____  5. _____

c. un empleado del hotel  3. _____  6. _____

**2** **¿Cierto o falso?** Mario and his wife, Natalia, are planning their next vacation with a travel agent. Indicate whether each statement is **cierto** or **falso** according to what you hear in the conversation.

|  | Cierto | Falso |
|---|---|---|
| 1. Mario y Natalia están en Puerto Rico. | ○ | ○ |
| 2. Ellos quieren hacer un viaje a Puerto Rico. | ○ | ○ |
| 3. Natalia prefiere ir a una montaña. | ○ | ○ |
| 4. Mario quiere pescar en Puerto Rico. | ○ | ○ |
| 5. La agente de viajes va a confirmar la reservación. | ○ | ○ |

**3** **Escoger** Choose the best answer for each sentence.

1. Un huésped es una persona que _____.
   a. toma fotos  b. está en un hotel  c. pesca en el mar
2. Abrimos la puerta con _____.
   a. una llave  b. un caballo  c. una llegada
3. Enrique tiene _____ porque va a viajar a otro (*another*) país.
   a. un pasaporte  b. una foto  c. una llegada
4. Antes de (*Before*) ir de vacaciones, hay que _____.
   a. pescar  b. ir en tren  c. hacer las maletas
5. Nosotros vamos en _____ al aeropuerto.
   a. autobús  b. pasaje  c. viajero
6. Me gusta mucho ir al campo. El _____ es increíble.
   a. paisaje  b. pasaje  c. equipaje

**4** **Analogías** Complete the analogies using the words below. Two words will not be used.

| auto | huésped | mar | sacar |
|---|---|---|---|
| botones | llegada | pasaporte | tren |

1. acampar ⟶ campo ⊜ pescar ⟶
2. agencia de viajes ⟶ agente ⊜ hotel ⟶
3. llave ⟶ habitación ⊜ pasaje ⟶
4. estudiante ⟶ libro ⊜ turista ⟶
5. aeropuerto ⟶ viajero ⊜ hotel ⟶
6. maleta ⟶ hacer ⊜ foto ⟶

Audio:
Vocabulary

## Las estaciones y los meses del año

el invierno: **diciembre, enero, febrero**

la primavera: **marzo, abril, mayo**

el verano: **junio, julio, agosto**

el otoño: **septiembre, octubre, noviembre**

—**¿Cuál es la fecha de hoy?**          *What is today's date?*
—**Es el primero de octubre.**          *It's the first of October.*
—**Es el dos de marzo.**                *It's March 2nd.*
—**Es el diez de noviembre.**           *It's November 10th.*

Audio:
Vocabulary

## El tiempo

—**¿Qué tiempo hace?**                  *How's the weather?*
—**Hace buen/mal tiempo.**              *The weather is good/bad.*

**Hace (mucho) calor.**
*It's (very) hot.*

**Hace (mucho) frío.**
*It's (very) cold.*

**Llueve. (llover o:ue)**
*It's raining.*

**Está lloviendo.**
*It's raining.*

**Nieva. (nevar e:ie)**
*It's snowing.*

**Está nevando.**
*It's snowing.*

### Más vocabulario

| | |
|---|---|
| **Está (muy) nublado.** | *It's (very) cloudy.* |
| **Hace fresco.** | *It's cool.* |
| **Hace (mucho) sol.** | *It's (very) sunny.* |
| **Hace (mucho) viento.** | *It's (very) windy.* |

**5** **El Hotel Regis** Label the floors of the hotel.

### Los números ordinales

| | |
|---|---|
| **primer** (before a masculine singular noun), **primero/a** | first |
| **segundo/a** | second |
| **tercer** (before a masculine singular noun), **tercero/a** | third |
| **cuarto/a** | fourth |
| **quinto/a** | fifth |
| **sexto/a** | sixth |
| **séptimo/a** | seventh |
| **octavo/a** | eighth |
| **noveno/a** | ninth |
| **décimo/a** | tenth |

Audio: Vocabulary

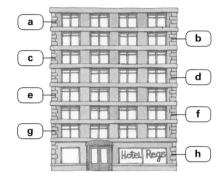

a. _____ piso
b. _____ piso
c. _____ piso
d. _____ piso
e. _____ piso
f. _____ piso
g. _____ piso
h. _____ baja

---

**6**

**Contestar** Look at the illustrations of the months and seasons on the previous page. In pairs, take turns asking each other these questions.

> **modelo**
>
> **Estudiante 1:** ¿Cuál es el primer mes de la primavera?
> **Estudiante 2:** marzo

1. ¿Cuál es el primer mes del invierno?
2. ¿Cuál es el segundo mes de la primavera?
3. ¿Cuál es el tercer mes del otoño?
4. ¿Cuál es el primer mes del año?
5. ¿Cuál es el quinto mes del año?
6. ¿Cuál es el octavo mes del año?
7. ¿Cuál es el décimo mes del año?
8. ¿Cuál es el segundo mes del verano?
9. ¿Cuál es el tercer mes del invierno?
10. ¿Cuál es el sexto mes del año?

---

**7**

**Las estaciones** Name the season that applies to the description.

1. Las clases terminan.
2. Vamos a la playa.
3. Acampamos.
4. Nieva mucho.
5. Las clases empiezan.
6. Hace mucho calor.
7. Llueve mucho.
8. Esquiamos.
9. el entrenamiento (*training*) de béisbol
10. el Día de Acción de Gracias (*Thanksgiving*)

---

**8**

**¿Cuál es la fecha?** Give the dates for these holidays.

> **modelo**
>
> **el día de San Valentín**    14 de febrero

1. el día de San Patricio
2. el día de Halloween
3. el primer día de verano
4. el Año Nuevo
5. mi cumpleaños (*birthday*)
6. mi día de fiesta favorito

**9**

**Seleccionar** Paco is talking about his family and friends. Choose the word or phrase that best completes each sentence.

1. A mis padres les gusta ir a Yucatán porque (hace sol, nieva).
2. Mi primo de Kansas dice que durante (*during*) un tornado, hace mucho (sol, viento).
3. Mis amigos van a esquiar si (nieva, está nublado).
4. Tomo el sol cuando (hace calor, llueve).
5. Nosotros vamos a ver una película si hace (buen, mal) tiempo.
6. Mi hermana prefiere correr cuando (hace mucho calor, hace fresco).
7. Mis tíos van de excursión si hace (buen, mal) tiempo.
8. Mi padre no quiere jugar al golf si (hace fresco, llueve).
9. Cuando hace mucho (sol, frío) no salgo de casa y tomo chocolate caliente (*hot*).
10. Hoy mi sobrino va al parque porque (está lloviendo, hace buen tiempo).

**10**

**El clima** With a partner, take turns asking and answering questions about the weather and temperatures in these cities. Use the model as a guide.

> **modelo**
>
> **Estudiante 1:** ¿Qué tiempo hace hoy en Nueva York?
> **Estudiante 2:** Hace frío y hace viento.
> **Estudiante 1:** ¿Cuál es la temperatura máxima?
> **Estudiante 2:** Treinta y un grados (*degrees*).
> **Estudiante 1:** ¿Y la temperatura mínima?
> **Estudiante 2:** Diez grados.

soleado    lluvia    nieve    nublado    viento

| Nueva York | Miami | Chicago | París | Madrid | Tokio |
|---|---|---|---|---|---|
| Máx. 31° | Máx. 84° | Máx. 23° | Máx. 38° | Máx. 42° | Máx. 49° |
| Mín. 10° | Mín. 62° | Mín. 5° | Mín. 26° | Mín. 27° | Mín. 34° |

| Montreal | México D.F. | Cozumel | Caracas | Quito | Buenos Aires |
|---|---|---|---|---|---|
| Máx. 18° | Máx. 76° | Máx. 91° | Máx. 80° | Máx. 60° | Máx. 85° |
| Mín. 2° | Mín. 41° | Mín. 73° | Mín. 72° | Mín. 51° | Mín. 59° |

**NOTA CULTURAL**

In most Spanish-speaking countries, temperatures are given in degrees Celsius. Use these formulas to convert between **grados centígrados** and **grados Fahrenheit**.

degrees C. × 9 ÷ 5 + 32 = degrees F.

degrees F. - 32 × 5 ÷ 9 = degrees C.

**11**

**Completar** Complete these sentences with your own ideas.

1. Cuando hace sol, yo…
2. Cuando llueve, mis amigos y yo…
3. Cuando hace calor, mi familia…
4. Cuando hace viento, la gente…
5. Cuando hace frío, yo…
6. Cuando hace mal tiempo, mis amigos…
7. Cuando nieva, muchas personas…
8. Cuando está nublado, mis amigos y yo…
9. Cuando hace fresco, mis padres…
10. Cuando hace buen tiempo, mis amigos…

**CONSULTA**

**Calor** and **frío** can apply to both weather and people. Use **hacer** to describe weather conditions or climate.

(**Hace frío en Santiago.** *It's cold in Santiago.*)

Use **tener** to refer to people.

(**El viajero tiene frío.** *The traveler is cold.*)

 Practice more at **vhlcentral.com.**

# Comunicación

**12**

**Preguntas personales** In pairs, ask each other these questions.

1. ¿Cuál es la fecha de hoy?
2. ¿Qué estación es?
3. ¿Te gusta esta estación? ¿Por qué?
4. ¿Qué estación prefieres? ¿Por qué?
5. ¿Prefieres el mar o las montañas? ¿La playa o el campo? ¿Por qué?
6. Cuando estás de vacaciones, ¿qué haces?
7. Cuando haces un viaje, ¿qué te gusta hacer y ver?
8. ¿Piensas ir de vacaciones este verano? ¿Adónde quieres ir? ¿Por qué?
9. ¿Qué deseas ver y qué lugares quieres visitar?
10. ¿Cómo te gusta viajar? ¿En avión? ¿En motocicleta...?

**recursos**

**v̂ Text**

CPA
p. 4

**13**

**Encuesta** Your teacher will give you a worksheet. How does the weather affect what you do? Walk around the class and ask your classmates what they prefer or like to do in the weather conditions given. Note their responses on your worksheet. Be sure to personalize your survey by adding a few original questions to the list. Be prepared to report your findings to the class.

**14**

**La reservación** In pairs, imagine that one of you is a receptionist at a hotel and the other is a tourist calling to make a reservation. Read only the information that pertains to you. Then role-play the situation.

### Turista

Vas a viajar a Yucatán con un amigo. Llegan a Cancún el 23 de febrero y necesitan una habitación con baño privado para cuatro noches. Ustedes quieren descansar y prefieren una habitación con vista (*view*) al mar. Averigua (*Find out*) toda la información que necesitas (el costo, cuántas camas, etc.) y decide si quieres hacer la reservación o no.

### Empleado/a

Trabajas en la recepción del Hotel Oceanía en Cancún. Para el mes de febrero, sólo quedan (*remain*) dos habitaciones: una individual ($168/ noche) en el primer piso y una doble ($134/noche) en el quinto piso que tiene descuento porque no hay ascensor. Todas las habitaciones tienen baño privado y vista (*view*) a la piscina.

**15**

**Minidrama** With two or three classmates, prepare a skit about people who are on vacation or are planning a vacation. The skit should take place in one of these locations.

- una agencia de viajes
- una casa
- un aeropuerto, una estación de tren o una estación de autobuses
- un hotel
- el campo o la playa

# Síntesis

**recursos**

**v̂ Text**

CPA
pp. 5–6

**16**

**Un viaje** You are planning a trip to Mexico and have many questions about your itinerary on which your partner, a travel agent, will advise you. Your teacher will give you and your partner each a sheet with different instructions for acting out the roles.

# ¡Vamos a la playa!

Los seis amigos hacen un viaje a la playa.

Video: *Fotonovela*
Record and Compare

**PERSONAJES**    **FELIPE**    **JUAN CARLOS**

**TÍA ANA MARÍA** ¿Están listos para su viaje a la playa?

**TODOS** Sí.

**TÍA ANA MARÍA** Excelente... ¡A la estación de autobuses!

**MARU** ¿Dónde está Miguel?

**FELIPE** Yo lo traigo.

(*se escucha un grito de Miguel*)

**FELIPE** Ya está listo. Y tal vez enojado. Ahorita vamos.

**EMPLEADO** Bienvenidas. ¿En qué puedo servirles?

**MARU** Hola. Tenemos una reservación para seis personas para esta noche.

**EMPLEADO** ¿A nombre de quién?

**JIMENA** ¿Díaz? ¿López? No estoy segura.

**EMPLEADO** Aquí están las llaves de sus habitaciones.

**MARU** Gracias. Una cosa más. Mi novio y yo queremos hacer windsurf, pero no tenemos tablas.

**EMPLEADO** El botones las puede conseguir para ustedes.

**JUAN CARLOS** ¿Qué hace este libro aquí? ¿Estás estudiando en la playa?

**JIMENA** Sí, es que tengo un examen la próxima semana.

**JUAN CARLOS** Ay, Jimena. ¡No! ¿Vamos a nadar?

**JIMENA** Bueno, como estudiar es tan aburrido y el tiempo está tan bonito...

MARISSA     JIMENA     MARU     MIGUEL     MAITE FUENTES     ANA MARÍA     EMPLEADO

## Expresiones útiles

**Talking with hotel personnel**

**¿En qué puedo servirles?**
*How can I help you?*
**Tenemos una reservación.**
*We have a reservation.*
**¿A nombre de quién?**
*In whose name?*
**¿Quizás López? ¿Tal vez Díaz?**
*Maybe López? Maybe Díaz?*
**Ahora lo veo, aquí está. Díaz.**
*Now I see it. Here it is. Díaz.*
**Dos habitaciones en el primer piso
para seis huéspedes.**
*Two rooms on the first floor
for six guests.*
**Aquí están las llaves.**
*Here are the keys.*

**Describing a hotel**

**No está nada mal el hotel.**
*The hotel isn't bad at all.*
**Todo está tan limpio y cómodo.**
*Everything is so clean and comfortable.*
**Es excelente/estupendo/fabuloso/
fenomenal/increíble/magnífico/
maravilloso/perfecto.**
*It's excellent/stupendous/fabulous/
phenomenal/incredible/magnificent/
marvelous/perfect.*

**Talking about how you feel**

**Yo estoy un poco cansado/a.**
*I am a little tired.*
**Estoy confundido/a.** *I'm confused.*
**Todavía estoy/Sigo enojado/a contigo.**
*I'm still angry with you.*

**Additional vocabulary**

**afuera** *outside*
**agradable** *pleasant*
**el balde** *bucket*
**la crema de afeitar** *shaving cream*
**entonces** *so, then*
**es igual** *it's the same*
**el frente (frío)** *(cold) front*
**el grito** *scream*
**la temporada** *period of time*

---

**4**

**EMPLEADO** No encuentro su
nombre. Ah, no, ahora sí
lo veo, aquí está. Díaz. Dos
habitaciones en el primer
piso para seis huéspedes.

**5**

**FELIPE** No está nada mal el hotel,
¿verdad? Limpio, cómodo...
¡Oye, Miguel! ¿Todavía estás
enojado conmigo? (*a Juan
Carlos*) Miguel está de mal
humor. No me habla.

**JUAN CARLOS** ¿Todavía?

**9**

**MARISSA** Yo estoy un poco
cansada. ¿Y tú? ¿Por qué no
estás nadando?

**FELIPE** Es por causa de Miguel.

**10**

**MARISSA** Hmm, estoy confundida.

**FELIPE** Esta mañana. ¡Sigue
enojado conmigo!

**MARISSA** No puede seguir
enojado tanto tiempo.

**recursos**

vText

CPA
pp. 7–8

vhlcentral.com

# ¿Qué pasó?

**1**

**Completar** Complete these sentences with the correct term from the word bank.

| | | |
|---|---|---|
| aburrido | la estación de autobuses | montar a caballo |
| el aeropuerto | habitaciones | reservación |
| amable | la llave | tablas de windsurf |

1. Los amigos van a _____ para ir a la playa.
2. La _____ del hotel está a nombre de los Díaz.
3. Los amigos tienen dos _____ para seis personas.
4. El botones puede conseguir _____ para Maru.
5. Jimena dice que estudiar en vacaciones es muy _____.

**CONSULTA**

The meaning of some adjectives, such as **aburrido,** changes depending on whether they are used with **ser** or **estar.** See **Estructura 5.3,** pp. 170–171.

**2**

**Identificar** Identify the person who would make each statement.

**EMPLEADO**    **MARU**    **TÍA ANA MARÍA**    **FELIPE**    **JUAN CARLOS**

1. No lo encuentro, ¿a nombre de quién está su reservación?
2. ¿Por qué estás estudiando en la playa? ¡Mejor vamos a nadar!
3. Nuestra reservación es para seis personas en dos habitaciones.
4. El hotel es limpio y cómodo, pero estoy triste porque Miguel no me habla.
5. Suban al autobús y ¡buen viaje a la playa!

**3**

**Ordenar** Place these events in the correct order.

_____ a. El empleado busca la reservación.
_____ b. Marissa dice que está confundida.
_____ c. Los amigos están listos para ir a la playa.
_____ d. El empleado da (*gives*) las llaves de las habitaciones a las chicas.
_____ e. Miguel grita (*screams*).

**4**

**Conversar** With a partner, use these cues to create a conversation between a hotel employee and a guest in Mexico.

| **Huésped** | **Empleado/a** |
|---|---|
| Say hi to the employee and ask for your reservation. | → Tell the guest that you can't find his/her reservation. |
| Tell the employee that the reservation is in your name. | → Tell him/her that you found the reservation and that it's for a double room. |
| Tell the employee that the hotel is very clean and orderly. | → Say that you agree with the guest, welcome him/her and give him/her the keys. |
| Ask the employee to call the bellhop to help you with your luggage. | → Call the bellhop to help the guest with his/her luggage. |

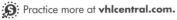 Practice more at **vhlcentral.com.**

# Pronunciación

## Spanish **b** and **v**

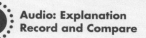 **Audio: Explanation
Record and Compare**

| **bueno** | **vóleibol** | **biblioteca** | **vivir** |

There is no difference in pronunciation between the Spanish letters **b** and **v**. However, each letter can be pronounced two different ways, depending on which letters appear next to them.

| **bonito** | **viajar** | **también** | **investigar** |

**B** and **v** are pronounced like the English hard *b* when they appear either as the first letter of a word, at the beginning of a phrase, or after **m** or **n**.

| **deber** | **novio** | **abril** | **cerveza** |

In all other positions, **b** and **v** have a softer pronunciation, which has no equivalent in English. Unlike the hard **b**, which is produced by tightly closing the lips and stopping the flow of air, the soft **b** is produced by keeping the lips slightly open.

| **bola** | **vela** | **Caribe** | **declive** |

In both pronunciations, there is no difference in sound between **b** and **v**. The English *v* sound, produced by friction between the upper teeth and lower lip, does not exist in Spanish. Instead, the soft **b** comes from friction between the two lips.

### Verónica y su esposo cantan boleros.

When **b** or **v** begins a word, its pronunciation depends on the previous word. At the beginning of a phrase or after a word that ends in **m** or **n**, it is pronounced as a hard **b**.

### Benito   es de Boquerón   pero vive   en Victoria.

Words that begin with **b** or **v** are pronounced with a soft **b** if they appear immediately after a word that ends in a vowel or any consonant other than **m** or **n**.

**Práctica** Read these words aloud to practice the **b** and the **v**.

1. hablamos
2. trabajar
3. botones
4. van
5. contabilidad
6. bien
7. doble
8. novia
9. béisbol
10. nublado
11. llave
12. invierno

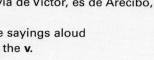
**Hombre prevenido vale por dos.**[2]

**Oraciones** Read these sentences aloud to practice the **b** and the **v**.

1. Vamos a Guaynabo en autobús.
2. Voy de vacaciones a la Isla Culebra.
3. Tengo una habitación individual en el octavo piso.
4. Víctor y Eva van por avión al Caribe.
5. La planta baja es bonita también.
6. ¿Qué vamos a ver en Bayamón?
7. Beatriz, la novia de Víctor, es de Arecibo, Puerto Rico.

**No hay mal que por bien no venga.**[1]

**Refranes** Read these sayings aloud to practice the **b** and the **v**.

2 *An ounce of prevention equals a pound of cure.*

1 *Every cloud has a silver lining.*

| **recursos** | | | |
| **v̂Text** | CPA p. 9 | CH p. 67 | vhlcentral.com |

Reading, Additional Reading

# Las cataratas del Iguazú

**Imagine the impressive and majestic Niagara Falls,** the most powerful waterfall in North America. Now, if you can, imagine a waterfall four times as wide and almost twice as tall that caused Eleanor Roosevelt to exclaim "Poor Niagara!" upon seeing it for the first time. Welcome to **las cataratas del Iguazú!**

Iguazú is located in Iguazú National Park, an area of subtropical jungle where Argentina meets Brazil. Its name comes from the indigenous Guaraní word for "great water." A UNESCO World Heritage Site, **las cataratas del Iguazú** span three kilometers and comprise 275 cascades split into two main sections by the San Martín Island. Most of the falls are about 82 meters (270 feet) high. The horseshoe-shaped cataract **Garganta del Diablo** (*Devil's Throat*) has the greatest water flow and is considered to be the most impressive; it also marks the border between Argentina and Brazil.

Each country offers different views and tourist options. Most visitors opt to use the numerous catwalks that are available on both

Garganta del Diablo

Isla San Martín

sides; however, from the Argentinean side, tourists can get very close to the falls, whereas Brazil provides more panoramic views. If you don't mind getting wet, a jet boat tour is a good choice; those looking for wildlife—such as toucans, ocelots, butterflies, and jaguars—should head for San Martín Island. Brazil boasts less conventional ways to view the falls, such as helicopter rides and rappelling, while Argentina focuses on sustainability with its **Tren Ecológico de la Selva** (*Ecological Jungle Train*), an environmentally friendly way to reach the walkways.

No matter which way you choose to enjoy the falls, you are certain to be captivated.

| Más cascadas° en Latinoamérica | | | |
|---|---|---|---|
| **Nombre** | **País** | **Altura°** | **Datos** |
| Salto Ángel | Venezuela | 979 metros | la más alta° del mundo° |
| Catarata del Gocta | Perú | 771 metros | descubierta° en 2006 |
| Piedra Volada | México | 453 metros | la más alta de México |

cascadas *waterfalls* Altura *Height* más alta *tallest* mundo *world* descubierta *discovered*

1 **¿Cierto o falso?** Indicate whether these statements are cierto or falso. Correct the false statements.

1. Iguazú Falls is located on the border of Argentina and Brazil.
2. Niagara Falls is four times as wide as Iguazú Falls.
3. Iguazú Falls has a few cascades, each about 82 meters.
4. Tourists visiting Iguazú can see exotic wildlife.
5. *Iguazú* is the Guaraní word for "blue water."
6. You can access the walkways by taking the **Garganta del Diablo.**
7. It is possible for tourists to visit Iguazú Falls by air.
8. **Salto Ángel** is the tallest waterfall in the world.
9. There are no waterfalls in Mexico.
10. For the best views of Iguazú Falls, tourists should visit the Brazilian side.

## Viajes y turismo

| | |
|---|---|
| **el asiento del medio, del pasillo, de la ventanilla** | *center, aisle, window seat* |
| **el itinerario** | *itinerary* |
| **media pensión** | *breakfast and one meal included* |
| **el ómnibus** (Perú) | **el autobús** |
| **pensión completa** | *all meals included* |
| **el puente** | *long weekend (lit., bridge)* |

## Destinos populares

- **Las playas del Parque Nacional Manuel Antonio** (Costa Rica) ofrecen° la oportunidad de nadar y luego caminar por el bosque tropical°.

- **Teotihuacán** (México) Desde la época° de los aztecas, aquí se celebra el equinoccio de primavera en la Pirámide del Sol.

- **Puerto Chicama** (Perú), con sus olas° de cuatro kilómetros de largo°, es un destino para surfistas expertos.

- **Tikal** (Guatemala) Aquí puedes ver las maravillas de la selva° y ruinas de la civilización maya.

- **Las playas de Rincón** (Puerto Rico) Son ideales para descansar y observar ballenas°.

ofrecen *offer* bosque tropical *rainforest* Desde la época *Since the time* olas *waves* de largo *in length* selva *jungle* ballenas *whales*

# Punta del Este

One of South America's largest and most fashionable beach resort towns is Uruguay's **Punta del Este**, a narrow strip of land containing twenty miles of pristine beaches. Its peninsular shape gives it two very different seascapes. **La Playa Mansa**, facing the bay and therefore the more protected side, has calm waters. Here, people practice water sports like swimming, water skiing, windsurfing, and diving. **La Playa Brava**, facing east, receives the Atlantic Ocean's powerful, wave-producing winds, making it popular for surfing, body boarding, and kite surfing. Besides the beaches, posh shopping, and world-famous nightlife, **Punta** offers its 600,000 yearly visitors yacht and fishing clubs, golf courses, and excursions to observe sea lions at the **Isla de Lobos** nature reserve.

### Conexión Internet

¿Cuáles son los sitios más populares para el turismo en Puerto Rico?

Go to **vhlcentral.com** to find more cultural information related to this **Cultura** section.

---

**2** **Comprensión** Complete the sentences.

1. En las playas de Rincón puedes ver _____.
2. Cerca de 600.000 turistas visitan _____ cada año.
3. En el avión pides el _____ si te gusta ver el paisaje.
4. En Punta del Este, la gente prefiere nadar en la Playa _____.
5. El _____ es un medio de transporte en Perú.

**3** **De vacaciones** Spring break is coming up, and your class is going on a trip abroad. Working in a small group, decide where you will go, how you will get there, and what each of you will do. Present your trip to the class.

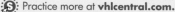  Practice more at **vhlcentral.com**.

## 5.1 **Estar** with conditions and emotions

Explanation Tutorial

**ANTE TODO** As you have already learned, the verb **estar** is used to talk about how you feel and to say where people, places, and things are located. **Estar** is also used with adjectives to talk about certain emotional and physical conditions.

▶ Use **estar** with adjectives to describe the physical condition of places and things.

La habitación **está** sucia.
*The room is dirty.*

La puerta **está** cerrada.
*The door is closed.*

▶ Use **estar** with adjectives to describe how people feel, both mentally and physically.

Yo estoy cansada.

¿Están listos para su viaje?

▶ **¡Atención!** Two important expressions with **estar** that you can use to talk about conditions and emotions are **estar de buen humor** (*to be in a good mood*) and **estar de mal humor** (*to be in a bad mood*).

### Adjectives that describe emotions and conditions

| | | | | | |
|---|---|---|---|---|---|
| **abierto/a** | open | **contento/a** | happy; content | **listo/a** | ready |
| **aburrido/a** | bored | **desordenado/a** | disorderly | **nervioso/a** | nervous |
| **alegre** | happy; joyful | **enamorado/a (de)** | in love (with) | **ocupado/a** | busy |
| **avergonzado/a** | embarrassed | | | **ordenado/a** | orderly |
| **cansado/a** | tired | **enojado/a** | mad; angry | **preocupado/a (por)** | worried (about) |
| **cerrado/a** | closed | **equivocado/a** | wrong | | |
| **cómodo/a** | comfortable | **feliz** | happy | **seguro/a** | sure |
| **confundido/a** | confused | **limpio/a** | clean | **sucio/a** | dirty |
| | | | | **triste** | sad |

 **¡INTÉNTALO!** Provide the present tense forms of **estar**, and choose which adjective best completes the sentence.

1. La biblioteca ___*está*___ (cerrada / nerviosa) los domingos por la noche. *cerrada*
2. Nosotros _____ muy (ocupados / equivocados) todos los lunes.
3. Ellas _____ (alegres / confundidas) porque tienen vacaciones.
4. Javier _____ (enamorado / ordenado) de Maribel.
5. Diana _____ (enojada / limpia) con su hermano.
6. Yo _____ (nerviosa / abierta) por el viaje.
7. La habitación siempre _____ (ordenada / segura) cuando vuelven sus padres.
8. Ustedes no comprenden; _____ (equivocados / tristes).

**recursos**

v̂Text

CPA pp. 10–12

CH pp. 69–70

vhlcentral.com

# Práctica y Comunicación

**AYUDA**

Make sure that you have agreement between:
• Subjects and verbs in person and number
• Nouns and adjectives in gender and number
Ell**os** no est**án** enferm**os**.
*They are not sick.*

**1**

**¿Cómo están?** Complete Martín's statements about how he and other people are feeling. In the first blank, fill in the correct form of **estar**. In the second blank, fill in the adjective that best fits the context.

1. Yo _____ un poco _____ porque tengo un examen mañana.
2. Mi hermana Patricia _____ muy _____ porque mañana va a hacer una excursión al campo.
3. Mis hermanos Juan y José salen de la casa a las cinco de la mañana. Por la noche, siempre _____ muy _____.
4. Mi amigo Ramiro _____ _____; su novia se llama Adela.
5. Mi papá y sus colegas _____ muy _____ hoy. ¡Hay mucho trabajo!
6. Patricia y yo _____ un poco _____ por ellos porque trabajan mucho.
7. Mi amiga Mónica _____ un poco _____ porque sus amigos no pueden salir esta noche.
8. Esta clase no es muy interesante. ¿Tú _____ _____ también?

**2**

**Describir** Describe these people and places.

1. Anabela

2. Juan y Luisa

3. la habitación de Teresa

4. la habitación de César

**3**

**Situaciones** With a partner, use **estar** to talk about how you feel in these situations.

1. Cuando hace sol…
2. Cuando tomas un examen…
3. Cuando viajas en avión…

4. Cuando estás en la clase de español…
5. Cuando ves una película con tu actor/actriz favorito/a…

**4**

**En la tele** In small groups, imagine that you are a family that stars on a reality TV show. You are vacationing together, but the trip isn't going well for everyone. Write the script of a scene from the show and then act it out. Use at least six adjectives from the previous page and be creative!

**modelo**

**Papá:** ¿Por qué estás enojada, María Rosa? El hotel es muy bonito y las habitaciones están limpias.

**Mamá:** ¡Pero mira, Roberto! Las maletas de Elisa están abiertas y, como siempre, sus cosas están muy desordenadas.

 Practice more at **vhlcentral.com**.

Explanation Tutorial

## 5.2 The present progressive

**ANTE TODO** Both Spanish and English use the present progressive, which consists of the present tense of the verb *to be* and the present participle of another verb (the *-ing* form in English).

Las chicas están hablando con el empleado del hotel.

¿Estás estudiando en la playa?

▶ Form the present progressive with the present tense of **estar** and a present participle.

FORM OF **ESTAR** + PRESENT PARTICIPLE

**Estoy pescando.**
*I am fishing.*

FORM OF **ESTAR** + PRESENT PARTICIPLE

**Estamos comiendo.**
*We are eating.*

▶ The present participle of regular **-ar**, **-er**, and **-ir** verbs is formed as follows:

| INFINITIVE | STEM | ENDING | PRESENT PARTICIPLE |
|---|---|---|---|
| hablar | habl- | **-ando** | habl**ando** |
| comer | com- | **-iendo** | com**iendo** |
| escribir | escrib- | **-iendo** | escrib**iendo** |

▶ **¡Atención!** When the stem of an **-er** or **-ir** verb ends in a vowel, the present participle ends in **-yendo**.

| INFINITIVE | STEM | ENDING | PRESENT PARTICIPLE |
|---|---|---|---|
| leer | le- | **-yendo** | le**yendo** |
| oír | o- | **-yendo** | o**yendo** |
| traer | tra- | **-yendo** | tra**yendo** |

▶ **Ir, poder,** and **venir** have irregular present participles (**yendo, pudiendo, viniendo**). Several other verbs have irregular present participles that you will need to learn.

▶ **-Ir** stem-changing verbs have a stem change in the present participle.

### -ir stem-changing verbs

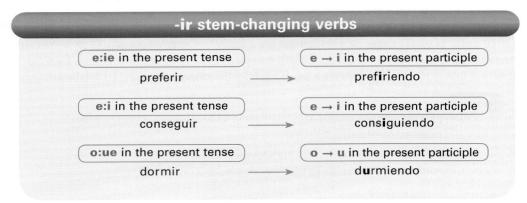

| e:ie in the present tense | e → i in the present participle |
|---|---|
| preferir | → | prefiriendo |

| e:i in the present tense | e → i in the present participle |
|---|---|
| conseguir | → | consiguiendo |

| o:ue in the present tense | o → u in the present participle |
|---|---|
| dormir | → | durmiendo |

The use of the present progressive is much more restricted in Spanish than in English. In Spanish, the present progressive is mainly used to emphasize that an action is in progress at the time of speaking.

Maru **está escuchando** música latina **ahora mismo**.
*Maru is listening to Latin music right now.*

Felipe y su amigo **todavía están jugando** al fútbol.
*Felipe and his friend are still playing soccer.*

In English, the present progressive is often used to talk about situations and actions that occur over an extended period of time or in the future. In Spanish, the simple present tense is often used instead.

Xavier **estudia** computación este semestre.
*Xavier is studying computer science this semester.*

Marissa **sale** mañana para los Estados Unidos.
*Marissa is leaving tomorrow for the United States.*

¿Está pensando en su futuro?
**Nosotros, sí.**

🏛 **BANCO CONGRESO** 🏛

*Preparándolo para el mañana*

**¡INTÉNTALO!**   Create complete sentences by putting the verbs in the present progressive.

1. mis amigos / descansar en la playa  *Mis amigos están descansando en la playa.*
2. nosotros / practicar deportes _____
3. Carmen / comer en casa _____
4. nuestro equipo / ganar el partido _____
5. yo / leer el periódico _____
6. él / pensar comprar una bicicleta roja _____
7. ustedes / jugar a las cartas _____
8. José y Francisco / dormir _____
9. Marisa / leer correo electrónico _____
10. yo / preparar sándwiches _____
11. Carlos / tomar fotos _____
12. ¿dormir / tú? _____

# Práctica

## 1

**Completar** Alfredo's Spanish class is preparing to travel to Puerto Rico. Use the present progressive of the verb in parentheses to complete Alfredo's description of what everyone is doing.

1. Yo _____ (investigar) la situación política de la isla (*island*).
2. La esposa del profesor _____ (hacer) las maletas.
3. Marta y José Luis _____ (buscar) información sobre San Juan en Internet.
4. Enrique y yo _____ (leer) un correo electrónico de nuestro amigo puertorriqueño.
5. Javier _____ (aprender) mucho sobre la cultura puertorriqueña.
6. Y tú _____ (practicar) el español, ¿verdad?

## 2

**¿Qué están haciendo?** María and her friends are vacationing at a resort in San Juan, Puerto Rico. Complete her description of what everyone is doing right now.

**CONSULTA**

For more information about Puerto Rico, see **Panorama**, pp. 186–187.

1. Yo     2. Javier     3. Alejandra y Rebeca

4. Celia y yo     5. Samuel     6. Lorenzo

## 3

**Personajes famosos** Say what these celebrities are doing right now, using the cues provided.

**AYUDA**

Stephenie Meyer: **novelas**
Rachel Ray: **televisión, negocios** (*business*)
James Cameron: **cine**
Venus y Serena Williams: **tenis**
Jason Bay: **béisbol**
Nelly Furtado: **canciones**
Steve Nash: **baloncesto**
Las Rockettes de Nueva York: **baile**

**modelo**

**Celine Dion**
*Celine Dion está cantando una canción ahora mismo.*

| A | | B | |
|---|---|---|---|
| Stephenie Meyer | Nelly Furtado | bailar | hacer |
| Rachel Ray | Steve Nash | cantar | jugar |
| James Cameron | Las Rockettes de | correr | preparar |
| Venus y Serena | Nueva York | escribir | ¿? |
| Williams | ¿? | hablar | ¿? |
| Jason Bay | ¿? | | |

 Practice more at **vhlcentral.com**.

# Comunicación

**4**

**Preguntar** With a partner, take turns asking each other what you are doing at these times.

> **Estudiante 1:** ¡Hola, Andrés! Son las ocho de la mañana. ¿Qué estás haciendo?
> **Estudiante 2:** Estoy desayunando.

| | | | |
|---|---|---|---|
| 1. 5:00 a.m. | 3. 11:00 a.m. | 5. 2:00 p.m. | 7. 9:00 p.m. |
| 2. 9:30 a.m. | 4. 12:00 p.m. | 6. 5:00 p.m. | 8. 11:30 p.m. |

**5**

**Describir** Work with a partner and use the present progressive to describe what is going on in this Spanish beach scene.

**NOTA CULTURAL**

Nearly 60 million tourists travel to Spain every year, many of them drawn by the warm climate and beautiful coasts. Tourists wanting a beach vacation go mostly to the **Costa del Sol** or the Balearic Islands, in the Mediterranean.

**6**

**Conversar** Imagine that you and a classmate are each babysitting a group of children. With a partner, prepare a telephone conversation using these cues. Be creative and add further comments.

| **Estudiante 1** | **Estudiante 2** |
|---|---|
| Say hello and ask what the kids are doing. | Say hello and tell your partner that two of your kids are doing their homework. Then ask what the kids at his/her house are doing. |
| Tell your partner that two of your kids are running and dancing in the house. | Tell your partner that one of the kids is reading. |
| Tell your partner that you are tired and that two of your kids are watching TV and eating pizza. | Tell your partner that one of the kids is sleeping. |
| Tell your partner you have to go; the kids are playing soccer in the house. | Say goodbye and good luck (**¡Buena suerte!**). |

# Síntesis

**recursos**

**v Text**

CPA
pp. 15–16

**7**

**¿Qué están haciendo?** A group of classmates is traveling to San Juan, Puerto Rico for a week-long Spanish immersion program. In order for the participants to be on time for their flight, you and your partner must locate them. Your teacher will give you each a handout to help you complete this task.

Explanation Tutorial

## 5.3 Ser and estar

**ANTE TODO** You have already learned that **ser** and **estar** both mean *to be* but are used for different purposes. These charts summarize the key differences in usage between **ser** and **estar**.

### Uses of ser

| | |
|---|---|
| 1. **Nationality and place of origin** . . . . . . . | Juan Carlos **es** argentino.<br>**Es** de Buenos Aires. |
| 2. **Profession or occupation** . . . . . . . . . . . | Adela **es** agente de viajes.<br>Francisco **es** médico. |
| 3. **Characteristics of people and things** . . . | José y Clara **son** simpáticos.<br>El clima de Puerto Rico **es** agradable. |
| 4. **Generalizations** . . . . . . . . . . . . . . . . . . . . | ¡**Es** fabuloso viajar!<br>**Es** difícil estudiar a la una de la mañana. |
| 5. **Possession** . . . . . . . . . . . . . . . . . . . . . . | **Es** la pluma de Jimena.<br>**Son** las llaves del señor Díaz. |
| 6. **What something is made of** . . . . . . . . | La bicicleta **es** de metal.<br>Los pasajes **son** de papel. |
| 7. **Time and date** . . . . . . . . . . . . . . . . . . . . | Hoy **es** martes. **Son** las dos.<br>Hoy **es** el primero de julio. |
| 8. **Where or when an event takes place** . . | El partido **es** en el estadio Santa Fe.<br>La conferencia **es** a las siete. |

Ellos son mis amigos.

Miguel está enojado conmigo.

### Uses of estar

| | |
|---|---|
| 1. **Location or spatial relationships** . . . . . | El aeropuerto **está** lejos de la ciudad.<br>Tu habitación **está** en el tercer piso. |
| 2. **Health** . . . . . . . . . . . . . . . . . . . . . . . . . . | ¿Cómo **estás**?<br>**Estoy** bien, gracias. |
| 3. **Physical states and conditions** . . . . . . . | El profesor **está** ocupado.<br>Las ventanas **están** abiertas. |
| 4. **Emotional states** . . . . . . . . . . . . . . . . . | Marissa **está** feliz hoy.<br>**Estoy** muy enojado con Maru. |
| 5. **Certain weather expressions** . . . . . . . . | **Está** lloviendo.<br>**Está** nublado. |
| 6. **Ongoing actions (progressive tenses)** . . | **Estamos** estudiando para un examen.<br>Ana **está** leyendo una novela. |

# Ser and estar with adjectives

▶ With many descriptive adjectives, **ser** and **estar** can both be used, but the meaning will change.

| | |
|---|---|
| Juan **es** delgado. | Ana **es** nerviosa. |
| *Juan is thin.* | *Ana is a nervous person.* |
| Juan **está** más delgado hoy. | Ana **está** nerviosa por el examen. |
| *Juan looks thinner today.* | *Ana is nervous because of the exam.* |

▶ In the examples above, the statements with **ser** are general observations about the inherent qualities of Juan and Ana. The statements with **estar** describe conditions that are variable.

▶ Here are some adjectives that change in meaning when used with **ser** and **estar**.

| With ser | With estar |
|---|---|
| El chico **es listo**. | El chico **está listo**. |
| *The boy is **smart**.* | *The boy is **ready**.* |
| La profesora **es mala**. | La profesora **está mala**. |
| *The professor is **bad**.* | *The professor is **sick**.* |
| Jaime **es aburrido**. | Jaime **está aburrido**. |
| *Jaime is **boring**.* | *Jaime is **bored**.* |
| Las peras **son verdes**. | Las peras **están verdes**. |
| *Pears are **green**.* | *The pears are **not ripe**.* |
| El gato **es muy vivo**. | El gato **está vivo**. |
| *The cat is very **lively**.* | *The cat is **alive**.* |
| Iván **es un hombre seguro**. | Iván no **está seguro**. |
| *Iván is a **confident** man.* | *Iván is not **sure**.* |

**¡ATENCIÓN!**

When referring to objects, **ser seguro/a** means *to be safe*. **El puente es seguro.** *The bridge is safe.*

**¡INTÉNTALO!**   Form complete sentences by using the correct form of **ser** or **estar** and making any other necessary changes.

1. Alejandra / cansado
   Alejandra está cansada.

2. ellos / pelirrojo
   _____

3. Carmen / alto
   _____

4. yo / la clase de español
   _____

5. película / a las once
   _____

6. hoy / viernes
   _____

7. nosotras / enojado
   _____

8. Antonio / médico
   _____

9. Romeo y Julieta / enamorado
   _____

10. libros / de Ana
    _____

11. Marisa y Juan / estudiando
    _____

12. partido de baloncesto / gimnasio
    _____

**recursos**

v Text

CPA
pp. 17–19

CH
pp. 73–74

vhlcentral.com

# Práctica

**1**

**¿Ser o estar?** Indicate whether each adjective takes **ser** or **estar**. **¡Ojo!** Three of them can take both verbs.

|  | ser | estar |  |  | ser | estar |
|---|---|---|---|---|---|---|
| 1. delgada | ○ | ○ | 5. seguro | | ○ | ○ |
| 2. canadiense | ○ | ○ | 6. enojada | | ○ | ○ |
| 3. enamorado | ○ | ○ | 7. importante | | ○ | ○ |
| 4. lista | ○ | ○ | 8. avergonzada | | ○ | ○ |

**2**

**Completar** Complete this conversation with the appropriate forms of **ser** and **estar**.

**EDUARDO** ¡Hola, Ceci! ¿Cómo (1)_____?

**CECILIA** Hola, Eduardo. Bien, gracias. ¡Qué guapo (2)_____ hoy!

**EDUARDO** Gracias. (3)_____ muy amable. Oye, ¿qué (4)_____ haciendo? (5)¿_____ ocupada?

**CECILIA** No, sólo le (6)_____ escribiendo una carta a mi prima Pilar.

**EDUARDO** ¿De dónde (7)_____ ella?

**CECILIA** Pilar (8)_____ de Ecuador. Su papá (9)_____ médico en Quito. Pero ahora Pilar y su familia (10)_____ de vacaciones en Ponce, Puerto Rico.

**EDUARDO** Y… ¿cómo (11)_____ Pilar?

**CECILIA** (12)_____ muy lista. Y también (13)_____ alta, rubia y muy bonita.

**3**

**En el parque** With a partner, take turns describing the people in the drawing. Your descriptions should answer the questions provided.

1. ¿Quiénes son?
2. ¿Dónde están?
3. ¿Cómo son?
4. ¿Cómo están?
5. ¿Qué están haciendo?
6. ¿Qué estación es?
7. ¿Qué tiempo hace?
8. ¿Quiénes están de vacaciones?

**S** Practice more at **vhlcentral.com.**

# Comunicación

**4**

**Describir**  With a classmate, take turns describing these people. Mention where they are from, what they are like, how they are feeling, and what they are doing right now.

> **modelo**
>
> **tu compañero/a de clase**
>
> *Mi compañera de clase es de San Juan, Puerto Rico. Es muy inteligente.*
> *Está cansada pero está estudiando porque tiene un examen.*

1. tu mejor (*best*) amigo/a
2. tu actor/actriz favorito/a
3. tu profesor(a) favorito/a
4. tu vecino/a
5. tus abuelos
6. tus padres

**5**

**Adivinar**  Get together with a partner and take turns describing a celebrity using these items as a guide. Don't mention the celebrity's name. Can your partner guess who you are describing?

- descripción física
- cómo está ahora
- origen
- dónde está ahora
- qué está haciendo ahora
- profesión u ocupación

**6**

**En el aeropuerto**  In groups of three, take turns assuming the identity of a character from this drawing. Your partners will ask you questions using **ser** and **estar** until they figure out who you are.

> **modelo**
>
> **Estudiante 3:** ¿Dónde estás?
> **Estudiante 1:** Estoy cerca de la puerta.
> **Estudiante 2:** ¿Qué estás haciendo?
> **Estudiante 1:** Estoy escuchando a otra persona.
>
> **Estudiante 3:** ¿Eres uno de los pasajeros?
> **Estudiante 1:** No, soy empleado del aeropuerto.
> **Estudiante 2:** ¿Eres Camilo?

# Síntesis

**7**

**Conversación**  In pairs, imagine that you and your partner are two of the characters in the drawing in **Actividad 6**. After boarding, you are seated next to each other and strike up a conversation. Act out what you would say to your fellow passenger.

## 5.4 Direct object nouns and pronouns

 **Explanation Tutorial**

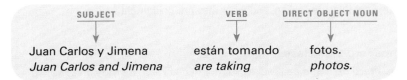

| SUBJECT | VERB | DIRECT OBJECT NOUN |
|---|---|---|
| Juan Carlos y Jimena | están tomando | fotos. |
| *Juan Carlos and Jimena* | *are taking* | *photos.* |

▶ A direct object noun receives the action of the verb directly and generally follows the verb. In the example above, the direct object noun answers the question *What are Juan Carlos and Jimena taking?*

▶ When a direct object noun in Spanish is a person or a pet, it is preceded by the word **a**. This is called the personal **a**; there is no English equivalent for this construction.

La señora Díaz visita **a** la doctora Salas.
*Mrs. Díaz is visiting Dr. Salas.*

La señora Díaz visita el café Delicias.
*Mrs. Díaz is visiting Delicias Café.*

▶ In the first sentence above, the personal **a** is required because the direct object is a person. In the second sentence, the personal **a** is not required because the direct object is a place, not a person.

No tenemos tablas de windsurf.

Miguel no me habla.

El botones las puede conseguir para ustedes.

▶ Direct object pronouns are words that replace direct object nouns. Like English, Spanish uses a direct object pronoun to avoid repeating a noun already mentioned.

| | DIRECT OBJECT | | | DIRECT OBJECT PRONOUN |
|---|---|---|---|---|
| Maribel hace | las maletas. | | Maribel | las hace. |
| Felipe compra | el sombrero. | ▶ | Felipe | lo compra. |
| Vicky tiene | la llave. | | Vicky | la tiene. |

### Direct object pronouns

| SINGULAR | | PLURAL | |
|---|---|---|---|
| **me** | *me* | **nos** | *us* |
| **te** | *you* | **os** | *you* (fam.) |
| **lo** | *you* | **los** | *you* (m., form.) |
| | *him; it* | | *them* (m.) |
| **la** | *you her; it* | **las** | *you* (f., form.) |
| | | | *them* (f.) |

▶ In affirmative sentences, direct object pronouns generally appear before the conjugated verb. In negative sentences, the pronoun is placed between the word **no** and the verb.

| | |
|---|---|
| Adela practica **el tenis**. | Gabriela no tiene **las llaves**. |
| Adela **lo** practica. | Gabriela **no las** tiene. |
| | |
| Carmen compra **los pasajes**. | Diego no hace **las maletas**. |
| Carmen **los** compra. | Diego **no las** hace. |

▶ When the verb is an infinitive construction, such as **ir a** + [*infinitive*], the direct object pronoun can be placed before the conjugated form or attached to the infinitive.

Ellos van a escribir **unas postales**.
   Ellos **las** van a escribir.
   Ellos van a escribir**las**.

Lidia quiere ver **una película**.
   Lidia **la** quiere ver.
   Lidia quiere ver**la**.

▶ When the verb is in the present progressive, the direct object pronoun can be placed before the conjugated form or attached to the present participle. **¡Atención!** When a direct object pronoun is attached to the present participle, an accent mark is added to maintain the proper stress.

Gerardo está leyendo **la lección**.
   Gerardo **la** está leyendo.
   Gerardo está leyéndo**la**.

Toni está mirando **el partido**.
   Toni **lo** está mirando.
   Toni está mirándo**lo**.

**¡INTÉNTALO!**  Choose the correct direct object pronoun for each sentence.

1. Tienes el libro de español. *c*
   a. La tienes.          b. Los tienes.          c. Lo tienes.
2. Voy a ver el partido de baloncesto.
   a. Voy a verlo.        b. Voy a verte.          c. Voy a vernos.
3. El artista quiere dibujar a Luisa con su mamá.
   a. Quiere dibujarme.   b. Quiere dibujarla.     c. Quiere dibujarlas.
4. Marcos busca la llave.
   a. Me busca.           b. La busca.             c. Las busca.
5. Rita me lleva al aeropuerto y también lleva a Tomás.
   a. Nos lleva.          b. Las lleva.            c. Te lleva.
6. Puedo oír a Gerardo y a Miguel.
   a. Puedo oírte.        b. Puedo oírlos.         c. Puedo oírlo.
7. Quieren estudiar la gramática.
   a. Quieren estudiarnos.  b. Quieren estudiarlo.  c. Quieren estudiarla.
8. ¿Practicas los verbos irregulares?
   a. ¿Los practicas?     b. ¿Las practicas?       c. ¿Lo practicas?
9. Ignacio ve la película.
   a. La ve.              b. Lo ve.                c. Las ve.
10. Sandra va a invitar a Mario a la excursión. También me va a invitar a mí.
   a. Los va a invitar.   b. Lo va a invitar.      c. Nos va a invitar.

# Práctica

**1**

**Simplificar** Señora Vega's class is planning a trip to Costa Rica. Describe their preparations by changing the direct object nouns into direct object pronouns.

> **modelo**
> La profesora Vega tiene su pasaporte.
> *La profesora Vega lo tiene.*

1. Gustavo y Héctor confirman las reservaciones.
2. Nosotros leemos los folletos (*brochures*).
3. Ana María estudia el mapa.
4. Yo aprendo los nombres de los monumentos de San José.
5. Alicia escucha a la profesora.
6. Miguel escribe las direcciones para ir al hotel.
7. Esteban busca el pasaje. ◀
8. Nosotros planeamos una excursión.

**¡LENGUA VIVA!**

There are many Spanish words that correspond to *ticket*. **Billete** and **pasaje** usually refer to a ticket for travel, such as an airplane ticket. **Entrada** refers to a ticket to an event, such as a concert or a movie. **Boleto** can be used in either case.

**2**

**Vacaciones** Ramón is going to San Juan, Puerto Rico with his friends, Javier and Marcos. Express his thoughts more succinctly using direct object pronouns.

> **modelo**
> Quiero hacer una excursión.
> *Quiero hacerla./La quiero hacer.*

1. Voy a hacer mi maleta.
2. Necesitamos llevar los pasaportes.
3. Marcos está pidiendo el folleto turístico.
4. Javier debe llamar a sus padres.
5. Ellos esperan visitar el Viejo San Juan.
6. Puedo llamar a Javier por la mañana. ◀
7. Prefiero llevar mi cámara.
8. No queremos perder nuestras reservaciones de hotel.

**NOTA CULTURAL**

Since Puerto Rico is a U.S. territory, passengers traveling there from the U.S. mainland do not need passports or visas. Passengers traveling to Puerto Rico from a foreign country, however, must meet travel requirements identical to those required for travel to the U.S. mainland. Puerto Ricans are U.S. citizens and can therefore travel to the U.S. mainland without any travel documents.

**3**

**¿Quién?** The Garza family is preparing to go on a vacation to Puerto Rico. Based on the clues, answer the questions. Use direct object pronouns in your answers.

> **modelo**
> ¿Quién hace las reservaciones para el hotel? (el Sr. Garza)
> *El Sr. Garza las hace.*

1. ¿Quién compra los pasajes de avión? (la Sra. Garza)
2. ¿Quién tiene que hacer las maletas de los niños? (María)
3. ¿Quiénes buscan los pasaportes? (Antonio y María)
4. ¿Quién va a confirmar las reservaciones de hotel? (la Sra. Garza)
5. ¿Quién busca la cámara? (María)
6. ¿Quién compra un mapa de Puerto Rico? (Antonio)

 Practice more at **vhlcentral.com.**

# Comunicación

**4**

**Entrevista** Take turns asking and answering these questions with a classmate. Be sure to use direct object pronouns in your responses.

1. ¿Ves mucho la televisión?
2. ¿Cuándo vas a ver tu programa favorito?
3. ¿Quién prepara la comida (*food*) en tu casa?
4. ¿Te visita mucho tu abuelo/a?
5. ¿Visitas mucho a tus abuelos?
6. ¿Nos entienden nuestros padres a nosotros?
7. ¿Cuándo ves a tus amigos/as?
8. ¿Cuándo te llaman tus amigos/as?

**5**

**Los pasajeros** With a partner, take turns asking each other questions about the drawing. Use the word bank and direct object pronouns.

**AYUDA**

For travel-related vocabulary, see **Contextos**, pp. 152–153.

> **modelo**
>
> **Estudiante 1:** ¿Quién está leyendo el libro?
> **Estudiante 2:** Susana lo está leyendo./Susana está leyéndolo.

| buscar | confirmar | escribir | leer | tener | vender |
|--------|-----------|----------|------|-------|--------|
| comprar | encontrar | escuchar | llevar | traer | ¿? |

Sra. Sánchez    Orlando    Sr. López

Marta    Sr. Sánchez    Susana    Miguelito

# Síntesis

**6**

**Adivinanzas** In pairs, take turns describing a person, place, or thing for your partner to guess. Each of you should give at least five descriptions.

> **modelo**
>
> **Estudiante 1:** Lo uso para (*I use it to*) escribir en mi cuaderno. No es muy grande y tiene borrador. ¿Qué es?
> **Estudiante 2:** ¿Es un lápiz?
> **Estudiante 1:** ¡Sí!

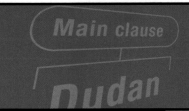

# Recapitulación

**Diagnostics
Remediation Activities**

Review the grammar concepts you have learned in this lesson by completing these activities.

**1**

**Completar** Complete the chart with the correct present participle of these verbs. **8 pts.**

| Infinitive | Present participle | Infinitive | Present participle |
|---|---|---|---|
| hacer | | estar | |
| acampar | | ser | |
| tener | | vivir | |
| venir | | estudiar | |

**2**

**Vacaciones en París** Complete this paragraph about Julia's trip to Paris with the correct form of **ser** or **estar**. **12 pts.**

Hoy (1) _____ (es/está) el 3 de julio y voy a París por tres semanas. (Yo) (2) _____ (Soy/Estoy) muy feliz porque voy a ver a mi mejor amiga. Ella (3) _____ (es/está) de Puerto Rico, pero ahora (4) _____ (es/está) viviendo en París. También (yo) (5) _____ (soy/estoy) un poco nerviosa porque (6) _____ (es/está) mi primer viaje a Francia. El vuelo (*flight*) (7) _____ (es/está) hoy por la tarde, pero ahora (8) _____ (es/está) lloviendo. Por eso (9) _____ (somos/estamos) preocupadas, porque probablemente el avión va a salir tarde. Mi equipaje ya (10) _____ (es/está) listo. (11) _____ (Es/Está) tarde y me tengo que ir. ¡Va a (12) _____ (ser/estar) un viaje fenomenal!

**3**

**¿Qué hacen?** Respond to these questions by indicating what people do with the items mentioned. Use direct object pronouns. **5 pts.**

> **modelo**
> ¿Qué hacen ellos con la película?
> La ven.

1. ¿Qué haces tú con el libro de viajes? (leer) _____
2. ¿Qué hacen los turistas en la ciudad? (explorar) _____
3. ¿Qué hace el botones con el equipaje? (llevar) _____
4. ¿Qué hace la agente con las reservaciones? (confirmar) _____
5. ¿Qué hacen ustedes con los pasaportes? (mostrar) _____

## RESUMEN GRAMATICAL

**5.1  Estar with conditions and emotions**  *p. 164*

► Yo **est**oy aburrido/a, feliz, nervioso/a.

► El cuarto **est**á desordenado, limpio, ordenado.

► Estos libros **est**án abiertos, cerrados, sucios.

**5.2  The present progressive**  *pp. 166–167*

► The present progressive is formed with the present tense of **estar** plus the present participle.

**Forming the present participle**

| infinitive | stem | ending | present participle |
|---|---|---|---|
| hablar | habl- | -ando | hablando |
| comer | com- | -iendo | comiendo |
| escribir | escrib- | -iendo | escribiendo |

**-ir stem-changing verbs**

| | infinitive | present participle |
|---|---|---|
| e:ie | preferir | **prefi**riendo |
| e:i | conseguir | **consi**guiendo |
| o:ue | dormir | **d**urmiendo |

► Irregular present participles: **yendo (ir)**, **pudiendo (poder)**, **viniendo (venir)**

**5.3  Ser and estar**  *pp. 170–171*

► Uses of **ser**: nationality, origin, profession or occupation, characteristics, generalizations, possession, what something is made of, time and date, time and place of events

► Uses of **estar**: location, health, physical states and conditions, emotional states, weather expressions, ongoing actions

► **Ser** and **estar** can both be used with many adjectives, but the meaning will change.

| Juan **es** delgado. | Juan **está** más delgado hoy. |
|---|---|
| *Juan is thin.* | *Juan looks thinner today.* |

**5.4 Direct object nouns and pronouns** *pp. 174–175*

**Direct object pronouns**

| Singular | | Plural | |
|---|---|---|---|
| me | lo | nos | los |
| te | la | os | las |

In affirmative sentences:
Adela practica el tenis. → Adela lo practica.

In negative sentences: Adela no lo practica.

With an infinitive:
Adela lo va a practicar./Adela va a practicarlo.

With the present progressive:
Adela lo está practicando./Adela está practicándolo.

**4** **Opuestos** Complete these sentences with the appropriate form of the verb **estar** and an antonym for the underlined adjective. **5 pts.**

**modelo**
Yo estoy <u>interesado</u>, pero Susana *está aburrida*.

1. Las tiendas están <u>abiertas</u>, pero la agencia de viajes _____ _____.
2. No me gustan las habitaciones <u>desordenadas</u>. Incluso (*Even*) mi habitación de hotel _____ _____.
3. Nosotras estamos <u>tristes</u> cuando trabajamos. Hoy comienzan las vacaciones y _____ _____.
4. En esta ciudad los autobuses están <u>sucios</u>, pero los taxis _____ _____.
5. —El avión sale a las 5:30, ¿verdad? —No, estás <u>confundida</u>. Yo _____ _____ de que el avión sale a las 5:00.

**5** **En la playa** Describe what these people are doing. Complete the sentences using the present progressive tense. **8 pts.**

1. El señor Camacho _____.
2. Felicia _____.
3. Leo _____.
4. Nosotros _____.

**6** **Antes del viaje** Write a paragraph of at least six sentences describing the time right before you go on a trip. Say how you feel and what you are doing. You can use **Actividad 2** as a model. **12 pts.**

**modelo**
Hoy es viernes, 27 de octubre. Estoy en mi habitación...

**7** **Refrán** Complete this Spanish saying by filling in the missing present participles. Refer to the translation and the drawing. **2 EXTRA points!**

**¡LA CIUDAD ESTÁ MUY SUCIA!**

" Se consigue más _____ que _____ . "

(*You can accomplish more by doing than by saying.*)

 Practice more at **vhlcentral.com.**

# Lectura

Audio: Synched Reading
Additional Reading

## Antes de leer

### Estrategia

**Scanning**

Scanning involves glancing over a document in search of specific information. For example, you can scan a document to identify its format, to find cognates, to locate visual clues about the document's content, or to find specific facts. Scanning allows you to learn a great deal about a text without having to read it word for word.

### Examinar el texto

Scan the reading selection for cognates and write down a few of them.

1. _____    4. _____
2. _____    5. _____
3. _____    6. _____

Based on the cognates you found, what do you think this document is about?

_____

### Preguntas

Read these questions. Then scan the document again to look for answers.

1. What is the format of the reading selection?
   _____

2. Which place is the document about?
   _____

3. What are some of the visual cues this document provides? What do they tell you about the content of the document?
   _____

4. Who produced the document, and what do you think it is for?
   _____

recursos

vText

CH pp. 77–78

vhlcentral.com

# Turismo ecológico en Puerto Rico

# Hotel Vistahermosa
~ Lajas, Puerto Rico ~

- 40 habitaciones individuales
- 15 habitaciones dobles
- Teléfono, TV por cable, Internet
- Aire acondicionado
- Restaurante (Bar)
- Piscina
- Área de juegos
- Cajero automático°

El hotel está situado en Playa Grande, un pequeño pueblo de pescadores del mar Caribe. Es el lugar perfecto para el viajero que viene de vacaciones. Las playas son seguras y limpias, ideales para tomar el sol, descansar, tomar fotografías y nadar. Está abierto los 365 días del año. Hay una rebaja° especial para estudiantes.

DIRECCIÓN: Playa Grande 406, Lajas, PR 00667, cerca del Parque Nacional Foresta.

Cajero automático *ATM*   rebaja *discount*

## Atracciones cercanas

**Playa Grande** ¿Busca la playa perfecta? Playa Grande es la playa que está buscando. Usted puede pescar, sacar fotos, nadar y pasear en bicicleta. Playa Grande es un paraíso para el turista que quiere practicar deportes acuáticos. El lugar es bonito e interesante y usted tiene muchas oportunidades para descansar y disfrutar en familia.

**Valle Niebla** Ir de excursión, tomar café, montar a caballo, caminar, acampar, hacer picnics. Más de cien lugares para acampar.

**Bahía Fosforescente** Sacar fotos, salidas de noche, excursión en barco. Una maravillosa experiencia llena de luz°.

**Arrecifes de Coral** Sacar fotos, bucear, explorar. Es un lugar único en el Caribe.

**Playa Vieja** Tomar el sol, pasear en bicicleta, jugar a las cartas, escuchar música. Ideal para la familia.

**Parque Nacional Foresta** Sacar fotos, visitar el Museo de Arte Nativo. Reserva Mundial de la Biosfera.

**Santuario de las Aves** Sacar fotos, observar aves°, seguir rutas de excursión.

llena de luz *full of light* aves *birds*

# Después de leer

## Listas
Which amenities of Hotel Vistahermosa would most interest these potential guests? Explain your choices.

1. dos padres con un hijo de seis años y una hija de ocho años

_____

2. un hombre y una mujer en su luna de miel (*honeymoon*)

_____

3. una persona en un viaje de negocios (*business trip*)

_____

## Conversaciones
With a partner, take turns asking each other these questions.

1. ¿Quieres visitar el Hotel Vistahermosa? ¿Por qué?
2. Tienes tiempo de visitar sólo tres de las atracciones turísticas que están cerca del hotel. ¿Cuáles vas a visitar? ¿Por qué?
3. ¿Qué prefieres hacer en Valle Niebla? ¿En Playa Vieja? ¿En el Parque Nacional Foresta?

## Situaciones
You have just arrived at Hotel Vistahermosa. Your classmate is the concierge. Use the phrases below to express your interests and ask for suggestions about where to go.

1. montar a caballo
2. bucear
3. pasear en bicicleta
4. pescar
5. observar aves

## Contestar
Answer these questions.

1. ¿Quieres visitar Puerto Rico? Explica tu respuesta.

_____

2. ¿Adónde quieres ir de vacaciones el verano que viene? Explica tu respuesta.

_____

 Practice more at **vhlcentral.com**.

# Escritura

## Estrategia

### Making an outline

When we write to share information, an outline can serve to separate topics and subtopics, providing a framework for the presentation of data. Consider the following excerpt from an outline of the tourist brochure on pages 180–181.

IV. Descripción del sitio (con foto)
    A. Playa Grande
        1. Playas seguras y limpias
        2. Ideal para tomar el sol, descansar, tomar fotografías, nadar
    B. El hotel
        1. Abierto los 365 días del año
        2. Rebaja para estudiantes

### Mapa de ideas

Idea maps can be used to create outlines. The major sections of an idea map correspond to the Roman numerals in an outline. The minor idea map sections correspond to the outline's capital letters, and so on. Examine the idea map that led to the outline above.

## Tema

### Escribir un folleto

Write a tourist brochure for a hotel or resort you have visited. If you wish, you may write about an imaginary location. You may want to include some of this information in your brochure:

▶ the name of the hotel or resort

▶ phone and fax numbers that tourists can use to make contact

▶ the hotel website that tourists can consult

▶ an e-mail address that tourists can use to request information

▶ a description of the exterior of the hotel or resort

▶ a description of the interior of the hotel or resort, including facilities and amenities

▶ a description of the surrounding area, including its climate

▶ a listing of nearby scenic natural attractions

▶ a listing of nearby cultural attractions

▶ a listing of recreational activities that tourists can pursue in the vicinity of the hotel or resort

# Escuchar

## Estrategia

### Listening for key words

By listening for key words or phrases, you can identify the subject and main ideas of what you hear, as well as some of the details.

 To practice this strategy, you will now listen to a short paragraph. As you listen, jot down the key words that help you identify the subject of the paragraph and its main ideas.

## Preparación

Based on the illustration, who do you think Hernán Jiménez is, and what is he doing? What key words might you listen for to help you understand what he is saying?

## Ahora escucha

Now you are going to listen to a weather report by Hernán Jiménez. Note which phrases are correct according to the key words and phrases you hear.

### Santo Domingo

1. hace sol
2. va a hacer frío
3. una mañana de mal tiempo
4. va a estar nublado
5. buena tarde para tomar el sol
6. buena mañana para la playa

### San Francisco de Macorís

1. hace frío
2. hace sol
3. va a nevar
4. va a llover
5. hace calor
6. mal día para excursiones

**recursos**

vText

vhlcentral.com

## Comprensión

### ¿Cierto o falso?

Indicate whether each statement is **cierto** or **falso**, based on the weather report. Correct the false statements.

1. Según el meteorólogo, la temperatura en Santo Domingo es de 26 grados.

   _____

2. La temperatura máxima en Santo Domingo hoy va a ser de 30 grados.

   _____

3. Está lloviendo ahora en Santo Domingo.

   _____

4. En San Francisco de Macorís la temperatura mínima de hoy va a ser de 20 grados.

   _____

5. Va a llover mucho hoy en San Francisco de Macorís.

   _____

### Preguntas

Answer these questions about the weather report.

1. ¿Hace viento en Santo Domingo ahora?
2. ¿Está nublado en Santo Domingo ahora?
3. ¿Está nevando ahora en San Francisco de Macorís?
4. ¿Qué tiempo hace en San Francisco de Macorís?

 Practice more at **vhlcentral.com**.

# En pantalla  Video: TV Clip

If you like adventure or extreme sports, Latin America might be a good destination for you. The area of Patagonia, located in Chile and Argentina, offers both breath-taking scenery and an adrenaline rush. Here, one can enjoy a variety of sports, including whitewater rafting, kayaking, trekking, and skiing. One weeklong itinerary in Argentina might include camping, hiking the granite rock of Mount Fitz Roy, and trekking across the deep blue Perito Moreno Glacier, a massive 18-mile-long sheet of ice and one of the world's few advancing glaciers.

   Now, hold on to your helmets as we travel to Mexico to see what sort of adventure you can experience there.

| Vocabulario útil | |
|---|---|
| **callejones** | *alleyways, narrow streets* |
| **calles** | *streets* |
| **carrera de bicicleta** | *bicycle race* |
| **descender (escaleras)** | *to descend (stairs)* |
| **reto, desafío** | *challenge* |

## Preparación

Some areas attract tourists because of their unusual sports and activities. Do you know of any such destinations? Where?

##  Preguntas

Answer these questions in complete sentences.

1. ¿Por qué viajan ciclistas (*cyclists*) a Taxco?

2. ¿Es Taxco una ciudad turística moderna o colonial?

3. ¿Hay competidores de otros (*other*) países en la carrera de bicicleta?

4. ¿Cómo está el reportero (*reporter*) después (*after*) de descender las escaleras, aburrido o cansado?

## Deportes extremos

In pairs, discuss these questions: **¿Cómo son las personas que hacen deportes extremos? ¿Por qué crees que los practican? ¿Viajarías (*Would you travel*) a algún destino para practicarlos?**

menor *least*  lo más alto *the highest point*  hasta *to*  diseño *design*

**Reportaje sobre Down Taxco**

**El reto es descender en el menor° tiempo posible...**

**... desde lo más alto° de la ciudad hasta° la plaza central.**

**El principal desafío es el diseño° de la ciudad...**

**Video:**
*Flash cultura*

Between 1438 and 1533, when the vast and powerful Incan Empire was at its height, the Incas built an elaborate network of **caminos** (*trails*) that traversed the Andes Mountains and converged on the empire's capital, Cuzco. Today, hundreds of thousands of tourists come to Peru annually to walk the surviving trails and enjoy the spectacular scenery. The most popular trail, **el Camino Inca**, leads from Cuzco to **Intipunku** (*Sun Gate*), the entrance to the ancient mountain city of Machu Picchu.

| Vocabulario útil | |
|---|---|
| **ciudadela** | *citadel* |
| **de cultivo** | *farming* |
| **el/la guía** | *guide* |
| **maravilla** | *wonder* |
| **quechua** | *Quechua (indigenous Peruvian)* |
| **sector (urbano)** | *(urban) sector* |

**Preparación**

Have you ever visited an archeological or historic site? Where? Why did you go there?

**Completar**

Complete these sentences. Make the necessary changes.

1. Las ruinas de Machu Picchu son una antigua _____ inca.

2. La ciudadela estaba (*was*) dividida en tres sectores: _____ , religioso y de cultivo.

3. Cada año los _____ reciben a cientos (*hundreds*) de turistas de diferentes países.

4. Hoy en día, la cultura _____ está presente en las comunidades andinas (*Andean*) de Perú.

**¡Vacaciones en Perú!**

**1**

**Machu Picchu [...] se encuentra aislada sobre° esta montaña...**

**2**

**... siempre he querido° venir [...] Me encantan° las civilizaciones antiguas°.**

**3**

**Somos una familia francesa [...] Perú es un país muy, muy bonito de verdad.**

se encuentra aislada sobre *it is isolated on* siempre he querido *I have always wanted* Me encantan *I love* antiguas *ancient*

Practice more at **vhlcentral.com**.

**recursos**

vText    CPA pp. 24–25    vhlcentral.com

# Puerto Rico

**Interactive Map**
**Video: *Panorama cultural***

## El país en cifras

▸ **Área**: 8.959 km² (3.459 millas²),
  *menor° que el área de Connecticut*
▸ **Población**: 3.746.000
*Puerto Rico es una de las islas más
densamente pobladas° del mundo. Más
de la mitad de la población vive en
San Juan, la capital.*
▸ **Capital**: San Juan—2.478.905

SOURCE: Population Division, UN Secretariat

▸ **Ciudades principales**: Arecibo, Bayamón,
  Fajardo, Mayagüez, Ponce
▸ **Moneda**: dólar estadounidense
▸ **Idiomas**: español (oficial); inglés (oficial)
*Aproximadamente la cuarta parte de la población
puertorriqueña habla inglés, pero en las zonas
turísticas este porcentaje es mucho más alto. El uso
del inglés es obligatorio para documentos federales.*

Bandera
de Puerto Rico

**Puertorriqueños célebres**
▸ **Raúl Juliá**, actor (1940–1994)
▸ **Roberto Clemente**, beisbolista
  (1934–1972)
▸ **Julia de Burgos**, escritora
  (1914–1953)
▸ **Benicio del Toro**, actor y productor (1967– )
▸ **Rosie Pérez**, actriz y bailarina (1964– )

menor *less* pobladas *populated* río subterráneo *underground river* más largo
*longest* cuevas *caves* bóveda *vault* fortaleza *fort* caber *fit*

Faro en Arecibo

Playa en San Juan

Océano Atlántico

Arecibo

San Juan ✪

Bayamón

Río Grande de Añasco

Mayagüez

**Cordillera Central**

**Sierra de Cayey**

Ponce

Mar Caribe

Iglesia en Ponce

Pescadores en Mayagüez

**recursos**

**vText**

CPA
pp. 26–29

vhlcentral.com

OCÉANO
ATLÁNTICO

**PUERTO RICO**

OCÉANO
PACÍFICO

## ¡Increíble pero cierto!

El río Camuy es el tercer río subterráneo° más
largo° del mundo y tiene el sistema de cuevas°
más grande del hemisferio occidental.
La Cueva de los Tres Pueblos es una gigantesca
bóveda°, tan grande que toda la fortaleza° del
Morro puede caber° en su interior.

## Lugares • **El Morro**

El Morro es una fortaleza que se construyó para proteger° la bahía° de San Juan desde principios del siglo° XVI hasta principios del siglo XX. Hoy día muchos turistas visitan este lugar, convertido en un museo. Es el sitio más fotografiado de Puerto Rico. La arquitectura de la fortaleza es impresionante. Tiene misteriosos túneles, oscuras mazmorras° y vistas fabulosas de la bahía.

## Artes • **Salsa**

La salsa, un estilo musical de origen puertorriqueño y cubano, nació° en el barrio latino de la ciudad de Nueva York. Dos de los músicos de salsa más famosos son Tito Puente y Willie Colón, los dos de Nueva York. Las estrellas° de la salsa en Puerto Rico son Felipe Rodríguez y Héctor Lavoe. Hoy en día, Puerto Rico es el centro internacional de este estilo musical. El Gran Combo de Puerto Rico es una de las orquestas de salsa más famosas del mundo°.

Isla de Culebra

Fajardo

Isla de Vieques

Río Grande de Loíza

## Ciencias • **El Observatorio de Arecibo**

El Observatorio de Arecibo tiene uno de los radiotelescopios más grandes del mundo. Gracias a este telescopio, los científicos° pueden estudiar las propiedades de la Tierra°, la Luna° y otros cuerpos celestes. También pueden analizar fenómenos celestiales como los quasares y pulsares, y detectar emisiones de radio de otras galaxias, en busca de inteligencia extraterrestre.

## Historia • **Relación con los Estados Unidos**

Puerto Rico pasó a ser° parte de los Estados Unidos después de° la guerra° de 1898 y se hizo° un estado libre asociado en 1952. Los puertorriqueños, ciudadanos° estadounidenses desde° 1917, tienen representación política en el Congreso, pero no votan en las elecciones presidenciales y no pagan impuestos° federales. Hay un debate entre los puertorriqueños: ¿debe la isla seguir como estado libre asociado, hacerse un estado como los otros° o volverse° independiente?

 **¿Qué aprendiste?** Responde a cada pregunta con una oración completa.

1. ¿Cuál es la moneda de Puerto Rico?
2. ¿Qué idiomas se hablan (*are spoken*) en Puerto Rico?
3. ¿Cuál es el sitio más fotografiado de Puerto Rico?
4. ¿Qué es el Gran Combo?
5. ¿Qué hacen los científicos en el Observatorio de Arecibo?

 **Conexión Internet** Investiga estos temas en **vhlcentral.com**.

1. Describe a dos puertorriqueños famosos. ¿Cómo son? ¿Qué hacen? ¿Dónde viven? ¿Por qué son célebres?
2. Busca información sobre lugares en los que se puede hacer ecoturismo en Puerto Rico. Luego presenta un informe a la clase.

 Practice more at **vhlcentral.com**.

proteger *protect* bahía *bay* siglo *century* mazmorras *dungeons* nació *was born* estrellas *stars* mundo *world* científicos *scientists* Tierra *Earth* Luna *Moon* pasó a ser *became* después de *after* guerra *war* se hizo *became* ciudadanos *citizens* desde *since* pagan impuestos *pay taxes* otros *others* volverse *to become*

## Los viajes y las vacaciones

| | |
|---|---|
| acampar | to camp |
| confirmar una reservación | to confirm a reservation |
| estar de vacaciones (f. pl.) | to be on vacation |
| hacer las maletas | to pack (one's suitcases) |
| hacer un viaje | to take a trip |
| hacer (wind)surf | to (wind)surf |
| ir de compras (f. pl.) | to go shopping |
| ir de vacaciones | to go on vacation |
| ir en autobús (m.), auto(móvil) (m.), avión (m.), barco (m.), moto(cicleta) (f.), taxi (m.) | to go by bus, car, plane, boat, motorcycle, taxi |
| jugar a las cartas | to play cards |
| montar a caballo (m.) | to ride a horse |
| pescar | to fish |
| sacar/tomar fotos (f. pl.) | to take photos |

| | |
|---|---|
| el/la agente de viajes | travel agent |
| el/la inspector(a) de aduanas | customs inspector |
| el/la viajero/a | traveler |

| | |
|---|---|
| el aeropuerto | airport |
| la agencia de viajes | travel agency |
| el campo | countryside |
| el equipaje | luggage |
| la estación de autobuses, del metro, de tren | bus, subway, train station |
| la llegada | arrival |
| el mar | sea |
| el paisaje | landscape |
| el pasaje (de ida y vuelta) | (round-trip) ticket |
| el pasaporte | passport |
| la playa | beach |
| la salida | departure; exit |
| la tabla de (wind)surf | surfboard/sailboard |

## El hotel

| | |
|---|---|
| el ascensor | elevator |
| el/la botones | bellhop |
| la cama | bed |
| el/la empleado/a | employee |
| la habitación individual, doble | single, double room |
| el hotel | hotel |
| el/la huésped | guest |
| la llave | key |
| el piso | floor (of a building) |
| la planta baja | ground floor |

## Adjetivos

| | |
|---|---|
| abierto/a | open |
| aburrido/a | bored; boring |
| alegre | happy; joyful |
| amable | nice; friendly |
| avergonzado/a | embarrassed |
| cansado/a | tired |
| cerrado/a | closed |
| cómodo/a | comfortable |
| confundido/a | confused |
| contento/a | happy; content |
| desordenado/a | disorderly |
| enamorado/a (de) | in love (with) |
| enojado/a | mad; angry |
| equivocado/a | wrong |
| feliz | happy |
| limpio/a | clean |
| listo/a | ready; smart |
| nervioso/a | nervous |
| ocupado/a | busy |
| ordenado/a | orderly |
| preocupado/a (por) | worried (about) |
| seguro/a | sure; safe |
| sucio/a | dirty |
| triste | sad |

 **Audio: Vocabulary Flashcards**

## Los números ordinales

| | |
|---|---|
| primer, primero/a | first |
| segundo/a | second |
| tercer, tercero/a | third |
| cuarto/a | fourth |
| quinto/a | fifth |
| sexto/a | sixth |
| séptimo/a | seventh |
| octavo/a | eighth |
| noveno/a | ninth |
| décimo/a | tenth |

## Palabras adicionales

| | |
|---|---|
| ahora mismo | right now |
| el año | year |
| ¿Cuál es la fecha (de hoy)? | What is the date (today)? |
| de buen/mal humor | in a good/bad mood |
| la estación | season |
| el mes | month |
| todavía | yet; still |

| | |
|---|---|
| Seasons, months, and dates | See page 154. |
| Weather expressions | See page 154. |
| Direct object pronouns | See page 174. |
| Expresiones útiles | See page 159. |

# ¡De compras!

## 6

**Communicative Goals**

*I will be able to:*
- **Talk about and describe clothing**
- **Express preferences in a store**
- **Negotiate and pay for items I buy**

VOICE BOARD

**A PRIMERA VISTA**
- ¿Está comprando algo la chica?
- ¿Crees que busca una maleta o una blusa?
- ¿Está contenta o enojada?
- ¿Cómo es ella?

# ¡De compras!

  **Audio: Vocabulary Tutorials, Games**

## Más vocabulario

| | |
|---|---|
| el abrigo | coat |
| los calcetines (el calcetín) | sock(s) |
| el cinturón | belt |
| las gafas (de sol) | (sun)glasses |
| los guantes | gloves |
| el impermeable | raincoat |
| la ropa | clothing; clothes |
| la ropa interior | underwear |
| las sandalias | sandals |
| el traje | suit |
| el vestido | dress |
| los zapatos de tenis | sneakers |
| el regalo | gift |
| el almacén | department store |
| el centro comercial | shopping mall |
| el mercado (al aire libre) | (open-air) market |
| el precio (fijo) | (fixed; set) price |
| la rebaja | sale |
| la tienda | shop; store |
| costar (o:ue) | to cost |
| gastar | to spend (money) |
| pagar | to pay |
| regatear | to bargain |
| vender | to sell |
| hacer juego (con) | to match (with) |
| llevar | to wear; to take |
| usar | to wear; to use |

## Variación léxica

calcetines ⟷ medias (*Amér. L.*)

cinturón ⟷ correa (*Col., Venez.*)

gafas/lentes ⟷ espejuelos (*Cuba, P.R.*), anteojos (*Arg., Chile*)

zapatos de tenis ⟷ zapatillas de deporte (*Esp.*), zapatillas (*Arg., Perú*)

los pantalones cortos

el traje de baño

los pantalones

la camiseta

el dependiente/el vendedor

la camisa

la clienta

la blusa

el dinero en efectivo

la bolsa

la falda

el suéter

las medias

**recursos**

vText · CPA pp. 31–33 · CH pp. 81–82 · vhlcentral.com

# Práctica

**1** **Escuchar** 🎧 Listen to Juanita and Vicente talk about what they're packing for their vacations. Indicate who is packing each item. If both are packing an item, write both names. If neither is packing an item, write an **X**.

1. abrigo _____
2. zapatos de tenis _____
3. impermeable _____
4. chaqueta _____
5. sandalias _____
6. bluejeans _____
7. gafas de sol _____
8. camisetas _____
9. traje de baño _____
10. botas _____
11. pantalones cortos _____
12. suéter _____

**2** **¿Lógico o ilógico?** 🎧 Listen to Guillermo and Ana talk about vacation destinations. Indicate whether each statement is **lógico** or **ilógico**.

1. _____
2. _____
3. _____
4. _____

**3** **Completar** Anita is talking about going shopping. Complete each sentence with the correct word(s), adding definite or indefinite articles when necessary.

| caja | medias | tarjeta de crédito |
| centro comercial | par | traje de baño |
| dependientas | ropa | vendedores |

1. Hoy voy a ir de compras al _____.
2. Voy a ir a la tienda de ropa para mujeres. Siempre hay muchas rebajas y las _____ son muy simpáticas.
3. Necesito comprar _____ de zapatos.
4. Y tengo que comprar _____ porque el sábado voy a la playa con mis amigos.
5. También voy a comprar unas _____ para mi mamá.
6. Voy a pagar todo (*everything*) en _____.
7. Pero hoy no tengo dinero. Voy a tener que usar mi _____.
8. Mañana voy al mercado al aire libre. Me gusta regatear con los _____.

**4** **Escoger** Choose the item in each group that does not belong.

1. almacén • centro comercial • mercado • sombrero
2. camisa • camiseta • blusa • botas
3. jeans • bolsa • falda • pantalones
4. abrigo • suéter • corbata • chaqueta
5. mercado • tienda • almacén • cartera
6. pagar • llevar • hacer juego (con) • usar
7. botas • sandalias • zapatos • traje
8. vender • regatear • ropa interior • gastar

el sombrero · un par de zapatos · los zapatos · la chaqueta · la caja · la cartera · la dependienta/la vendedora · la corbata · la tarjeta de crédito · los (blue)jeans · la bota

## Los colores

| anaranjado/a | gris | marrón, café | morado/a | rosado/a |

**¡LENGUA VIVA!**

The names of colors vary throughout the Spanish-speaking world. For example, in some countries, **anaranjado/a** may be referred to as **naranja**, **morado/a** as **púrpura**, and **rojo/a** as **colorado/a**.

Other terms that will prove helpful include **claro** (*light*) and **oscuro** (*dark*): **café claro, café oscuro.**

## Adjetivos

| barato/a | corto/a | largo/a |

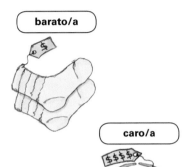

| caro/a |

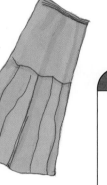

### Más adjetivos

| bueno/a | good |
|---|---|
| cada | each |
| elegante | elegant |
| hermoso/a | beautiful |
| loco/a | crazy |
| nuevo/a | new |
| otro/a | other; another |
| pobre | poor |
| rico/a | rich |

**5**

**Contrastes** Complete each phrase with the opposite of the underlined word.

1. una corbata <u>barata</u> • unas camisas...
2. unas vendedoras <u>malas</u> • unos dependientes...
3. un vestido <u>corto</u> • una falda...
4. un hombre muy <u>pobre</u> • una mujer muy...
5. una cartera <u>nueva</u> • un cinturón...
6. unos trajes <u>hermosos</u> • unos jeans...
7. un impermeable <u>caro</u> • unos suéteres...
8. unos calcetines <u>blancos</u> • unas medias...

**CONSULTA**

Like other adjectives you have seen, colors must agree in gender and number with the nouns they modify.
Ex: **las camisas grises, el vestido anaranjado.**

**6**

**Preguntas** Answer these questions with a classmate.

1. ¿De qué color es la rosa de Texas?
2. ¿De qué color es la bandera (*flag*) de Canadá?
3. ¿De qué color es la casa donde vive el presidente de los EE.UU.?
4. ¿De qué color es el océano Atlántico?
5. ¿De qué color es la nieve?
6. ¿De qué color es el café?
7. ¿De qué color es el dólar de los EE.UU.?
8. ¿De qué color son los elefantes (*elephants*)?

 Practice more at **vhlcentral.com.**

# Comunicación

**7**   **Las maletas** With a classmate, answer these questions about the drawings.

1. ¿Qué ropa hay al lado de la maleta de Carmela?

2. ¿Qué hay en la maleta?

3. ¿De qué color son las sandalias?

4. ¿Adónde va Carmela?

To review weather, see **Lección 5, Contextos,** p. 154.

▶ 5. ¿Qué tiempo va a hacer?

6. ¿Qué hay al lado de la maleta de Pepe?

7. ¿Qué hay en la maleta?

**NOTA CULTURAL**

**Bariloche** is a popular resort for skiing in South America. Located in Argentina's Patagonia region, the town is also known for its chocolate factories and its beautiful lakes, mountains, and forests.

8. ¿De qué color es el suéter?

▶ 9. ¿Qué va a hacer Pepe en Bariloche?

10. ¿Qué tiempo va a hacer?

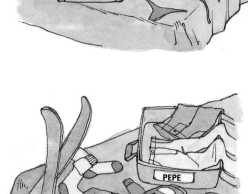

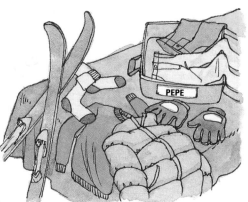

---

**8**   **El viaje** Get together with two classmates and imagine that the three of you are going on vacation. Pick a destination and then draw three suitcases. Write what clothing each of you is taking. Present your lists to the class, answering these questions.

- ¿Adónde van?
- ¿Qué tiempo va a hacer allí?
- ¿Qué van a hacer allí?
- ¿Qué hay en sus maletas?
- ¿De qué color es la ropa que llevan?

---

**9**   **Preferencias** Take turns asking and answering these questions with a classmate.

1. ¿Adónde vas a comprar ropa? ¿Por qué?
2. ¿Qué tipo de ropa prefieres? ¿Por qué?
3. ¿Cuáles son tus colores favoritos?
4. En tu opinión, ¿es importante comprar ropa nueva frecuentemente? ¿Por qué?
5. Y tu familia, ¿gasta mucho dinero en ropa cada mes? ¿Buscan rebajas tus padres?
6. ¿Regatea tu familia cuando compra ropa? ¿Usan tus padres tarjetas de crédito?

# En el mercado

Los chicos van de compras al mercado.
¿Quién hizo la mejor compra?

PERSONAJES    **FELIPE**    **JUAN CARLOS**

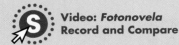
**Video: *Fotonovela***
**Record and Compare**

**MARISSA** Oigan, vamos al mercado.

**JUAN CARLOS** ¡Sí! Los chicos en un equipo y las chicas en otro.

**FELIPE** Tenemos dos horas para ir de compras.

**MARU** Y don Guillermo decide quién gana.

**JIMENA** Esta falda azul es muy elegante.

**MARISSA** ¡Sí! Además, este color está de moda.

**MARU** Éste rojo es de algodón.

**MARISSA** ¿Me das aquella blusa rosada? Me parece que hace juego con esta falda, ¿no? ¿No tienen otras tallas?

**JIMENA** Sí, aquí. ¿Qué talla usas?

**MARISSA** Uso talla 4.

**JIMENA** La encontré. ¡Qué ropa más bonita!

**VENDEDOR** Son 530 por las tres bolsas. Pero como ustedes son tan bonitas, son 500 pesos.

**MARU** Señor, no somos turistas ricas. Somos estudiantes pobres.

**VENDEDOR** Bueno, son 480 pesos.

**JUAN CARLOS** Miren, mi nueva camisa. Elegante, ¿verdad?

**FELIPE** A ver, Juan Carlos... te queda bien.

**MARU** ¿Qué compraste?

**MIGUEL** Sólo esto.

**MARU** ¡Qué bonitos aretes! Gracias, mi amor.

**MARISSA**

**JIMENA**

**MARU**

**MIGUEL**

**DON GUILLERMO**

**VENDEDORA**

**VENDEDOR**

4

5

(*En otra parte del mercado*)

**FELIPE** Juan Carlos compró una camisa de muy buena calidad.

**MIGUEL** (*a la vendedora*) ¿Puedo ver ésos, por favor?

**VENDEDORA** Sí, señor. Le doy un muy buen precio.

(*Las chicas encuentran unas bolsas.*)

**VENDEDOR** Ésta de rayas cuesta 190 pesos, ésta 120 pesos y ésta 220 pesos.

9

10

**JUAN CARLOS** Y ustedes, ¿qué compraron?

**JIMENA** Bolsas.

**MARU** Acabamos de comprar tres bolsas por sólo 480 pesos. ¡Una ganga!

**FELIPE** Don Guillermo, usted tiene que decidir quién gana. ¿Los chicos o las chicas?

**DON GUILLERMO** El ganador es... Miguel. ¡Porque no compró nada para él, sino para su novia!

## Expresiones útiles

**Talking about clothing**

**¡Qué ropa más bonita!**
*What nice clothing!*

**Esta falda azul es muy elegante.**
*This blue skirt is very elegant.*

**Está de moda.**
*It's in style.*

**Éste rojo es de algodón/lana.**
*This red one is cotton/wool.*

**Ésta de rayas/lunares/cuadros es de seda.**
*This striped / polka-dotted / plaid one is silk.*

**Es de muy buena calidad.**
*It's very good quality.*

**¿Qué talla usas/llevas?**
*What size do you wear?*

**Uso/Llevo talla 4.**
*I wear a size 4.*

**¿Qué número calza?**
*What size shoe do you wear?*

**Yo calzo siete.**
*I wear a size seven.*

**Negotiating a price**

**¿Cuánto cuesta?**
*How much does it cost?*

**Demasiado caro/a.**
*Too expensive.*

**Es una ganga.**
*It's a bargain.*

**Saying what you bought**

**¿Qué compraste?/¿Qué compró usted?**
*What did you buy?*

**Sólo compré esto.**
*I only bought this.*

**¡Qué bonitos aretes!**
*What beautiful earrings!*

**Y ustedes, ¿qué compraron?**
*And you guys, what did you buy?*

**Additional vocabulary**

**híjole** *wow*

**recursos**

vText

CPA pp. 34–35

vhlcentral.com

# ¿Qué pasó?

**1** **¿Cierto o falso?** Indicate whether each sentence is **cierto** or **falso**. Correct the false statements.

| | Cierto | Falso |
|---|---|---|
| 1. Jimena dice que la falda azul no es elegante. | ○ | ○ |
| 2. Juan Carlos compra una camisa. | ○ | ○ |
| 3. Marissa dice que el azul es un color que está de moda. | ○ | ○ |
| 4. Miguel compra unas sandalias para Maru. | ○ | ○ |

**2** **Identificar** Provide the first initial of the person who would make each statement.

___ 1. ¿Te gusta cómo se me ven mis nuevos aretes?
___ 2. Juan Carlos compró una camisa de muy buena calidad.
___ 3. No podemos pagar 500, señor, eso es muy caro.
___ 4. Aquí tienen ropa de muchas tallas.
___ 5. Esta falda me gusta mucho, el color azul es muy elegante.
___ 6. Hay que darnos prisa, sólo tenemos dos horas para ir de compras.

**MARU**

**FELIPE**

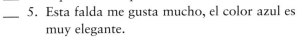

**JIMENA**

**3** **Completar** Answer the questions using the information in the **Fotonovela**.

1. ¿Qué talla usa Marissa?
2. Normalmente (*normally*), ¿cuánto cuestan las tres bolsas?
3. ¿Cuál es el precio que pagan las tres amigas por las bolsas?
4. ¿Qué dice Juan Carlos sobre su nueva camisa?
5. ¿Quién ganó al hacer las compras? ¿Por qué?

◄ **AYUDA**

When discussing prices, it's important to keep in mind singular and plural forms of verbs.

La **camisa cuesta** diez dólares.

Las **botas cuestan** sesenta dólares.

El **precio** de las botas **es** sesenta dólares.

Los **precios** de la ropa **son** altos.

**4** **Conversar** With a partner, role-play a conversation between a customer and a salesperson in an open-air market. Use these expressions and also look at **Expresiones útiles** on the previous page.

| ¿Qué desea? | Estoy buscando... | Prefiero el/la rojo/a. |
|---|---|---|
| *What would you like?* | *I'm looking for...* | *I prefer the red one.* |

| **Cliente/a** | **Vendedor(a)** |
|---|---|
| Say good afternoon. | Greet the customer and ask what he/she would like. |
| Explain that you are looking for a particular item of clothing. | Show him/her some items and ask what he/she prefers. |
| Discuss colors and sizes. | Discuss colors and sizes. |
| Ask for the price and begin bargaining. | Tell him/her a price. Negotiate a price. |
| Settle on a price and purchase the item. | Accept a price and say thank you. |

 Practice more at **vhlcentral.com**.

# Pronunciación

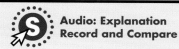 **Audio: Explanation Record and Compare**

## The consonants d and t

**¿Dónde?**     **vender**     **nadar**     **verdad**

Like **b** and **v**, the Spanish **d** can also have a hard sound or a soft sound, depending on which letters appear next to it.

**Don**     **dinero**     **tienda**     **falda**

At the beginning of a phrase and after **n** or **l**, the letter **d** is pronounced with a hard sound. This sound is similar to the English *d* in *dog*, but a little softer and duller. The tongue should touch the back of the upper teeth, not the roof of the mouth.

**medias**     **verde**     **vestido**     **huésped**

In all other positions, **d** has a soft sound. It is similar to the English *th* in *there*, but a little softer.

**Don Diego no tiene el diccionario.**

When **d** begins a word, its pronunciation depends on the previous word. At the beginning of a phrase or after a word that ends in **n** or **l**, it is pronounced as a hard **d**.

**Doña Dolores es de la capital.**

Words that begin with **d** are pronounced with a soft **d** if they appear immediately after a word that ends in a vowel or any consonant other than **n** or **l**.

**traje**     **pantalones**     **tarjeta**     **tienda**

When pronouncing the Spanish **t**, the tongue should touch the back of the upper teeth, not the roof of the mouth. Unlike the English *t*, no air is expelled from the mouth.

**Práctica** Read these phrases aloud to practice the **d** and the **t**.

1. Hasta pronto.
2. De nada.
3. Mucho gusto.
4. Lo siento.
5. No hay de qué.
6. ¿De dónde es usted?
7. ¡Todos a bordo!
8. No puedo.
9. Es estupendo.
10. No tengo computadora.
11. ¿Cuándo vienen?
12. Son las tres y media.

**Oraciones** Read these sentences aloud to practice the **d** and the **t**.

1. Don Teodoro tiene una tienda en un almacén en La Habana.
2. Don Teodoro vende muchos trajes, vestidos y zapatos todos los días.
3. Un día un turista, Federico Machado, entra en la tienda para comprar un par de botas.
4. Federico regatea con don Teodoro y compra las botas y también un par de sandalias.

**En la variedad está el gusto.**[1]

**Refranes** Read these sayings aloud to practice the **d** and the **t**.

**Aunque la mona se vista de seda, mona se queda.**[2]

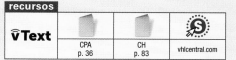

2 *You can't make a silk purse out of a sow's ear.*
1 *Variety is the spice of life.*

**recursos**

| v̂Text | CPA p. 36 | CH p. 83 | vhlcentral.com |
| --- | --- | --- | --- |

EN DETALLE

Reading, Additional Reading

# Los mercados al aire libre

**Mercados al aire libre** are an integral part of commerce and culture in the Spanish-speaking world. Whether they take place daily or weekly, these markets are an important forum where tourists, locals, and vendors interact. People come to the marketplace to shop, socialize, taste local foods, and watch street performers. Wandering from one **puesto** (*stand*) to the next, one can browse fresh fruits and vegetables, clothing, music and movies, and **artesanías** (*crafts*). Some markets offer a mix of products, while others specialize in food, fashion, or used merchandise, such as antiques and books.

When shoppers see an item they like, they can bargain with the vendor. Friendly bargaining is an expected ritual and may result in a significantly lower price. When selling food, vendors may give the customer a little extra of what they purchase; this free addition is known as **la ñapa**.

Many open-air markets are also tourist attractions. The market in Otavalo, Ecuador, is world-famous and has taken place every Saturday since pre-Incan times. This market is well-known for the colorful textiles woven by the **otavaleños**, the indigenous people of the area. One can also find leather goods and wood carvings from nearby towns. Another popular market is **El Rastro**, held every Sunday in Madrid, Spain. Sellers set up **puestos** along the streets to display their wares, which range from local artwork and antiques to inexpensive clothing and electronics.

**Mercado de Otavalo**

mariscos *seafood* pescado *fish* verduras *vegetables* flores *flowers*

### Otros mercados famosos

| Mercado | Lugar | Productos |
|---------|-------|-----------|
| Feria Artesanal de Recoleta | Buenos Aires, Argentina | artesanías |
| Mercado Central | Santiago, Chile | mariscos°, pescado°, frutas, verduras° |
| Tianguis Cultural del Chopo | Ciudad de México, México | ropa, música, revistas, libros, arte, artesanías |
| El mercado de Chichicastenango | Chichicastenango, Guatemala | frutas y verduras, flores°, cerámica, textiles |

---

**ACTIVIDADES**

**1** **¿Cierto o falso?** Indicate whether these statements are **cierto** or **falso**. Correct the false statements.

1. Generally, open-air markets specialize in one type of goods.
2. Bargaining is commonplace at outdoor markets.
3. Only new goods can be found at open-air markets.
4. A Spaniard in search of antiques could search at **El Rastro**.
5. If you are in Guatemala and want to buy ceramics, you can go to Chichicastenango.
6. A **ñapa** is a tax on open-air market goods.
7. The **otavaleños** weave colorful textiles to sell on Saturdays.
8. Santiago's **Mercado Central** is known for books and music.

 Practice more at **vhlcentral.com**.

## ASÍ SE DICE

### La ropa

| | |
|---|---|
| la chamarra (Méx.) | la chaqueta |
| de manga corta/larga | *short/long-sleeved* |
| los mahones (P. Rico); el pantalón de mezclilla (Méx.); los tejanos (Esp.); los vaqueros (Arg., Cuba, Esp., Uru.) | los bluejeans |
| la marca | *brand* |
| la playera (Méx.); la remera (Arg.) | la camiseta |

## EL MUNDO HISPANO

### Diseñadores de moda

- **Adolfo Domínguez** (España) Su ropa tiene un estilo minimalista y práctico. Usa telas° naturales y cómodas en sus diseños.

- **Silvia Tcherassi** (Colombia) Los colores vivos y las líneas asimétricas de sus vestidos y trajes muestran influencias tropicales.

- **Óscar de la Renta** (República Dominicana) Diseña ropa opulenta para la mujer clásica.

- **Narciso Rodríguez** (EE.UU.) En sus diseños delicados y finos predominan los colores blanco y negro. Hizo° el vestido de boda° de Carolyn Bessette Kennedy.

telas *fabrics* Hizo *He made* de boda *wedding*

## PERFIL

# Carolina Herrera

In 1980, at the urging of some friends, **Carolina Herrera** created a fashion collection as a "test." The Venezuelan designer received such a favorable response that within one year she moved her family from Caracas to New York City and created her own label, Carolina Herrera, Ltd.

"I love elegance and intricacy, but whether it is in a piece of clothing or a fragrance, the intricacy must appear as simplicity," Herrera once stated. She quickly found that many sophisticated women agreed; from the start, her sleek and glamorous designs have been in

constant demand. Over the years, Herrera has grown her brand into a veritable fashion empire that encompasses her fashion and bridal collections, cosmetics, perfume, and accessories that are sold around the globe.

 **Conexión Internet**

| ¿Qué marcas de ropa son populares en el mundo hispano? | Go to **vhlcentral.com** to find more cultural information related to this **Cultura** section. |

## ACTIVIDADES

**2** **Comprensión** Complete these sentences.

1. Adolfo Domínguez usa telas _____ y _____ en su ropa.
2. Si hace fresco en el D.F., puedes llevar una _____.
3. La diseñadora _____ hace ropa, perfumes y más.
4. La ropa de _____ muestra influencias tropicales.
5. Los _____ son una ropa casual en Puerto Rico.

**3** **Mi ropa favorita** Write a brief description of your favorite article of clothing. Mention what store it is from, the brand, colors, fabric, style, and any other information. Then get together with a small group, collect the descriptions, and take turns reading them aloud at random. Can the rest of the group guess whose favorite piece of clothing is being described?

## 6.1 Saber and conocer

**ANTE TODO**  Spanish has two verbs that mean *to know*: **saber** and **conocer**. They cannot be used interchangeably. Note the irregular **yo** forms.

### The verbs saber and conocer

| | | saber *(to know)* | conocer *(to know)* |
|---|---|---|---|
| **SINGULAR FORMS** | yo | sé | conozco |
| | tú | sabes | conoces |
| | Ud./él/ella | sabe | conoce |
| **PLURAL FORMS** | nosotros/as | sabemos | conocemos |
| | vosotros/as | sabéis | conocéis |
| | Uds./ellos/ellas | saben | conocen |

▶ **Saber** means *to know a fact or piece(s) of information* or *to know how to do something.*

No **sé** tu número de teléfono.
*I don't know your telephone number.*

Mi hermana **sabe** hablar francés.
*My sister knows how to speak French.*

▶ **Conocer** means *to know* or *be familiar/acquainted* with a person, place, or thing.

¿**Conoces** la ciudad de Nueva York?
*Do you know New York City?*

No **conozco** a tu amigo Esteban.
*I don't know your friend Esteban.*

▶ When the direct object of **conocer** is a person or pet, the personal **a** is used.

¿Conoces La Habana?    *but*    ¿Conoces **a** Celia Cruz?
*Do you know Havana?*         *Do you know Celia Cruz?*

▶ **¡Atención!** **Parecer** (*to seem*) and **ofrecer** (*to offer*) are conjugated like **conocer**.

▶ **¡Atención!** **Conducir** (*to drive*) and **traducir** (*to translate*) also have an irregular **yo** form, but since they are **-ir** verbs, they are conjugated differently from **conocer**.

**conducir** ▶ conduzco, conduces, conduce, conducimos, conducís, conducen
**traducir** ▶ traduzco, traduces, traduce, traducimos, traducís, traducen

 **¡INTÉNTALO!**  Provide the appropriate forms of these verbs.

**saber**
1. José no __sabe__ la hora.
2. Sara y yo _____ jugar al tenis.
3. ¿Por qué no _____ tú estos verbos?
4. Mis padres _____ hablar japonés.
5. Yo _____ a qué hora es la clase.
6. Usted no _____ dónde vivo.
7. Mi hermano no _____ nadar.
8. Nosotros _____ muchas cosas.

**conocer**
1. Usted y yo __conocemos__ bien Miami.
2. ¿Tú _____ a mi amigo Manuel?
3. Sergio y Taydé _____ mi pueblo.
4. Emiliano _____ a mis padres.
5. Yo _____ muy bien el centro.
6. ¿Ustedes _____ la tienda Gigante?
7. Nosotras _____ una playa hermosa.
8. ¿Usted _____ a mi profesora?

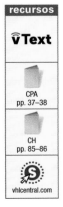

# Práctica y Comunicación

**1**

**Completar** Indicate the correct verb for each sentence.

1. Mis hermanos (conocen/saben) conducir, pero yo no (sé/conozco).
2. —¿(Conocen/Saben) ustedes dónde está el estadio? —No, no (conocemos/sabemos).
3. —¿(Conoces/Sabes) a Lady Gaga? —Bueno, (sé/conozco) quién es,
   pero no la (conozco/sé).
4. Mi profesora (sabe/conoce) Cuba y también (conoce/sabe) bailar salsa.

**2**

**Combinar** Combine elements from each column to create sentences.

| A | B | C |
|---|---|---|
| Shakira | (no) conocer | Conan O'Brien |
| los Yankees | (no) saber | cantar y bailar |
| el primer ministro | | La Habana Vieja |
| de Canadá | | muchas personas importantes |
| mis amigos y yo | | hablar dos lenguas extranjeras |
| tú | | jugar al béisbol |

**3**

**Preguntas** In pairs, ask each other these questions. Answer with complete sentences.

1. ¿Conoces a un(a) cantante famoso/a? ¿Te gusta cómo canta?
2. En tu familia, ¿quién sabe cantar bien? ¿Tu opinión es objetiva?
3. Tus padres, ¿conducen bien o mal? ¿Y tus hermanos mayores?
4. Si una persona no conduce muy bien, ¿le ofreces crítica constructiva?
5. ¿Cómo parece estar el/la profesor(a) hoy? ¿Y tus compañeros de clase?

**4**

**Entrevista** Jot down three things you know how to do, three people you know, and three places you are familiar with. Then, in a small group, find out what you have in common.

> **modelo**
>
> **Estudiante 1:** ¿Conocen ustedes a David Lomas?
> **Estudiante 2:** Sí, conozco a David. Vivimos en el mismo barrio (*neighborhood*).
> **Estudiante 3:** No, no lo conozco. ¿Cómo es?

**5**

**Anuncio** In groups, read the ad and answer these questions.

1. Busquen ejemplos de los verbos
   **saber** y **conocer**.
2. ¿Qué saben del Centro Comercial Málaga?
3. ¿Qué pueden hacer en el Centro
   Comercial Málaga?
4. ¿Conocen otros centros comerciales
   similares? ¿Cómo se llaman? ¿Dónde están?
5. ¿Conocen un centro comercial
   en otro país? ¿Cómo es?

Él sabe dónde **comer** lo que más le gusta.

Él sabe cómo **jugar** cuatro horas seguidas.

Él sabe dónde está su **regalo** de cumpleaños.

Él sabe dónde **divertirse…**

… y usted sabe dónde puede encontrar un poco de todo. ¿Conoce algún otro lugar como éste?

CENTRO COMERCIAL **MÁLAGA** SABE LO QUE TE GUSTA.

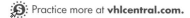
Practice more at **vhlcentral.com**.

**Explanation Tutorial**

# 6.2 Indirect object pronouns

**ANTE TODO**    In **Lección 5**, you learned that a direct object receives the action of the verb directly. In contrast, an indirect object receives the action of the verb indirectly.

| SUBJECT | I.O. PRONOUN | VERB | DIRECT OBJECT | INDIRECT OBJECT |
|---------|--------------|------|---------------|-----------------|
| Roberto | **le** | presta | cien pesos | **a Luisa**. |
| *Roberto* | | *lends* | *100 pesos* | *to Luisa.* |

An indirect object is a noun or pronoun that answers the question *to whom* or *for whom* an action is done. In the preceding example, the indirect object answers this question:
**¿A quién le presta Roberto cien pesos?** *To whom does Roberto lend 100 pesos?*

### Indirect object pronouns

| Singular forms | | Plural forms | |
|---|---|---|---|
| **me** | (to, for) *me* | **nos** | (to, for) *us* |
| **te** | (to, for) *you* (fam.) | **os** | (to, for) *you* (fam.) |
| **le** | (to, for) *you* (form.) | **les** | (to, for) *you* (form.) |
| | (to, for) *him; her* | | (to, for) *them* |

▶ **¡Atención!** The forms of indirect object pronouns for the first and second persons (**me, te, nos, os**) are the same as the direct object pronouns. Indirect object pronouns agree in number with the corresponding nouns, but not in gender.

Bueno, le doy un descuento.

Acabo de mostrarles que sí sabemos regatear.

## Using indirect object pronouns

▶ Spanish speakers commonly use both an indirect object pronoun and the noun to which it refers in the same sentence. This is done to emphasize and clarify to whom the pronoun refers.

| I.O. PRONOUN | INDIRECT OBJECT | I.O. PRONOUN | INDIRECT OBJECT |
|---|---|---|---|
| Ella **le** vende la ropa **a Elena**. | | **Les** prestamos el dinero **a Inés y a Álex**. | |

▶ Indirect object pronouns are also used without the indirect object noun when the person for whom the action is being done is known.

Ana **le** presta la falda **a Elena**.      También **le** presta unos jeans.
*Ana lends her skirt to Elena.*      *She also lends her a pair of jeans.*

▶ Indirect object pronouns are usually placed before the conjugated form of the verb. In negative sentences the pronoun is placed between **no** and the conjugated verb.

> Martín **me** compra un regalo.
> *Martín is buying me a gift.*

> Eva **no me** escribe cartas.
> *Eva doesn't write me letters.*

▶ When a conjugated verb is followed by an infinitive or the present progressive, the indirect object pronoun may be placed before the conjugated verb or attached to the infinitive or present participle. **¡Atención!** When an indirect object pronoun is attached to a present participle, an accent mark is added to maintain the proper stress.

> Él no quiere **pagarte**./
> Él no **te** quiere pagar.
> *He does not want to pay you.*

> Él está **escribiéndole** una postal a ella./
> Él **le** está escribiendo una postal a ella.
> *He is writing a postcard to her.*

▶ Because the indirect object pronouns **le** and **les** have multiple meanings, Spanish speakers often clarify to whom the pronouns refer with the preposition **a** + [*pronoun*] or **a** + [*noun*].

| UNCLARIFIED STATEMENTS | CLARIFIED STATEMENTS |
|---|---|
| Yo **le** compro un abrigo. | Yo **le** compro un abrigo **a usted/él/ella**. |
| Ella **le** describe un libro. | Ella **le** describe un libro **a Juan**. |

| UNCLARIFIED STATEMENTS | CLARIFIED STATEMENTS |
|---|---|
| Él **les** vende unos sombreros. | Él **les** vende unos sombreros **a ustedes/ellos/ellas**. |
| Ellos **les** hablan muy claro. | Ellos **les** hablan muy claro **a los clientes**. |

▶ The irregular verbs **dar** (*to give*) and **decir** (*to say; to tell*) are often used with indirect object pronouns.

### The verbs dar and decir

| Singular forms | | dar | decir | Plural forms | | dar | decir |
|---|---|---|---|---|---|---|---|
| yo | | **doy** | **digo** | nosotros/as | | **damos** | **decimos** |
| tú | | **das** | **dices** | vosotros/as | | **dais** | **decís** |
| Ud./él/ella | | **da** | **dice** | Uds./ellos/ellas | | **dan** | **dicen** |

> **Me dan** una fiesta cada año.
> *They give (throw) me a party every year.*

> **Te digo** la verdad.
> *I'm telling you the truth.*

> Voy a **darle** consejos.
> *I'm going to give her advice.*

> No **les digo** mentiras a mis padres.
> *I don't tell lies to my parents.*

 Use the cues in parentheses to provide the correct indirect object pronoun for each sentence.

1. Juan _____le_____ quiere dar un regalo. (*to Elena*)
2. María _____ prepara un café. (*for us*)
3. Beatriz y Felipe _____ escriben desde (*from*) Cuba. (*to me*)
4. Marta y yo _____ compramos unos guantes. (*for them*)
5. Los vendedores _____ venden ropa. (*to you, fam. sing.*)
6. La dependienta _____ muestra los guantes. (*to us*)

# Práctica

**1**

**Completar** Fill in the blanks with the correct pronouns to complete Mónica's description of her family's gift giving.

1. Juan y yo _____ damos una blusa a nuestra hermana Gisela.
2. Mi tía _____ da a nosotros una mesa para la casa.
3. Gisela _____ da dos corbatas a su novio.
4. A mi mamá yo _____ doy un par de guantes negros.
5. A mi profesora _____ doy dos libros de José Martí.
6. Juan _____ da un regalo a mis padres.
7. Mis padres _____ dan un traje nuevo a mí.
8. Y a ti, yo _____ doy un regalo también. ¿Quieres verlo?

**NOTA CULTURAL**

Cuban writer and patriot **José Martí** (1853–1895) was born in **La Habana Vieja**, the old colonial center of Havana.

**2**

**En La Habana** Describe what happens on Pascual's trip to Cuba based on the cues provided.

1. ellos / cantar / canción / (mí)
2. él / comprar / libros / (sus hijos) / Plaza de Armas
3. yo / preparar el almuerzo (*lunch*) / (ti)

4. él / explicar cómo llegar / (conductor)
5. mi novia / sacar / foto / (nosotros)
6. el guía (*guide*) / mostrar / catedral de San Cristóbal / (ustedes)

**3**

**Combinar** Use an item from each column and an indirect object pronoun to create logical sentences.

> **modelo**
>
> Mis padres les dan regalos a mis primos.

| A | B | C | D |
|---|---|---|---|
| yo | comprar | mensajes electrónicos | mí |
| el dependiente | dar | corbata | ustedes |
| el profesor Arce | decir | dinero en efectivo | clienta |
| la vendedora | escribir | tarea | novia |
| mis padres | explicar | problemas | primos |
| tú | pagar | regalos | ti |
| nosotros/as | prestar | ropa | nosotros |
| ¿? | vender | ¿? | ¿? |

 Practice more at **vhlcentral.com**.

# Comunicación

**4**

**Entrevista** In pairs, take turns asking and answering for whom you do these activities. Use the model as a guide.

| | |
|---|---|
| cantar | escribir mensajes electrónicos |
| comprar ropa | mostrar fotos de un viaje |
| dar una fiesta | pedir dinero |
| decir mentiras | preparar comida (*food*) mexicana |

**modelo**

escribir mensajes electrónicos
**Estudiante 1:** ¿A quién le escribes mensajes electrónicos?
**Estudiante 2:** Le escribo mensajes electrónicos a mi hermano.

**5**

**¡Somos ricos!** You and your classmates just received a large sum of money. Now you want to spend money on your loved ones. In groups of three, discuss what each person is buying for family and friends.

**modelo**

**Estudiante 1:** Quiero comprarle un vestido de Carolina Herrera a mi madre.
**Estudiante 2:** Y yo voy a darles un automóvil nuevo a mis padres.
**Estudiante 3:** Voy a comprarles una casa a mis padres, pero a mis amigos no les voy a dar nada.

**6**

**Entrevista** Use these questions to interview a classmate.

1. ¿Qué tiendas, almacenes o centros comerciales prefieres?
2. ¿A quién le compras regalos cuando hay rebajas?
3. ¿A quién le prestas dinero cuando lo necesita?
4. Quiero ir de compras. ¿Cuánto dinero me puedes prestar?
5. ¿Te dan tus padres su tarjeta de crédito cuando vas de compras?

# Síntesis

**7**

**Minidrama** In groups of three, take turns playing the roles of two shoppers and a clerk in a clothing store. The shoppers should talk about the articles of clothing they want and for whom they are buying them. The clerk should recommend several items based on the shoppers' descriptions. Use these expressions and also look at **Expresiones útiles** on page 195.

| | |
|---|---|
| **Me queda grande/pequeño.** | **¿Está en rebaja?** |
| *It's big/small on me.* | *Is it on sale?* |
| **¿Tiene otro color?** | **También estoy buscando...** |
| *Do you have another color?* | *I'm also looking for...* |

**S** Explanation Tutorial

# 6.3 Preterite tense of regular verbs

**ANTE TODO**   In order to talk about events in the past, Spanish uses two simple tenses: the preterite and the imperfect. In this lesson, you will learn how to form the preterite tense, which is used to express actions or states completed in the past.

## Preterite of regular -ar, -er, and -ir verbs

| | | -ar verbs<br>**comprar** | -er verbs<br>**vender** | -ir verbs<br>**escribir** |
|---|---|---|---|---|
| **SINGULAR FORMS** | yo | compr**é** *I bought* | vend**í** *I sold* | escrib**í** *I wrote* |
| | tú | compr**aste** | vend**iste** | escrib**iste** |
| | Ud./él/ella | compr**ó** | vend**ió** | escrib**ió** |
| **PLURAL FORMS** | nosotros/as | compr**amos** | vend**imos** | escrib**imos** |
| | vosotros/as | compr**asteis** | vend**isteis** | escrib**isteis** |
| | Uds./ellos/ellas | compr**aron** | vend**ieron** | escrib**ieron** |

▶ **¡Atención!** The **yo** and **Ud./él/ella** forms of all three conjugations have written accents on the last syllable to show that it is stressed.

▶ As the chart shows, the endings for regular **-er** and **-ir** verbs are identical in the preterite.

¿Qué compraste?

Compré estos aretes.

▶ Note that the **nosotros/as** forms of regular **-ar** and **-ir** verbs in the preterite are identical to the present tense forms. Context will help you determine which tense is being used.

> En invierno **compramos** ropa.      Anoche **compramos** unos zapatos.
> *In the winter, we buy clothing.*      *Last night we bought some shoes.*

▶ **-Ar** and **-er** verbs that have a stem change in the present tense are regular in the preterite. They do *not* have a stem change.

| | | PRESENT | PRETERITE |
|---|---|---|---|
| **cerrar** | (e:ie) | La tienda **cierra** a las seis. | La tienda **cerró** a las seis. |
| **volver** | (o:ue) | Carlitos **vuelve** tarde. | Carlitos **volvió** tarde. |
| **jugar** | (u:ue) | Él **juega** al fútbol. | Él **jugó** al fútbol. |

▶ **¡Atención!** **-Ir** verbs that have a stem change in the present tense also have a stem change in the preterite.

**CONSULTA**

There are a few high-frequency irregular verbs in the preterite. You will learn more about them in **Estructura 9.1**, p. 310.

**CONSULTA**

You will learn about the preterite of stem-changing verbs in **Estructura 8.1**, p. 274.

▶ Verbs that end in **-car**, **-gar**, and **-zar** have a spelling change in the first person singular (**yo** form) in the preterite.

| bus**car** | busc- | qu- | yo bus**qué** |
| lle**gar** | lleg- | gu- | yo lle**gué** |
| empe**zar** | empez- | c- | yo empe**cé** |

▶ Except for the **yo** form, all other forms of **-car**, **-gar**, and **-zar** verbs are regular in the preterite.

▶ Three other verbs—**creer**, **leer**, and **oír**—have spelling changes in the preterite. The **i** of the verb endings of **creer**, **leer**, and **oír** carries an accent in the **yo**, **tú**, **nosotros/as**, and **vosotros/as** forms, and changes to **y** in the **Ud./él/ella** and **Uds./ellos/ellas** forms.

| creer | cre- | cre**í**, cre**í**ste, cre**y**ó, cre**í**mos, cre**í**steis, cre**y**eron |
| leer | le- | le**í**, le**í**ste, le**y**ó, le**í**mos, le**í**steis, le**y**eron |
| oír | o- | o**í**, o**í**ste, o**y**ó, o**í**mos, o**í**steis, o**y**eron |

▶ **Ver** is regular in the preterite, but none of its forms has an accent.

**ver** ⟶ vi, viste, vio, vimos, visteis, vieron

## Words commonly used with the preterite

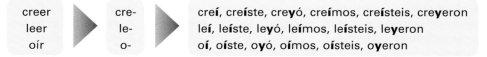

| anoche | *last night* | pasado/a (*adj.*) | *last; past* |
| anteayer | *the day before yesterday* | el año pasado | *last year* |
| ayer | *yesterday* | la semana pasada | *last week* |
| de repente | *suddenly* | una vez | *once; one time* |
| desde... hasta... | *from... until...* | dos veces | *twice; two times* |
| | | ya | *already* |

**Ayer** llegué a Santiago de Cuba.
*Yesterday I arrived in Santiago de Cuba.*

**Anoche** oí un ruido extraño.
*Last night I heard a strange noise.*

▶ **Acabar de** + [*infinitive*] is used to say that something has just occurred. Note that **acabar** is in the present tense in this construction.

**Acabo de comprar** una falda.
*I just bought a skirt.*

**Acabas de ir** de compras.
*You just went shopping.*

**¡INTÉNTALO!** Provide the appropriate preterite forms of the verbs.

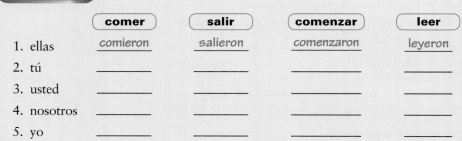

| | comer | salir | comenzar | leer |
|---|---|---|---|---|
| 1. ellas | comieron | salieron | comenzaron | leyeron |
| 2. tú | _____ | _____ | _____ | _____ |
| 3. usted | _____ | _____ | _____ | _____ |
| 4. nosotros | _____ | _____ | _____ | _____ |
| 5. yo | _____ | _____ | _____ | _____ |

# Práctica

**1**

**Completar** Andrea is talking about what happened last weekend. Complete each sentence by choosing the correct verb and putting it in the preterite.

1. El viernes a las cuatro de la tarde, la profesora Mora _____ (asistir, costar, usar) a una reunión (*meeting*) de profesores.
2. El sábado por la mañana, yo _____ (llegar, bucear, llevar) a la tienda con mis amigos.
3. Mis amigos y yo _____ (comprar, regatear, gastar) dos o tres cosas.
4. Yo _____ (costar, comprar, escribir) unos pantalones negros y mi amigo Mateo _____ (gastar, pasear, comprar) una camisa azul.
5. Después, nosotros _____ (llevar, vivir, comer) cerca de un mercado.
6. A las tres, Pepe _____ (hablar, pasear, nadar) con su novia por teléfono.
7. El sábado por la tarde, mi mamá _____ (escribir, beber, vivir) una carta.
8. El domingo mi tía _____ (decidir, salir, escribir) comprarme un traje.
9. A las cuatro de la tarde, mi tía _____ (beber, salir, encontrar) el traje y después nosotras _____ (acabar, ver, salir) una película.

**2**

**Preguntas** Imagine that you have a pesky friend who keeps asking you questions. Respond that you already did or have just done what he/she asks. Make sure you and your partner take turns playing the role of the pesky friend and responding to his/her questions.

> **modelo**
> leer la lección
> **Estudiante 1:** ¿Leíste la lección?
> **Estudiante 2:** Sí, ya la leí./Sí, acabo de leerla.

1. escribir el mensaje electrónico
2. lavar (*to wash*) la ropa
3. oír las noticias (*news*)
4. comprar pantalones cortos
5. practicar los verbos
6. leer el artículo
7. empezar la composición
8. ver la nueva película de Almodóvar

**3**

**¿Cuándo?** Use the time expressions from the word bank to talk about when you and others did the activities listed.

| anoche | anteayer | el mes pasado | una vez |
| ayer | la semana pasada | el año pasado | dos veces |

1. mi mejor amigo/a: llegar tarde a clase
2. mi hermano/a mayor: salir con un(a) chico/a guapo/a
3. mis padres: ver una película
4. yo: llevar un traje/vestido
5. el presidente/primer ministro de mi país: no escuchar a la gente
6. mis amigos y yo: comer en un restaurante
7. ¿?: comprar algo (*something*) bueno, bonito y barato

 Practice more at **vhlcentral.com.**

# Comunicación

**4**

**Ayer** Jot down at what time you did these activities yesterday. Then get together with a classmate and find out at what time he or she did these activities. Be prepared to share your findings with the class.

1. desayunar
2. empezar la primera clase
3. almorzar
4. ver a un(a) amigo/a
5. salir de clase
6. volver a casa

**5**

**Las vacaciones** Imagine that you took these photos on a vacation. Get together with a partner and use the pictures to tell him or her about your trip.

**6**

**El fin de semana** Your teacher will give you and your partner different incomplete charts about what four employees at **Almacén Gigante** did last weekend. After you fill out the chart based on each other's information, you will fill out the final column about your partner.

# Síntesis

**7**

**Conversación** With a partner, have a conversation about what you did last week, using verbs from the word bank. Don't forget to include school activities, shopping, and pastimes.

| | | | |
|---|---|---|---|
| acampar | comprar | hablar | tomar |
| asistir | correr | jugar | trabajar |
| bailar | escribir | leer | vender |
| buscar | estudiar | oír | ver |
| comer | gastar | pagar | viajar |

## 6.4 Demonstrative adjectives and pronouns

**Explanation Tutorial**

### Demonstrative adjectives

**ANTE TODO** In Spanish, as in English, demonstrative adjectives are words that "demonstrate" or "point out" nouns. Demonstrative adjectives precede the nouns they modify and, like other Spanish adjectives you have studied, agree with them in gender and number. Observe these examples and then study the chart below.

| **esta** camisa | **ese** vendedor | **aquellos** zapatos |
|---|---|---|
| *this shirt* | *that salesman* | *those shoes (over there)* |

### Demonstrative adjectives

|  | Singular |  | Plural |  |  |
|---|---|---|---|---|---|
|  | MASCULINE | FEMININE | MASCULINE | FEMININE |  |
|  | **este** | **esta** | **estos** | **estas** | *this; these* |
|  | **ese** | **esa** | **esos** | **esas** | *that; those* |
|  | **aquel** | **aquella** | **aquellos** | **aquellas** | *that; those (over there)* |

▶ There are three sets of demonstrative adjectives. To determine which one to use, you must establish the relationship between the speaker and the noun(s) being pointed out.

▶ The demonstrative adjectives **este**, **esta**, **estos**, and **estas** are used to point out nouns that are close to the speaker and the listener.

*Me gustan estos zapatos.*

▶ The demonstrative adjectives **ese**, **esa**, **esos**, and **esas** are used to point out nouns that are not close in space and time to the speaker. They may, however, be close to the listener.

*Prefiero esos zapatos.*

▶ The demonstrative adjectives **aquel**, **aquella**, **aquellos**, and **aquellas** are used to point out nouns that are far away from the speaker and the listener.

*Aquel auto es de mi hermana.*

## Demonstrative pronouns

▶ Demonstrative pronouns are identical to their corresponding demonstrative adjectives, with the exception that they carry an accent mark on the stressed vowel.

| Demonstrative pronouns | | | |
|---|---|---|---|
| **Singular** | | **Plural** | |
| MASCULINE | FEMININE | MASCULINE | FEMININE |
| **éste** | **ésta** | **éstos** | **éstas** |
| **ése** | **ésa** | **ésos** | **ésas** |
| **aquél** | **aquélla** | **aquéllos** | **aquéllas** |

—¿Quieres comprar **este suéter**?
*Do you want to buy this sweater?*

—No, no quiero **éste**. Quiero **ése**.
*No, I don't want this one. I want that one.*

—¿Vas a leer **estas revistas**?
*Are you going to read these magazines?*

—Sí, voy a leer **éstas**. También voy a leer **aquéllas**.
*Yes, I'm going to read these. I'll also read those (over there).*

▶ **¡Atención!** Like demonstrative adjectives, demonstrative pronouns agree in gender and number with the corresponding noun.

**Este libro** es de Pablito.          **Éstos** son de Juana.

▶ There are three neuter demonstrative pronouns: **esto**, **eso**, and **aquello**. These forms refer to unidentified or unspecified nouns, situations, ideas, and concepts. They do not change in gender or number and never carry an accent mark.

—¿Qué es **esto**?
*What's this?*

—**Eso** es interesante.
*That's interesting.*

—**Aquello** es bonito.
*That's pretty.*

**recursos**

v̂**Text**

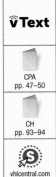

CPA
pp. 47–50

CH
pp. 93–94

vhlcentral.com

**¡INTÉNTALO!**   Provide the correct form of the demonstrative adjective for these nouns.

1. la falda / este ____*esta falda*____
2. los estudiantes / este _____
3. los países / aquel _____
4. la ventana / ese _____

5. los periodistas / ese _____
6. el chico / aquel _____
7. las sandalias / este _____
8. las chicas / aquel _____

# Práctica

**1**

**Cambiar** Make the singular sentences plural and the plural sentences singular.

> **modelo**
>
> Estas camisas son blancas.
> *Esta camisa es blanca.*

1. Aquellos sombreros son muy elegantes.
2. Ese abrigo es muy caro.
3. Estos cinturones son hermosos.
4. Esos precios son muy buenos.
5. Estas faldas son muy cortas.
6. ¿Quieres ir a aquel almacén?
7. Esas blusas son baratas.
8. Esta corbata hace juego con mi traje.

**2**

**Completar** Here are some things people might say while shopping. Complete the sentences with the correct demonstrative pronouns.

1. No me gustan esos zapatos. Voy a comprar _____. (*these*)
2. ¿Vas a comprar ese traje o _____? (*this one*)
3. Esta guayabera es bonita, pero prefiero _____. (*that one*)
4. Estas corbatas rojas son muy bonitas, pero _____ son fabulosas. (*those*)
5. Estos cinturones cuestan demasiado. Prefiero _____. (*those over there*)
6. ¿Te gustan esas botas o _____? (*these*)
7. Esa bolsa roja es bonita, pero prefiero _____. (*that one over there*)
8. No voy a comprar estas botas; voy a comprar _____. (*those over there*)
9. ¿Prefieres estos pantalones o _____? (*those*)
10. Me gusta este vestido, pero voy a comprar _____. (*that one*)
11. Me gusta ese almacén, pero _____ es mejor (*better*). (*that one over there*)
12. Esa blusa es bonita, pero cuesta demasiado. Voy a comprar _____. (*this one*)

◀ **NOTA CULTURAL**

The **guayabera** is a men's shirt typically worn in some parts of the Caribbean. Never tucked in, it is casual wear, but variations exist for more formal occasions, such as weddings, parties, or the office.

**3**

**Describir** With your partner, look for two items in the classroom that are one of these colors: **amarillo, azul, blanco, marrón, negro, verde, rojo.** Take turns pointing them out to each other, first using demonstrative adjectives, and then demonstrative pronouns.

> **modelo**
>
> azul
> **Estudiante 1:** *Esta silla es azul. Aquella mochila es azul.*
> **Estudiante 2:** *Ésta es azul. Aquélla es azul.*

Now use demonstrative adjectives and pronouns to discuss the colors of your classmates' clothing. One of you can ask a question about an article of clothing, using the wrong color. Your partner will correct you and point out that color somewhere else in the room.

> **modelo**
>
> **Estudiante 1:** *¿Esa camisa es negra?*
> **Estudiante 2:** *No, ésa es azul. Aquélla es negra.*

 Practice more at **vhlcentral.com.**

# Comunicación

**4**

**Conversación** With a classmate, use demonstrative adjectives and pronouns to ask each other questions about the people around you. Use expressions from the word bank and/or your own ideas.

| | |
|---|---|
| ¿A qué hora...? | ¿Cuántos años tiene(n)...? |
| ¿Cómo es/son...? | ¿De dónde es/son...? |
| ¿Cómo se llama...? | ¿De quién es/son...? |
| ¿Cuándo...? | ¿Qué clases toma(n)...? |

*modelo*

**Estudiante 1:** *¿Cómo se llama esa chica?*
**Estudiante 2:** *Se llama Rebeca.*
**Estudiante 1:** *¿A qué hora llegó aquel chico a la clase?*
**Estudiante 2:** *A las nueve.*

**5**

**En una tienda** Imagine that you and a classmate are in Madrid shopping at Zara. Study the floor plan, then have a conversation about your surroundings. Use demonstrative adjectives and pronouns.

*modelo*

**Estudiante 1:** *Me gusta este suéter azul.*
**Estudiante 2:** *Yo prefiero aquella chaqueta.*

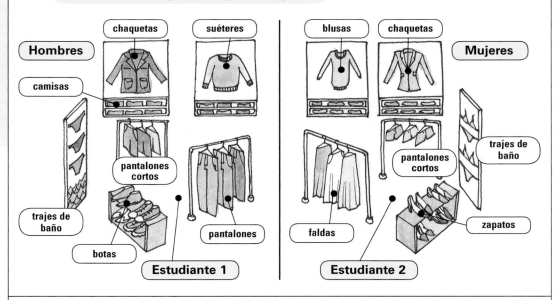

# Síntesis

**6**

**Diferencias** Your teacher will give you and a partner each a drawing of a store. They are almost identical, but not quite. Use demonstrative adjectives and pronouns to find seven differences.

*modelo*

**Estudiante 1:** *Aquellas gafas de sol son feas, ¿verdad?*
**Estudiante 2:** *No. Aquellas gafas de sol son hermosas.*

SUBJECT
Javier
CONJUGATED FORM
empiezo
Main clause
Dudan

# Recapitulación

**S** **Diagnostics**
**Remediation Activities**

Review the grammar concepts you have learned in this lesson by completing these activities.

**1** **Completar** Complete the chart with the correct preterite or infinitive form of the verbs. **15 pts.**

| Infinitive | yo | ella | ellos |
|---|---|---|---|
| | | | tomaron |
| | | abrió | |
| comprender | | | |
| | leí | | |
| pagar | | | |

**2** **En la tienda** Look at the drawing and complete the conversation with demonstrative adjectives and pronouns. **7 pts.**

**CLIENTE** Buenos días, señorita. Deseo comprar (1) _____ corbata.

**VENDEDORA** Muy bien, señor. ¿No le interesa mirar (2) _____ trajes que están allá? Hay unos que hacen juego con la corbata.

**CLIENTE** (3) _____ de allá son de lana, ¿no? Prefiero ver (4) _____ traje marrón que está detrás de usted.

**VENDEDORA** Estupendo. Como puede ver, es de seda. Cuesta ciento ochenta dólares.

**CLIENTE** Ah... eh... no, creo que sólo voy a comprar la corbata, gracias.

**VENDEDORA** Bueno... si busca algo más económico, hay rebaja en (5) _____ sombreros. Cuestan sólo treinta dólares.

**CLIENTE** ¡Magnífico! Me gusta (6) _____, el blanco que está hasta arriba (*at the top*). Y quiero pagar todo con (7) _____ tarjeta.

**VENDEDORA** Sí, señor. Ahora mismo le traigo el sombrero.

---

## RESUMEN GRAMATICAL

**6.1** **Saber and conocer** *p. 200*

| saber | conocer |
|---|---|
| sé | conozco |
| sabes | conoces |
| sabe | conoce |
| sabemos | conocemos |
| sabéis | conocéis |
| saben | conocen |

► **saber** = to know facts/how to do something
► **conocer** = to know a person, place, or thing

**6.2** **Indirect object pronouns** *pp. 202–203*

**Indirect object pronouns**

| Singular | Plural |
|---|---|
| me | nos |
| te | os |
| le | les |

► **dar** = doy, das, da, damos, dais, dan
► **decir (e:i)** = digo, dices, dice, decimos, decís, dicen

**6.3** **Preterite tense of regular verbs** *pp. 206–207*

| comprar | vender | escribir |
|---|---|---|
| compré | vendí | escribí |
| compraste | vendiste | escribiste |
| compró | vendió | escribió |
| compramos | vendimos | escribimos |
| comprasteis | vendisteis | escribisteis |
| compraron | vendieron | escribieron |

**Verbs with spelling changes in the preterite**

► **-car:** buscar → yo busqué
► **-gar:** llegar → yo llegué
► **-zar:** empezar → yo empecé
► **creer:** creí, creíste, creyó, creímos, creísteis, creyeron
► **leer:** leí, leíste, leyó, leímos, leísteis, leyeron
► **oír:** oí, oíste, oyó, oímos, oísteis, oyeron
► **ver:** vi, viste, vio, vimos, visteis, vieron

**3**   **¿Saber o conocer?** Complete each dialogue with the correct form of **saber** or **conocer**. **10 pts.**

1. —¿Qué _____ hacer tú?
   —(Yo) _____ jugar al fútbol.
2. —¿_____ tú esta tienda de ropa?
   —No, (yo) no la _____. ¿Es buena?
3. —¿Tus padres no _____ a tu profesor?
   —No, ¡ellos no _____ quién es!
4. —Mi hermanastro todavía no me
   _____ bien.
   —Y tú, ¿lo quieres _____ a él?
5. —¿_____ ustedes dónde está el mercado?
   —No, nosotros no _____ bien esta ciudad.

### 6.4 Demonstrative adjectives and pronouns pp. 210–211

**Demonstrative adjectives**

| Singular | | Plural | |
|---|---|---|---|
| Masc. | Fem. | Masc. | Fem. |
| este | esta | estos | estas |
| ese | esa | esos | esas |
| aquel | aquella | aquellos | aquellas |

**Demonstrative pronouns**

| Singular | | Plural | |
|---|---|---|---|
| Masc. | Fem. | Masc. | Fem. |
| éste | ésta | éstos | éstas |
| ése | ésa | ésos | ésas |
| aquél | aquélla | aquéllos | aquéllas |

**4**   **Oraciones** Form complete sentences using the information provided. Use indirect object pronouns and the present tense of the verbs. **10 pts.**

1. Javier / prestar / el abrigo / a Maripili

  _____

2. nosotros / vender / ropa / a los clientes

  _____

3. el vendedor / traer / las camisetas / a mis amigos y a mí

  _____

4. yo / querer dar / consejos (*advice*) / a ti

  _____

5. ¿tú / ir a comprar / un regalo / a mí?

  _____

**5**   **Mi última compra** Write a short paragraph describing the last time you went shopping. Use at least four verbs in the preterite tense. **8 pts.**

> **modelo**
> *El viernes pasado, busqué unos zapatos en el centro comercial...*

**6**   **Refranes** Write the missing words to complete the proverbs. **2 EXTRA points!**

  **" A la cama no te irás° sin _____ (conocer/saber) una cosa más. "**
  (*You learn something new every day.*)

  **" A todos _____ (les/te) llega su momento de gloria°. "**
  (*Every dog has its day.*)

no te irás *you will not go*    gloria *glory*

Practice more at **vhlcentral.com**.

# Lectura

**Audio:** Synched Reading Additional Reading

## Antes de leer

### Estrategia

**Skimming**

Skimming involves quickly reading through a document to absorb its general meaning. This allows you to understand the main ideas without having to read word for word. When you skim a text, you might want to look at its title and subtitles. You might also want to read the first sentence of each paragraph.

### Examinar el texto

Look at the format of the reading selection. How is it organized? What does the organization of the document tell you about its content?

### Buscar cognados

Scan the reading selection to locate at least five cognates. Based on the cognates, what do you think the reading selection is about?

1. _____    4. _____
2. _____    5. _____
3. _____

The reading selection is about _____.

### Impresiones generales

Now skim the reading selection to understand its general meaning. Jot down your impressions. What new information did you learn about the document by skimming it? Based on all the information you now have, answer these questions in Spanish.

1. Who created this document?
2. What is its purpose?
3. Who is its intended audience?

# Corona

**¡Corona tiene las ofertas más locas del verano!**

La tienda más elegante de la ciudad con precios increíbles

**Carteras**
**ELEGANCIA**
Colores anaranjado, blanco, rosado y amarillo
**Ahora: 15.000 pesos**
**50% de rebaja**

**Sandalias de playa**
**GINO**
Números del 35 al 38
**A sólo 12.000 pesos**
**50% de descuento**

**Faldas largas**
**ROPA BONITA**
Algodón. De distintos colores
Talla mediana
**Precio especial:**
**8.000 pesos**

**Blusas de seda**
**BAMBÚ**
De cuadros y de lunares
**Ahora: 21.000 pesos**
**40% de rebaja**

**Vestido de algodón**
**PANAMÁ**
Colores blanco, azul y verde
**Ahora: 18.000 pesos**
**30% de rebaja**

**Accesorios**
**BELLEZA**
Cinturones, gafas de sol, sombreros, medias
Diversos estilos
**Todos con un 40% de rebaja**

**Lunes a sábado de 9 a 21 horas.**
**Domingo de 10 a 14 horas.**

## ¡Grandes rebajas!
# Real° Liquidación°
### ¡La rebaja está de moda en Corona!

**y con la tarjeta de crédito más conveniente del mercado.**

**Chaquetas**
**CASINO**
Microfibra. Colores negro,
café y gris
Tallas: P, M, G, XG
**Ahora: 22.500 pesos**

**Zapatos**
**COLOR**
Italianos y franceses
Números del 40 al 45
**A sólo 20.000 pesos**

**Pantalones**
**OCÉANO**
Colores negro, gris y café
**Ahora: 11.500 pesos**
**30% de rebaja**

**Ropa interior**
**ATLÁNTICO**
Tallas: P, M, G
Colores blanco,
negro y gris
**40% de rebaja**

**Traje inglés**
**GALES**
Modelos originales
**Ahora: 105.000 pesos**
**30% de rebaja**

**Accesorios**
**GUAPO**
Gafas de sol, corbatas,
cinturones, calcetines
Diversos estilos
**Todos con un 40%**
**de rebaja**

Real *Royal* Liquidación *Clearance sale*

**Por la compra de 40.000 pesos, puede llevar un regalo gratis.**
- Un hermoso cinturón de mujer
- Un par de calcetines
- Una corbata de seda
- Una bolsa para la playa
- Una mochila
- Unas medias

# Después de leer

## Completar ✏️🅢
Complete this paragraph about the reading selection with the correct forms of the words from the word bank.

| | | |
|---|---|---|
| almacén | hacer juego | tarjeta de crédito |
| caro | increíble | tienda |
| dinero | pantalones | verano |
| falda | rebaja | zapato |

En este anuncio de periódico, el _____ Corona anuncia la liquidación de _____ con grandes _____. Con muy poco _____ usted puede conseguir ropa fina y elegante. Si no tiene dinero en efectivo, puede utilizar su _____ y pagar luego. Para el hombre de gustos refinados, hay _____ importados de París y Roma. La señora elegante puede encontrar blusas de seda que _____ con todo tipo de _____ o _____. Los precios de esta liquidación son realmente _____.

## ¿Cierto o falso? ✏️🅢
Indicate whether each statement is **cierto** or **falso**. Correct the false statements.

1. Hay sandalias de playa.
2. Las corbatas tienen una rebaja del 30%.
3. El almacén Corona tiene un departamento de zapatos.
4. Normalmente las sandalias cuestan 22.000 pesos.
5. Cuando gastas 30.000 pesos en la tienda, llevas un regalo gratis.
6. Tienen carteras amarillas.

## Preguntas
In pairs, take turns asking and answering these questions.

1. Imagina que vas a ir a la tienda Corona. ¿Qué departamentos vas a visitar? ¿El departamento de ropa para mujeres, el departamento de ropa para hombres...?
2. ¿Qué vas a buscar en Corona?
3. ¿Hay tiendas similares a la tienda Corona en tu pueblo o ciudad? ¿Cómo se llaman? ¿Tienen muchas gangas?

 Practice more at **vhlcentral.com**.

# Escritura

## Estrategia

### How to report an interview

There are several ways to prepare a written report about an interview. For example, you can transcribe the interview verbatim, you can simply summarize it, or you can summarize it but quote the speakers occasionally. In any event, the report should begin with an interesting title and a brief introduction, which may include the five Ws (*what, where, when, who, why*) and the H (*how*) of the interview. The report should end with an interesting conclusion. Note that when you transcribe dialogue in Spanish, you should pay careful attention to format and punctuation.

### Writing dialogue in Spanish

- If you need to transcribe an interview verbatim, you can use speakers' names to indicate a change of speaker.

| | |
|---|---|
| CARMELA | ¿Qué compraste? ¿Encontraste muchas gangas? |
| ROBERTO | Sí, muchas. Compré un suéter, una camisa y dos corbatas. Y tú, ¿qué compraste? |
| CARMELA | Una blusa y una falda muy bonitas. ¿Cuánto costó tu camisa? |
| ROBERTO | Sólo diez dólares. ¿Cuánto costó tu blusa? |
| CARMELA | Veinte dólares. |

- You can also use a dash (*raya*) to mark the beginning of each speaker's words.

  —¿Qué compraste?
  —Un suéter y una camisa muy bonitos. Y tú, ¿encontraste muchas gangas?
  —Sí... compré dos blusas, tres camisetas y un par de zapatos.
  —¡A ver!

## Tema

### Escribe un informe

Write a report for the school newspaper about an interview you conducted with a student about his or her shopping habits and clothing preferences. First, brainstorm a list of interview questions. Then conduct the interview using the questions below as a guide, but feel free to ask other questions as they occur to you.

Examples of questions:

▶ ¿Cuándo vas de compras?

▶ ¿Adónde vas de compras?

▶ ¿Con quién vas de compras?

▶ ¿Qué tiendas, almacenes o centros comerciales prefieres?

▶ ¿Compras ropa de catálogos o por Internet?

▶ ¿Prefieres comprar ropa cara o barata? ¿Por qué? ¿Te gusta buscar gangas?

▶ ¿Qué ropa llevas cuando vas a clase?

▶ ¿Qué ropa llevas cuando sales con tus amigos/as?

▶ ¿Qué ropa llevas cuando practicas un deporte?

▶ ¿Cuáles son tus colores favoritos? ¿Compras mucha ropa de esos colores?

▶ ¿Les das ropa a tu familia o a tus amigos/as?

# Escuchar

## Estrategia
### Listening for linguistic cues

You can enhance your listening comprehension by listening for specific linguistic cues. For example, if you listen for the endings of conjugated verbs, or for familiar constructions, such as **acabar de** + [*infinitive*] or **ir a** + [*infinitive*], you can find out whether an event already took place, is taking place now, or will take place in the future. Verb endings also give clues about who is participating in the action.

 To practice listening for linguistic cues, you will now listen to four sentences. As you listen, note whether each sentence refers to a past, present, or future action. Also jot down the subject of each sentence.

## Preparación

Based on the photograph, what do you think Marisol has recently done? What do you think Marisol and Alicia are talking about? What else can you guess about their conversation from the visual clues in the photograph?

## Ahora escucha

Now you are going to hear Marisol and Alicia's conversation. Make a list of the clothing items that each person mentions. Then put a check mark after the item if the person actually purchased it.

| Marisol | Alicia |
|---|---|
| 1._____ | 1._____ |
| 2._____ | 2._____ |
| 3._____ | 3._____ |
| 4._____ | 4._____ |

recursos

v Text

vhlcentral.com

Marisol

Alicia

## Comprensión

### ¿Cierto o falso?

Indicate whether each statement is **cierto** or **falso**. Then correct the false statements.

1. Marisol y Alicia acaban de ir de compras juntas (*together*).
2. Marisol va a comprar unos pantalones y una blusa mañana.
3. Marisol compró una blusa de cuadros.
4. Alicia compró unos zapatos nuevos hoy.
5. Alicia y Marisol van a ir al café.
6. Marisol gastó todo el dinero de la semana en ropa nueva.

### Preguntas

Discuss the following questions with a classmate. Be sure to explain your answers.

1. ¿Crees que Alicia y Marisol son buenas amigas? ¿Por qué?
2. ¿Cuál de las dos estudiantes es más ahorradora (*frugal*)? ¿Por qué?
3. ¿Crees que a Alicia le gusta la ropa que Marisol compró?
4. ¿Crees que la moda es importante para Alicia? ¿Para Marisol? ¿Por qué?
5. ¿Es importante para ti estar a la moda? ¿Por qué?

# En pantalla  Video: TV Clip

In Spain, during Francisco Franco's dictatorship (1939–1975), students in public schools were required to wear uniforms. After the fall of Franco's regime and the establishment of democracy, educational authorities rejected this former policy and decided it should no longer be obligatory to wear uniforms in public schools. Today, only some private schools in Spain enforce the use of uniforms; even Catholic schools do not have anything more than a basic dress code.

### Vocabulario útil

| | |
|---|---|
| anoraks | anoraks (Spain) |
| anchas | loose-fitting |
| vaqueros | jeans (Spain) |
| trencas | duffel coats (Spain) |
| lavables | washable |
| carteras | book bags (Spain) |
| chándals | tracksuits (Spain) |
| resiste | withstands |
| tanto como | as much as |

###  Identificar

Check off each word that you hear in the ad.

_____ 1. camisetas     _____ 5. chaquetas

_____ 2. hijos     _____ 6. clientas

_____ 3. zapatos     _____ 7. lana

_____ 4. algodón     _____ 8. precio

### Conversar

Take turns asking and answering these questions with a classmate. Use as much Spanish as you can.

1. ¿Qué ropa llevas normalmente cuando vienes a la escuela?

2. ¿Y los fines de semana?

3. ¿Tienes una prenda (*garment*) favorita? ¿Cómo es?

4. ¿Qué tipo de ropa no te gusta usar? ¿Por qué?

## Anuncio de tiendas Galerías

**Presentamos la moda para el próximo° curso.**

**Formas geométricas y colores vivos.**

**Tejidos° resistentes°.**

próximo *next* Tejidos *Fabrics* resistentes *strong, tough*

Practice more at **vhlcentral.com.**

 Video: *Flash cultura*

In the Spanish-speaking world, most city dwellers shop at large supermarkets and little stores that specialize in just one item, such as a butcher shop (**carnicería**), vegetable market (**verdulería**), perfume shop (**perfumería**), or hat shop (**sombrerería**). In small towns where supermarkets are less common, many people rely exclusively on specialty shops. This requires shopping more frequently—often every day or every other day for perishable items—but also means that the foods they consume are fresher and the goods are usually locally produced. Each neighborhood generally has its own shops, so people don't have to walk far to find fresh bread (at a **panadería**) for the midday meal.

## Vocabulario útil

| | |
|---|---|
| **colones (pl.)** | *currency from Costa Rica* |
| **¿Cuánto vale?** | **¿Cuánto cuesta?** |
| **descuento** | *discount* |
| **disculpe** | *excuse me* |
| **¿Dónde queda...?** | *Where is... located?* |
| **los helados** | *ice cream* |
| **el regateo** | *bargaining* |

**Preparación**

Have you ever been to an open-air market? What did you buy? Have you ever negotiated a price? What did you say?

**Comprensión**

Select the option that best summarizes this episode.
a. Randy Cruz va al mercado al aire libre para comprar papayas. Luego va al Mercado Central. Él les pregunta a varios clientes qué compran, prueba (*he tastes*) platos típicos y busca la heladería.
b. Randy Cruz va al mercado al aire libre para comprar papayas y pedir un descuento. Luego va al Mercado Central para preguntarles a los clientes qué compran en los mercados.

## Comprar en los mercados

Trescientos colones.

... pero me hace un buen descuento.

¿Qué compran en el Mercado Central?

 Practice more at **vhlcentral.com**.

**recursos**

vText | CPA pp. 55–56 | vhlcentral.com

# Cuba

**Interactive Map**
**Video: *Panorama cultural***

## El país en cifras

▶ **Área:** 110.860 km² (42.803 millas²),
*aproximadamente el área de Pensilvania*

▶ **Población:** 11.204.000

▶ **Capital:** La Habana—2.141.993

*La Habana Vieja fue declarada° Patrimonio°
Cultural de la Humanidad por la UNESCO
en 1982. Este distrito es uno de los lugares
más fascinantes de Cuba. En La Plaza de
Armas, se puede visitar el majestuoso Palacio
de Capitanes Generales, que ahora es un
museo. En la calle° Obispo, frecuentada por el
autor Ernest Hemingway, hay hermosos cafés,
clubes nocturnos y tiendas elegantes.*

▶ **Ciudades principales:** Santiago de Cuba;
Camagüey; Holguín; Guantánamo

SOURCE: Population Division, UN Secretariat

▶ **Moneda:** peso cubano

▶ **Idiomas:** español (oficial)

Bandera de Cuba

**Cubanos célebres**

▶ **Carlos Finlay,** doctor y científico (1833–1915)

▶ **José Martí,** político y poeta (1853–1895)

▶ **Fidel Castro,** ex presidente, ex comandante
en jefe° de las fuerzas armadas (1926– )

▶ **Zoé Valdés,** escritora (1959– )

▶ **Ibrahim Ferrer,** músico (1927–2005)

fue declarada *was declared* Patrimonio *Heritage* calle *street*
comandante en jefe *commander in chief* liviano *light*
colibrí abeja *bee hummingbird* ave *bird* mundo *world*
miden *measure* pesan *weigh*

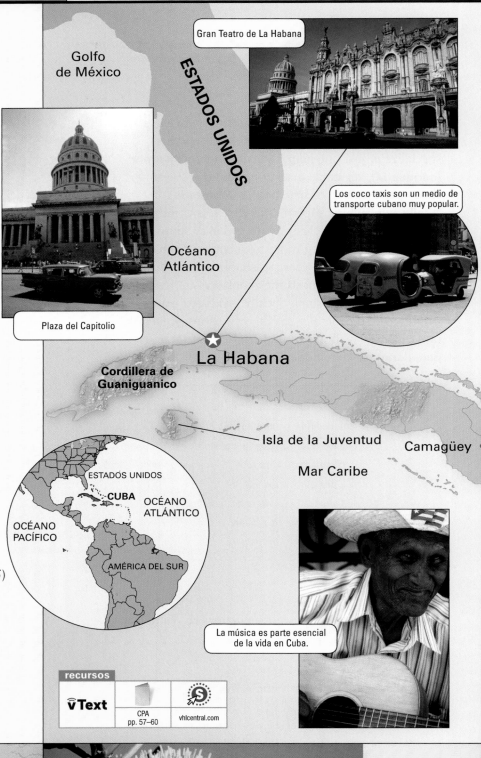

Gran Teatro de La Habana

Golfo de México

ESTADOS UNIDOS

Los coco taxis son un medio de transporte cubano muy popular.

Plaza del Capitolio

Océano Atlántico

La Habana

Cordillera de Guaniguanico

ESTADOS UNIDOS

CUBA

OCÉANO ATLÁNTICO

OCÉANO PACÍFICO

AMÉRICA DEL SUR

Isla de la Juventud

Camagüey

Mar Caribe

La música es parte esencial de la vida en Cuba.

**recursos**

**vText**

CPA
pp. 57–60

vhlcentral.com

## ¡Increíble pero cierto!

Pequeño y liviano°, el colibrí abeja° de Cuba
es una de las más de 320 especies de colibrí
y es también el ave° más pequeña del mundo°.
Menores que muchos insectos, estas aves
minúsculas miden° 5 centímetros y pesan°
sólo 1,95 gramos.

### Baile • Ballet Nacional de Cuba

La bailarina Alicia Alonso fundó el Ballet Nacional de Cuba en 1948, después de° convertirse en una estrella° internacional en el Ballet de Nueva York y en Broadway. El Ballet Nacional de Cuba es famoso en todo el mundo por su creatividad y perfección técnica.

### Economía • La caña de azúcar y el tabaco

La caña de azúcar° es el producto agrícola° que más se cultiva en la isla y su exportación es muy importante para la economía del país. El tabaco, que se usa para fabricar los famosos puros° cubanos, es otro cultivo° de mucha importancia.

### Gente • Población

La población cubana tiene raíces° muy heterogéneas. La inmigración a la isla fue determinante° desde la colonia hasta mediados° del siglo° XX. Los cubanos de hoy son descendientes de africanos, europeos, chinos y antillanos, entre otros.

### Música • Buena Vista Social Club

En 1997 nace° el fenómeno musical conocido como *Buena Vista Social Club*. Este proyecto reúne° a un grupo de importantes músicos de Cuba, la mayoría ya mayores, con una larga trayectoria interpretando canciones clásicas del son° cubano. Ese mismo año ganaron un *Grammy*. Hoy en día estos músicos son conocidos en todo el mundo, y personas de todas las edades bailan al ritmo° de su música.

Holguín
Santiago de Cuba
Guantánamo
**Sierra Maestra**

 **¿Qué aprendiste?** Responde a las preguntas con una oración completa.

1. ¿Qué autor está asociado con La Habana Vieja?
2. ¿Por qué es famoso el Ballet Nacional de Cuba?
3. ¿Cuáles son los dos cultivos más importantes para la economía cubana?
4. ¿Qué fabrican los cubanos con la planta del tabaco?
5. ¿De dónde son muchos de los inmigrantes que llegaron a Cuba?
6. ¿En qué año ganó un *Grammy* el disco *Buena Vista Social Club*?

 **Conexión Internet** Investiga estos temas en **vhlcentral.com**.

1. Busca información sobre un(a) cubano/a célebre. ¿Por qué es célebre? ¿Qué hace? ¿Todavía vive en Cuba?
2. Busca información sobre una de las ciudades principales de Cuba. ¿Qué atracciones hay en esta ciudad?

 Practice more at **vhlcentral.com**.

**después de** *after* **estrella** *star* **caña de azúcar** *sugar cane* **agrícola** *farming* **puros** *cigars* **cultivo** *crop* **raíces** *roots* **determinante** *deciding* **mediados** *halfway through* **siglo** *century* **nace** *is born* **reúne** *gets together* **son** *Cuban musical genre* **ritmo** *rhythm*

## La ropa

| | |
|---|---|
| el abrigo | coat |
| los (blue)jeans | jeans |
| la blusa | blouse |
| la bolsa | purse; bag |
| la bota | boot |
| los calcetines (el calcetín) | sock(s) |
| la camisa | shirt |
| la camiseta | t-shirt |
| la cartera | wallet |
| la chaqueta | jacket |
| el cinturón | belt |
| la corbata | tie |
| la falda | skirt |
| las gafas (de sol) | (sun)glasses |
| los guantes | gloves |
| el impermeable | raincoat |
| las medias | pantyhose; stockings |
| los pantalones | pants |
| los pantalones cortos | shorts |
| la ropa | clothing; clothes |
| la ropa interior | underwear |
| las sandalias | sandals |
| el sombrero | hat |
| el suéter | sweater |
| el traje | suit |
| el traje de baño | bathing suit |
| el vestido | dress |
| los zapatos de tenis | sneakers |

## Verbos

| | |
|---|---|
| conducir | to drive |
| conocer | to know; to be acquainted with |
| ofrecer | to offer |
| parecer | to seem |
| saber | to know; to know how |
| traducir | to translate |

## Ir de compras

| | |
|---|---|
| el almacén | department store |
| la caja | cash register |
| el centro comercial | shopping mall |
| el/la cliente/a | customer |
| el/la dependiente/a | clerk |
| el dinero | money |
| (en) efectivo | cash |
| el mercado (al aire libre) | (open-air) market |
| un par (de zapatos) | a pair (of shoes) |
| el precio (fijo) | (fixed; set) price |
| la rebaja | sale |
| el regalo | gift |
| la tarjeta de crédito | credit card |
| la tienda | shop; store |
| el/la vendedor(a) | salesperson |
| costar (o:ue) | to cost |
| gastar | to spend (money) |
| hacer juego (con) | to match (with) |
| llevar | to wear; to take |
| pagar | to pay |
| regatear | to bargain |
| usar | to wear; to use |
| vender | to sell |

## Adjetivos

| | |
|---|---|
| barato/a | cheap |
| bueno/a | good |
| cada | each |
| caro/a | expensive |
| corto/a | short (in length) |
| elegante | elegant |
| hermoso/a | beautiful |
| largo/a | long |
| loco/a | crazy |
| nuevo/a | new |
| otro/a | other; another |
| pobre | poor |
| rico/a | rich |

  **Audio: Vocabulary Flashcards**

## Los colores

| | |
|---|---|
| el color | color |
| anaranjado/a | orange |
| gris | gray |
| marrón, café | brown |
| morado/a | purple |
| rosado/a | pink |

## Palabras adicionales

| | |
|---|---|
| acabar de (+ inf.) | to have just done something |
| anoche | last night |
| anteayer | the day before yesterday |
| ayer | yesterday |
| de repente | suddenly |
| desde | from |
| dos veces | twice; two times |
| hasta | until |
| pasado/a (adj.) | last; past |
| el año pasado | last year |
| la semana pasada | last week |
| prestar | to lend; to loan |
| una vez | once; one time |
| ya | already |

| | |
|---|---|
| Indirect object pronouns | See page 202. |
| Demonstrative adjectives and pronouns | See page 210. |
| Expresiones útiles | See page 195. |

# La rutina diaria

**Communicative Goals**

*I will be able to:*
• Describe my daily routine
• Talk about personal hygiene
• Reassure someone

VOICE BOARD

**A PRIMERA VISTA**
• ¿Está él en casa o en una tienda?
• ¿Está contento o enojado?
• ¿Cómo es él?
• ¿Qué colores hay en la foto?

# La rutina diaria

  **Audio: Vocabulary Tutorials, Games**

## Más vocabulario

| | |
|---|---|
| el baño, el cuarto de baño | bathroom |
| el inodoro | toilet |
| el jabón | soap |
| el despertador | alarm clock |
| el maquillaje | makeup |
| la rutina diaria | daily routine |
| bañarse | to bathe; to take a bath |
| cepillarse el pelo | to brush one's hair |
| dormirse (o:ue) | to go to sleep; to fall asleep |
| lavarse la cara | to wash one's face |
| levantarse | to get up |
| maquillarse | to put on makeup |
| antes (de) | before |
| después | afterwards; then |
| después (de) | after |
| durante | during |
| entonces | then |
| luego | then |
| más tarde | later |
| por la mañana | in the morning |
| por la noche | at night |
| por la tarde | in the afternoon; in the evening |
| por último | finally |

## Variación léxica

afeitarse ⟷ rasurarse (Méx., Amér. C.)
ducha ⟷ regadera (Col., Méx., Venez.)
ducharse ⟷ bañarse (Amér. L.)
pantuflas ⟷ chancletas (Méx., Col.); zapatillas (Esp.)

**recursos**

v̂Text | CPA pp. 63–65 | CH pp. 99–100 | vhlcentral.com

**En la habitación por la mañana**

**En el baño por la mañana**

Se peina. (peinarse)

Se acuesta. (acostarse)

**En la habitación por la noche**

Se lava las manos. (lavarse las manos)

Se cepilla los dientes. (cepillarse los dientes)

la toalla

la pasta de dientes

las pantuflas

**En el baño por la noche**

# Práctica

**1** **Escuchar** 🎧 Escucha las oraciones e indica si cada oración es **cierta** o **falsa**, según el dibujo.

1. ____f____     6. ____f____
2. ____c____     7. ____f____
3. ____f____     8. ____c____
4. ____f____     9. ____f____
5. ____f____    10. ____c____

**2** **Ordenar** 🎧 Escucha la rutina diaria de Marta. Después ordena los verbos según lo que escuchaste.

__5__ a. almorzar      __3__ e. desayunar
__2__ b. ducharse      __8__ f. dormirse
__4__ c. peinarse      __1__ g. despertarse
__7__ d. ver la televisión      __6__ h. estudiar en la biblioteca

**3** **Seleccionar** Selecciona la palabra que no está relacionada con cada grupo.

1. lavabo • toalla • despertador • jabón _____
2. manos • antes de • después de • por último _____
3. acostarse • jabón • despertarse • dormirse _____
4. espejo • lavabo • despertador • entonces _____
5. dormirse • toalla • vestirse • levantarse _____
6. pelo • cara • manos • inodoro _____
7. espejo • champú • jabón • pasta de dientes _____
8. maquillarse • vestirse • peinarse • dientes _____
9. baño • dormirse • despertador • acostarse _____
10. ducharse • luego • bañarse • lavarse _____

**4** **Identificar** Con un(a) compañero/a, identifica las cosas que cada persona necesita. Sigue el modelo.

> **modelo**
> Jorge / lavarse la cara
> **Estudiante 1:** ¿Qué necesita Jorge para lavarse la cara?
> **Estudiante 2:** Necesita jabón y una toalla.

1. Mariana / maquillarse
2. Gerardo / despertarse
3. Celia / bañarse
4. Gabriel / ducharse
5. Roberto / afeitarse
6. Sonia / lavarse el pelo
7. Vanesa / lavarse las manos
8. Manuel / vestirse

**5** **La rutina de Andrés** Ordena esta rutina de una manera lógica.

a. Se afeita después de cepillarse los dientes. _4_

b. Se acuesta a las once y media de la noche. _9_

c. Por último, se duerme. _10_

d. Después de afeitarse, sale para las clases. _5_

e. Asiste a todas sus clases y vuelve a su casa. _6_

f. Andrés se despierta a las seis y media de la mañana. _1_

g. Después de volver a casa, come un poco. Luego estudia en su habitación. _7_

h. Se viste y entonces se cepilla los dientes. _3_

i. Se cepilla los dientes antes de acostarse. _8_

j. Se ducha antes de vestirse. _2_

**6** **La rutina diaria** Con un(a) compañero/a, mira los dibujos y describe lo que hacen Ángel y Lupe.

1.

2.

3.

4.

5.

6.

7.

8.

Practice more at **vhlcentral.com.**

# Comunicación

**7**

**La farmacia** Lee el anuncio y responde a las preguntas con un(a) compañero/a.

**LA FARMACIA NUEVO SOL** tiene todo
lo que necesitas para la vida diaria.

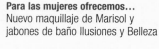

Esta semana tenemos grandes rebajas.

Con poco dinero puedes comprar lo que necesitas para el cuarto de baño ideal.

**Para los hombres ofrecemos…**
Excelentes cremas de afeitar
de Guapo y Máximo

**Para las mujeres ofrecemos…**
Nuevo maquillaje de Marisol y
jabones de baño Ilusiones y Belleza

Y para todos tenemos los mejores jabones, pastas de dientes
y cepillos de dientes.

¡Visita **LA FARMACIA NUEVO SOL!**
Tenemos los mejores precios. Visita nuestra tienda muy cerca de tu casa.

1. ¿Qué tipo de tienda es?
2. ¿Qué productos ofrecen para las mujeres?
3. ¿Qué productos ofrecen para los hombres?
4. Haz (*Make*) una lista de los verbos que asocias con los productos del anuncio.
5. ¿Dónde compras tus productos de higiene?
6. ¿Tienes una tienda favorita? ¿Cuál es?

**8**

**Rutinas diarias** Trabajen en parejas para describir la rutina diaria de dos o tres
de estas personas. Pueden usar palabras de la lista.

| | | |
|---|---|---|
| antes (de) | entonces | primero |
| después (de) | luego | tarde |
| durante el día | por último | temprano |

- un(a) maestro/a
- un(a) turista
- un hombre o una mujer de negocios (*businessman/woman*)
- un vigilante nocturno (*night watchman*)
- un(a) jubilado/a (*retired person*)
- el presidente/primer ministro de tu país
- un niño de cuatro años
- Daniel Espinosa

# ¡Necesito arreglarme!

Es viernes por la tarde y Marissa, Jimena y Felipe se preparan para salir.

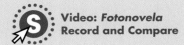

**Video:** *Fotonovela*
**Record and Compare**

**MARISSA** ¿Hola? ¿Está ocupado?

**JIMENA** Sí. Me estoy lavando la cara.

**MARISSA** Necesito usar el baño.

**MARISSA** Tengo que terminar de arreglarme. Voy al cine esta noche.

**JIMENA** Yo también tengo que salir. ¿Te importa si me maquillo primero? Me voy a encontrar con mi amiga Elena en una hora.

**JIMENA** ¡Felipe! ¿Qué estás haciendo?

**FELIPE** Me estoy afeitando. ¿Hay algún problema?

**JIMENA** ¡Siempre haces lo mismo!

**FELIPE** Pues, yo no vi a nadie aquí.

**MARISSA** Tú ganas. ¿Adónde vas a ir esta noche, Felipe?

**FELIPE** Juan Carlos y yo vamos a ir a un café en el centro. Siempre hay música en vivo. (*Se despide.*) Me siento guapísimo. Todavía me falta cambiarme la camisa.

**MARISSA** ¿Adónde vas esta noche?

**JIMENA** A la biblioteca.

**MARISSA** ¡Es viernes! ¡Nadie debe estudiar los viernes! Voy a ver una película de Pedro Almodóvar con unas amigas.

**MARISSA** ¿Por qué no vienen tú y Elena al cine con nosotras? Después, podemos ir a ese café y molestar a Felipe.

**FELIPE**

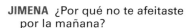

**JIMENA** ¿Por qué no te afeitaste por la mañana?

**FELIPE** Porque cada vez que quiero usar el baño, una de ustedes está aquí. O bañándose o maquillándose.

**JIMENA** No te preocupes, Marissa. Llegaste primero. Entonces, te arreglas el pelo y después me maquillo.

**FELIPE** ¿Y yo? Tengo crema de afeitar en la cara. No me voy a ir. Estoy aquí y aquí me quedo.

**JIMENA** No sé.

**MARISSA** ¿Cuándo fue la última vez que viste a Juan Carlos?

**JIMENA** Cuando fuimos a Mérida.

**MARISSA** A ti te gusta ese chico.

**JIMENA** No tengo idea de qué estás hablando. Si no te importa, nos vemos en el cine.

**recursos**

v̂Text

CPA
pp. 66–67

vhlcentral.com

## Expresiones útiles

### Talking about getting ready

**Necesito arreglarme.**
*I need to get ready.*
**Me estoy lavando la cara.**
*I'm washing my face.*
**¿Te importa si me maquillo primero?**
*Is it OK with you if I put on my makeup first?*
**Tú te arreglas el pelo y después yo me maquillo.**
*You fix your hair and then I'll put on my makeup.*
**Todavía me falta cambiarme la camisa.**
*I still have to change my shirt.*

### Reassuring someone

**Tranquilo/a.**
*Relax.*
**No te preocupes.**
*Don't worry.*

### Talking about past actions

**¿Cuándo fue la última vez que viste a Juan Carlos?**
*When was the last time you saw Juan Carlos?*
**Cuando fuimos a Mérida.**
*When we went to Mérida.*

### Talking about likes and dislikes

**Me fascinan las películas de Almodóvar.**
*I love Almodóvar's movies.*
**Me encanta la música en vivo.**
*I love live music.*
**Me molesta compartir el baño.**
*It bothers me to share the bathroom.*

### Additional vocabulary

**encontrarse con** *to meet up with*
**molestar** *to bother*
**nadie** *no one*

# ¿Qué pasó?

**1**   **¿Cierto o falso?** Indica si lo que dicen estas oraciones es **cierto** o **falso**. Corrige las oraciones falsas.

1. Marissa va a ver una película de Pedro Almodóvar con unas amigas.

2. Jimena se va a encontrar con Elena en dos horas.

3. Felipe se siente muy feo después de afeitarse.

4. Jimena quiere maquillarse.

5. Marissa quiere ir al café para molestar a Juan Carlos.

**2**   **Identificar** Identifica quién puede decir estas oraciones. Puedes usar cada nombre más de una vez.

1. No puedo usar el baño porque siempre están aquí, o bañándose o maquillándose. _____
2. Quiero arreglarme el pelo porque voy al cine esta noche. _____

**MARISSA**

3. Hoy voy a ir a la biblioteca. _____
4. ¡Necesito arreglarme! _____
5. Te gusta Juan Carlos. _____
6. ¿Por qué quieres afeitarte cuando estamos en el baño? _____

**FELIPE**

**JIMENA**

**3**   **Ordenar** Ordena correctamente los planes que tiene Marissa.

\_\_\_\_ a. Voy al café.
\_\_\_\_ b. Me arreglo el pelo.
\_\_\_\_ c. Molesto a Felipe.
\_\_\_\_ d. Me encuentro con unas amigas.
\_\_\_\_ e. Entro al baño.
\_\_\_\_ f. Voy al cine.

**4**   **En el baño** Trabajen en parejas para representar los papeles de dos compañeros/as de cuarto que deben usar el baño al mismo tiempo para hacer su rutina diaria. Usen las instrucciones como guía.

| Estudiante 1 | Estudiante 2 |
|---|---|
| Di (*Say*) que quieres arreglarte porque vas a ir al cine. | Di (*Say*) que necesitas arreglarte porque te vas a encontrar con tus amigos/as. |
| Pregunta si puedes secarte el pelo. | Responde que no porque necesitas lavarte la cara. |
| Di que puede lavarse la cara, pero que después necesitas secarte el pelo. | Di que puede secarse el pelo, pero que después necesitas peinarte. |

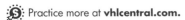 Practice more at **vhlcentral.com**.

# Pronunciación

 **Audio: Explanation Record and Compare**

**The consonant r**

| ropa | rutina | rico | Ramón |
|------|--------|------|-------|

In Spanish, **r** has a strong trilled sound at the beginning of a word. No English words have a trill, but English speakers often produce a trill when they imitate the sound of a motor.

| gustar | durante | primero | crema |
|--------|---------|---------|-------|

In any other position, **r** has a weak sound similar to the English *tt* in *better* or the English *dd* in *ladder*. In contrast to English, the tongue touches the roof of the mouth behind the teeth.

| pizarra | corro | marrón | aburrido |
|---------|-------|--------|----------|

The letter combination **rr**, which only appears between vowels, always has a strong trilled sound.

| caro | carro | pero | perro |
|------|-------|------|-------|

Between vowels, the difference between the strong trilled **rr** and the weak **r** is very important, as a mispronunciation could lead to confusion between two different words.

**Práctica** Lee las palabras en voz alta, prestando (*paying*) atención a la pronunciación de la **r** y la **rr**.

1. Perú
2. Rosa
3. borrador
4. madre
5. comprar
6. favor
7. rubio
8. reloj
9. Arequipa
10. tarde
11. cerrar
12. despertador

**Oraciones** Lee las oraciones en voz alta, prestando atención a la pronunciación de la **r** y la **rr**.

1. Ramón Robles Ruiz es programador. Su esposa Rosaura es artista.
2. A Rosaura Robles le encanta regatear en el mercado.
3. Ramón nunca regatea… le aburre regatear.
4. Rosaura siempre compra cosas baratas.
5. Ramón no es rico, pero prefiere comprar cosas muy caras.
6. ¡El martes Ramón compró un carro nuevo!

**Refranes** Lee en voz alta los refranes, prestando atención a la **r** y a la **rr**.

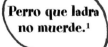

Perro que ladra no muerde.[1]

No se ganó Zamora en una hora.[2]

1 A dog's bark is worse than its bite.   2 Rome wasn't built in a day.

**recursos**

v̂Text

CPA p. 68   CH p. 101   vhlcentral.com

Reading, Additional Reading

# La siesta

**¿Sientes cansancio° después de comer?**
¿Te cuesta° volver al trabajo° o a clase después del almuerzo? Estas sensaciones son normales. A muchas personas les gusta relajarse° después de almorzar. Este momento de descanso es **la siesta**. La siesta es popular en los países hispanos y viene de una antigua costumbre° del área del Mediterráneo. La palabra *siesta* viene del latín, es una forma corta de decir "sexta hora". La sexta hora del día es después del mediodía, el momento de más calor. Debido al° calor y al cansancio, los habitantes de España, Italia, Grecia y Portugal tienen la costumbre de dormir la siesta desde hace° más de° dos mil años. Los españoles y los portugueses llevaron la costumbre a los países americanos.

Aunque° hoy día esta costumbre está desapareciendo° en las grandes ciudades, la siesta todavía es importante en la cultura hispana. En pueblos pequeños, por ejemplo, muchas oficinas° y tiendas tienen la costumbre de cerrar por dos o tres horas después del mediodía. Los empleados van a su casa, almuerzan con sus familias, duermen la siesta o hacen actividades, como ir al gimnasio, y luego regresan al trabajo entre las 2:30 y las 4:30 de la tarde.

Los estudios científicos explican que una siesta corta después de almorzar ayuda° a trabajar más y mejor° durante la tarde. Pero ¡cuidado! Esta siesta debe durar° sólo entre veinte y cuarenta minutos. Si dormimos más, entramos en la fase de sueño profundo y es difícil despertarse.

Hoy, algunas empresas° de los EE.UU., Canadá, Japón, Inglaterra y Alemania tienen salas° especiales donde los empleados pueden dormir la siesta.

### ¿Dónde duermen la siesta?

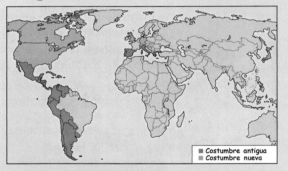

En los lugares donde la siesta es una costumbre antigua, las personas la duermen en su casa. En los países donde la siesta es una costumbre nueva, la gente duerme en sus lugares de trabajo o en centros de siesta.

■ Costumbre antigua
■ Costumbre nueva

Sientes cansancio *Do you feel tired* Te cuesta *Is it hard for you* trabajo *work* relajarse *to relax* antigua costumbre *old custom* Debido al *Because (of)* desde hace *for* más de *more than* Aunque *Although* está desapareciendo *is disappearing* oficinas *offices* ayuda *helps* mejor *better* durar *last* algunas empresas *some businesses* salas *rooms*

**1** **¿Cierto o falso?** Indica si lo que dicen las oraciones es **cierto** o **falso**. Corrige la información falsa.

1. La costumbre de la siesta empezó en Asia.
2. La palabra siesta está relacionada con la sexta hora del día.
3. Los españoles y los portugueses llevaron la costumbre de la siesta a Latinoamérica.
4. La siesta ayuda a trabajar más y mejor durante la tarde.
5. Los horarios de trabajo de las grandes ciudades hispanas son los mismos que los pueblos pequeños.
6. Una siesta larga siempre es mejor que una siesta corta.
7. En los Estados Unidos, los empleados de algunas empresas pueden dormir la siesta en el trabajo.
8. Es fácil despertar de un sueño profundo.

## El cuidado personal

| | |
|---|---|
| el aseo; el excusado; el servicio; el váter (Esp.) | el baño |
| el cortaúñas | nail clippers |
| el desodorante | deodorant |
| el enjuague bucal | mouthwash |
| el hilo dental/ la seda dental | dental floss |
| la máquina de afeitar/ de rasurar (Méx.) | electric razor |

## Costumbres especiales

- **México y El Salvador** Los vendedores pasan por las calles anunciando a gritos° su mercancía°: tanques de gas y flores° en México; pan y tortillas en El Salvador.

- **Costa Rica** Para encontrar las direcciones°, los costarricenses usan referencias a anécdotas, lugares o características geográficas. Por ejemplo: *200 metros norte de la iglesia Católica, frente al° supermercado Mi Mega.*

- **Argentina** En Tigre, una ciudad junto al Río° de la Plata, la gente usa barcos particulares°, barcos colectivos° y barcos-taxi para ir de una isla a otra. Todas las mañanas, un barco colectivo recoge° a los niños y los lleva a la escuela.

gritos *shouts* mercancía *merchandise* flores *flowers* direcciones *addresses* frente al *opposite* río *river* particulares *private* barcos colectivos *collective boats* recoge *picks up*

## El mate

El mate es una parte muy importante de la rutina diaria en muchos países. Es una bebida° muy similar al té que se consume en Argentina, Uruguay y Paraguay. Tradicionalmente se bebe caliente° con una *bombilla*° y en un recipiente° que también se llama *mate*. Por ser amarga, algunos le agregan° azúcar para suavizar su sabor°. El mate se puede tomar a cualquier° hora y en cualquier  lugar, aunque en Argentina las personas prefieren sentarse en círculo e ir pasando el mate de mano en mano mientras° conversan. Los uruguayos, por otra parte, acostumbran llevar

 el agua° caliente para el mate en un termo° bajo el brazo° y lo beben mientras caminan. Si ves a una persona con un termo bajo el brazo y un mate en la mano, ¡es casi seguro que es de Uruguay!

bebida *drink* caliente *hot* bombilla *straw (in Argentina)* recipiente *container* amarga *bitter* le agregan *add* suavizar su sabor *soften its flavor* cualquier *any* mientras *while* agua *water* termo *thermos* bajo el brazo *under their arm*

### Conexión Internet

¿Qué costumbres son populares en los países hispanos?

Go to **vhlcentral.com** to find more cultural information related to this **Cultura** section.

**2 Comprensión** Completa las oraciones.
1. Uso _____ para limpiar (*to clean*) entre los dientes.
2. En _____ las personas compran pan y tortillas a los vendedores que pasan por la calle.
3. El _____ es una bebida similar al té.
4. Los uruguayos beben mate mientras _____.

**3 ¿Qué costumbres tienes?** Escribe cuatro oraciones sobre una costumbre que compartes con tus amigos o con tu familia (por ejemplo: ir al cine, ir a eventos deportivos, leer, comer juntos, etc.). Explica qué haces, cuándo lo haces y con quién.

**recursos**

v̂Text

CH p. 102

vhlcentral.com

  Practice more at **vhlcentral.com**.

Explanation Tutorial

## 7.1 Reflexive verbs

**ANTE TODO** A reflexive verb is used to indicate that the subject does something to or for himself or herself. In other words, it "reflects" the action of the verb back to the subject. Reflexive verbs always use reflexive pronouns.

SUBJECT     REFLEXIVE VERB

Joaquín    **se ducha** por la mañana.

### The verb lavarse (*to wash oneself*)

| SINGULAR FORMS | | |
|---|---|---|
| yo | **me lavo** | *I wash (myself)* |
| tú | **te lavas** | *you wash (yourself)* |
| Ud. | **se lava** | *you wash (yourself)* |
| él/ella | **se lava** | *he/she washes (himself/herself)* |

| PLURAL FORMS | | |
|---|---|---|
| nosotros/as | **nos lavamos** | *we wash (ourselves)* |
| vosotros/as | **os laváis** | *you wash (yourselves)* |
| Uds. | **se lavan** | *you wash (yourselves)* |
| ellos/ellas | **se lavan** | *they wash (themselves)* |

**AYUDA**

Except for **se**, reflexive pronouns have the same forms as direct and indirect object pronouns.

• • •

**Se** is used for both singular and plural subjects—there is no individual plural form:
Pablo **se** lava.
Ellos **se** lavan.

▶ The pronoun **se** attached to an infinitive identifies the verb as reflexive: **lavarse.**

▶ When a reflexive verb is conjugated, the reflexive pronoun agrees with the subject.

**Me afeito.**                 **Te despiertas** a las siete.

¿Te importa si me maquillo primero?

A las chicas les encanta maquillarse durante horas y horas.

▶ Like object pronouns, reflexive pronouns generally appear before a conjugated verb. With infinitives and present participles, they may be placed before the conjugated verb or attached to the infinitive or present participle.

Ellos **se** van a vestir.          **Nos** estamos lavando las manos.
Ellos van a vestir**se.**           Estamos lavándo**nos** las manos.
*They are going to get dressed.*    *We are washing our hands.*

▶ **¡Atención!** When a reflexive pronoun is attached to a present participle, an accent mark is added to maintain the original stress.

bañando ⟶ bañ**á**ndo**se**          durmiendo ⟶ durmi**é**ndo**se**

## Common reflexive verbs

| | | | |
|---|---|---|---|
| **acordarse (de)** (o:ue) | to remember | **llamarse** | to be called; to be named |
| **acostarse** (o:ue) | to go to bed | **maquillarse** | to put on makeup |
| **afeitarse** | to shave | **peinarse** | to comb one's hair |
| **bañarse** | to bathe; to take a bath | **ponerse** | to put on |
| **cepillarse** | to brush | **ponerse (+ *adj.*)** | to become (+ *adj.*) |
| **despedirse (de)** (e:i) | to say goodbye (to) | **preocuparse (por)** | to worry (about) |
| **despertarse** (e:ie) | to wake up | **probarse** (o:ue) | to try on |
| **dormirse** (o:ue) | to go to sleep; to fall asleep | **quedarse** | to stay; to remain |
| **ducharse** | to shower; to take a shower | **quitarse** | to take off |
| | | **secarse** | to dry (oneself) |
| **enojarse (con)** | to get angry (with) | **sentarse** (e:ie) | to sit down |
| **irse** | to go away; to leave | **sentirse** (e:ie) | to feel |
| **lavarse** | to wash (oneself) | **vestirse** (e:i) | to get dressed |
| **levantarse** | to get up | | |

### COMPARE & CONTRAST

Unlike English, a number of verbs in Spanish can be reflexive or non-reflexive. If the verb acts upon the subject, the reflexive form is used. If the verb acts upon something other than the subject, the non-reflexive form is used. Compare these sentences.

Lola **lava** los platos.

Patricia **se lava** la cara.

As the preceding sentences show, reflexive verbs sometimes have different meanings than their non-reflexive counterparts. For example, **lavar** means *to wash*, while **lavarse** means *to wash oneself, to wash up*.

▶ **¡Atención!** Parts of the body or clothing are generally not referred to with possessives, but with articles.

La niña se quitó **un** zapato.                    Necesito cepillarme **los** dientes.

**¡INTÉNTALO!**   Indica el presente de estos verbos reflexivos.

**despertarse**

1. Mis hermanos __se despiertan__ tarde.
2. Tú _____ tarde.
3. Nosotros _____ tarde.
4. Benito _____ tarde.
5. Yo _____ tarde.

**ponerse**

1. Él ____se pone____ una chaqueta.
2. Yo _____ una chaqueta.
3. Usted _____ una chaqueta.
4. Nosotras _____ una chaqueta.
5. Las niñas _____ una chaqueta.

# Práctica

**1**

**Nuestra rutina** La familia de Blanca sigue la misma rutina todos los días. Según Blanca, ¿qué hacen ellos?

> **modelo**
> mamá / despertarse a las 5:00
> *Mamá se despierta a las cinco.*

1. Roberto y yo / levantarse a las 7:00
2. papá / ducharse primero y / luego afeitarse
3. yo / lavarse la cara y / vestirse antes de tomar café
4. mamá / peinarse y / luego maquillarse
5. todos (nosotros) / sentarse a la mesa para comer
6. Roberto / cepillarse los dientes después de comer
7. yo / ponerse el abrigo antes de salir
8. nosotros / despedirse de mamá

**2**

**La fiesta elegante** Selecciona el verbo apropiado y completa las oraciones con la forma correcta.

1. Tú _____ (lavar / lavarse) el auto antes de ir a la fiesta.
2. Nosotros no _____ (acordar / acordarse) de comprar los regalos.
3. Para llegar a tiempo, Raúl y Marta _____ (acostar / acostarse) a los niños antes de salir.
4. Yo _____ (sentir / sentirse) cómoda en mi vestido nuevo.
5. Mis amigos siempre _____ (vestir / vestirse) con ropa muy elegante.
6. Los cocineros _____ (probar / probarse) la comida antes de servirla.
7. Usted _____ (preocupar / preocuparse) mucho por llegar antes que (*before*) los demás invitados, ¿no?
8. En general, _____ (afeitar / afeitarse) yo mismo, pero hoy es un día especial y el barbero (*barber*) me _____ (afeitar / afeitarse). ¡Será una fiesta inolvidable!

**3**

**Describir** Mira los dibujos y describe lo que estas personas hacen.

1. el joven

2. Carmen

3. Juan

4. ellos

5. Estrella

6. Toni

# Comunicación

**4**

**Preguntas personales** En parejas, túrnense para hacerse estas preguntas.

1. ¿A qué hora te levantas durante la semana?
2. ¿A qué hora te levantas los fines de semana?
3. ¿Prefieres levantarte tarde o temprano? ¿Por qué?
4. ¿Te enojas frecuentemente con tus amigos?
5. ¿Te preocupas fácilmente? ¿Qué te preocupa?
6. ¿Qué te pone contento/a?
7. ¿Qué haces cuando te sientes triste?
8. ¿Y cuando te sientes alegre?
9. ¿Te acuestas tarde o temprano durante la semana?
10. ¿A qué hora te acuestas los fines de semana?

**5**

**Charadas** En grupos, jueguen a las charadas. Cada persona debe pensar en dos oraciones con verbos reflexivos. La primera persona que adivina la charada dramatiza la siguiente.

**6**

**Debate** En grupos, discutan este tema: ¿Quiénes necesitan más tiempo para arreglarse (*to get ready*) antes de salir, los hombres o las mujeres? Hagan una lista de las razones (*reasons*) que tienen para defender sus ideas e informen a la clase.

**7**

**La coartada** Hoy se cometió un crimen entre las 7 y las 11 de la mañana. En parejas, imaginen que uno de ustedes es un sospechoso y el otro un policía investigador. El policía le pregunta al sospechoso qué hace habitualmente a esas horas y el sospechoso responde. Luego, el policía presenta las respuestas del sospechoso ante el jurado (la clase) y entre todos deciden si es culpable o no.

# Síntesis

**recursos**

**v̂ Text**

CPA
pp. 72–73

**8**

**La familia ocupada** Tú y tu compañero/a asisten a un programa de verano en Lima, Perú. Viven con la familia Ramos. Tu profesor(a) te va a dar la rutina incompleta que la familia sigue en las mañanas. Trabaja con tu compañero/a para completarla.

**modelo**

**Estudiante 1:** ¿Qué hace el señor Ramos a las seis y cuarto?
**Estudiante 2:** El señor Ramos se levanta.

**Explanation Tutorial**

**7.2** # Indefinite and negative words

**ANTE TODO** Indefinite words refer to people and things that are not specific, for example, *someone* or *something*. In Spanish, indefinite words have corresponding negative words, which are opposite in meaning.

## Indefinite and negative words

| Indefinite words | | Negative words | |
|---|---|---|---|
| **algo** | something; anything | **nada** | nothing; not anything |
| **alguien** | someone; somebody; anyone | **nadie** | no one; nobody; not anyone |
| **alguno/a(s), algún** | some; any | **ninguno/a, ningún** | no; none; not any |
| **o... o** | either... or | **ni... ni** | neither... nor |
| **siempre** | always | **nunca, jamás** | never, not ever |
| **también** | also; too | **tampoco** | neither; not either |

▶ There are two ways to form negative sentences in Spanish. You can place the negative word before the verb, or you can place **no** before the verb and the negative word after.

**Nadie se levanta** temprano.
*No one gets up early.*

**No se levanta nadie** temprano.
*No one gets up early.*

Ellos **nunca gritan**.
*They never shout.*

Ellos **no gritan nunca**.
*They never shout.*

¿Hay algún problema?

Siempre haces esto.

▶ Because they refer to people, **alguien** and **nadie** are often used with the personal **a**. The personal **a** is also used before **alguno/a**, **algunos/as**, and **ninguno/a** when these words refer to people and they are the direct object of the verb.

—Perdón, señor, ¿busca usted **a alguien**?
—No, gracias, señorita, no busco **a nadie**.

—Tomás, ¿buscas **a alguno** de tus hermanos?
—No, mamá, no busco **a ninguno**.

▶ **¡Atención!** Before a masculine, singular noun, **alguno** and **ninguno** are shortened to **algún** and **ningún**.

—¿Tienen ustedes **algún** amigo peruano?

—No, no tenemos **ningún** amigo peruano.

**AYUDA**

Alguno/a, algunos/as are not always used in the same way English uses *some* or *any*. Often, **algún** is used where *a* would be used in English.

**¿Tienes algún libro que hable de los incas?**
*Do you have a book that talks about the Incas?*

Note that **ninguno/a** is rarely used in the plural.

—**¿Visitaste algunos museos?**
—**No, no visité ninguno.**

---

**COMPARE & CONTRAST**

In English, it is incorrect to use more than one negative word in a sentence. In Spanish, however, sentences frequently contain two or more negative words. Compare these Spanish and English sentences.

**Nunca** le escribo a **nadie**.
*I never write to anyone.*

**No** me preocupo por **nada nunca**.
*I do not ever worry about anything.*

As the preceding sentences show, once an English sentence contains one negative word (for example, *not* or *never*), no other negative word may be used. Instead, indefinite (or affirmative) words are used. In Spanish, however, once a sentence is negative, no other affirmative (that is, indefinite) word may be used. Instead, all indefinite ideas must be expressed in the negative.

▶ **Pero** is used to mean *but*. The meaning of **sino** is *but rather* or *on the contrary*. It is used when the first part of the sentence is negative and the second part contradicts it.

Los estudiantes no se acuestan temprano **sino** tarde.
*The students don't go to bed early, but rather late.*

Esas gafas son caras, **pero** bonitas.
*Those glasses are expensive, but pretty.*

María no habla francés **sino** español.
*María doesn't speak French, but rather Spanish.*

José es inteligente, **pero** no saca buenas notas.
*José is intelligent but doesn't get good grades.*

---

**¡INTÉNTALO!**     Cambia las oraciones para que sean negativas.

1. Siempre se viste bien.
   _____Nunca_____ se viste bien.
   _____No_____ se viste bien _____nunca_____.

2. Alguien se ducha.
   _____Nadie_____ se ducha.
   _____no_____ se ducha _nadie_.

3. Ellas van también.
   Ellas _tampoco_ van.
   Ellas _____no_____ van _tampoco_

4. Alguien se pone nervioso.
   _ninguno_ se pone nervioso.
   _no_ se pone nervioso _ningun_

5. Tú siempre te lavas las manos.
   Tú _nunca_ te lavas las manos.
   Tú _no_ te lavas las manos _nunca_.

6. Voy a traer algo.
   _____ voy a traer _____.

7. Juan se afeita también.
   Juan _tampoco_ se afeita.
   Juan _no_ se afeita _tampoco_

8. Mis amigos viven en una residencia o en casa.
   Mis amigos _no_ viven _ni_ en una residencia _ni_ en casa.

9. La profesora hace algo en su escritorio.
   La profesora _____ hace _____ en su escritorio.

10. Tú y yo vamos al mercado.
    _____ tú _Y_ yo vamos al mercado.

11. Tienen un espejo en su casa.
    _no_ tienen _nadie_ espejo en su casa.

12. Algunos niños se ponen sus abrigos.
    _ninguno_ niño se pone su abrigo.

**recursos**

vText

CPA
pp. 74–76

CH
pp. 105–106

vhlcentral.com

# Práctica

**1**

**¿Pero o sino?**  Forma oraciones sobre estas personas usando **pero** o **sino**.

> **modelo**
>
> muchos estudiantes comen en la cafetería / algunos de ellos quieren salir a comer a un restaurante local.
>
> *Muchos estudiantes comen en la cafetería, pero algunos de ellos quieren salir a comer a un restaurante local.*

1. Marcos nunca se despierta temprano / siempre llega puntual a clase
2. Lisa y Katarina no se acuestan temprano / muy tarde
3. Alfonso es inteligente / algunas veces es antipático
4. los directores de la escuela no son ecuatorianos / peruanos
5. no nos acordamos de comprar champú / compramos jabón
6. Emilia no es estudiante / profesora
7. no quiero levantarme / tengo que ir a clase
8. Miguel no se afeita por la mañana / por la noche

**2**

**Completar**  Completa esta conversación entre dos hermanos. Usa expresiones negativas en tus respuestas. Luego, dramatiza la conversación con un(a) compañero/a.

**AURELIO**   Ana María, ¿encontraste algún regalo para Eliana?
**ANA MARÍA** (1)_____

**AURELIO**   ¿Viste a alguna amiga en el centro comercial?
**ANA MARÍA** (2)_____

**AURELIO**   ¿Me llamó alguien?
**ANA MARÍA** (3)_____

**AURELIO**   ¿Quieres ir al teatro o al cine esta noche?
**ANA MARÍA** (4)_____

**AURELIO**   ¿No quieres salir a comer?
**ANA MARÍA** (5)_____

**AURELIO**   ¿Hay algo interesante en la televisión esta noche?
**ANA MARÍA** (6)_____

**AURELIO**   ¿Tienes algún problema?
**ANA MARÍA** (7)_____

 Practice more at **vhlcentral.com.**

# Comunicación

**3**

**Opiniones** Completa estas oraciones de una manera lógica. Luego, compara tus respuestas con las de un(a) compañero/a.

1. Mi habitación es _____, pero _____.
2. Por la noche me gusta _____, pero _____.
3. Un(a) profesor(a) ideal no es _____, sino _____.
4. Mis amigos son _____, pero _____.

**4**

**¿Qué hay?** En parejas, háganse preguntas sobre qué hay en su ciudad o pueblo: tiendas interesantes, almacenes, cines, librerías baratas, una biblioteca, una plaza central, playa, cafés, museos, una estación de tren. Sigan el modelo.

> **modelo**
>
> **Estudiante 1:** ¿Hay algunas tiendas interesantes?
> **Estudiante 2:** Sí, hay una/algunas. Está(n) detrás del estadio.
>
> **Estudiante 1:** ¿Hay algún museo?
> **Estudiante 2:** No, no hay ninguno.

**5**

**Quejas** En parejas, hagan una lista de cinco quejas (*complaints*) comunes que tienen los estudiantes. Usen expresiones negativas.

> **modelo**
> Nadie me entiende.

Ahora hagan una lista de cinco quejas que los padres tienen de sus hijos.

> **modelo**
> Nunca hacen sus camas.

**6**

**Anuncios** En parejas, lean el anuncio y contesten las preguntas.

1. ¿Es el anuncio positivo o negativo? ¿Por qué?
2. ¿Qué palabras indefinidas hay?
3. Escriban el texto del anuncio cambiando todo por expresiones negativas.

Ahora preparen su propio (*own*) anuncio usando expresiones afirmativas y negativas.

¿Buscas algún producto especial?

¡Siempre hay algo para todos en las tiendas García!

# Síntesis

**7**

**Encuesta** Tu profesor(a) te va a dar una hoja de actividades para hacer una encuesta. Circula por la clase y pídeles a tus compañeros/as que comparen las actividades que hacen durante la semana con las que hacen durante los fines de semana. Escribe las respuestas.

**7.3**   # Preterite of **ser** and **ir**

Explanation Tutorial

**ANTE TODO**   In **Lección 6**, you learned how to form the preterite tense of regular **-ar**, **-er**, and **-ir** verbs. The following chart contains the preterite forms of **ser** (*to be*) and **ir** (*to go*). Since these forms are irregular, you will need to memorize them.

| Preterite of ser and ir | | **ser** *(to be)* | **ir** *(to go)* |
|---|---|---|---|
| **SINGULAR FORMS** | yo | **fui** | **fui** |
| | tú | **fuiste** | **fuiste** |
| | Ud./él/ella | **fue** | **fue** |
| **PLURAL FORMS** | nosotros/as | **fuimos** | **fuimos** |
| | vosotros/as | **fuisteis** | **fuisteis** |
| | Uds./ellos/ellas | **fueron** | **fueron** |

**AYUDA**

Note that, whereas regular **-er** and **-ir** verbs have accent marks in the **yo** and **Ud./él/ella** forms of the preterite, **ser** and **ir** do not.

▶ Since the preterite forms of **ser** and **ir** are identical, context clarifies which of the two verbs is being used.

Él **fue** a comprar champú y jabón.
*He went to buy shampoo and soap.*

¿Cómo **fue** la película anoche?
*How was the movie last night?*

¿Cuándo fue la última vez que viste a Juan Carlos?

Cuando fuimos a Mérida.

**¡INTÉNTALO!**   Completa las oraciones usando el pretérito de **ser** e **ir**.

**ir**

1. Los viajeros ___fueron___ a Perú.
2. Patricia _fue_ a Cuzco.
3. Tú _fuiste_ a Iquitos.
4. Gregorio y yo _fuimos_ a Lima.
5. Yo _fui_ a Trujillo.
6. Ustedes _fueron_ a Arequipa.
7. Mi padre _fue_ a Lima.
8. Nosotras _fuimos_ a Cuzco.
9. Él _fue_ a Machu Picchu.
10. Usted _fue_ a Nazca.

**ser**

1. Usted ___fue___ muy amable.
2. Yo _fui_ muy cordial.
3. Ellos _fueron_ simpáticos.
4. Nosotros _fuimos_ muy tontos.
5. Ella _fue_ antipática.
6. Tú _fuiste_ muy generoso.
7. Ustedes _fueron_ cordiales.
8. La gente _fue_ amable.
9. Tomás y yo _fuimos_ muy felices.
10. Los profesores _fueron_ buenos.

**recursos**

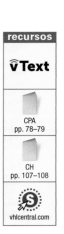

**vText**

CPA
pp. 78–79

CH
pp. 107–108

vhlcentral.com

# Práctica y Comunicación

**1**

**Completar** Completa estas conversaciones con la forma correcta del pretérito de **ser** o **ir**. Indica el infinitivo de cada forma verbal.

| Conversación 1 | | | ser | ir |
|---|---|---|---|---|

**RAÚL** ¿Adónde (1) _fueron_ ustedes de vacaciones?    ○   ☑

**PILAR** (2) _fue_ a Perú.    ○   ☑

**RAÚL** ¿Cómo (3) _fue_ el viaje?    ○   ☑

▶ **PILAR** ¡(4) _Fue_ estupendo! Machu Picchu y El Callao son increíbles.    ☑   ○

**RAÚL** ¿(5) _Fue_ caro el viaje?    ○   ☑

**PILAR** No, el precio (6) _fue_ muy bajo. Sólo costó tres mil dólares.    ☑   ○

| Conversación 2 | | | | |
|---|---|---|---|---|

**ISABEL** Tina y Vicente (7) _fueron_ novios, ¿no?    ☑   ○

**LUCÍA** Sí, pero ahora no. Anoche Tina (8) _fue_ a comer con Gregorio    ○   ☑

y la semana pasada ellos (9) _fueron_ al partido de fútbol.    ○   ☑

**ISABEL** ¿Ah sí? Javier y yo (10) _fuimos_ al partido y no los vimos.    ☑   ○

**2**

**Descripciones** Forma oraciones con estos elementos. Usa el pretérito.

| A | B | C | D |
|---|---|---|---|
| yo | (no) ir | a un restaurante | ayer |
| tú | (no) ser | en autobús | anoche |
| mi compañero/a | | estudiante | anteayer |
| nosotros | | muy simpático/a | la semana pasada |
| mis amigos | | a la playa | el año pasado |
| ustedes | | dependiente/a en una tienda | |

**3**

**Preguntas** En parejas, túrnense para hacerse estas preguntas.

1. ¿Cuándo fuiste al cine por última vez? ¿Con quién fuiste?
2. ¿Fuiste en auto, en autobús o en metro? ¿Cómo fue el viaje?
3. ¿Cómo fue la película?
4. ¿Fue una película de terror, de acción o un drama?
5. ¿Fue una de las mejores películas que viste? ¿Por qué?
6. ¿Fueron buenos los actores o no? ¿Cuál fue el mejor?
7. ¿Adónde fuiste/fueron después?
8. ¿Fue una buena idea ir al cine?
9. ¿Fuiste feliz ese día?

**4**

**El viaje** En parejas, escriban un diálogo de un(a) viajero/a hablando con el/la agente de viajes sobre un viaje que hizo recientemente. Usen el pretérito de **ser** e **ir**.

> **modelo**
>
> **Agente:** ¿Cómo fue el viaje?
>
> **Viajero:** El viaje fue maravilloso/horrible…

Practice more at **vhlcentral.com.**

## 7.4   Verbs like **gustar**

**Explanation Tutorial**

**ANTE TODO**   You have learned how to express preferences with **gustar**. You will now learn more about the verb **gustar** and other similar verbs. Observe these examples.

**Me gusta** ese champú. ◀

> **ENGLISH EQUIVALENT**
> *I like that shampoo.*
> **LITERAL MEANING**
> *That shampoo is pleasing to me.*

**¿Te gustaron** las clases? ◀

> **ENGLISH EQUIVALENT**
> *Did you like the classes?*
> **LITERAL MEANING**
> *Were the classes pleasing to you?*

▶ As the examples show, constructions with **gustar** do not have a direct equivalent in English. The literal meaning of this construction is *to be pleasing to (someone)*, and it requires the use of an indirect object pronoun.

| INDIRECT OBJECT PRONOUN | VERB | SUBJECT | | SUBJECT | VERB | DIRECT OBJECT |
|---|---|---|---|---|---|---|
| **Me** | **gusta** | ese champú. | | *I* | *like* | *that shampoo.* |

▶ In the diagram above, observe how in the Spanish sentence the object being liked (**ese champú**) is really the subject of the sentence. The person who likes the object, in turn, is an indirect object because it answers the question: *To whom is the shampoo pleasing?*

¿Te gusta Juan Carlos?

Me gustan los cafés que tienen música en vivo.

▶ Other verbs in Spanish are used in the same way as **gustar**. Here is a list of the most common ones.

### Verbs like gustar

| | | | | |
|---|---|---|---|---|
| **aburrir** | *to bore* | | **importar** | *to be important to; to matter* |
| **encantar** | *to like very much; to love* (inanimate objects) | | **interesar** | *to be interesting to; to interest* |
| **faltar** | *to lack; to need* | | **molestar** | *to bother; to annoy* |
| **fascinar** | *to fascinate; to like very much* | | **quedar** | *to be left over; to fit* (clothing) |

▶ The most commonly used forms of **gustar** and similar verbs are the third person (singular and plural). When the object or person being liked is singular, the singular form (**gusta**) is used. When two or more objects or persons are being liked, the plural form (**gustan**) is used. Observe the following diagram:

| | SINGULAR | encanta / interesó | ▶ | la película / el concierto |
| me, te, le, nos, os, les | PLURAL | importan / fascinaron | ▶ | las vacaciones / los museos de Lima |

▶ To express what someone likes or does not like to do, use an appropriate verb followed by an infinitive. The singular form is used even if there is more than one infinitive.

> **Nos molesta comer** a las nueve.          **Les encanta bailar** y **cantar** en las fiestas.
> *It bothers us to eat at nine o'clock.*        *They love to dance and sing at parties.*

**AYUDA**

Note that the **a** must be repeated if there is more than one person.
**A Armando** y **a Carmen** les molesta levantarse temprano.

▶ As you have already learned, the construction **a** + [*pronoun*] (**a mí, a ti, a usted, a él,** etc.) is used to clarify or to emphasize who is pleased, bored, etc. The construction **a** + [*noun*] can also be used before the indirect object pronoun to clarify or to emphasize who is pleased.

> **A los turistas** les gustó mucho          **A ti** te gusta cenar en casa, pero
>   Machu Picchu.                                **a mí** me aburre.
> *The tourists liked Machu Picchu a lot.*       *You like eating dinner at home, but I get bored.*

▶ **¡Atención!** **Mí** (*me*) has an accent mark to distinguish it from the possessive adjective **mi** (*my*).

---

 **¡INTÉNTALO!** Indica el pronombre de objeto indirecto y la forma del tiempo presente adecuados en cada oración.

**fascinar**

1. A él ___le fascina___ viajar.
2. A mí _____ bailar.
3. A nosotras _____ cantar.
4. A ustedes _____ leer.
5. A ti _____ correr y patinar.
6. A ellos _____ los aviones.
7. A mis padres _____ caminar.
8. A usted _____ jugar al tenis.
9. A mi esposo y a mí _____ dormir.
10. A Alberto _____ dibujar y pintar.
11. A todos _____ opinar.
12. A Pili _____ los sombreros.

**aburrir**

1. A ellos ___les aburren___ los deportes.
2. A ti _____ las películas.
3. A usted _____ los viajes.
4. A mí _____ las revistas.
5. A Jorge y a Luis _____ los perros.
6. A nosotros _____ las vacaciones.
7. A ustedes _____ el béisbol.
8. A Marcela _____ los libros.
9. A mis amigos _____ los museos.
10. A ella _____ el ciclismo.
11. A Omar _____ ir de compras.
12. A ti y a mí _____ el baile.

**recursos**

**v̂Text**

CPA
pp. 80–83

CH
pp. 109–110

vhlcentral.com
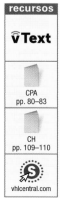

# Práctica

**1**

**Completar** Completa las oraciones con todos los elementos necesarios.

1. ____A____ Adela _le encanta_ (encantar) la música de Tito "El Bambino". ◄
2. A _mí_ me _interesa_ (interesar) la música de otros países.
3. A mis amigos _encantan_ (encantar) las canciones (*songs*) de Calle 13.
4. A Juan y ____a____ Rafael no les _molestan_ (molestar) la música alta (*loud*).
5. ____A____ nosotros _nos fascinan_ (fascinar) los grupos de pop latino.
6. ____A____ señor Ruiz _le interesa_ (interesar) más la música clásica.
7. A _mí_ me _aburre_ (aburrir) la música clásica.
8. ¿A ____ti____ te _falta_ (faltar) dinero para el concierto de Carlos Santana?
9. No. Ya compré el boleto y _le queda_ (quedar) cinco dólares.
10. ¿Cuánto dinero te _tú_ (quedar) a _queda_ ?

**2**

**Describir** Mira los dibujos y describe lo que está pasando. Usa los verbos de la lista.

| aburrir | faltar | molestar |
|---------|--------|----------|
| encantar | interesar | quedar |

1. a Ramón                  2. a nosotros

3. a ti                        4. a Sara

**3**

**Gustos** Forma oraciones con los elementos de las columnas.

> **modelo**
>
> A ti te interesan las ruinas de Machu Picchu.

| A | B | C |
|---|---|---|
| yo | aburrir | despertarse temprano |
| tú | encantar | mirarse en el espejo |
| mi mejor amigo/a | faltar | la música rock |
| mis amigos y yo | fascinar | las pantuflas rosadas |
| Bart y Homero Simpson | interesar | la pasta de dientes con menta (*mint*) |
| Shakira | molestar | las ruinas de Machu Picchu |
| Antonio Banderas | | los zapatos caros |

Practice more at **vhlcentral.com**.

# Comunicación

**4**

**Preguntas** En parejas, túrnense para hacer y contestar estas preguntas.

1. ¿Te gusta levantarte temprano o tarde? ¿Por qué?
2. ¿Te gusta acostarte temprano o tarde? ¿Y a tus hermanos/as?
3. ¿Te gusta dormir la siesta?
4. A tu familia, ¿le encanta acampar o prefiere quedarse en un hotel cuando va de vacaciones?
5. ¿Qué te gusta hacer en el verano?
6. ¿Qué te fascina de esta escuela? ¿Qué te molesta?
7. ¿Te interesan más las ciencias o las humanidades? ¿Por qué?
8. ¿Qué cosas te aburren?

**5**

**Completar** Trabajen en parejas. Túrnense para completar estas frases de una manera lógica.

1. A mi perro (*dog*) le fascina(n)…
2. A mi mejor (*best*) amigo/a no le interesa(n)…
3. A mis padres les importa(n)…
4. A nosotros nos molesta(n)…
5. A mis hermanos les aburre(n)…
6. A mi compañero/a de clase le aburre(n)…
7. A los turistas les interesa(n)…
8. A los jugadores profesionales les encanta(n)…
9. A nuestro/a profesor(a) le molesta(n)…
10. A mí me importa(n)…

**recursos**

**v̂Text**

CPA
pp. 84–85

**6**

**La residencia** Tú y tu compañero/a de clase son los directores de una residencia estudiantil en Perú. Su profesor(a) les va a dar a cada uno de ustedes las descripciones de cinco estudiantes. Con la información tienen que escoger quiénes van a ser compañeros de cuarto. Después, completen la lista.

# Síntesis

**7**

**Situación** Trabajen en parejas para representar los papeles de un(a) cliente/a y un(a) dependiente/a en una tienda de ropa. Usen las instrucciones como guía.

| Dependiente/a | Cliente/a |
|---|---|
| Saluda al/a la cliente/a y pregúntale en qué le puedes servir. | Saluda al/a la dependiente/a y dile (*tell him/her*) qué quieres comprar y qué colores prefieres. |
| Pregúntale si le interesan los estilos modernos y empieza a mostrarle la ropa. | Explícale que los estilos modernos te interesan. Escoge las cosas que te interesan. |
| Habla de los gustos del/de la cliente/a. | Habla de la ropa (me queda(n) bien/mal, me encanta(n)…). |
| Da opiniones favorables al/a la cliente/a (las botas te quedan fantásticas…). | Decide cuáles son las cosas que te gustan y qué vas a comprar. |

# Recapitulación

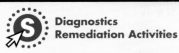

**Diagnostics**
**Remediation Activities**

Completa estas actividades para repasar los conceptos de gramática que aprendiste en esta lección.

**1 Completar** Completa la tabla con la forma correcta de los verbos. **6 pts.**

| yo | tú | nosotros | ellas |
|---|---|---|---|
| me levanto | | | |
| | te afeitas | | |
| | | nos vestimos | |
| | | | se secan |

**2 Hoy y ayer** Cambia los verbos del presente al pretérito. **5 pts.**

1. Vamos de compras hoy. _____ de compras hoy.
2. Por último, voy al supermercado. Por último, _____ al supermercado.
3. Lalo es el primero en levantarse. Lalo _____ el primero en levantarse.
4. ¿Vas a tu habitación? ¿_____ a tu habitación?
5. Ustedes son profesores. Ustedes _____ profesores.

**3 Reflexivos** Completa cada conversación con la forma correcta del presente del verbo reflexivo. **11 pts.**

**TOMÁS** Yo siempre (1) _____ (bañarse) antes de (2) _____ (acostarse). Esto me relaja porque no (3) _____ (dormirse) fácilmente. Y así puedo (4) _____ (levantarse) más tarde. Y tú, ¿cuándo (5) _____ (ducharse)?

**LETI** Pues por la mañana, para poder (6) _____ (despertarse).

**DAVID** ¿Cómo (7) _____ (sentirse) Pepa hoy?

**MARÍA** Todavía está enojada.

**DAVID** ¿De verdad? Ella nunca (8) _____ (enojarse) con nadie.

**BETO** ¿(Nosotros) (9) _____ (Irse) de esta tienda? Estoy cansado.

**SARA** Pero antes vamos a (10) _____ (probarse) estos sombreros. Si quieres, después (nosotros) (11) _____ (sentarse) un rato.

---

**7.1 Reflexive verbs** *pp. 236–237*

| lavarse | |
|---|---|
| me lavo | nos lavamos |
| te lavas | os laváis |
| se lava | se lavan |

**7.2 Indefinite and negative words** *pp. 240–241*

| Indefinite words | Negative words |
|---|---|
| algo | nada |
| alguien | nadie |
| alguno/a(s), algún | ninguno/a, ningún |
| o... o | ni... ni |
| siempre | nunca, jamás |
| también | tampoco |

**7.3 Preterite of ser and ir** *p. 244*

► The preterite of **ser** and **ir** are identical. Context will determine the meaning.

| ser and ir | |
|---|---|
| fui | fuimos |
| fuiste | fuisteis |
| fue | fueron |

**7.4 Verbs like gustar** *pp. 246–247*

| | |
|---|---|
| aburrir | importar |
| encantar | interesar |
| faltar | molestar |
| fascinar | quedar |

| | SINGULAR | |
|---|---|---|
| | encanta | la película |
| | interesó | el concierto |
| me, te, le, nos, os, les | | |
| | PLURAL | |
| | importan | las vacaciones |
| | fascinaron | los museos |

► Use the construction **a** + [*noun/pronoun*] to clarify the person in question.

    **A mí me encanta ver películas, ¿y a ti?**

**4**

**Conversaciones** Completa cada conversación de manera lógica con palabras de la lista. No tienes que usar todas las palabras. **8 pts.**

| algo | nada | ningún | siempre |
|------|------|--------|---------|
| alguien | nadie | nunca | también |
| algún | ni... ni | o... o | tampoco |

1. —¿Tienes _____ plan para esta noche?

   —No, prefiero quedarme en casa. Hoy no quiero ver a _____.

   —Yo _____ me quedo. Estoy muy cansado.

2. —¿Puedo entrar? ¿Hay _____ en el cuarto de baño?

   —Sí. ¡Un momento! Ahora mismo salgo.

3. —¿Puedes prestarme _____ para peinarme? No encuentro _____ mi cepillo (*brush*) _____ mi peine (*comb*).

   —Lo siento, yo _____ encuentro los míos (*mine*).

4. —¿Me prestas tu maquillaje?

   —Lo siento, no tengo. _____ me maquillo.

**5**

**Oraciones** Forma oraciones completas con los elementos dados (*given*). Usa el presente de los verbos. **8 pts.**

1. David y Juan / molestar / levantarse temprano
2. Lucía / encantar / las películas de terror
3. todos (nosotros) / importar / la educación
4. tú / aburrir / ver / la televisión

**6**

**Rutinas** Escribe seis oraciones que describan las rutinas de dos personas que conoces. **12 pts.**

**modelo**

Mi tía se despierta temprano, pero mi primo...

**7**

**Adivinanza** Completa la adivinanza con las palabras que faltan y adivina la respuesta. **¡2 puntos EXTRA!**

**❝ Cuanto más° _____ (*it dries you*), más se moja° ❞.**
**¿Qué es? _____**

Cuanto más *The more* se moja *it gets wet*

Practice more at **vhlcentral.com.**

# Lectura

 Audio: Synched Reading
Additional Reading

## Antes de leer

### Estrategia

**Predicting content from the title**

Prediction is an invaluable strategy in reading for comprehension. For example, we can usually predict the content of a newspaper article from its headline. We often decide whether to read the article based on its headline. Predicting content from the title will help you increase your reading comprehension in Spanish.

### Examinar el texto

Lee el título de la lectura y haz tres predicciones sobre el contenido. Escribe tus predicciones en una hoja de papel.

### Compartir

Comparte tus ideas con un(a) compañero/a de clase.

### Cognados

Haz una lista de seis cognados que encuentres en la lectura.

1. _____
2. _____
3. _____
4. _____
5. _____
6. _____

¿Qué te dicen los cognados sobre el tema de la lectura?

**recursos**

v̂Text

CH
pp. 111–112

vhlcentral.com

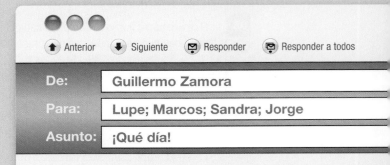

Anterior    Siguiente    Responder    Responder a todos

**De:** Guillermo Zamora

**Para:** Lupe; Marcos; Sandra; Jorge

**Asunto:** ¡Qué día!

**Hola, chicos:**

La semana pasada me di cuenta° de que necesito organizar mejor° mi rutina… pero especialmente debo prepararme mejor para los exámenes. Me falta disciplina, me molesta no tener control de mi tiempo y nunca deseo repetir los eventos de la semana pasada. ☹

El miércoles pasé todo el día y toda la noche estudiando para el examen de biología del jueves por la mañana. Me aburre la biología y no empecé a estudiar hasta el día antes del examen. El jueves a las 8, después de no dormir en toda la noche, fui exhausto al examen. Fue difícil, pero afortunadamente° me acordé de todo el material. Esa noche me acosté temprano y dormí mucho. 😴

Me desperté a las 7, y fue extraño° ver a mi hermano, Andrés, preparándose para ir a dormir. Como° siempre se enferma°, tiene problemas para dormir y no hablamos mucho, no le comenté nada. Fui al baño a cepillarme los dientes para ir a

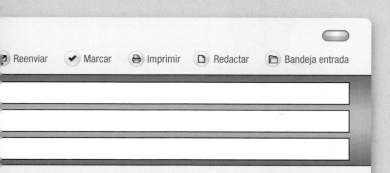

🔄 Reenviar    ✔ Marcar    🖨 Imprimir    🗋 Redactar    🗀 Bandeja entrada

clase. ¿Y Andrés? Él se acostó. "Debe estar enfermo°, ¡otra vez!", pensé. 😮

     Mi clase es a las 8, y fue necesario hacer las cosas rápido. Todo empezó a ir mal... 😠 eso pasa siempre cuando uno tiene prisa. Cuando busqué mis cosas para el baño, no las encontré. Entonces me duché sin jabón, me cepillé los dientes sin cepillo de dientes y me peiné con las manos. Tampoco encontré ropa limpia y usé la sucia. Rápido, tomé mis libros. ¿Y Andrés? Roncando°... ¡a las 7:50!

     Cuando salí corriendo para la clase, la prisa no me permitió ver el campus desierto. Cuando llegué a la clase, no vi a nadie. No vi al profesor ni a los estudiantes. Por último miré mi reloj, y vi la hora. Las 8 en punto... ¡de la noche!

¡Dormí 24 horas! 😮

     Guillermo

**me di cuenta** *I realized*   **mejor** *better*   **afortunadamente** *fortunately*
**extraño** *strange*   **Como** *Since*   **se enferma** *he gets sick*   **enfermo** *sick*
**Roncando** *Snoring*

# Después de leer

## Seleccionar

Selecciona la respuesta correcta.

1. ¿Quién es el/la narrador(a)?
   a. Andrés
   b. una profesora
   c. Guillermo
2. ¿Qué le molesta al narrador?
   a. Le molestan los exámenes de biología.
   b. Le molesta no tener control de su tiempo.
   c. Le molesta mucho organizar su rutina.
3. ¿Por qué está exhausto?
   a. Porque fue a una fiesta la noche anterior.
   b. Porque no le gusta la biología.
   c. Porque pasó la noche anterior estudiando.
4. ¿Por qué no hay nadie en clase?
   a. Porque es de noche.
   b. Porque todos están de vacaciones.
   c. Porque el profesor canceló la clase.
5. ¿Cómo es la relación de Guillermo y Andrés?
   a. Son buenos amigos.
   b. No hablan mucho.
   c. Tienen una buena relación.

## Ordenar

Ordena los sucesos de la narración. Utiliza los números del 1 al 9.

a. Toma el examen de biología. ____
b. No encuentra sus cosas para el baño. ____
c. Andrés se duerme. ____
d. Pasa todo el día y toda la noche estudiando para un examen. ____
e. Se ducha sin jabón. ____
f. Se acuesta temprano. ____
g. Vuelve a su cuarto después de las 8 de la noche. ____
h. Se despierta a las 7 y su hermano se prepara para dormir. ____
i. Va a clase y no hay nadie. ____

## Contestar

Contesta estas preguntas.

1. ¿Cómo es tu rutina diaria? ¿Muy organizada?
2. ¿Estudias mucho? ¿Cuándo empiezas a estudiar para los exámenes?
3. Para comunicarte con tus amigos/as, ¿prefieres el teléfono o el correo electrónico? ¿Por qué?

 Practice more at **vhlcentral.com**.

# Escritura

## Estrategia
### Sequencing events

Paying strict attention to sequencing in a narrative will ensure that your writing flows logically from one part to the next.

Every composition should have an introduction, a body, and a conclusion. The introduction presents the subject, the setting, the situation, and the people involved. The main part, or the body, describes the events and people's reactions to these events. The conclusion brings the narrative to a close.

Adverbs and adverbial phrases are sometimes used as transitions between the introduction, the body, and the conclusion. Here is a list of commonly used adverbs in Spanish:

### Adverbios

| | |
|---|---|
| además; también | in addition; also |
| al principio; en un principio | at first |
| antes (de) | before |
| después | then |
| después (de) | after |
| entonces; luego | then |
| más tarde | later |
| primero | first |
| pronto | soon |
| por fin; finalmente | finally |
| al final | finally |

## Tema

### Escribe tu rutina

Imagina tu rutina diaria en uno de estos lugares:

▶ una isla desierta
▶ el Polo Norte
▶ un crucero° transatlántico
▶ un desierto

Escribe una composición en la que describes tu rutina diaria en uno de estos lugares o en algún otro lugar interesante que imagines°. Mientras planeas tu composición, considera cómo cambian algunos de los elementos más básicos de tu rutina diaria en el lugar que escogiste°. Por ejemplo, ¿dónde te acuestas en el Polo Norte? ¿Cómo te duchas en el desierto?

Usa el presente de los verbos reflexivos que conoces e incluye algunos de los adverbios de esta página para organizar la secuencia de tus actividades. Piensa también en la información que debes incluir en cada sección de la narración. Por ejemplo, en la introducción puedes hacer una descripción del lugar y de las personas que están allí, y en la conclusión puedes dar tus opiniones acerca del° lugar y de tu vida diaria allí.

**recursos**

vText    CPA pp. 86–87    CH pp. 113–114    vhlcentral.com

crucero *cruise ship*   que imagines *that you dream up*   escogiste *you chose* acerca del *about the*

# Escuchar

## Estrategia

**Using background information**

Once you discern the topic of a conversation, take a minute to think about what you already know about the subject. Using this background information will help you guess the meaning of unknown words or linguistic structures.

 To help you practice this strategy, you will now listen to a short paragraph. Jot down the subject of the paragraph, and then use your knowledge of the subject to listen for and write down the paragraph's main points.

## Preparación

Según la foto, ¿dónde están Carolina y Julián? Piensa en lo que sabes de este tipo de situación. ¿De qué van a hablar?

## Ahora escucha

Ahora escucha la entrevista entre Carolina y Julián, teniendo en cuenta (*taking into account*) lo que sabes sobre este tipo de situación. Elige la información que completa correctamente cada oración.

1. Julián es _____.
   a. político
   b. deportista profesional
   c. artista de cine
2. El público de Julián quiere saber de _____.
   a. sus películas
   b. su vida
   c. su novia
3. Julián habla de _____.
   a. sus viajes y sus rutinas
   b. sus parientes y amigos
   c. sus comidas favoritas
4. Julián _____.
   a. se levanta y se acuesta a diferentes horas todos los días
   b. tiene una rutina diaria
   c. no quiere hablar de su vida

## Comprensión

### ¿Cierto o falso?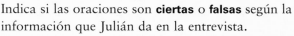

Indica si las oraciones son **ciertas** o **falsas** según la información que Julián da en la entrevista.

1. Es difícil despertarme; generalmente duermo hasta las diez.
2. Pienso que mi vida no es más interesante que las vidas de ustedes.
3. Me gusta tener tiempo para pensar y meditar.
4. Nunca hago mucho ejercicio; no soy una persona activa.
5. Me fascinan las actividades tranquilas, como escribir y escuchar música clásica.
6. Los viajes me parecen aburridos.

### Preguntas

1. ¿Qué tiene Julián en común con otras personas de su misma profesión?
2. ¿Te parece que Julián siempre fue rico? ¿Por qué?
3. ¿Qué piensas de Julián como persona?

 Practice more at **vhlcentral.com**.

recursos
vText
vhlcentral.com

# En pantalla  Video: TV Clip

Sunchales es una ciudad en la provincia de Santa Fe, Argentina, donde mucha gente trabaja en la agricultura y la ganadería°. Desde 1929, los habitantes de Sunchales se juntan para establecer cooperativas° en las que los trabajadores combinan sus esfuerzos° y recursos. Hoy, estas cooperativas constituyen el Grupo Sancor Seguros y todavía tratan de° incluir igualmente a todos los trabajadores de la región en los procesos, las decisiones y las ganancias° de sus labores°. Por eso, en 2005, Sunchales fue nombrada° "La capital nacional del cooperativismo". Este anuncio muestra este espíritu: no sólo se filmó en Sunchales, sino que los actores son nativos de la región y miembros del Grupo Sancor Seguros.

| Vocabulario útil | |
|---|---|
| **gran consigna** | *tall order* |
| **lo nuestro** | *what is ours* |
| **ver grande a la Argentina** | *to see a proud Argentina* |

### Opciones

Escoge la opción correcta para completar cada oración.

1. El anuncio tiene lugar _____.
   a. por la mañana  b. por la tarde  c. por la noche

2. El niño _____.
   a. se acuesta  b. se despierta  c. se duerme

3. Cada día, los profesionales _____.
   a. se quedan en casa  b. salen de casa  c. se aburren en casa

4. Según el anuncio, el país se mejora con _____.
   a. los bancos  b. la rutina diaria  c. el trabajo y la dedicación

### Banderas

En parejas, comenten cómo se utiliza la imagen de la bandera en el anuncio. ¿Qué simbolizan las banderas tradicionalmente? ¿Conoces un anuncio de tu país que muestra la bandera nacional? ¿Cuál es el objetivo o el efecto de mostrar la bandera al público?

ganadería *livestock farming* cooperativas *cooperatives* esfuerzos *efforts*
tratan de *try to* ganancias *profits* labores *work* fue nombrada *was named*

## Anuncio de Sancor Seguros

1

2

**Cada mañana...**

3

**...un gran grupo de argentinos...**

 Practice more at **vhlcentral.com.**

Video:
*Flash cultura*

En este episodio de *Flash cultura* vas a conocer unos entremeses° españoles llamados **tapas**. Hay varias teorías sobre el origen de su nombre. Una dice que viene de la costumbre antigua° de **tapar**° los vasos de vino para evitar° que insectos o polvo entren en° ellos. Otra teoría cuenta que el rey Alfonso X debía° beber un poco de vino por indicación médica y decidió acompañarlo° con algunos bocados° para tapar los efectos del alcohol. Cuando estuvo° mejor, ordenó que siempre en Castilla se sirviera° algo de comer con las bebidas° alcohólicas.

| Vocabulario útil | |
|---|---|
| **económicas** | *inexpensive* |
| **montaditos** | *bread slices with assorted toppings* |
| **pagar propinas** | *to tip* |
| **tapar el hambre** | *to take the edge off (lit. putting the lid on one's hunger)* |

**Preparación**

En el área donde vives, ¿qué hacen las personas normalmente después del trabajo (*work*)? ¿Van a sus casas? ¿Salen con amigos? ¿Comen?

**Ordenar**

Ordena estos sucesos de manera lógica.

_____ a. El empleado cuenta los palillos (*counts the toothpicks*) de los montaditos que Mari Carmen comió.

_____ b. Mari Carmen va al barrio de la Ribera.

_____ c. Un hombre en un bar explica cuándo sale a tomar tapas.

_____ d. Un hombre explica la tradición de los montaditos o pinchos.

_____ e. Carmen le pregunta a la chica si los montaditos son buenos para la salud.

entremeses *hors d'oeuvres* antigua *ancient* tapar *cover* evitar *avoid*
entren en *get in* debía *should* acompañarlo *accompany it* bocados *snacks*
estuvo *he was* se sirviera *they should serve* bebidas *drinks* sueles *do you tend*

## Tapas para todos los días

**Estamos en la Plaza Cataluña, el puro centro de Barcelona.**

—¿Cuándo sueles° venir a tomar tapas?
—Generalmente después del trabajo.

**Estos son los montaditos, o también llamados pinchos. ¿Te gustan?**

 Practice more at **vhlcentral.com**.

**recursos**

vText

CPA
pp. 88–89

vhlcentral.com

# Perú

**Interactive Map**
**Video:** *Panorama cultural*

## El país en cifras

▸ **Área:** 1.285.220 km$^2$ (496.224 millas$^2$),
*un poco menos que el área de Alaska*
▸ **Población:** 29.077.000
▸ **Capital:** Lima—8.473.000
▸ **Ciudades principales:** Arequipa—837.000,
Trujillo, Chiclayo, Callao, Iquitos

SOURCE: Population Division, UN Secretariat

*Iquitos es un puerto muy importante en el río Amazonas. Desde Iquitos se envían° muchos productos a otros lugares, incluyendo goma°, nueces°, madera°, arroz°, café y tabaco. Iquitos es también un destino popular para los ecoturistas que visitan la selva°.*

▸ **Moneda:** nuevo sol
▸ **Idiomas:** español (oficial); quechua, aimara y otras lenguas indígenas (oficiales en los territorios donde se usan)

Bandera de Perú

## Peruanos célebres

▸ **Clorinda Matto de Turner,** escritora (1854–1909)
▸ **César Vallejo,** poeta (1892–1938)
▸ **Javier Pérez de Cuéllar,** diplomático (1920– )
▸ **Mario Vargas Llosa,** escritor (1936– )

Mario Vargas Llosa, Premio Nobel de Literatura 2010

se envían *are shipped* goma *rubber* nueces *nuts* madera *timber* arroz *rice* selva *jungle* Hace más de *More than... ago* grabó *engraved* tamaño *size*

Bailando marinera norteña en Trujillo

Calle en la ciudad de Iquitos

ECUADOR COLOMBIA
Río Putumayo
Río Napo
Río Tigre
Río Pastaza
Río Amazonas
Iquitos
Río Marañón
Cordillera Oriental de los Andes
Río Huallaga
Chiclayo
Río Ucayali
Trujillo
Cordillera Central de los Andes
Río Urubamba
Pasaje Santa Rosa de Lima
Callao ☆ Lima
Océano Pacífico
Cordillera Occidental de los Andes
Machu Picchu
Cuzco
Lago Titicaca
Mercado indígena en Cuzco
Arequipa
ESTADOS UNIDOS
OCÉANO ATLÁNTICO
OCÉANO PACÍFICO
PERÚ
AMÉRICA DEL SUR
CHI

recursos
v̂Text
CPA pp. 90–93
vhlcentral.com

## ¡Increíble pero cierto!

Hace más de° dos mil años la civilización nazca de Perú grabó° más de dos mil kilómetros de líneas en el desierto. Los dibujos sólo son descifrables desde el aire. Uno de ellos es un cóndor del tamaño° de un estadio. Las Líneas de Nazca son uno de los grandes misterios de la humanidad.

## Lugares • **Lima**

Lima es una ciudad moderna y antigua° a la vez°. La Iglesia de San Francisco es notable por su arquitectura barroca colonial. También son fascinantes las exhibiciones sobre los incas en el Museo Oro del Perú y en el Museo Nacional de Antropología y Arqueología. Barranco, el barrio° bohemio de la ciudad, es famoso por su ambiente cultural y sus bares y restaurantes.

**BRASIL**

## Historia • **Machu Picchu**

A 80 kilómetros al noroeste de Cuzco está Machu Picchu, una ciudad antigua del Imperio inca. Está a una altitud de 2.350 metros (7.710 pies), entre dos cimas° de los Andes. Cuando los españoles llegaron a Perú y recorrieron la región, nunca encontraron Machu Picchu. En 1911, el arqueólogo estadounidense Hiram Bingham la descubrió. Todavía no se sabe ni cómo se construyó° una ciudad a esa altura, ni por qué los incas la abandonaron. Sin embargo°, esta ciudad situada en desniveles° naturales es el ejemplo más conocido de la arquitectura inca.

## Artes • **La música andina**

Machu Picchu aún no existía° cuando se originó la música cautivadora° de las culturas indígenas de los Andes. Los ritmos actuales° de la música andina tienen influencias españolas y africanas. Varios tipos de flauta°, entre ellos la quena y la zampoña, caracterizan esta música. En las décadas de los 60 y los 70 se popularizó un movimiento para preservar la música andina, y hasta° Simon y Garfunkel incorporaron a su repertorio la canción *El cóndor pasa*.

## Economía • **Llamas y alpacas**

Perú se conoce por sus llamas, alpacas, guanacos y vicuñas, todos ellos animales mamíferos° parientes del camello. Estos animales todavía tienen una enorme importancia en la economía del país. Dan lana para exportar a otros países y para hacer ropa, mantas°, bolsas y otros artículos artesanales. La llama se usa también para la carga y el transporte.

**BOLIVIA**

 **¿Qué aprendiste?** Responde a cada pregunta con una oración completa.
1. ¿Qué productos envía Iquitos a otros lugares?
2. ¿Cuáles son las lenguas oficiales de Perú?
3. ¿Por qué es notable la Iglesia de San Francisco en Lima?
4. ¿Qué información sobre Machu Picchu no se sabe todavía?
5. ¿Qué son la quena y la zampoña?
6. ¿Qué hacen los peruanos con la lana de sus llamas y alpacas?

 **Conexión Internet** Investiga estos temas en **vhlcentral.com**.

1. Investiga la cultura incaica. ¿Cuáles son algunos de los aspectos interesantes de su cultura?
2. Busca información sobre dos artistas, escritores o músicos peruanos y presenta un breve informe a tu clase.

antigua *old*  a la vez *at the same time*  barrio *neighborhood*  cimas *summits*  se construyó *was built*  Sin embargo *However*  desniveles *uneven pieces of land*  aún no existía *didn't exist yet*  cautivadora *captivating*  actuales *present-day*  flauta *flute*  hasta *even*  mamíferos *mammalian*  mantas *blankets*

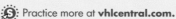
Practice more at **vhlcentral.com**.

## Los verbos reflexivos

| | |
|---|---|
| acordarse (de) (o:ue) | to remember |
| acostarse (o:ue) | to go to bed |
| afeitarse | to shave |
| bañarse | to bathe; to take a bath |
| cepillarse el pelo | to brush one's hair |
| cepillarse los dientes | to brush one's teeth |
| despedirse (de) (e:i) | to say goodbye (to) |
| despertarse (e:ie) | to wake up |
| dormirse (o:ue) | to go to sleep; to fall asleep |
| ducharse | to shower; to take a shower |
| enojarse (con) | to get angry (with) |
| irse | to go away; to leave |
| lavarse la cara | to wash one's face |
| lavarse las manos | to wash one's hands |
| levantarse | to get up |
| llamarse | to be called; to be named |
| maquillarse | to put on makeup |
| peinarse | to comb one's hair |
| ponerse | to put on |
| ponerse (+ *adj.*) | to become (+ *adj.*) |
| preocuparse (por) | to worry (about) |
| probarse (o:ue) | to try on |
| quedarse | to stay; to remain |
| quitarse | to take off |
| secarse | to dry oneself |
| sentarse (e:ie) | to sit down |
| sentirse (e:ie) | to feel |
| vestirse (e:i) | to get dressed |

## Palabras de secuencia

| | |
|---|---|
| antes (de) | before |
| después | afterwards; then |
| después (de) | after |
| durante | during |
| entonces | then |
| luego | then |
| más tarde | later (on) |
| por último | finally |

## Palabras afirmativas y negativas

| | |
|---|---|
| algo | something; anything |
| alguien | someone; somebody; anyone |
| alguno/a(s), algún | some; any |
| jamás | never; not ever |
| nada | nothing; not anything |
| nadie | no one; nobody; not anyone |
| ni... ni | neither... nor |
| ninguno/a, ningún | no; none; not any |
| nunca | never; not ever |
| o... o | either... or |
| siempre | always |
| también | also; too |
| tampoco | neither; not either |

## En el baño

| | |
|---|---|
| el baño, el cuarto de baño | bathroom |
| el champú | shampoo |
| la crema de afeitar | shaving cream |
| la ducha | shower |
| el espejo | mirror |
| el inodoro | toilet |
| el jabón | soap |
| el lavabo | sink |
| el maquillaje | makeup |
| la pasta de dientes | toothpaste |
| la toalla | towel |

 **Audio: Vocabulary Flashcards**

## Verbos similares a gustar

| | |
|---|---|
| aburrir | to bore |
| encantar | to like very much; to love (inanimate objects) |
| faltar | to lack; to need |
| fascinar | to fascinate; to like very much |
| importar | to be important to; to matter |
| interesar | to be interesting to; to interest |
| molestar | to bother; to annoy |
| quedar | to be left over; to fit (clothing) |

## Palabras adicionales

| | |
|---|---|
| el despertador | alarm clock |
| las pantuflas | slippers |
| la rutina diaria | daily routine |
| por la mañana | in the morning |
| por la noche | at night |
| por la tarde | in the afternoon; in the evening |

| | |
|---|---|
| Expresiones útiles | See page 231. |

# La comida

**Communicative Goals**

*I will be able to:*
- Order food in a restaurant
- Talk about and describe food

## A PRIMERA VISTA
- ¿Dónde están ellos?
- ¿Qué hacen?
- ¿Es parte de su rutina diaria?
- ¿Qué colores hay en la foto?

# La comida

  **Audio: Vocabulary Tutorials, Games**

## Más vocabulario

| | |
|---|---|
| el/la camarero/a | waiter/waitress |
| la comida | food; meal |
| el/la dueño/a | owner; landlord |
| los entremeses | hors d'oeuvres; appetizers |
| el menú | menu |
| el plato (principal) | (main) dish |
| la sección de (no) fumar | (non) smoking section |
| el agua (mineral) | (mineral) water |
| la bebida | drink |
| la cerveza | beer |
| la leche | milk |
| el refresco | soft drink; soda |
| el ajo | garlic |
| las arvejas | peas |
| los cereales | cereal; grains |
| los frijoles | beans |
| el melocotón | peach |
| el pollo (asado) | (roast) chicken |
| el queso | cheese |
| el sándwich | sandwich |
| el yogur | yogurt |
| el aceite | oil |
| la margarina | margarine |
| la mayonesa | mayonnaise |
| el vinagre | vinegar |
| delicioso/a | delicious |
| sabroso/a | tasty; delicious |
| saber | to taste; to know |
| saber a | to taste like |

## Variación léxica

| | |
|---|---|
| camarones ⟷ | gambas (Esp.) |
| camarero ⟷ | mesero (Amér. L.), mesonero (Ven.), mozo (Arg., Chile, Urug., Perú) |
| refresco ⟷ | gaseosa (Amér. C., Amér. S.) |

Las frutas — la pera, la banana, las uvas, la naranja, el limón, el maíz, la cebolla, la lechuga, la zanahoria, el champiñón, el tomate

Las verduras

**recursos**

vText — CPA pp. 95–97 — CH pp. 115–116 — vhlcentral.com

# Práctica

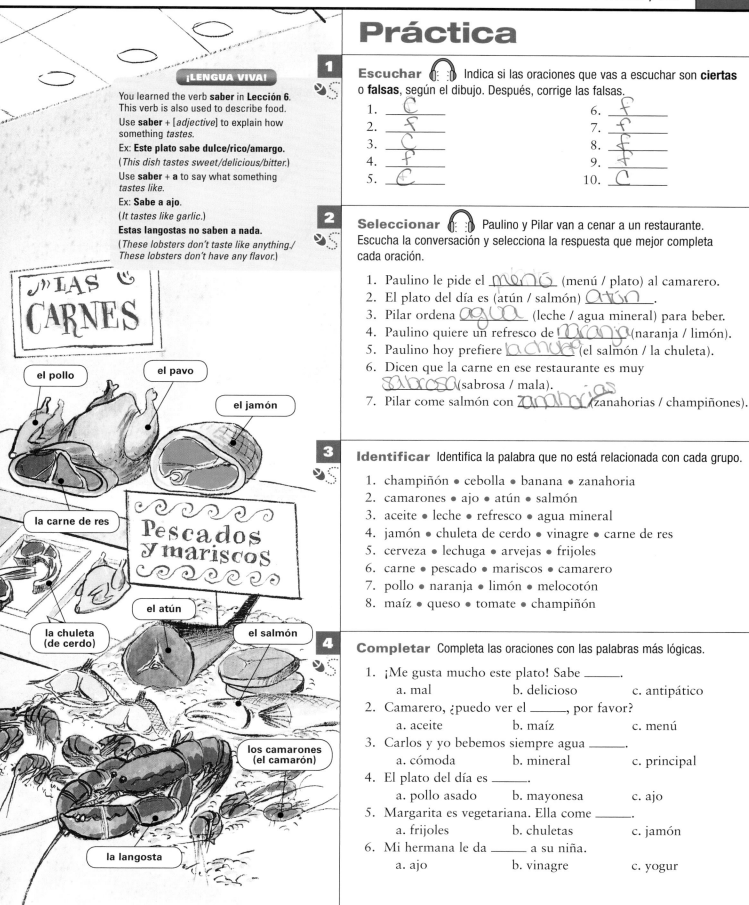

**1 Escuchar** 🎧 Indica si las oraciones que vas a escuchar son **ciertas** o **falsas**, según el dibujo. Después, corrige las falsas.

1. C
2. f
3. C
4. f
5. C

6. f
7. f f f
8. f f
9. f
10. C

**2 Seleccionar** 🎧 Paulino y Pilar van a cenar a un restaurante. Escucha la conversación y selecciona la respuesta que mejor completa cada oración.

1. Paulino le pide el _menú_ (menú / plato) al camarero.
2. El plato del día es (atún / salmón) _atún_.
3. Pilar ordena _agua_ (leche / agua mineral) para beber.
4. Paulino quiere un refresco de _naranja_ (naranja / limón).
5. Paulino hoy prefiere _la chuleta_ (el salmón / la chuleta).
6. Dicen que la carne en ese restaurante es muy _sabrosa_ (sabrosa / mala).
7. Pilar come salmón con _zanahorias_ (zanahorias / champiñones).

**3 Identificar** Identifica la palabra que no está relacionada con cada grupo.

1. champiñón • cebolla • banana • zanahoria
2. camarones • ajo • atún • salmón
3. aceite • leche • refresco • agua mineral
4. jamón • chuleta de cerdo • vinagre • carne de res
5. cerveza • lechuga • arvejas • frijoles
6. carne • pescado • mariscos • camarero
7. pollo • naranja • limón • melocotón
8. maíz • queso • tomate • champiñón

**4 Completar** Completa las oraciones con las palabras más lógicas.

1. ¡Me gusta mucho este plato! Sabe _____.
   a. mal          b. delicioso          c. antipático
2. Camarero, ¿puedo ver el _____, por favor?
   a. aceite          b. maíz          c. menú
3. Carlos y yo bebemos siempre agua _____.
   a. cómoda          b. mineral          c. principal
4. El plato del día es _____.
   a. pollo asado          b. mayonesa          c. ajo
5. Margarita es vegetariana. Ella come _____.
   a. frijoles          b. chuletas          c. jamón
6. Mi hermana le da _____ a su niña.
   a. ajo          b. vinagre          c. yogur

¡LENGUA VIVA!

You learned the verb **saber** in **Lección 6**. This verb is also used to describe food.

Use **saber** + [*adjective*] to explain how something *tastes*.

Ex: **Este plato sabe dulce/rico/amargo.**
(*This dish tastes sweet/delicious/bitter.*)

Use **saber** + **a** to say what something *tastes like*.

Ex: **Sabe a ajo.**
(*It tastes like garlic.*)

**Estas langostas no saben a nada.**
(*These lobsters don't taste like anything./ These lobsters don't have any flavor.*)

LAS CARNES

el pollo
el pavo
el jamón
la carne de res
la chuleta (de cerdo)
el atún

Pescados y mariscos

el salmón
los camarones (el camarón)
la langosta

Audio: Vocabulary

## el desayuno

el jugo (de fruta)

el café

el pan (tostado)

el azúcar

la mantequilla

la salchicha

el huevo

Audio: Vocabulary

**NOTA CULTURAL**

En Guatemala, un desayuno típico incluye huevos, frijoles, fruta, tortillas, jugo y café.

Otros desayunos populares son:

**madalenas** (*muffins*) España

**pan dulce** (*assorted breads/pastries*) México

**champurradas** (*sugar cookies*) Guatemala

**gallo pinto** (*fried rice and beans*) Costa Rica

**perico** (*scrambled eggs with peppers and onions*) Venezuela

## el almuerzo

el té helado

la manzana

la hamburguesa

el pan

las papas/patatas fritas

### Más vocabulario

| | |
|---|---|
| escoger | to choose |
| merendar (e:ie) | to snack |
| probar (o:ue) | to taste; to try |
| recomendar (e:ie) | to recommend |
| servir (e:i) | to serve |
| el té | tea |
| el vino blanco | white wine |

Audio: Vocabulary

## la cena

la sal

el vino tinto

la pimienta

la sopa

el arroz

la ensalada

los espárragos

el bistec

**5**

**Completar** Trabaja con un(a) compañero/a de clase para relacionar cada producto con el grupo alimenticio (*food group*) correcto.

modelo

___La carne___ es del grupo uno.

| | | | |
|---|---|---|---|
| el aceite | las bananas | los cereales | la leche |
| el arroz | el café | los espárragos | el pescado |
| el azúcar | la carne | los frijoles | el vino |

1. La leche y el queso son del grupo cuatro.
2. Los frijoles son del grupo ocho.
3. La carne y el pollo son del grupo tres.
4. el aceite es del grupo cinco.
5. el azúcar es del grupo dos.
6. Las manzanas y los bananas son del grupo siete.
7. el café es del grupo seis.
8. los cereales son del grupo diez.
9. los espárragos y los tomates son del grupo nueve.
10. El pan y el arroz son del grupo diez.

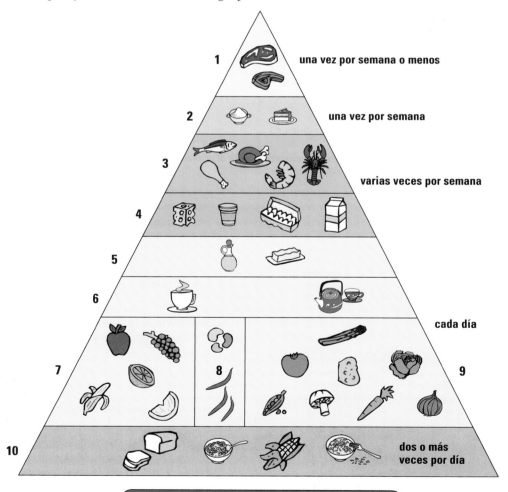

1 — una vez por semana o menos
2 — una vez por semana
3 — varias veces por semana
4
5
6
7   8   9 — cada día
10 — dos o más veces por día

**La Pirámide Alimenticia Latinoamericana**

**6**

**¿Cierto o falso?** Consulta la Pirámide Alimenticia Latinoamericana de la página 265 e indica si lo que dice cada oración es **cierto** o **falso**. Si la oración es falsa, escribe las comidas que sí están en el grupo indicado.

> **modelo**
>
> El queso está en el grupo diez.
> Falso. En ese grupo están el maíz, el pan, los cereales y el arroz.

1. La manzana, la banana, el limón y las arvejas están en el grupo siete.

2. En el grupo cuatro están los huevos, la leche y el aceite.

3. El azúcar está en el grupo dos.

4. En el grupo diez están el pan, el arroz y el maíz.

5. El pollo está en el grupo uno.

6. En el grupo nueve están la lechuga, el tomate, las arvejas, la naranja, la papa, los espárragos y la cebolla.

7. El café y el té están en el mismo grupo.

8. En el grupo cinco está el arroz.

9. El pescado, el yogur y el bistec están en el grupo tres.

**7** **Combinar** Combina palabras de cada columna, en cualquier (*any*) orden, para formar nueve oraciones lógicas sobre las comidas. Añade otras palabras si es necesario.

> **modelo**
>
> La camarera nos sirve la ensalada.

| **A** | **B** | **C** |
|---|---|---|
| el/la camarero/a | almorzar | la sección de no fumar |
| el/la dueño/a | escoger | el desayuno |
| mi familia | gustar | la ensalada |
| mi novio/a | merendar | las uvas |
| mis amigos y yo | pedir | el restaurante |
| mis padres | preferir | el jugo de naranja |
| mi hermano/a | probar | el refresco |
| el/la médico/a | recomendar | el plato |
| yo | servir | el arroz |

**NOTA CULTURAL**

El arroz es un alimento básico en el Caribe, Centroamérica y México, entre otros países. Aparece frecuentemente como acompañamiento del plato principal y muchas veces se sirve con frijoles. Un plato muy popular en varios países es **el arroz con pollo** *(chicken and rice casserole).*

**8** **Un menú** En parejas, usen la Pirámide Alimenticia Latinoamericana de la página 265 para crear un menú para una cena especial. Incluyan alimentos de los diez grupos para los entremeses, los platos principales y las bebidas. Luego presenten el menú a la clase.

> **modelo**
>
> La cena especial que vamos a preparar es deliciosa. Primero, hay dos entremeses: ensalada César y sopa de langosta. El plato principal es salmón con salsa de ajo y espárragos. También vamos a servir arroz…

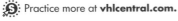 Practice more at **vhlcentral.com**.

# Comunicación

**9**

**Conversación** En parejas, túrnense para hacerse estas preguntas.

1. ¿Meriendas mucho durante el día? ¿Qué comes? ¿A qué hora?
2. ¿Qué te gusta cenar?
3. ¿A qué hora, dónde y con quién almuerzas?
4. ¿Cuáles son las comidas más (*most*) típicas de tu almuerzo?
5. ¿Desayunas? ¿Qué comes y bebes por la mañana?
6. ¿Qué comida te gusta más? ¿Qué comida no conoces y quieres probar?
7. ¿Comes cada día alimentos de los diferentes grupos de la pirámide alimenticia? ¿Cuáles son los alimentos y bebidas más frecuentes en tu dieta?
8. ¿Qué comida recomiendas a tus amigos? ¿Por qué?
9. ¿Eres vegetariano/a? ¿Crees que ser vegetariano/a es una buena idea? ¿Por qué?
10. ¿Te gusta cocinar (*to cook*)? ¿Qué comidas preparas para tus amigos? ¿Para tu familia?

**10**

**Describir** Con dos compañeros/as de clase, describe las dos fotos, contestando estas preguntas.

▶ ¿Quiénes están en las fotos?

▶ ¿Dónde están?

▶ ¿Qué hora es?

▶ ¿Qué comen y qué beben?

**11**

**Crucigrama** Tu profesor(a) les va a dar a ti y a tu compañero/a un crucigrama (*crossword puzzle*) incompleto. Tú tienes las palabras que necesita tu compañero/a y él/ella tiene las palabras que tú necesitas. Tienen que darse pistas (*clues*) para completarlo. No pueden decir la palabra; deben utilizar definiciones, ejemplos y frases.

> **modelo**
>
> **6 vertical:** Es un condimento que normalmente viene con la sal.
> **2 horizontal:** Es una fruta amarilla.

# Una cena... romántica

Maru y Miguel quieren tener una cena romántica,
pero les espera una sorpresa.

PERSONAJES

**MARU**

**MIGUEL**

**S** Video: *Fotonovela*
Record and Compare

**1**

**MARU** No sé qué pedir. ¿Qué
me recomiendas?

**MIGUEL** No estoy seguro. Las
chuletas de cerdo se ven
muy buenas.

**MARU** ¿Vas a pedirlas?

**MIGUEL** No sé.

**2**

**MIGUEL** ¡Qué bonitos! ¿Quién te
los dio?

**MARU** Me los compró un chico
muy guapo e inteligente.

**MIGUEL** ¿Es tan guapo como yo?

**MARU** Sí, como tú, guapísimo.

**3**

(*El camarero llega a la mesa.*)

**CAMARERO** ¿Les gustaría saber
nuestras especialidades del día?

**MARU** Sí, por favor.

**CAMARERO** Para el entremés,
tenemos ceviche de camarón.
De plato principal ofrecemos
bistec con verduras a la plancha.

**6**

(*en otra parte del restaurante*)

**JUAN CARLOS** Disculpe. ¿Qué me
puede contar del pollo? ¿Dónde
lo consiguió el chef?

**CAMARERO** ¡Oiga! ¿Qué
está haciendo?

**7**

**FELIPE** Los espárragos están
sabrosísimos esta noche.
Usted pidió el pollo, señor.
Estos champiñones saben
a mantequilla.

**8**

**GERENTE** ¿Qué pasa aquí, Esteban?

**CAMARERO** Lo siento señor.
Me quitaron la comida.

**GERENTE** (*a Felipe*) Señor,
¿quién es usted? ¿Qué
cree que está haciendo?

**CAMARERO**    **JUAN CARLOS**    **FELIPE**   **GERENTE**

**MARU** Voy a probar el jamón.

**CAMARERO** Perfecto. ¿Y para usted, caballero?

**MIGUEL** Pollo asado con champiñones y papas, por favor.

**CAMARERO** Excelente.

**MIGUEL** Por nosotros.

**MARU** Dos años.

**JUAN CARLOS** Felipe y yo les servimos la comida a nuestros amigos. Pero desafortunadamente, salió todo mal.

**FELIPE** Soy el peor camarero del mundo. ¡Lo siento! Nosotros vamos a pagar la comida.

**JUAN CARLOS** ¿Nosotros?

**FELIPE** Todo esto fue idea tuya, Juan Carlos.

**JUAN CARLOS** ¿Mi idea? ¡Felipe! (al gerente) Señor, él es más responsable que yo.

**GERENTE** Tú y tú, vamos.

## Expresiones útiles

### Ordering food
**¿Qué me recomiendas?**
*What do you recommend?*
**Las chuletas de cerdo se ven muy buenas.**
*The pork chops look good.*
**¿Les gustaría saber nuestras especialidades del día?**
*Would you like to hear our specials?*
**Para el entremés, tenemos ceviche de camarón.**
*For an appetizer, we have shrimp ceviche.*
**De plato principal ofrecemos bistec con verduras a la plancha.**
*For a main course, we have beef with grilled vegetables.*
**Voy a probar el jamón.**
*I am going to try the ham.*

### Describing people and things
**¡Qué bonitos! ¿Quién te los dio?**
*How pretty! Who gave them to you?*
**Me los compró un chico muy guapo e inteligente.**
*A really handsome, intelligent guy bought them for me.*
**¿Es tan guapo como yo?**
*Is he as handsome as I am?*
**Sí, como tú, guapísimo.**
*Yes, like you, gorgeous.*
**Soy el peor camarero del mundo.**
*I am the worst waiter in the world.*
**Él es más responsable que yo.**
*He is more responsible than I am.*

### Additional vocabulary
**el/la gerente** *manager*
**caballero** *gentleman, sir*

# ¿Qué pasó?

**1**

**Escoger** Escoge la respuesta que completa mejor cada oración.

1. Miguel lleva a Maru a un restaurante para _____.
   a. almorzar   b. desayunar   c. cenar
2. El camarero les ofrece _____ como plato principal.
   a. ceviche de camarón   b. bistec con verduras a la plancha
   c. pescado, arroz y ensalada
3. Miguel va a pedir _____.
   a. pollo asado con champiñones y papas
   b. langosta al horno   c. pescado con verduras a la mantequilla
4. Felipe les lleva la comida a sus amigos y prueba _____.
   a. el jamón y los vinos   b. el atún y la lechuga
   c. los espárragos y los champiñones

**NOTA CULTURAL**

El **ceviche** es un plato típico de varios países hispanos como México, Perú y Costa Rica. En México, se prepara con pescado o mariscos frescos, jugo de limón, tomate, cebolla, chile y cilantro. Se puede comer como plato principal, pero también como entremés o merienda. Casi siempre se sirve con tostadas (*fried tortillas*) o galletas saladas (*crackers*).

**2**

**Identificar** Indica quién puede decir estas oraciones.

1. ¡Qué desastre! Soy un camarero muy malo.
2. Les recomiendo el bistec con verduras a la plancha.
3. Tal vez escoja las chuletas de cerdo, creo que son muy sabrosas.
4. ¿Qué pasa aquí?
5. Dígame las especialidades del día, por favor.
6. No fue mi idea. Felipe es más responsable que yo.

**FELIPE**    **MARU**    **JUAN CARLOS**

**CAMARERO**    **MIGUEL**    **GERENTE**

**3**

**Preguntas** Contesta estas preguntas sobre la **Fotonovela**.

1. ¿Por qué fueron Maru y Miguel a un restaurante?
2. ¿Qué entremés es una de las especialidades del día?
3. ¿Qué pidió Maru?
4. ¿Quiénes van a pagar la cuenta?

**4**

**En el restaurante**

1. Prepara con un(a) compañero/a una conversación en la que le preguntas si conoce algún buen restaurante en tu comunidad. Tu compañero/a responde que él/ella sí conoce un restaurante que sirve una comida deliciosa. Lo/La invitas a cenar y tu compañero/a acepta. Determinan la hora para verse en el restaurante y se despiden.

2. Trabaja con un(a) compañero/a para representar los papeles de un(a) cliente/a y un(a) camarero/a en un restaurante. El/La camarero/a te pregunta qué te puede servir y tú preguntas cuál es la especialidad de la casa. El/La camarero/a te dice cuál es la especialidad y te recomienda algunos platos del menú. Tú pides entremeses, un plato principal y escoges una bebida. El/La camarero/a te sirve la comida y tú le das las gracias.

**CONSULTA**

To review indefinite words like **algún**, see **Estructura 7.2**, p. 240.

 Practice more at **vhlcentral.com**.

# Pronunciación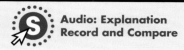

**Audio: Explanation
Record and Compare**

## ll, ñ, c, and z

| | | | |
|---|---|---|---|
| **pollo** | **llave** | **ella** | **cebolla** |

Most Spanish speakers pronounce the letter **ll** like the *y* in *yes*.

| | | | |
|---|---|---|---|
| **mañana** | **señor** | **baño** | **niña** |

The letter **ñ** is pronounced much like the *ny* in *canyon*.

| | | | |
|---|---|---|---|
| **café** | **colombiano** | **cuando** | **rico** |

Before **a**, **o**, or **u**, the Spanish **c** is pronounced like the *c* in *car*.

| | | | |
|---|---|---|---|
| **cereales** | **delicioso** | **conducir** | **conocer** |

Before **e** or **i**, the Spanish **c** is pronounced like the *s* in *sit*. (In parts of Spain, **c** before **e** or **i** is pronounced like the *th* in *think*.)

| | | | |
|---|---|---|---|
| **zeta** | **zanahoria** | **almuerzo** | **cerveza** |

The Spanish **z** is pronounced like the *s* in *sit*. (In parts of Spain, **z** is pronounced like the *th* in *think*.)

**Práctica** Lee las palabras en voz alta.

1. mantequilla
2. cuñada
3. aceite
4. manzana
5. español
6. cepillo
7. zapato
8. azúcar
9. quince
10. compañera
11. almorzar
12. calle

**Oraciones** Lee las oraciones en voz alta.

1. Mi compañero de cuarto se llama Toño Núñez. Su familia es de la ciudad de Guatemala y de Quetzaltenango.
2. Dice que la comida de su mamá es deliciosa, especialmente su pollo al champiñón y sus tortillas de maíz.
3. Creo que Toño tiene razón porque hoy cené en su casa y quiero volver mañana para cenar allí otra vez.

**Refranes** Lee los refranes en voz alta.

Panza llena, corazón contento.[2]

Las apariencias engañan.[1]

1 *Looks can be deceiving.*
2 *A full belly makes a happy heart.*

**recursos**

vText

CPA p. 102

CH p. 117

vhlcentral.com

EN DETALLE

Reading, Additional Reading

# Frutas y verduras
# de América

**Imagínate una pizza sin salsa° de tomate** o una hamburguesa sin papas fritas. Ahora piensa que quieres ver una película, pero las palomitas de maíz° y el chocolate no existen. ¡Qué mundo° tan insípido°! Muchas de las comidas más populares del mundo tienen ingredientes esenciales que son originarios del continente llamado Nuevo Mundo. Estas frutas y verduras no fueron introducidas en Europa sino hasta° el siglo° XVI.

El tomate, por ejemplo, era° usado como planta ornamental cuando llegó por primera vez a Europa porque pensaron que era venenoso°. El maíz, por su parte, era ya la base de la comida de muchos países latinoamericanos muchos siglos antes de la llegada de los españoles.

La papa fue un alimento° básico para los incas. Incluso consiguieron deshidratarla para almacenarla° por largos períodos de tiempo. El cacao (planta con la que se hace el chocolate) fue muy importante para los aztecas y los mayas. Ellos usaban sus semillas° como moneda° y como ingrediente de diversas salsas. También las molían° para preparar una bebida, mezclándolas° con agua ¡y con chile!

El aguacate°, la guayaba°, la papaya, la piña y el maracuyá (o fruta de la pasión) son otros ejemplos de frutas originarias de América que son hoy día conocidas en todo el mundo.

**Mole**

### ¿En qué alimentos encontramos estas frutas y verduras?

**Tomate:** pizza, ketchup, salsa de tomate, sopa de tomate

**Maíz:** palomitas de maíz, tamales, tortillas, arepas (Colombia y Venezuela), pan

**Papa:** papas fritas, frituras de papa°, puré de papas°, sopa de papas, tortilla de patatas (España)

**Cacao:** mole (México), chocolatinas°, cereales, helados°, tartas°

**Aguacate:** guacamole (México), coctel de camarones, sopa de aguacate, nachos, enchiladas hondureñas

salsa *sauce* palomitas de maíz *popcorn* mundo *world* insípido *flavorless* hasta *until* siglo *century* era *was* venenoso *poisonous* alimento *food* almacenarla *to store it* semillas *seeds* moneda *currency* las molían *they used to grind them* mezclándolas *mixing them* aguacate *avocado* guayaba *guava* frituras de papa *chips* puré de papas *mashed potatoes* chocolatinas *chocolate bars* helados *ice cream* tartas *cakes*

ACTIVIDADES

**1**

**¿Cierto o falso?** Indica si lo que dicen las oraciones es cierto o **falso**. Corrige la información falsa.

1. El tomate se introdujo a Europa como planta ornamental.
2. Los incas sólo consiguieron almacenar las papas por poco tiempo.
3. Los aztecas y los mayas usaron las papas como moneda.
4. El maíz era una comida poco popular en Latinoamérica.
5. El aguacate era el alimento básico de los incas.
6. En México se hace una salsa con chocolate.
7. El aguacate, la guayaba, la papaya, la piña y el maracuyá son originarios de América.
8. Las arepas se hacen con cacao.
9. El aguacate es un ingrediente del cóctel de camarones.
10. En España hacen una tortilla con papas.

## ASÍ SE DICE

### Viajes y turismo

| | |
|---|---|
| el banano (Col.), el cambur (Ven.), el guineo (Nic.), el plátano (Amér. L., Esp.) | la banana |
| el choclo (Amér. S.), el elote (Méx.), el jojoto (Ven.), la mazorca (Esp.) | *corncob* |
| las caraotas (Ven.), los porotos (Amér. S.), las habichuelas (P. R.) | los frijoles |
| el durazno (Méx.) | el melocotón |
| el jitomate (Méx.) | el tomate |

## EL MUNDO HISPANO

### Algunos platos típicos

- **Ceviche peruano:** Es un plato de pescado crudo° que se marina° en jugo de limón, con sal, pimienta, cebolla y ají°. Se sirve con lechuga, maíz, camote° y papa amarilla.

- **Gazpacho andaluz:** Es una sopa fría típica del sur de España. Se hace con verduras crudas y molidas°: tomate, ají, pepino° y ajo. También lleva pan, sal, aceite y vinagre.

- **Sancocho colombiano:** Es una sopa de pollo, pescado o carne con plátano, maíz, zanahoria, yuca, papas, cebolla, cilantro y ajo. Se sirve con arroz blanco.

crudo *raw* se marina *gets marinated* ají *pepper* camote *sweet potato* molidas *mashed* pepino *cucumber*

## PERFIL

# Ferran Adrià: arte en la cocina°

¿Qué haces si un amigo te invita a comer croquetas líquidas o paella de *Kellogg's*? ¿Piensas que es una broma°? ¡Cuidado! Puedes estar perdiendo la oportunidad de probar los platos de uno de los chefs más innovadores del mundo°: **Ferran Adrià.**

Este artista de la cocina basa su éxito° en la creatividad y en la química. Adrià modifica combinaciones de ingredientes y juega con contrastes de gustos y sensaciones: frío-caliente, crudo-cocido°, dulce°-salado°... A partir de nuevas

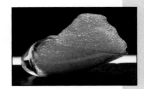

**Aire de zanahorias**

técnicas, altera la textura de los alimentos sin alterar su sabor°. Sus platos sorprendentes° y divertidos atraen a muchos nuevos chefs a su academia de cocina experimental. Quizás un día compraremos° en el supermercado té esférico°, carne líquida y espuma° de tomate.

cocina *kitchen* broma *joke* mundo *world* éxito *success* cocido *cooked* dulce *sweet* salado *savory* sabor *taste* sorprendentes *surprising* compraremos *we will buy* esférico *spheric* espuma *foam*

###  Conexión Internet

| | |
|---|---|
| ¿Qué platos comen los hispanos en los Estados Unidos? | Go to **vhlcentral.com** to find more cultural information related to this **Cultura** section. |

## ACTIVIDADES

**2**   **Comprensión** Empareja cada palabra con su definición.

1. fruta amarilla
2. sopa típica de Colombia
3. ingrediente del ceviche
4. chef español

   a. gazpacho
   b. Ferran Adrià
   c. sancocho
   d. guineo
   e. pescado

**3**   **¿Qué plato especial hay en tu región?** Escribe cuatro oraciones sobre un plato típico de tu región. Explica los ingredientes que contiene y cómo se sirve.

 Practice more at **vhlcentral.com.**

**recursos**

**v̂Text**

CH p. 118

vhlcentral.com

# 8.1 Preterite of stem-changing verbs

**ANTE TODO** As you learned in **Lección 6**, **–ar** and **–er** stem-changing verbs have no stem change in the preterite. **–Ir** stem-changing verbs, however, do have a stem change. Study the following chart and observe where the stem changes occur.

**CONSULTA**

There are a few high-frequency irregular verbs in the preterite. You will learn more about them in **Estructura 9.1**, p. 310.

## Preterite of –ir stem-changing verbs

| | | **servir** *(to serve)* | **dormir** *(to sleep)* |
|---|---|---|---|
| SINGULAR FORMS | yo | serví | dormí |
| | tú | serviste | dormiste |
| | Ud./él/ella | s**i**rvió | d**u**rmió |
| PLURAL FORMS | nosotros/as | servimos | dormimos |
| | vosotros/as | servisteis | dormisteis |
| | Uds./ellos/ellas | s**i**rvieron | d**u**rmieron |

▶ Stem-changing **–ir** verbs, in the preterite only, have a stem change in the third-person singular and plural forms. The stem change consists of either **e** to **i** or **o** to **u**.

(e → i) pedir: p**i**dió, p**i**dieron      (o → u) morir *(to die)*: m**u**rió, m**u**rieron

¿Quién pidió el jamón?

Yo lo pedí.

**¡INTÉNTALO!** Cambia cada infinitivo al pretérito.

1. Yo _____serví, dormí, pedí..._____. (servir, dormir, pedir, preferir, repetir, seguir)

2. Usted _____. (morir, conseguir, pedir, sentirse, despedirse, vestirse)

3. Tú _____. (conseguir, servir, morir, pedir, dormir, repetir)

4. Ellas _____. (repetir, dormir, seguir, preferir, morir, servir)

5. Nosotros _____. (seguir, preferir, servir, vestirse, despedirse, dormirse)

6. Ustedes _____. (sentirse, vestirse, conseguir, pedir, despedirse, dormirse)

7. Él _____. (dormir, morir, preferir, repetir, seguir, pedir)

**recursos**

v̂Text

CPA
pp. 103–105

CH
pp. 119–120

vhlcentral.com

# Práctica

**1**

**Completar** Completa estas oraciones para describir lo que pasó anoche en el restaurante El Famoso.

1. Paula y Humberto Suárez llegaron al restaurante El Famoso a las ocho y _____ (seguir) al camarero a una mesa en la sección de no fumar.
2. El señor Suárez _____ (pedir) una chuleta de cerdo.
3. La señora Suárez _____ (preferir) probar los camarones.
4. De tomar, los dos _____ (pedir) vino tinto.
5. El camarero _____ (repetir) el pedido (*the order*) para confirmarlo.
6. La comida tardó mucho (*took a long time*) en llegar y los señores Suárez _____ (dormirse) esperando la comida.
7. A las nueve y media el camarero les _____ (servir) la comida.
8. Después de comer la chuleta, el señor Suárez _____ (sentirse) muy mal.
9. Pobre señor Suárez... ¿por qué no _____ (pedir) los camarones?

**2**

**El camarero loco** En el restaurante La Hermosa trabaja un camarero muy loco que siempre comete muchos errores. Indica lo que los clientes pidieron y lo que el camarero les sirvió.

Armando / papas fritas

Armando pidió papas fritas, pero el camarero le sirvió maíz.

1. nosotros / jugo de naranja   2. Beatriz / queso   3. tú / arroz

4. Elena y Alejandro / atún   5. usted / refresco   6. yo / hamburguesa

# Comunicación

**3**

**El almuerzo** Trabajen en parejas. Túrnense para completar las oraciones de César de una manera lógica.

> *modelo*
>
> Mi abuelo se despertó temprano, pero yo...
> *Mi abuelo se despertó temprano, pero yo me desperté tarde.*

1. Yo llegué al restaurante a tiempo, pero mis amigos...
2. Beatriz pidió la ensalada de frutas, pero yo...
3. Yolanda les recomendó el bistec, pero Eva y Paco...
4. Nosotros preferimos las papas fritas, pero Yolanda...
5. El camarero sirvió la carne, pero yo...
6. Beatriz y yo pedimos café, pero Yolanda y Paco...
7. Eva se sintió enferma, pero Paco y yo...
8. Nosotros repetimos postre (*dessert*), pero Eva... ◀
9. Ellos salieron tarde, pero yo...
10. Yo me dormí temprano, pero mi hermano...

**¡LENGUA VIVA!**

In Spanish, the verb **repetir** is used to express *to have a second helping* (*of something*).

**Cuando mi mamá prepara sopa de champiñones, yo siempre repito.**
*When my mom makes mushroom soup, I always have a second helping.*

**4**

**Entrevista** Trabajen en parejas y túrnense para entrevistar a su compañero/a.

1. ¿Te acostaste tarde o temprano anoche? ¿A qué hora te dormiste? ¿Dormiste bien?
2. ¿A qué hora te despertaste esta mañana? Y, ¿a qué hora te levantaste?
3. ¿A qué hora vas a acostarte esta noche?
4. ¿Qué almorzaste ayer? ¿Quién te sirvió el almuerzo?
5. ¿Qué cenaste ayer?
6. ¿Cenaste en un restaurante recientemente? ¿Con quién(es)?
7. ¿Qué pediste en el restaurante? ¿Qué pidieron los demás?
8. ¿Se durmió alguien en alguna de tus clases la semana pasada? ¿En qué clase?

# Síntesis

**5**

**Describir** En grupos, estudien la foto y las preguntas. Luego, describan la primera (¿y la última?) ◀ cita de César y Libertad.

▶ ¿Adónde salieron a cenar?

▶ ¿Qué pidieron?

▶ ¿Les gustó la comida?

▶ ¿Quién prefirió una comida vegetariana? ¿Por qué?

▶ ¿Cómo se vistieron?

▶ ¿De qué hablaron? ¿Les gustó la conversación?

▶ ¿Van a volver a verse? ¿Por qué?

**CONSULTA**

To review words commonly associated with the preterite, such as **anoche**, see **Estructura 6.3**, p. 207.

# 8.2 Double object pronouns  Explanation Tutorial

**ANTE TODO** In **Lecciones 5** and **6**, you learned that direct and indirect object pronouns replace nouns and that they often refer to nouns that have already been referenced. You will now learn how to use direct and indirect object pronouns together. Observe the following diagram.

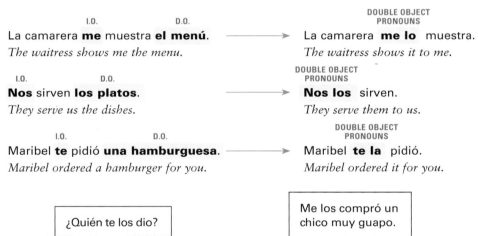

| Indirect Object Pronouns | | + | Direct Object Pronouns | |
|---|---|---|---|---|
| me | nos | | lo | los |
| te | os | | la | las |
| le (se) | les (se) | | | |

▶ When direct and indirect object pronouns are used together, the indirect object pronoun always precedes the direct object pronoun.

| I.O.   D.O. | | DOUBLE OBJECT PRONOUNS |
|---|---|---|
| La camarera **me** muestra **el menú**. | ⟶ | La camarera **me lo** muestra. |
| *The waitress shows me the menu.* | | *The waitress shows it to me.* |

| I.O.   D.O. | | DOUBLE OBJECT PRONOUNS |
|---|---|---|
| **Nos** sirven **los platos**. | ⟶ | **Nos los** sirven. |
| *They serve us the dishes.* | | *They serve them to us.* |

| I.O.   D.O. | | DOUBLE OBJECT PRONOUNS |
|---|---|---|
| Maribel **te** pidió **una hamburguesa**. | ⟶ | Maribel **te la** pidió. |
| *Maribel ordered a hamburger for you.* | | *Maribel ordered it for you.* |

¿Quién te los dio?

Me los compró un chico muy guapo.

▶ In Spanish, two pronouns that begin with the letter **l** cannot be used together. Therefore, the indirect object pronouns **le** and **les** always change to **se** when they are used with **lo, los, la,** and **las**.

| I.O.   D.O. | | DOUBLE OBJECT PRONOUNS |
|---|---|---|
| **Le** escribí **la carta**. | ⟶ | **Se la** escribí. |
| *I wrote him the letter.* | | *I wrote it to him.* |

| I.O.   D.O. | | DOUBLE OBJECT PRONOUNS |
|---|---|---|
| **Les** sirvió **los sándwiches**. | ⟶ | **Se los** sirvió. |
| *He served them the sandwiches.* | | *He served them to them.* |

▶ Because **se** has multiple meanings, Spanish speakers often clarify to whom the pronoun refers by adding **a usted, a él, a ella, a ustedes, a ellos,** or **a ellas.**

¿El sombrero? Carlos **se** lo
vendió **a ella.**
*The hat? Carlos sold it to her.*

¿Las verduras? Ellos **se** las
compran **a usted.**
*The vegetables? They are buying
them for you.*

▶ Double object pronouns are placed before a conjugated verb. With infinitives and present participles, they may be placed before the conjugated verb or attached to the end of the infinitive or present participle.

DOUBLE OBJECT
PRONOUNS
**Te  lo**  voy a mostrar.

DOUBLE OBJECT
PRONOUNS
Voy a mostrár**telo**.

DOUBLE OBJECT
PRONOUNS
**Nos las** están comprando.

DOUBLE OBJECT
PRONOUNS
Están comprándo**noslas**.

Mi abuelo **me lo** está leyendo.
Mi abuelo está leyéndo**melo**.

El camarero **se los** va a servir.
El camarero va a servír**selos**.

▶ As you can see above, when double object pronouns are attached to an infinitive or a present participle, an accent mark is added to maintain the original stress.

---

**¡INTÉNTALO!**     Escribe el pronombre de objeto directo o indirecto que falta en cada oración.

### Objeto directo

1. ¿La ensalada? El camarero nos _____la_____ sirvió.
2. ¿El salmón? La dueña me _____ recomienda.
3. ¿La comida? Voy a preparárte_____.
4. ¿Las bebidas? Estamos pidiéndose_____.
5. ¿Los refrescos? Te _____ puedo traer ahora.
6. ¿Los platos de arroz? Van a servírnos_____ después.

### Objeto indirecto

1. —¿Puedes traerme tu plato? —No, no __te__ lo puedo traer.
2. —¿Quieres mostrarle la carta? —Sí, voy a mostrár_____la ahora.
3. —¿Les serviste la carne? —No, no _____ la serví.
4. —¿Vas a leerle el menú? —No, no _____ lo voy a leer.
5. —¿Me recomiendas la langosta? —Sí, _____ la recomiendo.
6. —¿Cuándo vas a prepararnos la cena? —_____ la voy a preparar en una hora.

# Práctica

**1**

**Responder** Imagínate que trabajas de camarero/a en un restaurante. Responde a los pedidos (*requests*) de estos clientes usando pronombres.

> **modelo**
>
> Sra. Gómez: Una ensalada, por favor.
> Sí, señora. Enseguida *(Right away)* se la traigo.

**AYUDA**

Here are some other useful expressions:

**ahora mismo**
*right now*

**inmediatamente**
*immediately*

**¡A la orden!**
*At your service!*

**¡Ya voy!**
*I'm on my way!*

1. Sres. López: La mantequilla, por favor.
2. Srta. Rivas: Los camarones, por favor.
3. Sra. Lugones: El pollo asado, por favor.
4. Tus compañeros/as de clase: Café, por favor.
5. Tu profesor(a) de español: Papas fritas, por favor.
6. Dra. González: La chuleta de cerdo, por favor.
7. Tu padre: Los champiñones, por favor.
8. Dr. Torres: La cuenta (*check*), por favor.

**2**

**¿Quién?** La señora Cevallos está planeando una cena. Se pregunta cómo va a resolver ciertas situaciones. En parejas, túrnense para decir lo que ella está pensando. Cambien los sustantivos subrayados por pronombres de objeto directo y hagan los otros cambios necesarios.

> **modelo**
>
> ¡No tengo carne! ¿Quién va a traerme la carne del supermercado? (mi esposo)
> Mi esposo va a traérmela./Mi esposo me la va a traer.

1. ¡Las invitaciones! ¿Quién les manda las invitaciones a los invitados (*guests*)? (mi hija)
2. No tengo tiempo de ir a la tienda. ¿Quién me puede comprar el vinagre? (mi hijo)
3. ¡Ay! No tengo suficientes platos (*plates*). ¿Quién puede prestarme los platos que necesito? (mi mamá)
4. Nos falta mantequilla. ¿Quién nos trae la mantequilla? (mi cuñada)
5. ¡Los entremeses! ¿Quién está preparándonos los entremeses? (Silvia y Renata)
6. No hay suficientes sillas. ¿Quién nos trae las sillas que faltan? (Héctor y Lorena)
7. No tengo tiempo de pedirle el aceite a Mónica. ¿Quién puede pedirle el aceite? (mi hijo)
8. ¿Quién va a servirles la cena a los invitados? (mis hijos)
9. Quiero poner buena música de fondo (*background*). ¿Quién me va a recomendar la música? (mi esposo)
10. ¡Los postres! ¿Quién va a preparar los postres para los invitados? (Sra. Villalba)

 Practice more at **vhlcentral.com.**

# Comunicación

**3**

**Contestar** Trabajen en parejas. Túrnense para hacer preguntas, usando las palabras interrogativas **¿Quién?** o **¿Cuándo?**, y para responderlas. Sigan el modelo.

> **modelo**
>
> nos enseña español
>
> **Estudiante 1:** ¿Quién nos enseña español?
> **Estudiante 2:** La profesora Camacho nos lo enseña.

1. te puede explicar la tarea cuando no la entiendes
2. les vende el almuerzo a los estudiantes
3. vas a comprarme boletos para un concierto
4. te escribe mensajes de texto
5. nos prepara los entremeses
6. me vas a prestar tu computadora
7. te compró esa bebida
8. nos va a recomendar el menú de la cafetería
9. le enseñó español al/a la profesor(a)
10. me vas a mostrar tu casa o apartamento

**4**

**Preguntas** En parejas, túrnense para hacerse estas preguntas.

> **modelo**
>
> **Estudiante 1:** ¿Les prestas tu computadora a tus amigos?
> **Estudiante 2:** No, no se la presto a mis amigos porque no son muy responsables.

1. ¿Me prestas tu chaqueta? ¿Ya le prestaste tu chaqueta a otro/a amigo/a?
2. ¿Quién te presta dinero cuando lo necesitas?
3. ¿Les prestas dinero a tus amigos? ¿Por qué?
4. ¿Nos compras el almuerzo a mí y a los otros compañeros de clase?
5. ¿Les mandas correo electrónico a tus amigos? ¿Y a tu familia?
6. ¿Les das regalos a tus amigos? ¿Cuándo?
7. ¿Quién te va a preparar la cena esta noche?
8. ¿Quién te va a preparar el desayuno mañana?

# Síntesis

**5**

**Regalos de Navidad** Tu profesor(a) te va a dar a ti y a un(a) compañero/a una parte de la lista de los regalos de Navidad (*Christmas gifts*) que Berta pidió y los regalos que sus parientes le compraron. Conversen para completar sus listas.

> **modelo**
>
> **Estudiante 1:** ¿Qué le pidió Berta a su mamá?
> **Estudiante 2:** Le pidió una computadora. ¿Se la compró?
> **Estudiante 1:** Sí, se la compró.

**recursos**

v**Text**

CPA
pp. 109–110

# [8.3] Comparisons  Explanation Tutorial

**ANTE TODO**  Both Spanish and English use comparisons to indicate which of two people or things has a lesser, equal, or greater degree of a quality.

( Comparisons )

**menos interesante**          **más grande**          **tan sabroso como**
*less interesting*              *bigger*                *as delicious as*

## Comparisons of inequality

▶ Comparisons of inequality are formed by placing **más** (*more*) or **menos** (*less*) before adjectives, adverbs, and nouns and **que** (*than*) after them.

$$\textbf{más/menos} + \begin{bmatrix} \textit{adjective} \\ \textit{adverb} \\ \textit{noun} \end{bmatrix} + \textbf{que}$$

▶ **¡Atención!** Note that while English has a comparative form for short adjectives (*tall**er***), such forms do not exist in Spanish (**más** alto).

( adjectives )

Los bistecs son **más caros que** el pollo. | Estas uvas son **menos ricas que** esa pera.
*Steaks are more expensive than chicken.* | *These grapes are less tasty than that pear.*

( adverbs )

Me acuesto **más tarde que** tú. | Luis se despierta **menos temprano que** yo.
*I go to bed later than you (do).* | *Luis wakes up less early than I (do).*

( nouns )

Juan prepara **más platos que** José. | Susana come **menos carne que** Enrique.
*Juan prepares more dishes than José (does).* | *Susana eats less meat than Enrique (does).*

La ensalada es menos cara que la sopa.

¿El pollo es más rico que el jamón?

▶ When the comparison involves a numerical expression, **de** is used before the number instead of **que**.

Hay más **de** cincuenta naranjas. | Llego en menos **de** diez minutos.
*There are more than fifty oranges.* | *I'll be there in less than ten minutes.*

▶ With verbs, this construction is used to make comparisons of inequality.

$$\begin{bmatrix} \textit{verb} \end{bmatrix} + \textbf{más/menos que}$$

Mis hermanos **comen más que** yo. | Arturo **duerme menos que** su padre.
*My brothers eat more than I (do).* | *Arturo sleeps less than his father (does).*

# Comparisons of equality

▶ This construction is used to make comparisons of equality.

tan + [ *adjective* / *adverb* ] + **como**          **tanto/a(s)** + [ *singular noun* / *plural noun* ] + **como**

¿Es tan guapo como yo?

¿Aquí vienen tantos mexicanos como extranjeros?

▶ **¡Atención!** Note that unlike **tan**, **tanto** acts as an adjective and therefore agrees in number and gender with the noun it modifies.

Estas uvas son **tan ricas como** aquéllas.
*These grapes are as tasty as those ones (are).*

Yo probé **tantos platos como** él.
*I tried as many dishes as he did.*

▶ **Tan** and **tanto** can also be used for emphasis, rather than to compare, with these meanings: **tan** *so*, **tanto** *so much*, **tantos/as** *so many*.

¡Tu almuerzo es **tan** grande!
*Your lunch is so big!*

¡Comes **tantas** manzanas!
*You eat so many apples!*

¡Comes **tanto**!
*You eat so much!*

¡Preparan **tantos** platos!
*They prepare so many dishes!*

▶ Comparisons of equality with verbs are formed by placing **tanto como** after the verb. Note that in this construction **tanto** does not change in number or gender.

[ *verb* ] + **tanto como**

Tú viajas **tanto como** mi tía.
*You travel as much as my aunt (does).*

Ellos hablan **tanto como** mis hermanas.
*They talk as much as my sisters.*

Sabemos **tanto como** ustedes.
*We know as much as you (do).*

No estudio **tanto como** Felipe.
*I don't study as much as Felipe (does).*

# Irregular comparisons

▶ Some adjectives have irregular comparative forms.

## Irregular comparative forms

| Adjective | | Comparative form | |
|---|---|---|---|
| **bueno/a** | good | **mejor** | better |
| **malo/a** | bad | **peor** | worse |
| **grande** | big | **mayor** | bigger |
| **pequeño/a** | small | **menor** | smaller |
| **joven** | young | **menor** | younger |
| **viejo/a** | old | **mayor** | older |

▶ When **grande** and **pequeño/a** refer to age, the irregular comparative forms, **mayor** and **menor**, are used. However, when these adjectives refer to size, the regular forms, **más grande** and **más pequeño/a**, are used.

Yo soy **menor** que tú.
*I'm younger than you.*

Pedí un plato **más pequeño**.
*I ordered a smaller dish.*

Nuestro hijo es **mayor** que
el hijo de los Andrade.
*Our son is older than the Andrades' son.*

La ensalada de Isabel es **más
grande** que ésa.
*Isabel's salad is bigger than that one.*

▶ The adverbs **bien** and **mal** have the same irregular comparative forms as the adjectives **bueno/a** and **malo/a**.

Julio nada **mejor** que los otros chicos.
*Julio swims better than the other boys.*

Ellas cantan **peor** que las otras chicas.
*They sing worse than the other girls.*

 **¡INTÉNTALO!** Escribe el equivalente de las palabras en inglés.

1. Ernesto mira más televisión ___que___ (*than*) Alberto.
2. Tú eres ___men___ (*less*) simpático que Federico.
3. La camarera sirve _____ (*as much*) carne como pescado.
4. Conozco _____ (*more*) restaurantes que tú.
5. No estudio _____ (*as much as*) tú.
6. ¿Sabes jugar al tenis tan bien _____ (*as*) tu hermana?
7. ¿Puedes beber _____ (*as many*) refrescos como yo?
8. Mis amigos parecen _____ (*as*) simpáticos como ustedes.

# Práctica

**1**

**Escoger** Escoge la palabra correcta para comparar a dos hermanas muy diferentes. Haz los cambios necesarios.

1. Lucila es más alta y más bonita ___que___ Tita. (de, más, menos, que)
2. Tita es más delgada porque come ___menos___ verduras que su hermana. (de, más, menos, que)
3. Lucila es más _____ que Tita porque es alegre. (listo, simpático, bajo)
4. A Tita le gusta comer en casa. Va a ___menos___ restaurantes que su hermana. (más, menos, que) Es tímida, pero activa. Hace ___más___ ejercicio (*exercise*) que su hermana. (más, tanto, menos) Todos los días toma más _____ cinco vasos (*glasses*) de agua mineral. (que, tan, de)
5. Lucila come muchas papas fritas y se preocupa _____ que Tita por comer frutas. (de, más, menos) ¡Son _____ diferentes! Pero se llevan (*they get along*) muy bien. (como, tan, tanto)

**2**

**Emparejar** Compara a Mario y a Luis, los novios de Lucila y Tita, completando las oraciones de la columna A con las palabras o frases de la columna B.

| **A** | **B** |
|---|---|
| 1. Mario es ___tan interesante___ como Luis. | ~~tantas~~ |
| 2. Mario viaja tanto ___como___ Luis. | ~~diferencia~~ |
| 3. Luis toma ___tantas___ clases de cocina (*cooking*) como Mario. | ~~tan interesante~~ |
| 4. Luis habla ___francés___ tan bien como Mario. | ~~amigos extranjeros~~ |
| 5. Mario tiene tantos ___amigos extranjeros___ como Luis. | ~~como~~ |
| 6. ¡Qué casualidad (*coincidence*)! Mario y Luis también son hermanos, pero no hay tanta ___diferencia___ entre ellos como entre Lucila y Tita. | ~~francés~~ |

**3**

**Oraciones** Combina elementos de las columnas A, B y C para hacer comparaciones. Escribe oraciones completas.

> **modelo**
>
> George Clooney tiene tantos autos como el presidente de los EE.UU.
> Emma Stone es menor que George Clooney.

| **A** | **B** | **C** |
|---|---|---|
| la comida japonesa | costar | la gente de Montreal |
| el fútbol | saber | la música *country* |
| George Clooney | ser | el brócoli |
| el pollo | tener | el presidente de los EE.UU. |
| la gente de Vancouver | ¿? | la comida italiana |
| la primera dama (*lady*) de los EE.UU. | | el hockey |
| las escuelas privadas | | Emma Stone |
| las espinacas | | las escuelas públicas |
| la música rap | | la carne de res |

 Practice more at **vhlcentral.com**.

# Comunicación

**4**

**Intercambiar** En parejas, hagan comparaciones sobre diferentes cosas. Pueden usar las sugerencias de la lista u otras ideas.

> *modelo*
>
> **Estudiante 1:** Los pollos de *Pollitos del Corral* son muy ricos.
> **Estudiante 2:** Pues yo creo que los pollos de *Rostipollos* son tan buenos como los pollos de *Pollitos del Corral*.
> **Estudiante 1:** Mmm… no tienen tanta mantequilla como los pollos de *Pollitos del Corral*. Tienes razón. Son muy sabrosos.

restaurantes en tu ciudad/pueblo
cafés en tu comunidad
tiendas en tu ciudad/pueblo

periódicos en tu ciudad/pueblo
revistas favoritas
libros favoritos

comidas favoritas
los profesores
las clases que toman

**5**

**Conversar** En grupos, túrnense para hacer comparaciones entre ustedes mismos (*yourselves*) y una persona de cada categoría de la lista.

▶ una persona de tu familia

▶ un(a) amigo/a especial

▶ una persona famosa

# Síntesis

**6**

**La familia López** En grupos, túrnense para hablar de Sara, Sabrina, Cristina, Ricardo y David y hacer comparaciones entre ellos.

> *modelo*
>
> **Estudiante 1:** Sara es tan alta como Sabrina.
> **Estudiante 2:** Sí, pero David es más alto que ellas.
> **Estudiante 3:** En mi opinión, él es guapo también.

Explanation
Tutorial

## 8.4 Superlatives

**ANTE TODO**   Both English and Spanish use superlatives to express the highest or
lowest degree of a quality.

| **el/la mejor** | **el/la peor** | **el/la más alto/a** |
|-----------------|----------------|----------------------|
| *the best*      | *the worst*    | *the tallest*        |

▶ This construction is used to form superlatives. Note that the noun is always preceded
by a definite article and that **de** is equivalent to the English *in* or *of*.

**el/la/los/las** + [ *noun* ] + **más/menos** + [ *adjective* ] + **de**

▶ The noun can be omitted if the person, place, or thing referred to is clear.

¿El restaurante Las Delicias?                    Recomiendo el pollo asado.
  Es **el más elegante** de la ciudad.             Es **el más sabroso** del menú.
  *The restaurant Las Delicias?*                   *I recommend the roast chicken.*
  *It's the most elegant (one) in the city.*       *It's the most delicious on the menu.*

▶ Here are some irregular superlative forms.

| **Irregular superlatives** | | | |
|---|---|---|---|
| **Adjective** | | **Superlative form** | |
| **bueno/a** | *good* | **el/la mejor** | *(the) best* |
| **malo/a** | *bad* | **el/la peor** | *(the) worst* |
| **grande** | *big* | **el/la mayor** | *(the) biggest* |
| **pequeño/a** | *small* | **el/la menor** | *(the) smallest* |
| **joven** | *young* | **el/la menor** | *(the) youngest* |
| **viejo/a** | *old* | **el/la mayor** | *(the) eldest* |

▶ The absolute superlative is equivalent to *extremely, super,* or *very*. To form the absolute
superlative of most adjectives and adverbs, drop the final vowel, if there is one, and
add **-ísimo/a(s)**.

malo ⟶ mal- ⟶ **malísimo**              mucho ⟶ much- ⟶ **muchísimo**

¡El bistec está **malísimo**!            Comes **muchísimo**.

▶ Note these spelling changes.

rico ⟶ **riquísimo**    largo ⟶ **larguísimo**    feliz ⟶ **felicísimo**

fácil ⟶ **facilísimo**    joven ⟶ **jovencísimo**    trabajador ⟶ **trabajadorcísimo**

**¡ATENCIÓN!**

While **más** alone
means *more*, after **el**,
**la**, **los** or **las**, it means
*most*. Likewise, **menos**
can mean *less* or *least*.

Es **el café más rico
del** país.
*It's the most delicious
coffee in the country.*

Es **el menú menos
caro de** todos éstos.
*It is the least
expensive menu of all
of these.*

**CONSULTA**

The rule you learned
in **Estructura 8.3**
(p. 283) regarding the
use of **mayor/menor**
with age, but not with
size, is also true with
superlative forms.

**recursos**

v̂**Text**

CPA
pp. 114–117

CH
pp. 125–126

vhlcentral.com

---

   Escribe el equivalente de las palabras en inglés.

1. Marisa es ___la más inteligente___ (*the most intelligent*) de todas.
2. Ricardo y Tomás son _____ (*the least boring*) de la fiesta.
3. Miguel y Antonio son _____ (*the worst*) estudiantes de la clase.
4. Mi profesor de biología es _____ (*the oldest*) de la escuela.

# Práctica y Comunicación

**1**

**El más...** Responde a las preguntas afirmativamente. Usa las palabras entre paréntesis.

> **modelo**
>
> El cuarto está sucísimo, ¿no? (casa)
> *Sí, es el más sucio de la casa.*

1. El almacén Velasco es buenísimo, ¿no? (centro comercial)
2. La silla de tu madre es comodísima, ¿no? (casa)
3. Ángela y Julia están nerviosísimas por el examen, ¿no? (clase)
4. Jorge es jovencísimo, ¿no? (mis amigos)

**2**

**Completar** Tu profesor(a) te va a dar una hoja de actividades con descripciones de José Valenzuela Carranza y Ana Orozco Hoffman. Completa las oraciones con las palabras de la lista.

| | | | |
|---|---|---|---|
| altísima | del | mayor | peor |
| atlética | guapísimo | mejor | periodista |
| bajo | la | menor | trabajadorcísimo |
| de | más | Orozco | Valenzuela |

1. José tiene 22 años; es el _____ y el más _____ de su familia. Es _____ y _____. Es el mejor _____ de la ciudad y el _____ jugador de baloncesto.
2. Ana es la más _____ y _____ mejor jugadora de baloncesto del estado. Es la _____ de sus hermanos (tiene 28 años) y es _____. Estudió la profesión _____ difícil _____ todas: medicina.
3. Jorge es el _____ jugador de videojuegos de su familia.
4. Mauricio es el menor de la familia _____.
5. El abuelo es el _____ de todos los miembros de la familia Valenzuela.
6. Fifí es la perra más antipática _____ mundo.

**3**

**Superlativos** Trabajen en parejas para hacer comparaciones. Usen superlativos.

> **modelo**
>
> Angelina Jolie, Bill Gates, Jimmy Carter
> **Estudiante 1:** Bill Gates es el más rico de los tres.
> **Estudiante 2:** Sí, ¡es riquísimo! Y Jimmy Carter es el mayor de los tres.

1. Guatemala, Argentina, España
2. Jaguar, Prius, Smart
3. la comida mexicana, la comida francesa, la comida árabe
4. Paris Hilton, Meryl Streep, Ellen Page
5. Ciudad de México, Buenos Aires, Nueva York
6. *Don Quijote de la Mancha*, *Cien años de soledad*, *Como agua para chocolate*
7. el fútbol americano, el golf, el béisbol
8. las películas románticas, las películas de acción, las películas cómicas

 Practice more at **vhlcentral.com**.

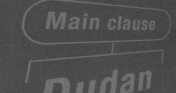

# Recapitulación

**Diagnostics**
**Remediation Activities**

Completa estas actividades para repasar los conceptos de gramática que aprendiste en esta lección.

**1** **Completar** Completa la tabla con la forma correcta del pretérito. **9 pts.**

| Infinitive | yo | usted | ellos |
|---|---|---|---|
| **dormir** | | | |
| **servir** | | | |
| **vestirse** | | | |

**2** **La cena** Completa la conversación con el pretérito de los verbos. **7 pts.**

**PAULA** ¡Hola, Daniel! ¿Qué tal el fin de semana?

**DANIEL** Muy bien. Marta y yo (1) _____ (conseguir) hacer muchas cosas, pero lo mejor fue la cena del sábado.

**PAULA** Ah, ¿sí? ¿Adónde fueron?

**DANIEL** Al restaurante Vistahermosa. Es elegante, así que (nosotros) (2) _____ (vestirse) bien.

**PAULA** Y ¿qué platos (3) _____ (pedir, ustedes)?

**DANIEL** Yo (4) _____ (pedir) camarones y Marta (5) _____ (preferir) el pollo. Y al final, el camarero nos (6) _____ (servir) flan.

**PAULA** ¡Qué rico!

**DANIEL** Sí. Pero después de la cena Marta no (7) _____ (sentirse) bien.

**3** **Camareros** Genaro y Úrsula son camareros en un restaurante. Usa pronombres para completar la conversación que tienen con su jefe. **8 pts.**

**JEFE** Úrsula, ¿le ofreciste agua fría al cliente de la mesa 22?

**ÚRSULA** Sí, (1) _____ de inmediato.

**JEFE** Genaro, ¿los clientes de la mesa 5 te pidieron ensaladas?

**GENARO** Sí, (2) _____.

**ÚRSULA** Genaro, ¿recuerdas si ya me mostraste los vinos nuevos?

**GENARO** Sí, ya (3) _____.

**JEFE** Genaro, ¿van a pagarte la cuenta (*bill*) los clientes de la mesa 5?

**GENARO** Sí, (4) _____ ahora mismo.

---

**RESUMEN GRAMATICAL**

**8.1** **Preterite of stem-changing verbs** *p. 274*

| servir | dormir |
|---|---|
| serví | dormí |
| serviste | dormiste |
| sirvió | durmió |
| servimos | dormimos |
| servisteis | dormisteis |
| sirvieron | durmieron |

**8.2** **Double object pronouns** *pp. 277–278*

Indirect Object Pronouns: me, te, le (se), nos, os, les (se)

Direct Object Pronouns: lo, la, los, las

Le escribí la carta. → Se la escribí.

Nos van a servir los platos. → Nos los van a servir./ Van a servírnoslos.

**8.3** **Comparisons** *pp. 281–283*

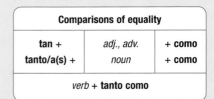

| Comparisons of inequality | | |
|---|---|---|
| más/menos + | adj., adv., n. | + que |
| verb + **más/menos + que** | | |

| Comparisons of equality | | |
|---|---|---|
| tan + | adj., adv. | + como |
| tanto/a(s) + | noun | + como |
| verb + **tanto como** | | |

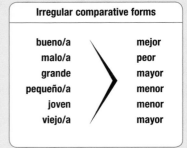

| Irregular comparative forms | |
|---|---|
| bueno/a | mejor |
| malo/a | peor |
| grande | mayor |
| pequeño/a | menor |
| joven | menor |
| viejo/a | mayor |

**4**    **El menú** Observa el menú y sus características.
Completa las oraciones basándote en los elementos dados.
Usa comparativos y superlativos.   **14 pts.**

**8.4** **Superlatives**   *p. 286*

| el/la/ los/las + | noun | + más/ menos + | adjective | + de |
|---|---|---|---|---|

► Irregular superlatives follow the same pattern as irregular comparatives.

| *Ensaladas* | *Precio* | *Calorías* |
|---|---|---|
| Ensalada de tomates | $9.00 | 170 |
| Ensalada de mariscos | $12.99 | 325 |
| Ensalada de zanahorias | $9.00 | 200 |

| *Platos principales* | | |
|---|---|---|
| Pollo con champiñones | $13.00 | 495 |
| Cerdo con papas | $10.50 | 725 |
| Atún con espárragos | $18.95 | 495 |

1. ensalada de mariscos / otras ensaladas / costar
   La ensalada de mariscos _____ las otras ensaladas.
2. pollo con champiñones / cerdo con papas / calorías
   El pollo con champiñones tiene _____ el cerdo con papas.
3. atún con espárragos / pollo con champiñones / calorías
   El atún con espárragos tiene _____ el pollo con champiñones.
4. ensalada de tomates / ensalada de zanahorias / caro
   La ensalada de tomates es _____ la ensalada de zanahorias.
5. cerdo con papas / platos principales / caro
   El cerdo con papas es _____ los platos principales.
6. ensalada de zanahorias / ensalada de tomates / costar
   La ensalada de zanahorias _____ la ensalada de tomates.
7. ensalada de mariscos / ensaladas / caro
   La ensalada de mariscos es _____ las ensaladas.

**5**    **Dos restaurantes** ¿Cuál es el mejor restaurante que conoces? ¿Y el peor? Escribe un párrafo de
por lo menos (*at least*) seis oraciones donde expliques por qué piensas así. Puedes hablar de la calidad
de la comida, el ambiente, los precios, el servicio, etc.   **12 pts.**

**6**   **Adivinanza** Completa la adivinanza y adivina la respuesta.   **¡2 puntos EXTRA!**

**“ En el campo yo nací°,
mis hermanos son
los _____ (*garlic, pl.*),
y aquél que llora° por mí
me está partiendo°
en pedazos° ”.
¿Quién soy? _____**

 Practice more at **vhlcentral.com.**   nací *was born* llora *cries* partiendo *cutting* pedazos *pieces*

# Lectura  Audio: Synched Reading Additional Reading

## Antes de leer

### Estrategia

**Reading for the main idea**

As you know, you can learn a great deal about a reading selection by looking at the format and looking for cognates, titles, and subtitles. You can skim to get the gist of the reading selection and scan it for specific information. Reading for the main idea is another useful strategy; it involves locating the topic sentences of each paragraph to determine the author's purpose for writing a particular piece. Topic sentences can provide clues about the content of each paragraph, as well as the general organization of the reading. Your choice of which reading strategies to use will depend on the style and format of each reading selection.

### Examinar el texto

En esta sección tenemos dos textos diferentes. ¿Qué estrategias puedes usar para leer la crítica culinaria°? ¿Cuáles son las apropiadas para familiarizarte con el menú? Utiliza las estrategias más eficaces° para cada texto. ¿Qué tienen en común? ¿Qué tipo de comida sirven en el restaurante?

### Identificar la idea principal

Lee la primera frase de cada párrafo de la crítica culinaria del restaurante **La feria del maíz**. Apunta° el tema principal de cada párrafo. Luego lee todo el primer párrafo. ¿Crees que el restaurante le gustó al autor de la crítica culinaria? ¿Por qué? Ahora lee la crítica entera. En tu opinión, ¿cuál es la idea principal de la crítica? ¿Por qué la escribió el autor? Compara tus opiniones con las de un(a) compañero/a.

crítica culinaria *restaurant review*   eficaces *efficient*   Apunta *Jot down*

## MENÚ

### *Entremeses*

Tortilla servida con
- Ajiaceite (chile, aceite)   • Ajicomino (chile, comino)

Pan tostado servido con
- Queso frito a la pimienta   • Salsa de ajo y mayonesa

### *Sopas*

- Tomate   • Cebolla   • Verduras   • Pollo y huevo
- Carne de res   • Mariscos

### *Entradas*

Tomaticán
(tomate, papas, maíz, chile, arvejas y zanahorias)

Tamales
(maíz, azúcar, ajo, cebolla)

Frijoles enchilados
(frijoles negros, carne de cerdo o de res, arroz, chile)

Chilaquil
(tortilla de maíz, queso, hierbas y chile)

Tacos
(tortillas, pollo, verduras y salsa)

Cóctel de mariscos
(camarones, langosta, vinagre, sal, pimienta, aceite)

### *Postres°*

- Plátanos caribeños   • Cóctel de frutas al ron°
- Uvate (uvas, azúcar de caña y ron)   • Flan napolitano
- Helado° de piña y naranja   • Pastel° de yogur

## Después de leer

### Preguntas

En parejas, contesten estas preguntas sobre la crítica culinaria de **La feria del maíz.**

1. ¿Quién es el dueño y chef de **La feria del maíz**?

2. ¿Qué tipo de comida se sirve en el restaurante?

3. ¿Cuál es el problema con el servicio?

4. ¿Cómo es el ambiente del restaurante?

5. ¿Qué comidas probó el autor?

6. ¿Quieren ir ustedes al restaurante **La feria del maíz**? ¿Por qué?

23F

# Gastronomía

Por Eduardo Fernández

## La feria del maíz

Sobresaliente°. En el nuevo restaurante **La feria del maíz** va a encontrar la perfecta combinación entre la comida tradicional y el encanto° de la vieja ciudad de Antigua. Ernesto Sandoval, antiguo jefe de cocina° del famoso restaurante **El fogón**, está teniendo mucho éxito° en su nueva aventura culinaria.

El gerente°, el experimentado José Sierra, controla a la perfección la calidad del servicio. El camarero que me atendió esa noche fue muy amable en todo momento. Sólo hay que comentar que,

**La feria del maíz
13 calle 4-41 Zona 1
La Antigua, Guatemala
2329912**

*lunes a sábado
10:30am-11:30pm
domingo 10:00am-10:00pm*

Comida ♉♉♉♉♉

Servicio ♉♉♉

Ambiente ♉♉♉♉

Precio ♉♉♉

debido al éxito inmediato de **La feria del maíz**, se necesitan más camareros para atender a los clientes de una forma más eficaz. En esta ocasión, el mesero se

tomó unos veinte minutos en traerme la bebida.

Afortunadamente, no me importó mucho la espera entre plato y plato, pues el ambiente es tan agradable que me sentí como en casa. El restaurante mantiene el estilo colonial de Antigua. Por dentro°, es elegante y rústico a la vez. Cuando el tiempo lo permite, se puede comer también en el patio, donde hay muchas flores.

El servicio de camareros y el ambiente agradable del local pasan a un segundo plano cuando llega la comida, de una calidad extraordinaria. Las tortillas de casa se sirven con un ajiaceite delicioso. La sopa

de mariscos es excelente y los tamales, pues, tengo que confesar que son mejores que los de mi abuelita. También recomiendo los tacos de pollo, servidos con un mole buenísimo. De postre, don Ernesto me preparó su especialidad, unos plátanos caribeños sabrosísimos.

Los precios pueden parecer altos° para una comida tradicional, pero la calidad de los productos con que se cocinan los platos y el exquisito ambiente de **La feria del maíz** garantizan° una experiencia inolvidable°.

### *Bebidas*

- Cerveza negra
- Chilate (bebida de maíz, chile y cacao)
- Jugos de fruta
- Agua mineral
- Té helado
- Vino tinto/blanco
- Ron

**Postres** *Desserts* **ron** *rum* **Helado** *Ice cream* **Pastel** *Cake* **Sobresaliente** *Outstanding* **encanto** *charm* **jefe de cocina** *head chef* **éxito** *success* **gerente** *manager* **Por dentro** *Inside* **altos** *high* **garantizan** *guarantee* **inolvidable** *unforgettable*

---

## Un(a) guía turístico/a

Tú eres un(a) guía turístico/a en Guatemala. Estás en el restaurante **La feria del maíz** con un grupo de turistas norteamericanos. Ellos no hablan español y quieren pedir de comer, pero necesitan tu ayuda. Lee nuevamente el menú e indica qué error comete cada turista.

1. La señora Johnson es diabética y no puede comer azúcar. Pide sopa de verduras y tamales. No pide nada de postre.

2. Los señores Petit son vegeterianos y piden sopa de tomate, frijoles enchilados y plátanos caribeños.

3. El señor Smith, que es alérgico al chocolate, pide tortilla servida con ajiaceite, chilaquil y chilate para beber.

4. La adorable hija del señor Smith tiene sólo cuatro años y le gustan mucho las verduras y las frutas naturales. Su papá le pide tomaticán y un cóctel de frutas.

5. La señorita Jackson está a dieta y pide uvate, flan napolitano y helado.

# Escritura

## Estrategia
### Expressing and supporting opinions

Written reviews are just one of the many kinds of writing which require you to state your opinions. In order to convince your reader to take your opinions seriously, it is important to support them as thoroughly as possible. Details, facts, examples, and other forms of evidence are necessary. In a restaurant review, for example, it is not enough just to rate the food, service, and atmosphere. Readers will want details about the dishes you ordered, the kind of service you received, and the type of atmosphere you encountered. If you were writing a concert or album review, what kinds of details might your readers expect to find?

It is easier to include details that support your opinions if you plan ahead. Before going to a place or event that you are planning to review, write a list of questions that your readers might ask. Decide which aspects of the experience you are going to rate and list the details that will help you decide upon a rating. You can then organize these lists into a questionnaire and a rating sheet. Bring these forms with you to help you make your opinions and to remind you of the kinds of information you need to gather in order to support those opinions. Later, these forms will help you organize your review into logical categories. They can also provide the details and other evidence you need to convince your readers of your opinions.

## Tema

### Escribir una crítica ✎ⓢ

Escribe una crítica culinaria° sobre un restaurante local para el periódico de la escuela. Clasifica el restaurante, dándole de una a cinco estrellas°, y anota tus recomendaciones para futuros clientes del restaurante. Incluye tus opiniones acerca de°:

▸ La comida
  ¿Qué tipo de comida es? ¿Qué tipo de ingredientes usan? ¿Es de buena calidad? ¿Cuál es el mejor plato? ¿Y el peor? ¿Quién es el/la chef?

▸ El servicio
  ¿Es necesario esperar mucho para conseguir una mesa? ¿Tienen los camareros un buen conocimiento del menú? ¿Atienden° a los clientes con rapidez° y cortesía?

▸ El ambiente
  ¿Cómo es la decoración del restaurante? ¿Es el ambiente informal o elegante? ¿Hay música o algún tipo de entretenimiento°? ¿Hay un balcón? ¿Un patio?

▸ Información práctica
  ¿Cómo son los precios? ¿Se aceptan tarjetas de crédito? ¿Cuál es la dirección° y el número de teléfono? ¿Quién es el/la dueño/a? ¿El/La gerente?

crítica culinaria *restaurant review* estrellas *stars* acerca de *about* Atienden *They take care of* rapidez *speed* entretenimiento *entertainment* dirección *address*

# Escuchar

## Estrategia

**Jotting down notes as you listen**

Jotting down notes while you listen to a conversation in Spanish can help you keep track of the important points or details. It will help you to focus actively on comprehension rather than on remembering what you have heard.

 To practice this strategy, you will now listen to a paragraph. Jot down the main points you hear.

## Preparación

Mira la foto. ¿Dónde están estas personas y qué hacen? ¿Sobre qué crees que están hablando?

## Ahora escucha

Rosa y Roberto están en un restaurante. Escucha la conversación entre ellos y la camarera y toma nota de cuáles son los especiales del día, qué pidieron y qué bebidas se mencionan.

**Especiales del día**

**Entremeses**
_____

**Plato principal**
_____
_____
_____

**¿Qué pidieron?**

**Roberto**
_____

**Rosa**
_____

**Bebidas**
_____
_____

## Comprensión

### Seleccionar

Usa tus notas para seleccionar la opción correcta para completar cada oración.

1. Dos de los mejores platos del restaurante son _____.
   a. los entremeses del día y el cerdo
   b. el salmón y el arroz con pollo
   c. la carne y el arroz con pollo

2. La camarera _____.
   a. los lleva a su mesa, les muestra el menú y les sirve el postre
   b. les habla de los especiales del día, les recomienda unos platos y ellos deciden qué van a comer
   c. les lleva unas bebidas, les recomienda unos platos y les sirve pan

3. Roberto va a comer _____ Rosa.
   a. tantos platos como
   b. más platos que
   c. menos platos que

### Preguntas

En grupos de tres o cuatro, respondan a las preguntas: ¿Conocen los platos que Rosa y Roberto pidieron? ¿Conocen platos con los mismos ingredientes? ¿En qué son diferentes o similares? ¿Cuál les gusta más? ¿Por qué?

 Practice more at **vhlcentral.com**.

# En pantalla  Video: TV Clip

La sopa es un plato muy importante en las cocinas° del mundo hispano. Se pueden tomar° frías, como el famoso gazpacho español, a base de tomate y otras verduras y servida totalmente líquida. La mayoría se sirven calientes, como el pozole de México, un plato precolombino preparado con nixtamal°, cerdo, chiles y otras especias°. Otra sopa de origen indígena es la changua, de la región andina central de Colombia. Aunque° las sopas normalmente forman parte del almuerzo, la changua siempre se toma en el desayuno: se hace con agua, leche, huevo y cilantro.

| Vocabulario útil | |
|---|---|
| bajar | to descend |
| la escalera | staircase |
| lo que yo quiera | whatever I want |
| sabor marinero | seafood flavor |

##  Ordenar

Ordena cronológicamente estas oraciones.

_____ a. El niño abre la puerta.

_____ b. El niño decide almorzar.

_____ c. El niño baja la escalera con una maleta.

_____ d. El niño se va a lavar las manos.

_____ e. La madre dice que la sopa está servida.

##  Sopas

En parejas, túrnense para describir su sopa favorita. ¿Cuál es tu sopa favorita? ¿Quién la prepara o dónde la compras? ¿Qué ingredientes tiene? ¿Con qué se sirve? ¿Cómo la prefieres, caliente o fría? ¿La tomas en el almuerzo o en la cena? ¿En invierno o en verano?

cocinas *cuisines* tomar *to eat (soup)* nixtamal *hominy* especias *spices*
Aunque *Although* está servida *it is served*

### Anuncio de Sopas Roa

**Me voy de esta casa.**

**Ya está servida° la sopa...**

**...y lavarme las manos.**

 Practice more at **vhlcentral.com.**

Video:
*Flash cultura*

Los países hispanos tienen una producción muy abundante de frutas y verduras. Por eso, en los hogares° hispanos se cocina° con productos frescos° más que con alimentos° que vienen en latas° o frascos°. Las salsas mexicanas, el gazpacho español y el sancocho colombiano, por ejemplo, deben prepararse con ingredientes frescos para que mantengan° su sabor° auténtico. Actualmente, en los Estados Unidos está creciendo el interés en cocinar con productos frescos y orgánicos. Cada vez hay más mercados° donde los agricultores° pueden vender sus frutas y verduras directamente° al público. En este episodio de *Flash cultura* vas a ver algunos ingredientes típicos de la comida hispana.

## Vocabulario útil

| | |
|---|---|
| blanda | *soft* |
| cocinar | *to cook* |
| dura | *hard* |
| ¿Está lista para ordenar? | *Are you ready to order?* |
| el plato | *dish (in a meal)* |
| pruébala | *try it, taste it* |
| las ventas | *sales* |

### Preparación

¿Probaste alguna vez comida latina? ¿La compraste en un supermercado o fuiste a un restaurante? ¿Qué plato(s) probaste? ¿Te gustó?

### ¿Cierto o falso?

Indica si cada oración es **cierta** o **falsa**.

1. En Los Ángeles hay comida de países latinoamericanos y de España.
2. Leticia explica que la tortilla del taco americano es blanda y la del taco mexicano es dura.
3. Las ventas de salsa son bajas en los Estados Unidos.
4. Leticia fue a un restaurante ecuatoriano.
5. Leticia probó Inca Kola en un supermercado.

hogares *homes* se cocina *they cook* frescos *fresh* alimentos *foods* latas *cans* frascos *jars* para que mantengan *so that they keep* sabor *flavor* mercados *markets* agricultores *farmers* directamente *directly* mostrará *will show*

## La comida latina

**La mejor comida latina no sólo se encuentra en los grandes restaurantes.**

**Marta nos mostrará° algunos de los platos de la comida mexicana.**

**... hay más lugares donde podemos comprar productos hispanos.**

 Practice more at **vhlcentral.com**.

# Guatemala

**Interactive Map**
**Video: *Panorama cultural***

## El país en cifras

▶ **Área:** 108.890 km$^2$ (42.042 millas$^2$),
*un poco más pequeño que Tennessee*

▶ **Población:** 14.389.000

▶ **Capital:** Ciudad de Guatemala—1.110.000

▶ **Ciudades principales:** Quetzaltenango,
Escuintla, Mazatenango, Puerto Barrios

SOURCE: Population Division, UN Secretariat

▶ **Moneda:** quetzal

▶ **Idiomas:** español (oficial),
lenguas mayas, xinca, garífuna

*El español es la lengua de un
60 por ciento° de la población; el
otro 40 por ciento tiene como lengua
materna el xinca, el garífuna o, en su
mayoría°, una de las lenguas mayas
(cakchiquel, quiché y kekchícomo, entre
otras). Una palabra que las lenguas
mayas tienen en común es ixim, que
significa "maíz", un cultivo° de mucha
importancia en estas culturas.*

Bandera de Guatemala

**Guatemaltecos célebres**

▶ **Carlos Mérida,** pintor (1891–1984)

▶ **Miguel Ángel Asturias,** escritor (1899–1974)

▶ **Margarita Carrera,** poeta y ensayista (1929– )

▶ **Rigoberta Menchú Tum,** activista (1959– ),
premio Nobel de la Paz° en 1992

por ciento *percent*  en su mayoría *most of them*  cultivo *crop*
Paz *Peace*  telas *fabrics*  tinte *dye*  aplastados *crushed*
hace... destiñan *keeps the colors from running*

ESTADOS UNIDOS
OCÉANO ATLÁNTICO
GUATEMALA
OCÉANO PACÍFICO
AMÉRICA DEL SUR

Palacio Nacional de la Cultura
en la Ciudad de Guatemala

Sierra de Lacandón

Lago Petén Itzá

Río Usumacinta

MÉXICO

Río de la Pasión

BELICE

Mujeres indígenas limpiando cebollas

Lago de Izabal

Sierra de las Minas

Quetzaltenango

Río Motagua

Sierra Madre

Lago de Atitlán  ★ Guatemala

Mazatenango  Antigua Guatemala

Escuintla

Iglesia de la Merced en
Antigua Guatemala

EL SALVADOR

Océano Pacífico

recursos

vText

CPA
pp. 122–125

vhlcentral.com

## ¡Increíble pero cierto!

¿Qué "ingrediente" secreto se encuentra en las
telas° tradicionales de Guatemala? ¡El mosquito! El
excepcional tinte° de estas telas es producto de una
combinación de flores y de mosquitos aplastados°.
El insecto hace que los colores no se destiñan°.
Quizás es por esto que los artesanos representan
la figura del mosquito en muchas de sus telas.

## Ciudades • **Antigua Guatemala**

Antigua Guatemala fue fundada en 1543. Fue una capital de gran importancia hasta 1773, cuando un terremoto° la destruyó. Sin embargo, conserva el carácter original de su arquitectura y hoy es uno de los centros turísticos del país. Su celebración de la Semana Santa° es, para muchas personas, la más importante del hemisferio.

## Naturaleza • **El quetzal**

El quetzal simbolizó la libertad para los antiguos° mayas porque creían° que este pájaro° no podía° vivir en cautiverio°. Hoy el quetzal es el símbolo nacional. El pájaro da su nombre a la moneda nacional y aparece también en los billetes° del país. Desafortunadamente, está en peligro° de extinción. Para su protección, el gobierno mantiene una reserva ecológica especial.

## Historia • **Los mayas**

Desde 1500 a.C. hasta 900 d.C., los mayas habitaron gran parte de lo que ahora es Guatemala. Su civilización fue muy avanzada. Los mayas fueron arquitectos y constructores de pirámides, templos y observatorios. También descubrieron° y usaron el cero antes que los europeos, e inventaron un calendario complejo° y preciso.

## Artesanía • **La ropa tradicional**

La ropa tradicional de los guatemaltecos se llama *huipil* y muestra el amor° de la cultura maya por la naturaleza. Ellos se inspiran en las flores°, plantas y animales para crear sus diseños° de colores vivos° y formas geométricas. El diseño y los colores de cada *huipil* indican el pueblo de origen y a veces también el sexo y la edad° de la persona que lo lleva.

 **¿Qué aprendiste?** Responde a cada pregunta con una oración completa.

1. ¿Qué significa la palabra *ixim*?

2. ¿Quién es Rigoberta Menchú?

3. ¿Qué pájaro representa a Guatemala?

4. ¿Qué simbolizó el quetzal para los mayas?

5. ¿Cuál es la moneda nacional de Guatemala?

6. ¿De qué fueron arquitectos los mayas?

7. ¿Qué celebración de la Antigua Guatemala es la más importante del hemisferio para muchas personas?

8. ¿Qué descubrieron los mayas antes que los europeos?

9. ¿Qué muestra la ropa tradicional de los guatemaltecos?

10. ¿Qué indica un *huipil* con su diseño y sus colores?

 **Conexión Internet** Investiga estos temas en **vhlcentral.com**.

1. Busca información sobre Rigoberta Menchú. ¿De dónde es? ¿Qué libros publicó? ¿Por qué es famosa?

2. Estudia un sitio arqueológico de Guatemala para aprender más sobre los mayas y prepara un breve informe para tu clase.

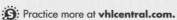 **S: Practice more at vhlcentral.com.**

terremoto *earthquake* Semana Santa *Holy Week* antiguos *ancient* creían *they believed* pájaro *bird* no podía *couldn't* cautiverio *captivity* los billetes *bills* peligro *danger* descubrieron *they discovered* complejo *complex* amor *love* flores *flowers* diseños *designs* vivos *bright* edad *age*

## Las comidas

| | |
|---|---|
| el/la camarero/a | waiter/waitress |
| la comida | food; meal |
| el/la dueño/a | owner; landlord |
| el menú | menu |
| la sección de (no) fumar | (non) smoking section |
| el almuerzo | lunch |
| la cena | dinner |
| el desayuno | breakfast |
| los entremeses | hors d'oeuvres; appetizers |
| el plato (principal) | (main) dish |
| delicioso/a | delicious |
| rico/a | tasty; delicious |
| sabroso/a | tasty; delicious |

## Las frutas

| | |
|---|---|
| la banana | banana |
| las frutas | fruits |
| el limón | lemon |
| la manzana | apple |
| el melocotón | peach |
| la naranja | orange |
| la pera | pear |
| la uva | grape |

## Las verduras

| | |
|---|---|
| las arvejas | peas |
| la cebolla | onion |
| el champiñón | mushroom |
| la ensalada | salad |
| los espárragos | asparagus |
| los frijoles | beans |
| la lechuga | lettuce |
| el maíz | corn |
| las papas/patatas (fritas) | (fried) potatoes; French fries |
| el tomate | tomato |
| las verduras | vegetables |
| la zanahoria | carrot |

## La carne y el pescado

| | |
|---|---|
| el atún | tuna |
| el bistec | steak |
| los camarones | shrimp |
| la carne | meat |
| la carne de res | beef |
| la chuleta (de cerdo) | (pork) chop |
| la hamburguesa | hamburger |
| el jamón | ham |
| la langosta | lobster |
| los mariscos | shellfish |
| el pavo | turkey |
| el pescado | fish |
| el pollo (asado) | (roast) chicken |
| la salchicha | sausage |
| el salmón | salmon |

## Otras comidas

| | |
|---|---|
| el aceite | oil |
| el ajo | garlic |
| el arroz | rice |
| el azúcar | sugar |
| los cereales | cereal; grains |
| el huevo | egg |
| la mantequilla | butter |
| la margarina | margarine |
| la mayonesa | mayonnaise |
| el pan (tostado) | (toasted) bread |
| la pimienta | black pepper |
| el queso | cheese |
| la sal | salt |
| el sándwich | sandwich |
| la sopa | soup |
| el vinagre | vinegar |
| el yogur | yogurt |

## Las bebidas

| | |
|---|---|
| el agua (mineral) | (mineral) water |
| la bebida | drink |
| el café | coffee |
| la cerveza | beer |
| el jugo (de fruta) | (fruit) juice |
| la leche | milk |
| el refresco | soft drink; soda |
| el té (helado) | (iced) tea |
| el vino (blanco/tinto) | (white/red) wine |

**Audio: Vocabulary Flashcards**

## Verbos

| | |
|---|---|
| escoger | to choose |
| merendar (e:ie) | to snack |
| morir (o:ue) | to die |
| pedir (e:i) | to order (food) |
| probar (o:ue) | to taste; to try |
| recomendar (e:ie) | to recommend |
| saber | to taste; to know |
| saber a | to taste like |
| servir (e:i) | to serve |

## Las comparaciones

| | |
|---|---|
| como | like; as |
| más de (+ number) | more than |
| más... que | more... than |
| menos de (+ number) | fewer than |
| menos... que | less... than |
| tan... como | as... as |
| tantos/as... como | as many... as |
| tanto... como | as much... as |
| el/la mayor | the eldest |
| el/la mejor | the best |
| el/la menor | the youngest |
| el/la peor | the worst |
| mejor | better |
| peor | worse |

| | |
|---|---|
| Expresiones útiles | See page 269. |

# Las fiestas

**9**

**Communicative Goals**

*I will be able to:*
- Express congratulations
- Express gratitude
- Ask for and pay the bill at a restaurant

**VOICE BOARD**

**A PRIMERA VISTA**
- ¿Se conocen ellos?
- ¿Cómo se sienten, alegres o tristes?
- ¿Está el hombre más contento que la mujer?
- ¿De qué color es su ropa?

# Las fiestas

  **Audio: Vocabulary Tutorials, Games**

## Más vocabulario

| | |
|---|---|
| la alegría | happiness |
| la amistad | friendship |
| el amor | love |
| el beso | kiss |
| la sorpresa | surprise |
| el aniversario (de bodas) | (wedding) anniversary |
| la boda | wedding |
| el cumpleaños | birthday |
| el día de fiesta | holiday |
| el divorcio | divorce |
| el matrimonio | marriage |
| la Navidad | Christmas |
| la quinceañera | young woman celebrating her fifteenth birthday |
| el/la recién casado/a | newlywed |
| cambiar (de) | to change |
| celebrar | to celebrate |
| divertirse (e:ie) | to have fun |
| graduarse (de/en) | to graduate (from/in) |
| invitar | to invite |
| jubilarse | to retire (from work) |
| nacer | to be born |
| odiar | to hate |
| pasarlo bien/mal | to have a good/bad time |
| reírse (e:i) | to laugh |
| relajarse | to relax |
| sonreír (e:i) | to smile |
| sorprender | to surprise |
| juntos/as | together |

## Variación léxica

pastel ⟷ torta (*Arg., Col., Venez.*)

comprometerse ⟷ prometerse (*Esp.*)

la pareja

el pastel de chocolate

la botella de vino

el flan de caramelo

las galletas

los postres

el champán

los dulces

FELIZ CUMPLEAÑOS

brindar

el invitado

regalar

**Relaciones personales**

| | |
|---|---|
| **casarse (con)** | *to get married (to)* |
| **comprometerse (con)** | *to get engaged (to)* |
| **divorciarse (de)** | *to get divorced (from)* |
| **enamorarse (de)** | *to fall in love (with)* |
| **llevarse bien/mal (con)** | *to get along well/ badly (with)* |
| **romper (con)** | *to break up (with)* |
| **salir (con)** | *to go out (with); to date* |
| **separarse (de)** | *to separate (from)* |
| **tener una cita** | *to have a date; to have an appointment* |

el helado

# Práctica

**1  Escuchar** 🎧 Escucha la conversación e indica si las oraciones son **ciertas** o **falsas**.

1. A Silvia no le gusta mucho el chocolate. F
2. Silvia sabe que sus amigos le van a hacer una fiesta.
3. Los amigos de Silvia le compraron un pastel de chocolate. T
4. Los amigos brindan por Silvia con refrescos.
5. Silvia y sus amigos van a comer helado. T
6. Los amigos de Silvia le van a servir flan y galletas.

**2  Ordenar** 🎧 Escucha la narración y ordena las oraciones de acuerdo con los eventos de la vida de Beatriz.

_____ a. Beatriz se compromete con Roberto.

_____ b. Beatriz se gradúa.

_____ c. Beatriz sale con Emilio.

_____ d. Sus padres le hacen una gran fiesta.

_____ e. La pareja se casa.

_____ f. Beatriz nace en Montevideo.

**3  Emparejar** Indica la letra de la frase que mejor completa cada oración.

| | | |
|---|---|---|
| a. **cambió de** | d. **nos divertimos** | g. **se llevan bien** |
| b. **lo pasaron mal** | e. **se casaron** | h. **sonrió** |
| c. **nació** | f. **se jubiló** | i. **tenemos una cita** |

1. María y sus compañeras de clase _____. Son buenas amigas.
2. Pablo y yo _____ en la fiesta. Bailamos y comimos mucho.
3. Manuel y Felipe _____ en el cine. La película fue muy mala.
4. ¡Tengo una nueva sobrina! Ella _____ ayer por la mañana.
5. Mi madre _____ profesión. Ahora es artista.
6. Mi padre _____ el año pasado. Ahora no trabaja.
7. Jorge y yo _____ esta noche. Vamos a ir a un restaurante muy elegante.
8. Jaime y Laura _____ el septiembre pasado. La boda fue maravillosa.

**4  Definiciones** En parejas, definan las palabras y escriban una oración para cada ejemplo.

> **modelo**
>
> **romper (con)** una pareja termina la relación
> Marta rompió con su novio.

1. regalar
2. helado
3. pareja
4. invitado

5. casarse
6. pasarlo bien
7. sorpresa
8. amistad

**Las etapas de la vida de Sergio**

Audio: Vocabulary

el nacimiento      la niñez      la adolescencia

la juventud      la madurez      la vejez

### Más vocabulario

| | |
|---|---|
| la edad | age |
| el estado civil | marital status |
| las etapas de la vida | the stages of life |
| la muerte | death |
| casado/a | married |
| divorciado/a | divorced |
| separado/a | separated |
| soltero/a | single |
| viudo/a | widower/widow |

**5** **Las etapas de la vida** Identifica las etapas de la vida que se describen en estas oraciones.

1. Mi abuela se jubiló y se mudó (*moved*) a Viña del Mar. ◄
2. Mi padre trabaja para una compañía grande en Santiago.
3. ¿Viste a mi nuevo sobrino en el hospital? Es precioso y ¡tan pequeño!
4. Mi abuelo murió este año.
5. Mi hermana celebró su fiesta de quince años. ◄
6. Mi hermana pequeña juega con muñecas (*dolls*).

**NOTA CULTURAL**

**Viña del Mar** es una ciudad en la costa de Chile, situada al oeste de Santiago. Tiene playas hermosas, excelentes hoteles, casinos y buenos restaurantes. El poeta Pablo Neruda pasó muchos años allí.

**¡LENGUA VIVA!**

The term **quinceañera** refers to a girl who is celebrating her 15th birthday. The party is called **la fiesta de quince años**.

**6** **Cambiar** En parejas, imaginen que son dos hermanos/as de diferentes edades. Cada vez que el/la hermano/a menor dice algo, se equivoca. El/La hermano/a mayor lo/la corrige (*corrects him/her*), cambiando las expresiones subrayadas (*underlined*). Túrnense para ser mayor y menor, decir algo equivocado y corregir.

> **modelo**
>
> **Estudiante 1:** La <u>niñez</u> es cuando trabajamos mucho.
> **Estudiante 2:** No, te equivocas (*you're wrong*). La madurez es cuando trabajamos mucho.

◄

1. <u>El nacimiento</u> es el fin de la vida.
2. <u>La juventud</u> es la etapa cuando nos jubilamos.
3. A los sesenta y cinco años, muchas personas <u>comienzan a trabajar.</u>
4. Julián y nuestra prima <u>se divorcian</u> mañana.
5. Mamá <u>odia</u> a su hermana.
6. El abuelo murió, por eso la abuela es <u>separada</u>.
7. Cuando te gradúas de la universidad, estás en la etapa de <u>la adolescencia</u>.
8. Mi tío nunca se casó; es <u>viudo</u>.

**AYUDA**

Other ways to contradict someone:
**No es verdad.**
*It's not true.*

**Creo que no.**
*I don't think so.*

**¡Claro que no!**
*Of course not!*

**¡Qué va!**
*No way!*

**S:** Practice more at **vhlcentral.com.**

# Comunicación

**7**

**Una cena especial** Planea con dos compañeros/as una cena para celebrar la graduación de tu hermano/a mayor de la escuela secundaria. Recuerda incluir la siguiente información.

1. ¿Qué tipo de cena es? ¿Dónde va a ser? ¿Cuándo va a ser?
2. ¿A cuántas personas piensan invitar? ¿A quiénes van a invitar?
3. ¿Van a pedir un menú especial? ¿Qué van a comer?
4. ¿Cuánto dinero piensan gastar? ¿Cómo van a compartir los gastos?
5. ¿Qué van a hacer todos durante la fiesta?
6. Después de la cena, ¿quiénes van a limpiar (*to clean*)?

**recursos**

**v̂ Text**

CPA
p. 130

**8**

**Encuesta** Tu profesor(a) va a darte una hoja. Haz las preguntas de la hoja a dos o tres compañeros/as de clase para saber qué actitudes tienen en sus relaciones personales. Luego comparte los resultados de la encuesta con la clase y comenta tus conclusiones.

| Preguntas | Nombres | Actitudes |
|---|---|---|
| 1. ¿Te importa la amistad? ¿Por qué? | | |
| 2. ¿Es mejor tener un(a) buen(a) amigo/a o muchos/as amigos/as? | | |
| 3. ¿Cuáles son las características que buscas en tus amigos/as? | | |
| 4. ¿A qué edad es posible enamorarse? | | |
| 5. ¿Deben las parejas hacer todo juntos? ¿Deben tener las mismas opiniones? ¿Por qué? | | |

**¡LENGUA VIVA!**

While a **buen(a) amigo/a** is a *good friend*, the term **amigo/a íntimo/a** refers to a *close friend*, or a very good friend, without any romantic overtones.

**9**

**Minidrama** En parejas, consulten la ilustración de la página 302 y luego, usando las palabras de la lista, preparen un minidrama para representar las etapas de la vida de Sergio. Pueden inventar más información sobre su vida.

| | | | |
|---|---|---|---|
| amor | celebrar | enamorarse | romper |
| boda | comprometerse | graduarse | salir |
| cambiar | cumpleaños | jubilarse | separarse |
| casarse | divorciarse | nacer | tener una cita |

# El Día de Muertos

La familia Díaz conmemora el Día de Muertos.

PERSONAJES

 MARISSA    JIMENA    FELIPE    JUAN CARLOS

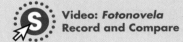 Video: *Fotonovela*
Record and Compare

**1**

**MAITE FUENTES** El Día de Muertos se celebra en México el primero y el segundo de noviembre. Como pueden ver, hay calaveras de azúcar, flores, música y comida por todas partes. Ésta es una fiesta única que todos deben ver por lo menos una vez en la vida.

**2**

**MARISSA** *Holy moley!* ¡Está delicioso!

**TÍA ANA MARÍA** Mi mamá me enseñó a prepararlo. El mole siempre fue el plato favorito de mi papá. Mi hijo Eduardo nació el día de su cumpleaños. Por eso le pusimos su nombre.

**3**

**TÍO RAMÓN** ¿Dónde están mis hermanos?

**JIMENA** Mi papá y Felipe están en el otro cuarto. Esos dos antipáticos no quieren decirnos qué están haciendo. Y la tía Ana María...

**TÍO RAMÓN** ... está en la cocina.

**6**

**TÍA ANA MARÍA** Ramón, ¿cómo estás?

**TÍO RAMÓN** Bien, gracias. ¿Y Mateo? ¿No vino contigo?

**TÍA ANA MARÍA** No. Ya sabes que me casé con un doctor y, pues, trabaja muchísimo.

**7**

**SR. DÍAZ** Familia Díaz, deben prepararse...

**FELIPE** ... ¡para la sorpresa de sus vidas!

**8**

**JUAN CARLOS** Gracias por invitarme.

**SR. DÍAZ** Juan Carlos, como eres nuestro amigo, ya eres parte de la familia.

**SRA. DÍAZ**  **SR. DÍAZ**  **TÍA ANA MARÍA**  **TÍO RAMÓN**  **TÍA NAYELI**  **DON DIEGO**  **MARTA**  **VALENTINA**  **MAITE FUENTES**

**TÍA ANA MARÍA** Marissa, ¿le puedes llevar esa foto que está ahí a Carolina? La necesita para el altar.

**MARISSA** Sí. ¿Son sus padres?

**TÍA ANA MARÍA** Sí, el día de su boda.

**MARISSA** ¿Cómo se conocieron?

**TÍA ANA MARÍA** En la fiesta de un amigo. Fue amor a primera vista.

**MARISSA** (Señala la foto.) La voy a llevar al altar.

(En el cementerio)

**JIMENA** Yo hice las galletas y el pastel. ¿Dónde los puse?

**MARTA** Postres... ¿Cuál prefiero? ¿Galletas? ¿Pastel? ¡Dulces!

**VALENTINA** Me gustan las galletas.

**SR. DÍAZ** Brindamos por ustedes, mamá y papá.

**TÍO RAMÓN** Todas las otras noches estamos separados. Pero esta noche estamos juntos.

**TÍA ANA MARÍA** Con gratitud y amor.

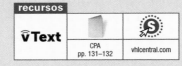

**recursos**

vText

CPA pp. 131–132

vhlcentral.com

## Expresiones útiles

### Discussing family history

**El mole siempre fue el plato favorito de mi papá.**
Mole *was always my dad's favorite dish.*

**Mi hijo Eduardo nació el día de su cumpleaños.**
*My son Eduardo was born on his birthday.*

**Por eso le pusimos su nombre.**
*That's why we named him after him (after my father).*

**¿Cómo se conocieron sus padres?**
*How did your parents meet?*

**En la fiesta de un amigo. Fue amor a primera vista.**
*At a friend's party. It was love at first sight.*

### Talking about a party/ celebration

**Ésta es una fiesta única que todos deben ver por lo menos una vez.**
*This is a unique celebration that everyone should see at least once.*

**Gracias por invitarme.**
*Thanks for inviting me.*

**Brindamos por ustedes.**
*A toast to you.*

### Additional vocabulary

**alma** *soul*
**altar** *altar*
**ángel** *angel*
**calavera de azúcar**
 *skull made out of sugar*
**cementerio** *cemetery*
**cocina** *kitchen*
**disfraz** *costume*

# ¿Qué pasó?

**1**

**Completar** Completa las oraciones con la información correcta, según la **Fotonovela**.

1. El Día de Muertos es una _____ única que todos deben ver.
2. La tía Ana María preparó _____ para celebrar.
3. Marissa lleva la _____ al altar.
4. Jimena hizo las _____ y el _____.
5. Marta no sabe qué _____ prefiere.

**2**

**Identificar** Identifica quién puede decir estas oraciones. Vas a usar un nombre dos veces.

1. Mis padres se conocieron en la fiesta de un amigo.

2. El Día de Muertos se celebra con flores, calaveras de azúcar, música y comida.

3. Gracias por invitarme a celebrar este Día de Muertos.

4. Los de la foto son mis padres el día de su boda.

5. A mí me gustan mucho las galletas.

6. ¡Qué bueno que estás aquí, Juan Carlos! Eres uno más de la familia.

**SR. DÍAZ**      **MAITE FUENTES**

**JUAN CARLOS**      **VALENTINA**

**TÍA ANA MARÍA**

**3**

**Seleccionar** Selecciona algunas de las opciones de la lista para completar las oraciones.

| amor | días de fiesta | pasarlo bien | salieron |
|---|---|---|---|
| el champán | divorciarse | postres | se enamoraron |
| cumpleaños | flan | la quinceañera | una sorpresa |

1. El Sr. Díaz y Felipe prepararon _____ para la familia.
2. Los _____, como el Día de Muertos, se celebran con la familia.
3. Eduardo, el hijo de Ana María, nació el día del _____ de su abuelo.
4. La tía Ana María siente gratitud y _____ hacia (*toward*) sus padres.
5. Los días de fiesta también son para _____ con los amigos.
6. El Día de Muertos se hacen muchos _____.
7. Los padres de la tía Ana María _____ a primera vista.

**4**

**Una cena** Trabajen en grupos para representar una conversación en una cena de Año Nuevo.

- Una persona brinda por el año que está por comenzar y por estar con su familia y amigos.
- Cada persona del grupo habla de cuál es su comida favorita en año nuevo.
- Después de la cena, una persona del grupo dice que es hora de (*it's time to*) comer las uvas.
- Cada persona del grupo dice qué desea para el año que empieza.
- Después, cada persona del grupo debe desear Feliz Año Nuevo a las demás.

 Practice more at **vhlcentral.com**.

# Pronunciación

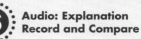

**Audio: Explanation
Record and Compare**

## The letters h, j, and g

| | | | |
|---|---|---|---|
| **helado** | **hombre** | **hola** | **hermosa** |

The Spanish **h** is always silent.

| | | | |
|---|---|---|---|
| **José** | **jubilarse** | **dejar** | **pareja** |

The letter **j** is pronounced much like the English *h* in *his*.

| | | | |
|---|---|---|---|
| **agencia** | **general** | **Gil** | **Gisela** |

The letter **g** can be pronounced three different ways. Before **e** or **i**, the letter **g** is pronounced much like the English *h*.

**Gustavo, gracias por llamar el domingo.**

At the beginning of a phrase or after the letter **n**, the Spanish **g** is pronounced like the English *g* in *girl*.

**Me gradué en agosto.**

In any other position, the Spanish **g** has a somewhat softer sound.

| | | | |
|---|---|---|---|
| **guerra** | **conseguir** | **guantes** | **agua** |

In the combinations **gue** and **gui**, the **g** has a hard sound and the **u** is silent. In the combination **gua**, the **g** has a hard sound and the **u** is pronounced like the English *w*.

**Práctica** Lee las palabras en voz alta, prestando atención a la **h**, la **j** y la **g**.

1. hamburguesa
2. jugar
3. oreja
4. guapa
5. geografía
6. magnífico
7. espejo
8. hago
9. seguir
10. gracias
11. hijo
12. galleta
13. Jorge
14. tengo
15. ahora
16. guantes

**Oraciones** Lee las oraciones en voz alta, prestando atención a la **h**, la **j** y la **g**.

1. Hola. Me llamo Gustavo Hinojosa Lugones y vivo en Santiago de Chile.
2. Tengo una familia grande; somos tres hermanos y tres hermanas.
3. Voy a graduarme en mayo.
4. Para celebrar mi graduación, mis padres van a regalarme un viaje a Egipto.
5. ¡Qué generosos son!

**Refranes** Lee los refranes en voz alta, prestando atención a la **h**, la **j** y la **g**.

A la larga, lo más dulce amarga.[1]

El hábito no hace al monje.[2]

1 *Too much of a good thing.*
2 *The clothes don't make the man.*

**recursos**

v̂Text

CPA
p. 133

CH
p. 133

vhlcentral.com

**Reading,
Additional Reading**

# Semana Santa:
# vacaciones y tradición

**¿Te imaginas pasar veinticuatro horas tocando un tambor°** entre miles de personas? Así es como mucha gente celebra el Viernes Santo° en el pequeño pueblo de **Calanda**, España.

De todas las celebraciones hispanas, la Semana Santa° es una de las más espectaculares y únicas. Semana Santa es la semana antes de Pascua°, una celebración religiosa que conmemora la Pasión de Jesucristo. Generalmente, la gente tiene unos días de vacaciones en esta semana. Algunas personas aprovechan° estos días para viajar, pero otras prefieren participar en las tradicionales celebraciones religiosas en las calles. En **Antigua**, Guatemala, hacen alfombras° de flores° y altares; también organizan Vía Crucis° y danzas. En las famosas procesiones y desfiles° religiosos de **Sevilla**, España, los fieles° sacan a las calles imágenes religiosas. Las imágenes van encima de plataformas ricamente decoradas con abundantes flores y velas°. En la procesión, los penitentes llevan túnicas y unos sombreros cónicos que les cubren° la cara°. En sus manos llevan faroles° o velas encendidas.

**Procesión en Sevilla, España**

**Alfombra de flores en Antigua, Guatemala**

Si visitas algún país hispano durante la Semana Santa, debes asistir a un desfile. Las playas pueden esperar hasta la semana siguiente.

---

### Otras celebraciones famosas

**Ayacucho, Perú:** Además de alfombras de flores y procesiones, aquí hay una antigua tradición llamada "quema de la chamiza"°.

**Iztapalapa, Ciudad de México:** Es famoso el Vía Crucis del cerro° de la Estrella. Es una representación del recorrido° de Jesucristo con la cruz°

**Popayán, Colombia:** En las procesiones "chiquitas" los niños llevan imágenes que son copias pequeñas de las que llevan los mayores.

---

tocando un tambor *playing a drum* Viernes Santo *Good Friday* Semana Santa *Holy Week* Pascua *Easter Sunday* aprovechan *take advantage of* alfombras *carpets* flores *flowers* Vía Crucis *Stations of the Cross* desfiles *parades* fieles *faithful* velas *candles* cubren *cover* cara *face* faroles *lamps* quema de la chamiza *burning of brushwood* cerro *hill* recorrido *route* cruz *cross*

---

**ACTIVIDADES**

**1**

**¿Cierto o falso?** Indica si lo que dicen las oraciones sobre Semana Santa en países hispanos es **cierto** o **falso**. Corrige las falsas.

1. La Semana Santa se celebra después de Pascua.

2. Las personas tienen días libres durante la Semana Santa.

3. Todas las personas asisten a las celebraciones religiosas.

4. En los países hispanos, las celebraciones se hacen en las calles.

5. En Antigua y en Ayacucho es típico hacer alfombras de flores.

6. En Sevilla, sacan imágenes religiosas a las calles.

7. En Sevilla, las túnicas cubren la cara.

8. En la procesión en Sevilla algunas personas llevan flores en sus manos.

9. El Vía Crucis de Iztapalapa es en el interior de una iglesia.

10. Las procesiones "chiquitas" son famosas en Sevilla, España.

## ASÍ SE DICE

### Fiestas y celebraciones

| | |
|---|---|
| la despedida de soltero/a | *bachelor(ette) party* |
| el día feriado/festivo | el día de fiesta |
| disfrutar | *to enjoy* |
| festejar | celebrar |
| los fuegos artificiales | *fireworks* |
| pasarlo en grande | **divertirse mucho** |
| la vela | *candle* |

## EL MUNDO HISPANO

### Celebraciones latinoamericanas

- **Oruro, Bolivia** Durante el carnaval de Oruro se realiza la famosa Diablada, una antigua danza° que muestra la lucha° entre el Bien y el Mal: ángeles contra° demonios.

- **Panchimalco, El Salvador** La primera semana de mayo, Panchimalco se cubre de flores y de color. También hacen el Desfile de las palmas° y bailan danzas antiguas.

- **Quito, Ecuador** El mes de agosto es el Mes de las Artes. Danza, teatro, música, cine, artesanías° y otros eventos culturales inundan la ciudad.

- **San Pedro Sula, Honduras** En junio se celebra la Feria Juniana. Hay comida típica, bailes, desfiles, conciertos, rodeos, exposiciones ganaderas° y eventos deportivos y culturales.

danza *dance* lucha *fight* contra *versus* palmas palm *leaves* artesanías *handcrafts* exposiciones ganaderas *cattle shows*

## PERFIL

# Festival de Viña del Mar

En 1959 unos estudiantes de **Viña del Mar**, Chile, celebraron una fiesta en una casa de campo conocida como la Quinta Vergara donde hubo° un espectáculo° musical. En 1960 repitieron el evento. Asistió tanta gente que muchos vieron el espectáculo parados° o sentados en el suelo°. Algunos se subieron a los árboles°.

Años después, se convirtió en el **Festival Internacional de la Canción.** Se celebra en febrero, en el mismo lugar donde empezó. ¡Pero ahora nadie necesita subirse a un árbol para verlo! Hay un anfiteatro con capacidad para quince mil personas y el evento se transmite por la televisión.

**Nelly Furtado**

En el festival hay concursos° musicales y conciertos de artistas famosos como Calle 13 y Nelly Furtado.

hubo *there was* espectáculo *show* parados *standing* suelo *floor* se subieron a los árboles *climbed trees* concursos *competitions*

 **Conexión Internet**

| | |
|---|---|
| ¿Qué celebraciones hispanas hay en los Estados Unidos y Canadá? | Go to **vhlcentral.com** to find more cultural information related to this **Cultura** section. |

## ACTIVIDADES

**2** **Comprensión** Responde a las preguntas.

1. ¿Cuántas personas por día pueden asistir al Festival de Viña del Mar?
2. ¿Qué es la Diablada?
3. ¿Qué celebran en Quito en agosto?
4. Nombra dos atracciones en la Feria Juniana de San Pedro Sula.
5. ¿Qué es la Quinta Vergara?

**3** **¿Cuál es tu celebración favorita?** Escribe un pequeño párrafo sobre la celebración que más te gusta de tu comunidad. Explica cómo se llama, cuándo ocurre y cómo es.

 Practice more at **vhlcentral.com**.

**Explanation Tutorial**

## 9.1 Irregular preterites

**ANTE TODO** You already know that the verbs **ir** and **ser** are irregular in the preterite. You will now learn other verbs whose preterite forms are also irregular.

### Preterite of **tener**, **venir**, and **decir**

|  |  | tener (u-stem) | venir (i-stem) | decir (j-stem) |
|---|---|---|---|---|
| **SINGULAR FORMS** | yo | tuve | vine | dije |
|  | tú | tuviste | viniste | dijiste |
|  | Ud./él/ella | tuvo | vino | dijo |
| **PLURAL FORMS** | nosotros/as | tuvimos | vinimos | dijimos |
|  | vosotros/as | tuvisteis | vinisteis | dijisteis |
|  | Uds./ellos/ellas | tuvieron | vinieron | dijeron |

▶ **¡Atención!** The endings of these verbs are the regular preterite endings of **-er/-ir** verbs, except for the **yo** and **usted/él/ella** forms. Note that these two endings are unaccented.

▶ These verbs observe similar stem changes to **tener, venir,** and **decir.**

| INFINITIVE | U-STEM | PRETERITE FORMS |
|---|---|---|
| poder | pud- | pude, pudiste, pudo, pudimos, pudisteis, pudieron |
| poner | pus- | puse, pusiste, puso, pusimos, pusisteis, pusieron |
| saber | sup- | supe, supiste, supo, supimos, supisteis, supieron |
| estar | estuv- | estuve, estuviste, estuvo, estuvimos, estuvisteis, estuvieron |

| INFINITIVE | I-STEM | PRETERITE FORMS |
|---|---|---|
| querer | quis- | quise, quisiste, quiso, quisimos, quisisteis, quisieron |
| hacer | hic- | hice, hiciste, hizo, hicimos, hicisteis, hicieron |

| INFINITIVE | J-STEM | PRETERITE FORMS |
|---|---|---|
| traer | traj- | traje, trajiste, trajo, trajimos, trajisteis, trajeron |
| conducir | conduj- | conduje, condujiste, condujo, condujimos, condujisteis, condujeron |
| traducir | traduj- | traduje, tradujiste, tradujo, tradujimos, tradujisteis, tradujeron |

▶ **¡Atención!** Most verbs that end in **–cir** are **j**-stem verbs in the preterite. For example, **producir** → **produje, produjiste,** etc.

> **Produjimos** un documental sobre los accidentes en la casa.
> *We produced a documentary about accidents in the home.*

▶ Notice that the preterites with **j**-stems omit the letter **i** in the **ustedes/ellos/ellas** form.

> Mis amigos **trajeron** comida a la fiesta.      Ellos **dijeron** la verdad.
> *My friends brought food to the party.*      *They told the truth.*

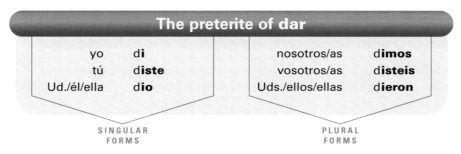

## The preterite of dar

| | | | | |
|---|---|---|---|---|
| yo | **di** | | nosotros/as | **dimos** |
| tú | **diste** | | vosotros/as | **disteis** |
| Ud./él/ella | **dio** | | Uds./ellos/ellas | **dieron** |

SINGULAR FORMS       PLURAL FORMS

▶ The endings for **dar** are the same as the regular preterite endings for **-er** and **-ir** verbs, except that there are no accent marks.

La camarera me **dio** el menú.
*The waitress gave me the menu.*

Le **di** a Juan algunos consejos.
*I gave Juan some advice.*

Los invitados le **dieron** un regalo.
*The guests gave him/her a gift.*

Nosotros **dimos** una gran fiesta.
*We gave a great party.*

▶ The preterite of **hay** (*inf.* **haber**) is **hubo** (*there was; there were*).

Marissa le dio la foto a la Sra. Díaz.

Hubo una celebración en casa de los Díaz.

---

**¡INTÉNTALO!** Escribe la forma correcta del pretérito de cada verbo que está entre paréntesis.

1. (querer) tú _quisiste_
2. (decir) usted _____
3. (hacer) nosotras _____
4. (traer) yo _____
5. (conducir) ellas _____
6. (estar) ella _____
7. (tener) tú _____
8. (dar) ella y yo _____
9. (traducir) yo _____
10. (haber) ayer _____
11. (saber) usted _____
12. (poner) ellos _____

13. (venir) yo _____
14. (poder) tú _____
15. (querer) ustedes _____
16. (estar) nosotros _____
17. (decir) tú _____
18. (saber) ellos _____
19. (hacer) él _____
20. (poner) yo _____
21. (traer) nosotras _____
22. (tener) yo _____
23. (dar) tú _____
24. (poder) ustedes _____

# Práctica

**1**

**Completar** Completa estas oraciones con el pretérito de los verbos entre paréntesis.

1. El sábado _____ (haber) una fiesta sorpresa para Elsa en mi casa.
2. Sofía _____ (hacer) un pastel para la fiesta y Miguel _____ (traer) un flan. ◄
3. Los amigos y parientes de Elsa _____ (venir) y _____ (traer) regalos.
4. El hermano de Elsa no _____ (venir) porque _____ (tener) que trabajar.
5. Su tía María Dolores tampoco _____ (poder) venir.
6. Cuando Elsa abrió la puerta, todos gritaron: "¡Feliz cumpleaños!" y su esposo le _____ (dar) un beso.
7. Elsa no _____ (saber) cómo reaccionar (*to react*). _____ (Estar) un poco nerviosa al principio, pero pronto sus amigos _____ (poner) música y ella _____ (poder) relajarse bailando con su esposo.
8. Al final de la noche, todos _____ (decir) que se divirtieron mucho.

**NOTA CULTURAL**

El **flan** es un postre muy popular en los países de habla hispana. Se prepara con huevos, leche y azúcar y se sirve con salsa de caramelo. Existen variedades deliciosas como el flan de chocolate o el flan de coco.

**2**

**Describir** En parejas, usen verbos de la lista para describir lo que estas personas hicieron. Deben dar por lo menos dos oraciones por cada dibujo.

| | | | |
|---|---|---|---|
| dar | estar | poner | traer |
| decir | hacer | tener | venir |

1. el señor López

2. Norma

3. anoche nosotros

4. Roberto y Elena

 Practice more at **vhlcentral.com**.

# Comunicación

**3**   **Preguntas** En parejas, túrnense para hacerse y responder a estas preguntas.

1. ¿Fuiste a una fiesta de cumpleaños el año pasado? ¿De quién?
2. ¿Quiénes fueron a la fiesta?
3. ¿Quién condujo el auto?
4. ¿Cómo estuvo el ambiente de la fiesta?
5. ¿Quién llevó regalos, bebidas o comida? ¿Llevaste algo especial?
6. ¿Hubo comida? ¿Quién la hizo?
7. ¿Qué regalo hiciste tú? ¿Qué otros regalos trajeron los invitados?
8. ¿Cuántos invitados hubo en la fiesta?
9. ¿Qué tipo de música hubo?
10. ¿Qué te dijeron algunos invitados de la fiesta?

**4**   **Encuesta** Tu profesor(a) va a darte una hoja de actividades. Para cada una de las actividades de la lista, encuentra a alguien que hizo esa actividad en el tiempo indicado.

> **modelo**
>
> traer dulces a clase
> **Estudiante 1:** ¿Trajiste dulces a clase?
> **Estudiante 2:** Sí, traje galletas y helado a la fiesta del fin del semestre.

| Actividades | Nombres |
|---|---|
| 1. ponerse un disfraz (*costume*) de Halloween | |
| 2. traer dulces a clase | |
| 3. llegar a la escuela en auto | |
| 4. estar en la biblioteca ayer | |
| 5. dar un regalo a alguien ayer | |
| 6. poder levantarse temprano esta mañana | |
| 7. hacer un viaje a un país hispano en el verano | |
| 8. ver una película anoche | |
| 9. ir a una fiesta el fin de semana pasado | |
| 10. tener que estudiar el sábado pasado | |

# Síntesis

**5**   **Conversación** En parejas, preparen una conversación en la que uno/a de ustedes va a visitar a su hermano/a para explicarle por qué no fue a su fiesta de graduación y para saber cómo estuvo la fiesta. Incluyan esta información en la conversación:

- cuál fue el menú
- quiénes vinieron a la fiesta y quiénes no pudieron venir
- quiénes prepararon la comida o trajeron algo
- si él/ella tuvo que preparar algo
- lo que la gente hizo antes y después de comer
- cómo lo pasaron, bien o mal

**Explanation Tutorial**

## 9.2 Verbs that change meaning in the preterite

**ANTE TODO** The verbs **conocer, saber, poder,** and **querer** change meanings when used in the preterite. Because of this, each of them corresponds to more than one verb in English, depending on its tense.

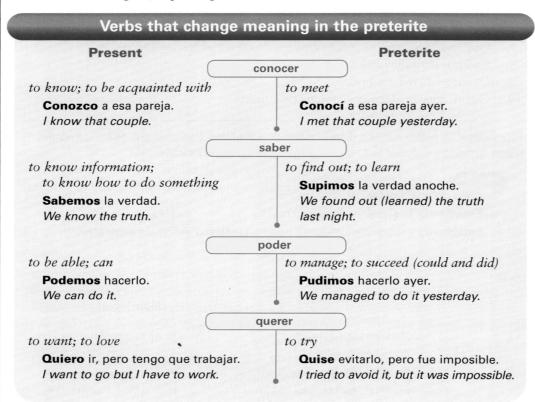

**Verbs that change meaning in the preterite**

| Present | Preterite |
|---|---|
| **conocer** | |
| to know; to be acquainted with | to meet |
| **Conozco** a esa pareja. | **Conocí** a esa pareja ayer. |
| *I know that couple.* | *I met that couple yesterday.* |
| **saber** | |
| to know information; to know how to do something | to find out; to learn |
| **Sabemos** la verdad. | **Supimos** la verdad anoche. |
| *We know the truth.* | *We found out (learned) the truth last night.* |
| **poder** | |
| to be able; can | to manage; to succeed (could and did) |
| **Podemos** hacerlo. | **Pudimos** hacerlo ayer. |
| *We can do it.* | *We managed to do it yesterday.* |
| **querer** | |
| to want; to love | to try |
| **Quiero** ir, pero tengo que trabajar. | **Quise** evitarlo, pero fue imposible. |
| *I want to go but I have to work.* | *I tried to avoid it, but it was impossible.* |

**¡ATENCIÓN!**

In the preterite, the verbs **poder** and **querer** have different meanings when they are used in affirmative or negative sentences.

**pude** *I succeeded*
**no pude** *I failed (to)*
**quise** *I tried (to)*
**no quise** *I refused (to)*

**¡INTÉNTALO!** Elige la respuesta más lógica.

1. Yo no hice lo que me pidieron mis padres. ¡Tengo mis principios!
   a. No quise hacerlo.  *(circled)*    b. No supe hacerlo.

2. Hablamos por primera vez con Nuria y Ana en la boda.
   a. Las conocimos en la boda.  *(circled)*    b. Les dijimos en la boda.

3. Por fin hablé con mi hermano después de llamarlo siete veces.
   a. No quise hablar con él.    b. Pude hablar con él.  *(circled)*

4. Josefina se acostó para relajarse. Se durmió inmediatamente.
   a. Pudo relajarse.  *(circled)*    b. No pudo relajarse.

5. Después de mucho buscar, encontraste la definición en el diccionario.
   a. No supiste la respuesta.    b. Supiste la respuesta.  *(circled)*

6. Las chicas fueron a la fiesta. Cantaron y bailaron mucho.
   a. Ellas pudieron divertirse.  *(circled)*    b. Ellas no supieron divertirse.

**recursos**

**v̂ Text**

CPA
pp. 138–139

CH
pp. 139–140

vhlcentral.com

# Práctica y Comunicación

**1**

**Carlos y Eva** Forma oraciones con los siguientes elementos. Usa el pretérito y haz todos los cambios necesarios. Al final, inventa la razón del divorcio de Carlos y Eva.

1. anoche / mi esposa y yo / saber / que / Carlos y Eva / divorciarse

▶ 2. los / conocer / viaje / isla de Pascua

3. no / poder / hablar / mucho / con / ellos / ese día

4. pero / ellos / ser / simpático / y / nosotros / hacer planes / vernos / con más / frecuencia

5. yo / poder / encontrar / su / número / teléfono / páginas / amarillo

6. (yo) querer / llamar / los / ese día / pero / no / tener / tiempo

7. cuando / los / llamar / nosotros / poder / hablar / Eva

8. nosotros / saber / razón / divorcio / después / hablar / ella

9. _____

**NOTA CULTURAL**

**La isla de Pascua** es un remoto territorio chileno situado en el océano Pacífico Sur. Sus inmensas estatuas son uno de los mayores misterios del mundo: nadie sabe cómo o por qué se crearon. Para más información, véase **Panorama**, p. 329.

**2**

**Completar** Completa estas frases de una manera lógica.

1. Ayer mi compañero/a de clase supo…
2. Esta mañana no pude…
3. Conocí a mi mejor amigo/a en…
4. Mis padres no quisieron…
5. Mi mejor amigo/a no pudo…
6. Mi novio/a y yo nos conocimos en…
7. La semana pasada supe…
8. Ayer mis amigos quisieron…

**3**

**Telenovela** En parejas, escriban el diálogo para una escena de una telenovela (*soap opera*). La escena trata de una situación amorosa entre tres personas: Mirta, Daniel y Raúl. Usen el pretérito de **conocer, poder, querer** y **saber** en su diálogo.

INTRIGA · SUSPENSO          AVENTURA · VENGANZA

LA MUJER DOBLE

 Practice more at **vhlcentral.com**.

# Síntesis

**4**

**Conversación** En una hoja de papel, escribe dos listas: las cosas que hiciste durante el fin de semana y las cosas que quisiste hacer, pero no pudiste. Luego, compara tu lista con la de un(a) compañero/a, y expliquen ambos por qué no pudieron hacer esas cosas.

**9.3** | # ¿Qué? and ¿cuál?

 **Explanation Tutorial**

 **ANTE TODO**   You've already learned how to use interrogative words and phrases. As you know, **¿qué?** and **¿cuál?** or **¿cuáles?** mean *what?* or *which?* However, they are not interchangeable.

▶ **¿Qué?** is used to ask for a definition or an explanation.

¿**Qué** es el flan?
*What is flan?*

¿**Qué** estudias?
*What do you study?*

▶ **¿Cuál(es)?** is used when there is more than one possibility to choose from.

¿**Cuál** de los dos prefieres,
  las galletas o el helado?
*Which of these (two) do you prefer,*
  *cookies or ice cream?*

¿**Cuáles** son tus medias,
  las negras o las blancas?
*Which ones are your socks,*
  *the black ones or the white ones?*

▶ **¿Cuál?** cannot be used before a noun; in this case, **¿qué?** is used.

¿**Qué** sorpresa te dieron tus amigos?
*What surprise did your friends give you?*

¿**Qué** colores te gustan?
*What colors do you like?*

▶ **¿Qué?** used before a noun has the same meaning as **¿cuál?**

¿**Qué regalo** te gusta?
*What (Which) gift do you like?*

¿**Qué dulces** quieren ustedes?
*What (Which) sweets do you want?*

### Review of interrogative words and phrases

| | | | |
|---|---|---|---|
| **¿a qué hora?** | at what time? | **¿cuántos/as?** | how many? |
| **¿adónde?** | (to) where? | **¿de dónde?** | from where? |
| **¿cómo?** | how? | **¿dónde?** | where? |
| **¿cuál(es)?** | what?; which? | **¿por qué?** | why? |
| **¿cuándo?** | when? | **¿qué?** | what?; which? |
| **¿cuánto/a?** | how much? | **¿quién(es)?** | who? |

 **¡INTÉNTALO!**   Completa las preguntas con **¿qué?** o **¿cuál(es)?**, según el contexto.

1. ¿ _____Cuál_____ de los dos te gusta más?
2. ¿ _____ es tu teléfono?
3. ¿ _____ tipo de pastel pediste?
4. ¿ _____ es una galleta?
5. ¿ _____ haces ahora?
6. ¿ _____ son tus platos favoritos?
7. ¿ _____ bebidas te gustan más?
8. ¿ _____ es esto?
9. ¿ _____ es el mejor?
10. ¿ _____ es tu opinión?
11. ¿ _____ fiestas celebras tú?
12. ¿ _____ regalo prefieres?
13. ¿ _____ es tu helado favorito?
14. ¿ _____ pones en la mesa?
15. ¿ _____ restaurante prefieres?
16. ¿ _____ estudiantes estudian más?
17. ¿ _____ quieres comer esta noche?
18. ¿ _____ es la sorpresa mañana?
19. ¿ _____ postre prefieres?
20. ¿ _____ opinas?

**recursos**

**vText**

CPA
pp. 140–141

CH
pp. 141–142

vhlcentral.com

# Práctica y Comunicación

**1**

**Completar** Tu clase de español va a crear un sitio web. Completa estas preguntas con palabras interrogativas. Luego, con un(a) compañero/a, hagan y contesten las preguntas para obtener la información para el sitio web.

1. ¿_____ es la fecha de tu cumpleaños?
2. ¿_____ naciste?
3. ¿_____ es tu estado civil?
4. ¿_____ te relajas?
5. ¿_____ es tu mejor amigo/a?
6. ¿_____ cosas te hacen reír?
7. ¿_____ postres te gustan? ¿_____ te gusta más?
8. ¿_____ problemas tuviste el primer día en esta escuela?

**2**

**Una invitación** En parejas, lean esta invitación. Luego, túrnense para hacer y contestar preguntas con **qué** y **cuál** basadas en la información de la invitación.

> **modelo**
>
> **Estudiante 1:** ¿Cuál es el nombre del padre de la novia?
> **Estudiante 2:** Su nombre es Fernando Sandoval Valera.

> *Fernando Sandoval Valera*   *Lorenzo Vásquez Amaral*
> *Isabel Arzipe de Sandoval*   *Elena Soto de Vásquez*
>
> *tienen el agrado de invitarlos*
> *a la boda de sus hijos*
>
> *María Luisa y José Antonio*
>
> *La ceremonia religiosa tendrá lugar*
> *el sábado 10 de junio a las dos de la tarde*
> *en el Templo de Santo Domingo*
> *(Calle Santo Domingo, 961).*
>
> *Después de la ceremonia, sírvanse pasar a la recepción en el salón*
> *de baile del Hotel Metrópoli (Sotero del Río, 465).*

**recursos**

**vText**

CPA
pp. 142–143

**3**

**Quinceañera** Trabaja con un(a) compañero/a. Uno/a de ustedes es el/la director(a) del salón de fiestas "Renacimiento". La otra persona es el padre/la madre de Sandra, quien quiere hacer la fiesta de quince años de su hija gastando menos de $25 por invitado. Su profesor(a) va a darles la información necesaria para confirmar la reservación.

> **modelo**
>
> **Estudiante 1:** ¿Cuánto cuestan los entremeses?
> **Estudiante 2:** Depende. Puede escoger champiñones por 50 centavos o
>                   camarones por dos dólares.
> **Estudiante 1:** ¡Uf! A mi hija le gustan los camarones, pero son muy caros.
> **Estudiante 2:** Bueno, también puede escoger quesos por un dólar por invitado.

 Practice more at **vhlcentral.com**.

Explanation Tutorial

 **Pronouns after prepositions**

**ANTE TODO**   In Spanish, as in English, the object of a preposition is the noun or pronoun that follows the preposition. Observe the following diagram.

| PREPOSITION | NOUN | PREPOSITION | PRONOUN |
|:---:|:---:|:---:|:---:|
| La sopa es para | Alicia | y para | él. |

### Prepositional pronouns

| | Singular | | | Plural | |
|:---:|:---:|:---|:---:|:---:|:---|
| | **mí** | me | | **nosotros/as** | us |
| | **ti** | you (fam.) | | **vosotros/as** | you (fam.) |
| preposition + | **Ud.** | you (form.) | | **Uds.** | you (form.) |
| | **él** | him | | **ellos** | them (m.) |
| | **ella** | her | | **ellas** | them (f.) |

▶ Note that, except for **mí** and **ti,** these pronouns are the same as the subject pronouns. **¡Atención! Mí** (*me*) has an accent mark to distinguish it from the possessive adjective **mi** (*my*).

▶ The preposition **con** combines with **mí** and **ti** to form **conmigo** and **contigo,** respectively.

—¿Quieres venir **conmigo** a Concepción?     —Sí, gracias, me gustaría ir **contigo.**
*Do you want to come with me to Concepción?*     *Yes, thanks, I would like to go with you.*

▶ The preposition **entre** is followed by **tú** and **yo** instead of **ti** and **mí.**

Papá va a sentarse **entre tú y yo**.
*Dad is going to sit between you and me.*

**¡INTÉNTALO!**   Completa estas oraciones con las preposiciones y los pronombres apropiados.

1. *(with him)* No quiero ir ___con él___.
2. *(for her)* Las galletas son _____.
3. *(for me)* Los mariscos son _____.
4. *(with you, pl. form.)* Preferimos estar _____.
5. *(with you, sing. fam.)* Me gusta salir _____.
6. *(with me)* ¿Por qué no quieres tener una cita _____?
7. *(for her)* La cuenta es _____.
8. *(for them, m.)* La habitación es muy pequeña _____.
9. *(with them, f.)* Anoche celebré la Navidad _____.
10. *(for you, sing. fam.)* Este beso es _____.
11. *(with you, sing. fam.)* Nunca me aburro _____.
12. *(with you, pl. form.)* ¡Qué bien que vamos _____!
13. *(for you, sing. fam.)* _____ la vida es muy fácil.
14. *(for them, f.)* _____ no hay sorpresas.

**recursos**

**v̂Text**

CPA
pp. 144–146

CH
p. 143

vhlcentral.com

# Práctica y Comunicación

**1**

**Completar** David sale con sus amigos a comer. Para saber quién come qué, lee el mensaje electrónico que David le envió (*sent*) a Cecilia dos días después y completa el diálogo en el restaurante con los pronombres apropiados.

> **modelo**
>
> **Camarero:** Los camarones en salsa verde, ¿para quién son?
> **David:** Son para ___ella___.

**NOTA CULTURAL**

Las **machas a la parmesana** son un plato muy típico de Chile. Se prepara con machas, un tipo de almeja (*clam*) que se encuentra en Suramérica. Las machas a la parmesana se hacen con queso parmesano, limón, sal, pimienta y mantequilla, y luego se ponen en el horno (*oven*).

| Para: Cecilia | Asunto: El menú |
| --- | --- |

Hola, Cecilia:

¿Recuerdas la comida del viernes? Quiero repetir el menú en mi casa el miércoles. Ahora voy a escribir lo que comimos, luego me dices si falta algún plato. Yo pedí el filete de pescado y Maribel camarones en salsa verde. Tatiana pidió un plato grandísimo de machas a la parmesana. Diana y Silvia pidieron langostas, ¿te acuerdas? Y tú, ¿qué pediste? Ah, sí, un bistec grande con papas. Héctor también pidió un bistec, pero más pequeño. Miguel pidió pollo y agua mineral para todos. Y la profesora comió ensalada verde porque está a dieta. ¿Falta algo? Espero tu mensaje. Hasta pronto. David.

| | |
| --- | --- |
| **CAMARERO** | El filete de pescado, ¿para quién es? |
| **DAVID** | Es para (1)_____. |
| **CAMARERO** | Aquí está. ¿Y las machas a la parmesana y las langostas? |
| **DAVID** | Las machas son para (2)_____. |
| **SILVIA Y DIANA** | Las langostas son para (3)_____. |
| **CAMARERO** | Tengo un bistec grande… |
| **DAVID** | Cecilia, es para (4)_____, ¿no es cierto? Y el bistec más pequeño es para (5)_____. |
| **CAMARERO** | ¿Y la botella de agua mineral? |
| **MIGUEL** | Es para todos (6)_____, y el pollo es para (7)_____. |
| **CAMARERO** | (*a la profesora*) Entonces la ensalada verde es para (8)_____. |

**recursos**

**vText**

**CPA**
pp. 147–148

**2**

**Compartir** Tu profesor(a) va a darte una hoja de actividades en la que hay un dibujo. En parejas, hagan preguntas para saber dónde está cada una de las personas en el dibujo. Ustedes tienen dos versiones diferentes de la ilustración. Al final deben saber dónde está cada persona.

> **modelo**
>
> **Estudiante 1:** ¿Quién está al lado de Óscar?
> **Estudiante 2:** Alfredo está al lado de él.

**AYUDA**

Here are some other useful prepositions: **al lado de, debajo de, a la derecha de, a la izquierda de, cerca de, lejos de, delante de, detrás de, entre.**

| | | | |
| --- | --- | --- | --- |
| Alfredo | Dolores | Graciela | Raúl |
| Sra. Blanco | Enrique | Leonor | Rubén |
| Carlos | Sra. Gómez | Óscar | Yolanda |

 Practice more at **vhlcentral.com**.

# Recapitulación

 **Diagnostics
Remediation Activities**

Completa estas actividades para repasar los conceptos de gramática que aprendiste en esta lección.

**1** **Completar** Completa la tabla con el pretérito de los verbos. **9 pts.**

| Infinitive | yo | ella | nosotros |
|---|---|---|---|
| conducir | | | |
| hacer | | | |
| saber | | | |

**2** **Mi fiesta** Completa este mensaje electrónico con el pretérito de los verbos de la lista. Vas a usar cada verbo sólo una vez. **10 pts.**

| | | |
|---|---|---|
| dar | haber | tener |
| decir | hacer | traer |
| estar | poder | venir |
| | poner | |

Hola, Omar:

Como tú no (1) _____ venir a mi fiesta de cumpleaños, quiero contarte cómo fue. El día de mi cumpleaños, muy temprano por la mañana, mis hermanos me (2) _____ una gran sorpresa: ellos (3) _____ un regalo delante de la puerta de mi habitación: ¡una bicicleta roja preciosa! Mi madre nos preparó un desayuno riquísimo. Después de desayunar, mis hermanos y yo (4) _____ que limpiar toda la casa, así que (*therefore*) no (5) _____ más celebración hasta la tarde. A las seis y media (nosotros) (6) _____ una barbacoa en el patio de la casa. Todos los invitados (7) _____ bebidas y regalos. (8) _____ todos mis amigos, excepto tú, ¡qué pena! :-( La fiesta (9) _____ muy animada hasta las diez de la noche, cuando mis padres (10) _____ que los vecinos (*neighbors*) iban a (*were going to*) protestar y entonces todos se fueron a sus casas.

Tu amigo,
Andrés

**RESUMEN GRAMATICAL**

**9.1** **Irregular preterites**　*pp. 310–311*

| u-stem | estar<br>poder<br>poner<br>saber<br>tener | estuv-<br>pud-<br>pus-<br>sup-<br>tuv- | -e, -iste,<br>-o, -imos,<br>-isteis, -(i)eron |
|---|---|---|---|
| i-stem | hacer<br>querer<br>venir | hic-<br>quis-<br>vin- | |
| j-stem | conducir<br>decir<br>traducir<br>traer | conduj-<br>dij-<br>traduj-<br>traj- | |

► Preterite of **dar**: di, diste, dio, dimos, disteis, dieron

► Preterite of **hay** (*inf.* **haber**): hubo

**9.2** **Verbs that change meaning in the preterite**　*p. 314*

| Present | Preterite |
|---|---|
| **conocer** | |
| *to know;<br>to be acquainted with* | *to meet* |
| **saber** | |
| *to know info.; to know<br>how to do something* | *to find out; to learn* |
| **poder** | |
| *to be able; can* | *to manage; to succeed* |
| **querer** | |
| *to want; to love* | *to try* |

**9.3** **¿Qué? and ¿cuál?**　*p. 316*

► Use **¿qué?** to ask for a definition or an explanation.

► Use **¿cuál(es)?** when there is more than one possibility to choose from.

► **¿Cuál?** cannot be used before a noun; use **¿qué?** instead.

► **¿Qué?** used before a noun has the same meaning as **¿cuál?**

**9.4** **Pronouns after prepositions** *p. 318*

**Prepositional pronouns**

|  | Singular | Plural |
|---|---|---|
| *Preposition +* | mí | nosotros/as |
|  | ti | vosotros/as |
|  | Ud. | Uds. |
|  | él | ellos |
|  | ella | ellas |

▶ Exceptions: **conmigo, contigo, entre tú y yo**

**3**

**¿Presente o pretérito?** Escoge la forma correcta de los verbos entre paréntesis. **6 pts.**

1. Después de muchos intentos (*tries*), (podemos/pudimos) hacer una piñata.
2. —¿Conoces a Pepe?
   —Sí, lo (conozco/conocí) en tu fiesta.
3. Como no es de aquí, Cristina no (sabe/supo) mucho de las celebraciones locales.
4. Yo no (quiero/quise) ir a un restaurante grande, pero tú decides.
5. Ellos (quieren/quisieron) darme una sorpresa, pero Nina me lo dijo todo.
6. Mañana se terminan las vacaciones; por fin (podemos/pudimos) volver a la escuela.

**4**

**Preguntas** Escribe una pregunta para cada respuesta con los elementos dados. Empieza con **qué**, **cuál** o **cuáles** de acuerdo con el contexto y haz los cambios necesarios. **8 pts.**

1. —¿? / pastel / querer  —Quiero el pastel de chocolate.
2. —¿? / ser / flan  —El flan es un postre típico hispano.
3. —¿? / ser / restaurante favorito  —Mis restaurantes favoritos son Dalí y Jaleo.
4. —¿? / ser / dirección electrónica  —Mi dirección electrónica es paco@email.com.

**5**

**¿Dónde me siento?** Completa la conversación con los pronombres apropiados. **7 pts.**

**JUAN** A ver, te voy a decir dónde te vas a sentar. Manuel, ¿ves esa silla? Es para _____. Y esa otra silla es para tu novia, que todavía no está aquí.

**MANUEL** Muy bien, yo la reservo para _____.

**HUGO** ¿Y esta silla es para _____?

**JUAN** No, Hugo. No es para _____. Es para Carmina, que viene con Julio.

**HUGO** No, Carmina y Julio no pueden venir. Hablé con _____ y me avisaron.

**JUAN** Pues ellos se lo pierden (*it's their loss*). ¡Más comida para _____ (*us*)!

**CAMARERO** Aquí tienen el menú. Les doy un minuto y enseguida estoy con _____.

**6**

**Cumpleaños feliz** Escribe cinco oraciones que describan cómo celebraste tu último cumpleaños. Usa el pretérito y los pronombres que aprendiste en esta lección. **10 pts.**

**7**

**Adivinanza** Completa la adivinanza con la palabra que falta y adivina la respuesta.
**¡2 puntos EXTRA!**

**❝ Sólo una vez al año tú celebras ese día, y conmemoras° la fecha en que llegaste a la vida. ¿_____ es? ❞**

(El _____)

 Practice more at **vhlcentral.com.**    conmemoras *commemorate*

# Lectura

**Audio: Synched Reading Additional Reading**

## Antes de leer

### Estrategia
**Recognizing word families**

Recognizing root words can help you guess the meaning of words in context, ensuring better comprehension of a reading selection. Using this strategy will enrich your Spanish vocabulary as you will see below.

#### Examinar el texto

Familiarízate con el texto usando las estrategias de lectura más efectivas para ti. ¿Qué tipo de documento es? ¿De qué tratan° las cuatro secciones del documento? Explica tus respuestas.

#### Raíces°

Completa el siguiente cuadro° para ampliar tu vocabulario. Usa palabras de la lectura de esta lección y vocabulario de las lecciones anteriores. ¿Qué significan las palabras que escribiste en el cuadro?

| Verbo | Sustantivos | Otras formas |
|---|---|---|
| 1. agradecer *to thank, to be grateful for* | *agradecimiento/ gracias* *gratitude/thanks* | *agradecido* *grateful, thankful* |
| 2. estudiar | _____ | _____ |
| 3. _____ | _____ | celebrado |
| 4. _____ | baile | _____ |
| 5. bautizar | _____ | _____ |

¿De qué tratan...? *What are... about?* **Raíces** *Roots* **cuadro** *chart*

# VIDA SOCIAL

## Matrimonio
### Espinoza Álvarez–Reyes Salazar

El día sábado 17 de junio a las 19 horas, se celebró el matrimonio de Silvia Reyes y Carlos Espinoza en la catedral de Santiago. La ceremonia fue oficiada por el pastor Federico Salas y participaron los padres de los novios, el señor Jorge Espinoza y señora, y el señor José Alfredo Reyes y señora. Después de la ceremonia, los padres de los recién casados ofrecieron una fiesta bailable en el restaurante La Misión.

## Bautismo
### José María recibió el bautismo el 26 de junio.

Sus padres, don Roberto Lagos Moreno y doña María Angélica Sánchez, compartieron la alegría de la fiesta con todos sus parientes y amigos. La ceremonia religiosa tuvo lugar° en la catedral de Aguas Blancas. Después de la ceremonia, padres, parientes y amigos celebraron una fiesta en la residencia de la familia Lagos.

## Fiesta de quince años

**32B**

El doctor don Amador Larenas Fernández y la señora Felisa Vera de Larenas celebraron los quince años de su hija Ana Ester junto a sus parientes y amigos. La quinceañera reside en la ciudad de Valparaíso y es estudiante del Colegio Francés. La fiesta de presentación en sociedad de la señorita Ana Ester fue el día viernes 2 de mayo a las 19 horas en el Club Español. Entre los invitados especiales asistieron el alcalde° de la ciudad, don Pedro Castedo, y su esposa. La música estuvo a cargo de la Orquesta Americana. ¡Feliz cumpleaños, le deseamos a la señorita Ana Ester en su fiesta bailable!

## Expresión de gracias
### Carmen Godoy Tapia

Agradecemos° sinceramente a todas las personas que nos acompañaron en el último adiós a nuestra apreciada esposa, madre, abuela y tía, la señora Carmen Godoy Tapia. El funeral tuvo lugar el día 28 de junio en la ciudad de Viña del Mar. La vida de Carmen Godoy fue un ejemplo de trabajo, amistad, alegría y amor para todos nosotros. Su esposo, hijos y familia agradecen de todo corazón° su asistencia° al funeral a todos los parientes y amigos.

tuvo lugar *took place*  alcalde *mayor*  Agradecemos *We thank*
de todo corazón *sincerely*  asistencia *attendance*

# Después de leer

## Corregir
Escribe estos comentarios otra vez para corregir la información errónea.

1. El alcalde y su esposa asistieron a la boda de Silvia y Carlos.

2. Todos los anuncios (*announcements*) describen eventos felices.

3. Felisa Vera de Larenas cumple quince años.

4. Roberto Lagos y María Angélica Sánchez son hermanos.

5. Carmen Godoy Tapia les dio las gracias a las personas que asistieron al funeral.

## Identificar
Escribe los nombres de la(s) persona(s) descrita(s) (*described*).

1. Dejó viudo a su esposo el 28 de junio.

2. Sus padres y todos los invitados brindaron por él, pero él no entendió por qué.

3. El Club Español les presentó una cuenta considerable.

4. Unió a los novios en santo matrimonio.

5. Su fiesta de cumpleaños se celebró en Valparaíso.

## Un anuncio
Trabajen en grupos pequeños para inventar un anuncio breve sobre una celebración importante. Puede ser una graduación, un cumpleaños o una gran fiesta en la que ustedes participan. Incluyan la siguiente información.

1. nombres de los participantes
2. la fecha, la hora y el lugar
3. qué se celebra
4. otros detalles de interés

 Practice more at **vhlcentral.com**.

# Escritura

## Estrategia

### Planning and writing a comparative analysis

Writing any kind of comparative analysis requires careful planning. Venn diagrams are useful for organizing your ideas visually before comparing and contrasting people, places, objects, events, or issues. To create a Venn diagram, draw two circles that overlap one another and label the top of each circle. List the differences between the two elements in the outer rings of the two circles, then list their similarities where the two circles overlap. Review the following example.

**Diferencias y similitudes**

**Boda de Silvia Reyes y Carlos Espinoza**

**Diferencias:**
1. Primero hay una celebración religiosa.
2. Se celebra en un restaurante.

**Similitudes:**
1. Las dos fiestas se celebran por la noche.
2. Las dos fiestas son bailables.

**Fiesta de quince años de Ana Ester Larenas Vera**

**Diferencias:**
1. Se celebra en un club.
2. Vienen invitados especiales.

La lista de palabras y expresiones a la derecha puede ayudarte a escribir este tipo de ensayo (*essay*).

## Tema

### Escribir una composición

Compara una celebración familiar (como una boda, una fiesta de cumpleaños o una graduación) a la que tú asististe recientemente con otro tipo de celebración. Utiliza palabras y expresiones de esta lista.

**Para expresar similitudes**

| | |
|---|---|
| **además; también** | *in addition; also* |
| **al igual que** | *the same as* |
| **como** | *as; like* |
| **de la misma manera** | *in the same manner (way)* |
| **del mismo modo** | *in the same manner (way)* |
| **tan + [*adjetivo*] + como** | *as + [adjective] + as* |
| **tanto/a(s) + [*sustantivo*] + como** | *as many/much + [noun] + as* |

**Para expresar diferencias**

| | |
|---|---|
| **a diferencia de** | *unlike* |
| **a pesar de** | *in spite of* |
| **aunque** | *although* |
| **en cambio** | *on the other hand* |
| **más/menos… que** | *more/less … than* |
| **no obstante** | *nevertheless; however* |
| **por otro lado** | *on the other hand* |
| **por el contrario** | *on the contrary* |
| **sin embargo** | *nevertheless; however* |

# Escuchar

## Estrategia

**Guessing the meaning of words through context**

When you hear an unfamiliar word, you can often guess its meaning by listening to the words and phrases around it.

 To practice this strategy, you will now listen to a paragraph. Jot down the unfamiliar words that you hear. Then listen to the paragraph again and jot down the word or words that give the most useful clues to the meaning of each unfamiliar word.

## Preparación

Lee la invitación. ¿De qué crees que van a hablar Rosa y Josefina?

## Ahora escucha

Ahora escucha la conversación entre Josefina y Rosa. Cuando oigas una de las palabras de la columna A, usa el contexto para identificar el sinónimo o la definición en la columna B.

| A | B |
|---|---|
| ____ festejar | a. conmemoración religiosa de una muerte |
| ____ dicha | |
| ____ bien parecido | b. tolera |
| ____ finge (fingir) | c. suerte |
| ____ soporta (soportar) | d. celebrar |
| ____ yo lo disfruté (disfrutar) | e. me divertí |
| | f. horror |
| | g. crea una ficción |
| | h. guapo |

*Margarita Robles de García*
*y Roberto García Olmos*

*Piden su presencia en la celebración*
*del décimo aniversario de bodas*
*el día 13 de marzo*
*con una misa en la Iglesia Virgen del Coromoto*
*a las 6:30*

*seguida por cena y baile*
*en el restaurante El Campanero,*
*Calle Principal, Las Mercedes*
*a las 8:30*

## Comprensión

### ¿Cierto o falso? ❧⟲

Lee cada oración e indica si lo que dice es **cierto** o **falso**. Corrige las oraciones falsas.

1. No invitaron a mucha gente a la fiesta de Margarita y Roberto porque ellos no conocen a muchas personas.

2. Algunos fueron a la fiesta con pareja y otros fueron sin compañero/a.

3. Margarita y Roberto decidieron celebrar el décimo aniversario porque no hicieron una fiesta el día de su boda.

4. Rafael les parece interesante a Rosa y a Josefina.

5. Josefina se divirtió mucho en la fiesta porque bailó toda la noche con Rafael.

### Preguntas ❧⟲

Responde a estas preguntas con oraciones completas.

1. ¿Son solteras Rosa y Josefina? ¿Cómo lo sabes?

2. ¿Tienen las chicas una amistad de mucho tiempo con la pareja que celebra su aniversario? ¿Cómo lo sabes?

# En pantalla  Video: TV Clip

Desfiles°, música, asados°, fuegos artificiales° y baile son los elementos de una buena fiesta. ¿Celebrar durante toda una semana? ¡Eso sí que es una fiesta espectacular! El 18 de septiembre Chile conmemora su independencia de España y los chilenos demuestran su orgullo° nacional durante una semana llena° de celebraciones. Durante las Fiestas Patrias° casi todas las oficinas° y escuelas se cierran para que la gente se reúna° a festejar. Desfiles y rodeos representan la tradición de los vaqueros° del país, y la gente baila cueca, el baile nacional. Las familias y los amigos se reúnen para preparar y disfrutar platos tradicionales como las empanadas y asados. Otra de las tradiciones de estas fiestas es hacer volar cometas°, llamadas volantines. Mira el video para descubrir cómo se celebran otras fiestas en Chile.

| Vocabulario útil | |
|---|---|
| **conejo** | *bunny* |
| **disfraces** | *costumes* |
| **mariscal** | *traditional Chilean soup with raw seafood* |
| **sustos** | *frights* |
| **vieja (Chi.)** | *mother* |

##  Seleccionar

Selecciona la palabra que no está relacionada con cada grupo.

1. disfraces • noviembre • arbolito • sustos
2. volantines • arbolito • regalos • diciembre
3. conejo • enero • huevitos • chocolates
4. septiembre • volantines • disfraces • asado

## Fiesta

Trabajen en grupos de tres. Imaginen que van a organizar una fiesta para celebrar el 4 de julio. Escriban una invitación electrónica para invitar a sus parientes y amigos a la fiesta. Describan los planes que tienen para la fiesta y díganles a sus amigos qué tiene que traer cada uno.

Desfiles/Paradas *Parades* asados *barbecues* fuegos artificiales *fireworks* orgullo *pride* llena *full* Fiestas Patrias *Independence Day celebrations* oficinas *offices* se reúna *would get together* vaqueros *cowboys* cometas/volantines *kites*

## Fiestas patrias: Chilevisión

**Noviembre: disfraces, dulces...**

**Mayo: besito, tarjeta, tecito con la mamá...**

**Septiembre... Septiembre: familia, parada militar...**

 Practice more at **vhlcentral.com.**

recursos

v̂Text

vhlcentral.com

Video:
*Flash cultura*

El Día de los Reyes Magos* es una celebración muy popular en muchos países hispanos. No sólo es el día en que los reyes les traen regalos a los niños, también es una fiesta llena° de tradiciones. La tarde del 5 de enero, en muchas ciudades como Barcelona, España, se hace un desfile° en que los reyes regalan dulces a los niños y reciben sus cartas con peticiones. Esa noche, antes de irse a dormir, los niños deben dejar° un zapato junto a la ventana y un bocado° para los reyes. En Puerto Rico, por ejemplo, los niños ponen una caja con hierba° bajo su cama para alimentar a los camellos° de los reyes.

### Vocabulario útil

| | |
|---|---|
| los cabezudos | carnival figures with large heads |
| los carteles | posters |
| fiesta de pueblo | popular celebration |
| santos de palo | wooden saints |

### Preparación

¿Se celebra la Navidad en tu país? ¿Qué otras fiestas importantes se celebran? En cada caso, ¿cuántos días dura la fiesta? ¿Cuáles son las tradiciones y actividades típicas? ¿Hay alguna comida típica en esa celebración?

### Elegir

Indica cuál de las dos opciones resume mejor este episodio.

a. Las Navidades puertorriqueñas son las más largas y terminan después de las fiestas de la calle San Sebastián. Esta fiesta de pueblo se celebra con baile, música y distintas expresiones artísticas típicas.

b. En la celebración de las Navidades puertorriqueñas, los cabezudos son una tradición de España y son el elemento más importante de la fiesta. A la gente le gusta bailar y hacer procesiones por la noche.

*According to the Christian tradition, the Three Wise Men were the three kings that traveled to Bethlehem after the birth of Baby Jesus, carrying with them gifts of gold, frankincense, and myrrh to pay him homage.*

llena *full* desfile *parade* dejar *leave* bocado *snack* hierba *grass*
alimentar los camellos *feed the camels*

## Las fiestas

**Los cabezudos son una tradición [...] de España.**

**Hay mucha gente y mucho arte.**

**Es una fiesta de pueblo... una tradición. Vengo todos los años.**

recursos

vText

CPA
pp. 151–152

vhlcentral.com

# Chile

**Interactive Map**
**Video:** *Panorama cultural*

## El país en cifras

▸ **Área:** 756.950 km² (292.259 millas²), *dos veces el área de Montana*

▸ **Población:** 17.926.000 *Aproximadamente el 80 por ciento de la población del país es urbana.*

▸ **Capital:** Santiago de Chile—6.237.000

▸ **Ciudades principales:** Valparaíso— 911.000, Concepción, Viña del Mar, Temuco

SOURCE: Population Division, UN Secretariat

▸ **Moneda:** peso chileno

▸ **Idiomas:** español (oficial), mapuche

Bandera de Chile

### Chilenos célebres

▸ **Bernardo O'Higgins,** militar° y héroe nacional (1778–1842)

▸ **Gabriela Mistral,** Premio Nobel de Literatura, 1945; poeta y diplomática (1889–1957)

▸ **Pablo Neruda,** Premio Nobel de Literatura, 1971; poeta (1904–1973)

▸ **Isabel Allende,** novelista (1942– )

Pablo Neruda

militar *soldier* terremoto *earthquake* heridas *wounded*
hogar *home* desierto *desert* más seco *driest* mundo *world*
han tenido *have had* ha sido usado *has been used* Marte *Mars*

PERÚ

La costa de Viña del Mar

Pampa del Tamarugal

BOLIVIA

Cordillera de los Andes

Edificio antiguo en Santiago

El puerto de Valparaíso

Océano Pacífico

Viña del Mar
Valparaíso

★ Santiago

ARGENTINA

Concepción

Temuco

Torres del Paine

Una celebración en Temuco

Lago Buenos Aires

Océano Atlántico

Punta Arenas

recursos

**v̂Text**

CPA pp. 153–156

vhlcentral.com

Estrecho de Magallanes

Isla Grande de Tierra del Fuego

## ¡Increíble pero cierto!

El desierto° de Atacama, en el norte de Chile, es el más seco° del mundo°. Con más de cien mil km² de superficie, algunas zonas de este desierto nunca han tenido° lluvia. Atacama ha sido usado° como escenario para representar a Marte° en películas y series de televisión.

## Lugares • **La isla de Pascua**

La isla de Pascua° recibió ese nombre porque los exploradores holandeses° llegaron a la isla por primera vez el día de Pascua de 1722. Ahora es parte del territorio de Chile. La isla de Pascua es famosa por los *moái*, estatuas enormes que representan personas con rasgos° muy exagerados. Estas estatuas las construyeron los *rapa nui*, los antiguos habitantes de la zona. Todavía no se sabe mucho sobre los *rapa nui*, ni tampoco se sabe por qué decidieron abandonar la isla.

## Deportes • **Los deportes de invierno**

Hay muchos lugares para practicar deportes de invierno en Chile porque las montañas nevadas de los Andes ocupan gran parte del país. El Parque Nacional Villarrica, por ejemplo, situado al pie de un volcán y junto a° un lago, es un sitio popular para el esquí y el *snowboard*. Para los que prefieren deportes más extremos, el centro de esquí Valle Nevado organiza excursiones para practicar heliesquí.

## Ciencias • **Astronomía**

Los observatorios chilenos, situados en los Andes, son lugares excelentes para las observaciones astronómicas. Científicos° de todo el mundo van a Chile para estudiar las estrellas° y otros cuerpos celestes°. Hoy día Chile está construyendo nuevos observatorios y telescopios para mejorar las imágenes del universo.

## Economía • **El vino**

La producción de vino comenzó en Chile en el siglo° XVI. Ahora la industria del vino constituye una parte importante de la actividad agrícola del país y la exportación de sus productos está aumentando° cada vez más. Los vinos chilenos son muy apreciados internacionalmente por su gran variedad, sus ricos y complejos sabores° y su precio moderado. Los más conocidos son los vinos de Aconcagua y del valle del Maipo.

 **¿Qué aprendiste?** Responde a cada pregunta con una oración completa.

1. ¿Qué porcentaje (*percentage*) de la población chilena es urbana?

2. ¿Qué son los *moái*? ¿Dónde están?

3. ¿Qué deporte extremo ofrece el centro de esquí Valle Nevado?

4. ¿Por qué van a Chile científicos de todo el mundo?

5. ¿Cuándo comenzó la producción de vino en Chile?

6. ¿Por qué son apreciados internacionalmente los vinos chilenos?

 **Conexión Internet** Investiga estos temas en **vhlcentral.com**.

1. Busca información sobre Pablo Neruda e Isabel Allende. ¿Dónde y cuándo nacieron? ¿Cuáles son algunas de sus obras (*works*)? ¿Cuáles son algunos de los temas de sus obras?

2. Busca información sobre sitios donde los chilenos y los turistas practican deportes de invierno en Chile. Selecciona un sitio y descríbeselo a tu clase.

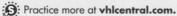 Practice more at **vhlcentral.com**.

La isla de Pascua *Easter Island* holandeses *Dutch* rasgos *features* junto a *beside* Científicos *Scientists* estrellas *stars* cuerpos celestes *celestial bodies* siglo *century* aumentando *increasing* complejos sabores *complex flavors*

## Las celebraciones

| | |
|---|---|
| el aniversario (de bodas) | *(wedding) anniversary* |
| la boda | *wedding* |
| el cumpleaños | *birthday* |
| el día de fiesta | *holiday* |
| la fiesta | *party* |
| el/la invitado/a | *guest* |
| la Navidad | *Christmas* |
| la quinceañera | *young woman celebrating her fifteenth birthday* |
| la sorpresa | *surprise* |
| brindar | *to toast* (drink) |
| celebrar | *to celebrate* |
| divertirse (e:ie) | *to have fun* |
| invitar | *to invite* |
| pasarlo bien/mal | *to have a good/bad time* |
| regalar | *to give* (a gift) |
| reírse (e:i) | *to laugh* |
| relajarse | *to relax* |
| sonreír (e:i) | *to smile* |
| sorprender | *to surprise* |

## Los postres y otras comidas

| | |
|---|---|
| la botella (de vino) | *bottle (of wine)* |
| el champán | *champagne* |
| los dulces | *sweets; candy* |
| el flan (de caramelo) | *baked (caramel) custard* |
| la galleta | *cookie* |
| el helado | *ice cream* |
| el pastel (de chocolate) | *(chocolate) cake; pie* |
| el postre | *dessert* |

## Las relaciones personales

| | |
|---|---|
| la amistad | *friendship* |
| el amor | *love* |
| el divorcio | *divorce* |
| el estado civil | *marital status* |
| el matrimonio | *marriage* |
| la pareja | *(married) couple; partner* |
| el/la recién casado/a | *newlywed* |
| casarse (con) | *to get married (to)* |
| comprometerse (con) | *to get engaged (to)* |
| divorciarse (de) | *to get divorced (from)* |
| enamorarse (de) | *to fall in love (with)* |
| llevarse bien/mal (con) | *to get along well/ badly (with)* |
| odiar | *to hate* |
| romper (con) | *to break up (with)* |
| salir (con) | *to go out (with); to date* |
| separarse (de) | *to separate (from)* |
| tener una cita | *to have a date; to have an appointment* |
| casado/a | *married* |
| divorciado/a | *divorced* |
| juntos/as | *together* |
| separado/a | *separated* |
| soltero/a | *single* |
| viudo/a | *widower/widow* |

  **Audio: Vocabulary Flashcards**

## Las etapas de la vida

| | |
|---|---|
| la adolescencia | *adolescence* |
| la edad | *age* |
| el estado civil | *marital status* |
| las etapas de la vida | *the stages of life* |
| la juventud | *youth* |
| la madurez | *maturity; middle age* |
| la muerte | *death* |
| el nacimiento | *birth* |
| la niñez | *childhood* |
| la vejez | *old age* |
| cambiar (de) | *to change* |
| graduarse (de/en) | *to graduate (from/in)* |
| jubilarse | *to retire (from work)* |
| nacer | *to be born* |

## Palabras adicionales

| | |
|---|---|
| la alegría | *happiness* |
| el beso | *kiss* |
| conmigo | *with me* |
| contigo | *with you* |

| | |
|---|---|
| **Expresiones útiles** | *See page 305.* |

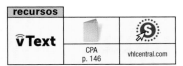

# Glossary of Grammatical Terms

**ADJECTIVE** A word that modifies, or describes, a noun or pronoun.

**muchos** libros
*many* books

las mujeres **altas**
the *tall* women

un hombre **rico**
a *rich* man

**Demonstrative adjective** An adjective that specifies which noun a speaker is referring to.

**esta** fiesta
*this* party

**aquellas** flores
*those* flowers

**ese** chico
*that* boy

**Possessive adjective** An adjective that indicates ownership or possession.

**mi** mejor vestido
*my* best dress

Éste es **mi** hermano.
This is *my* brother.

**Stressed possessive adjective** A possessive adjective that emphasizes the owner or possessor.

Es un libro **mío**.
It's *my* book./It's *a book of mine*.

Es amiga **tuya**; yo no la conozco.
She's a friend *of yours*; I don't know her.

**ADVERB** A word that modifies, or describes, a verb, adjective, or other adverb.

Pancho escribe **rápidamente**.
*Pancho writes* **quickly**.

Este cuadro es **muy** bonito.
*This picture is* **very** *pretty*.

**ARTICLE** A word that points out a noun in either a specific or a non-specific way.

**Definite article** An article that points out a noun in a specific way.

**el** libro
*the* book

**los** diccionarios
*the* dictionaries

**la** maleta
*the* suitcase

**las** palabras
*the* words

**Indefinite article** An article that points out a noun in a general, non-specific way.

**un** lápiz
*a* pencil

**unos** pájaros
*some* birds

**una** computadora
*a* computer

**unas** escuelas
*some* schools

**CLAUSE** A group of words that contains both a conjugated verb and a subject, either expressed or implied.

**Main (or Independent) clause** A clause that can stand alone as a complete sentence.

Pienso ir a cenar pronto.
*I plan to go to dinner soon.*

**Subordinate (or Dependent) clause** A clause that does not express a complete thought and therefore cannot stand alone as a sentence.

Trabajo en la cafetería **porque necesito dinero para la escuela**.
I work in the cafeteria *because I need money for school*.

**COMPARATIVE** A construction used with an adjective or adverb to express a comparison between two people, places, or things.

Este programa es **más interesante que** el otro.
*This program is* **more interesting than** *the other one.*

Tomás no es **tan alto como** Alberto.
*Tomás is not* **as tall as** *Alberto.*

**CONJUGATION** A set of the forms of a verb for a specific tense or mood or the process by which these verb forms are presented.

Preterite conjugation of **cantar**:

| | |
|---|---|
| cant**é** | cant**amos** |
| cant**aste** | cant**asteis** |
| cant**ó** | cant**aron** |

**CONJUNCTION** A word used to connect words, clauses, or phrases.

Susana es de Cuba **y** Pedro es de España.
*Susana is from Cuba* **and** *Pedro is from Spain.*

No quiero estudiar **pero** tengo que hacerlo.
*I don't want to study,* **but** *I have to.*

**CONTRACTION** The joining of two words into one. The only contractions in Spanish are **al** and **del**.

Mi hermano fue **al** concierto ayer.
*My brother went **to the** concert yesterday.*

Saqué dinero **del** banco.
*I took money **from the** bank.*

**DIRECT OBJECT** A noun or pronoun that directly receives the action of the verb.

Tomás lee **el libro.**   La pagó ayer.
*Tomás reads **the book.**   She paid **it** yesterday.*

**GENDER** The grammatical categorizing of certain kinds of words, such as nouns and pronouns, as masculine, feminine, or neuter.

Masculine
*articles* **el, un**
*pronouns* **él, lo, mío, éste, ése, aquél**
*adjective* **simpático**

Feminine
*articles* **la, una**
*pronouns* **ella, la, mía, ésta, ésa, aquélla**
*adjective* **simpática**

**IMPERSONAL EXPRESSION** A third-person expression with no expressed or specific subject.

**Es muy importante.**   **Llueve** mucho.
*It's **very important.**   **It's raining** hard.*

Aquí **se habla** español.
*Spanish **is spoken** here.*

**INDIRECT OBJECT** A noun or pronoun that receives the action of the verb indirectly; the object, often a living being, to or for whom an action is performed.

Eduardo **le** dio un libro **a Linda.**
*Eduardo gave a book **to Linda.***

La profesora **me** puso una C en el examen.
*The professor gave **me** a C on the test.*

**INFINITIVE** The basic form of a verb. Infinitives in Spanish end in **-ar**, **-er**, or **-ir**.

hablar        correr        abrir
*to speak*    *to run*      *to open*

**INTERROGATIVE** An adjective or pronoun used to ask a question.

¿**Quién** habla?        ¿**Cuántos** compraste?
***Who** is speaking?*   ***How many** did you buy?*

¿**Qué** piensas hacer hoy?
***What** do you plan to do today?*

**INVERSION** Changing the word order of a sentence, often to form a question.

*Statement:* Elena pagó la cuenta del restaurante.

*Inversion:* ¿Pagó Elena la cuenta del restaurante?

**MOOD** A grammatical distinction of verbs that indicates whether the verb is intended to make a statement or command or to express a doubt, emotion, or condition contrary to fact.

**Imperative mood** Verb forms used to make commands.

**Di** la verdad.        **Caminen** ustedes conmigo.
***Tell** the truth.*    ***Walk** with me.*

¡**Comamos** ahora!
***Let's eat** now!*

**Indicative mood** Verb forms used to state facts, actions, and states considered to be real.

**Sé** que **tienes** el dinero.
***I know** that **you have** the money.*

**Subjunctive mood** Verb forms used principally in subordinate (dependent) clauses to express wishes, desires, emotions, doubts, and certain conditions, such as contrary-to-fact situations.

Prefieren que **hables** en español.
*They prefer that **you speak** in Spanish.*

Dudo que Luis **tenga** el dinero necesario.
*I doubt that Luis **has** the necessary money.*

**NOUN** A word that identifies people, animals, places, things, and ideas.

hombre        gato
*man*         *cat*

México        casa
*Mexico*      *house*

libertad      libro
*freedom*     *book*

**NUMBER** A grammatical term that refers to singular or plural. Nouns in Spanish and English have number. Other parts of a sentence, such as adjectives, articles, and verbs, can also have number.

| Singular | Plural |
|---|---|
| **una** cosa | **unas** cosas |
| *a thing* | *some things* |
| **el** profesor | **los** profesores |
| *the professor* | *the professors* |

**NUMBERS** Words that represent amounts.

**Cardinal numbers** Words that show specific amounts.

**cinco** minutos
*five minutes*

el año **dos mil veintitrés**
*the year 2023*

**Ordinal numbers** Words that indicate the order of a noun in a series.

| el **cuarto** jugador | la **décima** hora |
|---|---|
| *the **fourth** player* | *the **tenth** hour* |

**PAST PARTICIPLE** A past form of the verb used in compound tenses. The past participle may also be used as an adjective, but it must then agree in number and gender with the word it modifies.

Han **buscado** por todas partes.
*They have **searched** everywhere.*

Yo no había **estudiado** para el examen.
*I hadn't **studied** for the exam.*

Hay una **ventana abierta** en la sala.
*There is an **open window** in the living room.*

**PERSON** The form of the verb or pronoun that indicates the speaker, the one spoken to, or the one spoken about. In Spanish, as in English, there are three persons: first, second, and third.

| Person | Singular | Plural |
|---|---|---|
| 1st | yo  *I* | nosotros/as  *we* |
| 2nd | tú, Ud.  *you* | vosotros/as, Uds.  *you* |
| 3rd | él, ella  *he, she* | ellos, ellas  *they* |

**PREPOSITION** A word or words that describe(s) the relationship, most often in time or space, between two other words.

Anita es **de** California.
*Anita is **from** California.*

La chaqueta está **en** el carro.
*The jacket is **in** the car.*

Marta se peinó **antes de** salir.
*Marta combed her hair **before** going out.*

**PRESENT PARTICIPLE** In English, a verb form that ends in *-ing*. In Spanish, the present participle ends in **-ndo,** and is often used with **estar** to form a progressive tense.

Mi hermana está **hablando** por teléfono ahora mismo.
*My sister is **talking** on the phone right now.*

**PRONOUN** A word that takes the place of a noun or nouns.

**Demonstrative pronoun** A pronoun that takes the place of a specific noun.

Quiero **ésta.**
*I want **this one.***

¿Vas a comprar **ése?**
*Are you going to buy **that one?***

Juan prefirió **aquéllos.**
*Juan preferred **those** (over there).*

**Object pronoun** A pronoun that functions as a direct or indirect object of the verb.

**Te** digo la verdad.
*I'm telling **you** the truth.*

**Me lo** trajo Juan.
*Juan brought **it** to **me.***

**Reflexive pronoun** A pronoun that indicates that the action of a verb is performed by the subject on itself. These pronouns are often expressed in English with *-self: myself, yourself,* etc.

Yo **me bañé** antes de salir.
*I bathed **(myself)** before going out.*

Elena **se acostó** a las once y media.
*Elena **went to bed** at eleven-thirty.*

**Relative pronoun** A pronoun that connects a subordinate clause to a main clause.

El chico **que** nos escribió viene a visitar mañana.
*The boy **who** wrote us is coming to visit tomorrow.*

Ya sé **lo que** tenemos que hacer.
*I already know **what** we have to do.*

**Subject pronoun** A pronoun that replaces the name or title of a person or thing, and acts as the subject of a verb.

**Tú** debes estudiar más.
***You** should study more.*

**Él** llegó primero.
***He** arrived first.*

**SUBJECT** A noun or pronoun that performs the action of a verb and is often implied by the verb.

**María** va al supermercado.
***María** goes to the supermarket.*

(**Ellos**) Trabajan mucho.
***They** work hard.*

Esos **libros** son muy caros.
*Those **books** are very expensive.*

**SUPERLATIVE** A word or construction used with an adjective or adverb to express the highest or lowest degree of a specific quality among three or more people, places, or things.

De todas mis clases, ésta es la **más interesante**.
*Of all my classes, this is the **most interesting**.*

Raúl es el **menos simpático** de los chicos.
*Raúl is the **least pleasant** of the boys.*

**TENSE** A set of verb forms that indicates the time of an action or state: past, present, or future.

**Compound tense** A two-word tense made up of an auxiliary verb and a present or past participle. In Spanish, there are two auxiliary verbs: **estar** and **haber**.

En este momento, **estoy estudiando**.
*At this time, **I am studying**.*

El paquete no **ha llegado** todavía.
*The package **has not arrived** yet.*

**Simple tense** A tense expressed by a single verb form.

María **estaba** enferma anoche.
*María **was** sick last night.*

Juana **hablará** con su mamá mañana.
*Juana **will speak** with her mom tomorrow.*

**VERB** A word that expresses actions or states-of-being.

**Auxiliary verb** A verb used with a present or past participle to form a compound tense. **Haber** is the most commonly used auxiliary verb in Spanish.

Los chicos **han** visto los elefantes.
*The children **have** seen the elephants.*

Espero que **hayas** comido.
*I hope you **have** eaten.*

**Reflexive verb** A verb that describes an action performed by the subject on itself and is always used with a reflexive pronoun.

**Me compré** un carro nuevo.
*I **bought myself** a new car.*

Pedro y Adela **se levantan** muy temprano.
*Pedro and Adela **get (themselves) up** very early.*

**Spelling-change verb** A verb that undergoes a predictable change in spelling, in order to reflect its actual pronunciation in the various conjugations.

| | | | |
|---|---|---|---|
| **practicar** | c→qu | practico | practiqué |
| **dirigir** | g→j | dirigí | dirijo |
| **almorzar** | z→c | almorzó | almorcé |

**Stem-changing verb** A verb whose stem vowel undergoes one or more predictable changes in the various conjugations.

| | |
|---|---|
| entender (i:ie) | entiendo |
| pedir (e:i) | piden |
| dormir (o:ue, u) | duermo, durmieron |

# Verb Conjugation Tables

### The verb lists

The list of verbs below and the model verb tables that start on page 338 show you how to conjugate every verb taught in **DESCUBRE**. Each verb in the list is followed by a model verb conjugated according to the same pattern. The number in parentheses indicates where in the verb tables you can find the conjugated forms of the model verb. If you want to find out how to conjugate **divertirse**, for example, look up number 33, **sentir**, the model for verbs that follow the e:ie stem-change pattern.

### How to use the verb tables

In the tables you will find the infinitive, present and past participles, and all the simple forms of each model verb. The formation of the compound tenses of any verb can be inferred from the table of compound tenses, pages 338–339, either by combining the past participle of the verb with a conjugated form of **haber** or by combining the present participle with a conjugated form of **estar**.

**abrazar** (z:c) like cruzar (37)

**abrir** like vivir (3) *except* past participle is abierto

**aburrir(se)** like vivir (3)

**acabar de** like hablar (1)

**acampar** like hablar (1)

**acompañar** like hablar (1)

**aconsejar** like hablar (1)

**acordarse** (o:ue) like contar (24)

**acostarse** (o:ue) like contar (24)

**adelgazar** (z:c) like cruzar (37)

**afeitarse** like hablar (1)

**ahorrar** like hablar (1)

**alegrarse** like hablar (1)

**aliviar** like hablar (1)

**almorzar** (o:ue) like contar (24) *except* (z:c)

**alquilar** like hablar (1)

**andar** like hablar (1) *except* preterite stem is anduv-

**anunciar** like hablar (1)

**apagar** (g:gu) like llegar (41)

**aplaudir** like vivir (3)

**apreciar** like hablar (1)

**aprender** like comer (2)

**apurarse** like hablar (1)

**arrancar** (c:qu) like tocar (43)

**arreglar** like hablar (1)

**asistir** like vivir (3)

**aumentar** like hablar (1)

**ayudar(se)** like hablar (1)

**bailar** like hablar (1)

**bajar(se)** like hablar (1)

**bañarse** like hablar (1)

**barrer** like comer (2)

**beber** like comer (2)

**besar(se)** like hablar (1)

**borrar** like hablar (1)

**brindar** like hablar (1)

**bucear** like hablar (1)

**buscar** (c:qu) like tocar (43)

**caber** (4)

**caer(se)** (5)

**calentarse** (e:ie) like pensar (30)

**calzar** (z:c) like cruzar (37)

**cambiar** like hablar (1)

**caminar** like hablar (1)

**cantar** like hablar (1)

**casarse** like hablar (1)

**cazar** (z:c) like cruzar (37)

**celebrar** like hablar (1)

**cenar** like hablar (1)

**cepillarse** like hablar (1)

**cerrar** (e:ie) like pensar (30)

**cobrar** like hablar (1)

**cocinar** like hablar (1)

**comenzar** (e:ie) (z:c) like empezar (26)

**comer** (2)

**compartir** like vivir (3)

**comprar** like hablar (1)

**comprender** like comer (2)

**comprometerse** like comer (2)

**comunicarse** (c:qu) like tocar (43)

**conducir** (c:zc) (6)

**confirmar** like hablar (1)

**conocer** (c:zc) (35)

**conseguir** (e:i) (gu:g) like seguir (32)

**conservar** like hablar (1)

**consumir** like vivir (3)

**contaminar** like hablar (1)

**contar** (o:ue) (24)

**contestar** like hablar (1))

**contratar** like hablar (1)

**controlar** like hablar (1)

**conversar** like hablar (1)

**correr** like comer (2)

**costar** (o:ue) like contar (24)

**creer** (y) (36)

**cruzar** (z:c) (37)

**cuidar** like hablar (1)

**cumplir** like vivir (3)

**dañar** like hablar (1)

**dar** (7)

**deber** like comer (2)

**decidir** like vivir (3)

**decir** (e:i) (8)

**declarar** like hablar (1)

**dejar** like hablar (1)

**depositar** like hablar (1)

**desarrollar** like hablar (1)

**desayunar** like hablar (1)

**descansar** like hablar (1)

**descargar** (g:gu) like llegar (41)

**describir** like vivir (3) *except* past participle is descrito

**descubrir** like vivir (3) *except* past participle is descubierto

**desear** like hablar (1)

**despedirse** (e:i) like pedir (29)

**despertarse** (e:ie) like pensar (30)

**destruir** (y) (38)

**dibujar** like hablar (1)

**dirigir** like vivir (3) *except* (g:j)

**disfrutar** like hablar (1)

**divertirse** (e:ie) like sentir (33)

**divorciarse** like hablar (1)

**doblar** like hablar (1)

**doler** (o:ue) like volver (34) *except* past participle is regular

**dormir(se)** (o:ue) (25)

**ducharse** like hablar (1)

**dudar** like hablar (1)

**durar** like hablar (1)

**echar** like hablar (1)

**elegir** (e:i) like pedir (29) *except* (g:j)

**emitir** like vivir (3)

**empezar** (e:ie) (z:c) (26)

**enamorarse** like hablar (1)
**encantar** like hablar (1)
**encontrar(se)** (o:ue) like contar (24)
**enfermarse** like hablar (1)
**engordar** like hablar (1)
**enojarse** like hablar (1)
**enseñar** like hablar (1)
**ensuciar** like hablar (1)
**entender** (e:ie) (27)
**entrenarse** like hablar (1)
**entrevistar** like hablar (1)
**enviar** (envío) (39)
**escalar** like hablar (1)
**escanear** like hablar (1)
**escoger** (g:j) like proteger (42)
**escribir** like vivir (3) *except* past participle is escrito
**escuchar** like hablar (1)
**esculpir** like vivir (3)
**esperar** like hablar (1)
**esquiar** (esquío) like enviar (39)
**establecer** (c:zc) like conocer (35)
**estacionar** like hablar (1)
**estar** (9)
**estornudar** like hablar (1)
**estudiar** like hablar (1)
**evitar** like hablar (1)
**explicar** (c:qu) like tocar (43)
**faltar** like hablar (1)
**fascinar** like hablar (1)
**firmar** like hablar (1)
**fumar** like hablar (1)
**funcionar** like hablar (1)
**ganar** like hablar (1)
**gastar** like hablar (1)
**grabar** like hablar (1)
**graduarse** (gradúo) (40)
**guardar** like hablar (1)
**gustar** like hablar (1)
**haber** (hay) (10)
**hablar** (1)
**hacer** (11)
**importar** like hablar (1)
**imprimir** like vivir (3)
**indicar** (c:qu) like tocar (43)
**informar** like hablar (1)
**insistir** like vivir (3)
**interesar** like hablar (1)
**invertir** (e:ie) like sentir (33)
**invitar** like hablar (1)
**ir(se)** (12)

**jubilarse** like hablar (1)
**jugar** (u:ue) (g:gu) (28)
**lastimarse** like hablar (1)
**lavar(se)** like hablar (1)
**leer** (y) like creer (36)
**levantar(se)** like hablar (1)
**limpiar** like hablar (1)
**llamar(se)** like hablar (1)
**llegar** (g:gu) (41)
**llenar** like hablar (1)
**llevar(se)** like hablar (1)
**llover** (o:ue) like volver (34) *except* past participle is regular
**luchar** like hablar (1)
**mandar** like hablar (1)
**manejar** like hablar (1)
**mantener(se)** like tener (20)
**maquillarse** like hablar (1)
**mejorar** like hablar (1)
**merendar** (e:ie) like pensar (30)
**mirar** like hablar (1)
**molestar** like hablar (1)
**montar** like hablar (1)
**morir** (o:ue) like dormir (25) *except* past participle is *muerto*
**mostrar** (o:ue) like contar (24)
**mudarse** like hablar (1)
**nacer** (c:zc) like conocer (35)
**nadar** like hablar (1)
**navegar** (g:gu) like llegar (41)
**necesitar** like hablar (1)
**negar** (e:ie) like pensar (30) *except* (g:gu)
**nevar** (e:ie) like pensar (30)
**obedecer** (c:zc) like conocer (35)
**obtener** like tener (20)
**ocurrir** like vivir (3)
**odiar** like hablar (1)
**ofrecer** (c:zc) like conocer (35)
**oír** (y) (13)
**olvidar** like hablar (1)
**pagar** (g:gu) like llegar (41)
**parar** like hablar (1)
**parecer** (c:zc) like conocer (35)
**pasar** like hablar (1)
**pasear** like hablar (1)
**patinar** like hablar (1)

**pedir** (e:i) (29)
**peinarse** like hablar (1)
**pensar** (e:ie) (30)
**perder** (e:ie) like entender (27)
**pescar** (c:qu) like tocar (43)
**pintar** like hablar (1)
**planchar** like hablar (1)
**poder** (o:ue) (14)
**poner(se)** (15)
**practicar** (c:qu) like tocar (43)
**preferir** (e:ie) like sentir (33)
**preguntar** like hablar (1)
**prender** like comer (2)
**preocuparse** like hablar (1)
**preparar** like hablar (1)
**presentar** like hablar (1)
**prestar** like hablar (1)
**probar(se)** (o:ue) like contar (24)
**prohibir** like vivir (3)
**proteger** (g:j) (42)
**publicar** (c:qu) like tocar (43)
**quedar(se)** like hablar (1)
**querer** (e:ie) (16)
**quitar(se)** like hablar (1)
**recetar** like hablar (1)
**recibir** like vivir (3)
**reciclar** like hablar (1)
**recoger** (g:j) like proteger (42)
**recomendar** (e:ie) like pensar (30)
**recordar** (o:ue) like contar (24)
**reducir** (c:zc) like conducir (6)
**regalar** like hablar (1)
**regatear** like hablar (1)
**regresar** like hablar (1)
**reír(se)** (e:i) (31)
**relajarse** like hablar (1)
**renunciar** like hablar (1)
**repetir** (e:i) like pedir (29)
**resolver** (o:ue) like volver (34)
**respirar** like hablar (1)
**revisar** like hablar (1)
**rogar** (o:ue) like contar (24) *except* (g:gu)
**romper(se)** like comer (2) *except* past participle is roto
**saber** (17)
**sacar** (c:qu) like tocar (43)
**sacudir** like vivir (3)

**salir** (18)
**saludar(se)** like hablar (1)
**secar(se)** (c:q) like tocar (43)
**seguir** (e:i) (32)
**sentarse** (e:ie) like pensar (30)
**sentir(se)** (e:ie) (33)
**separarse** like hablar (1)
**ser** (19)
**servir** (e:i) like pedir (29)
**solicitar** like hablar (1)
**sonar** (o:ue) like contar (24)
**sonreír** (e:i) like reír(se) (31)
**sorprender** like comer (2)
**subir** like vivir (3)
**sudar** like hablar (1)
**sufrir** like vivir (3)
**sugerir** (e:ie) like sentir (33)
**suponer** like poner (15)
**temer** like comer (2)
**tener** (20)
**terminar** like hablar (1)
**tocar** (c:qu) (43)
**tomar** like hablar (1)
**torcerse** (o:ue) like volver (34) *except* (c:z) and past participle is regular; e.g. yo tuerzo
**toser** like comer (2)
**trabajar** like hablar (1)
**traducir** (c:zc) like conducir (6)
**traer** (21)
**transmitir** like vivir (3)
**tratar** like hablar (1)
**usar** like hablar (1)
**vender** like comer (2)
**venir** (22)
**ver** (23)
**vestirse** (e:i) like pedir (29)
**viajar** like hablar (1)
**visitar** like hablar (1)
**vivir** (3)
**volver** (o:ue) (34)
**votar** like hablar (1)

# Regular verbs: simple tenses

| Infinitive | INDICATIVE | | | | | | SUBJUNCTIVE | | IMPERATIVE |
|---|---|---|---|---|---|---|---|---|---|
| | Present | Imperfect | Preterite | Future | Conditional | | Present | Past | |

**1**

| Infinitive | Present | Imperfect | Preterite | Future | Conditional | Present | Past | IMPERATIVE |
|---|---|---|---|---|---|---|---|---|
| hablar | hablo | hablaba | hablé | hablaré | hablaría | hable | hablara | |
| | hablas | hablabas | hablaste | hablarás | hablarías | hables | hablaras | habla tú (no hables) |
| **Participles:** | habla | hablaba | habló | hablará | hablaría | hable | hablara | hable Ud. |
| hablando | hablamos | hablábamos | hablamos | hablaremos | hablaríamos | hablemos | habláramos | hablemos |
| hablado | habláis | hablabais | hablasteis | hablaréis | hablaríais | habléis | hablarais | hablad (no habléis) |
| | hablan | hablaban | hablaron | hablarán | hablarían | hablen | hablaran | hablen Uds. |

**2**

| Infinitive | Present | Imperfect | Preterite | Future | Conditional | Present | Past | IMPERATIVE |
|---|---|---|---|---|---|---|---|---|
| comer | como | comía | comí | comeré | comería | coma | comiera | |
| | comes | comías | comiste | comerás | comerías | comas | comieras | come tú (no comas) |
| **Participles:** | come | comía | comió | comerá | comería | coma | comiera | coma Ud. |
| comiendo | comemos | comíamos | comimos | comeremos | comeríamos | comamos | comiéramos | comamos |
| comido | coméis | comíais | comisteis | comeréis | comeríais | comáis | comierais | comed (no comáis) |
| | comen | comían | comieron | comerán | comerían | coman | comieran | coman Uds. |

**3**

| Infinitive | Present | Imperfect | Preterite | Future | Conditional | Present | Past | IMPERATIVE |
|---|---|---|---|---|---|---|---|---|
| vivir | vivo | vivía | viví | viviré | viviría | viva | viviera | |
| | vives | vivías | viviste | vivirás | vivirías | vivas | vivieras | vive tú (no vivas) |
| **Participles:** | vive | vivía | vivió | vivirá | viviría | viva | viviera | viva Ud. |
| viviendo | vivimos | vivíamos | vivimos | viviremos | viviríamos | vivamos | viviéramos | vivamos |
| vivido | vivís | vivíais | vivisteis | viviréis | viviríais | viváis | vivierais | vivid (no viváis) |
| | viven | vivían | vivieron | vivirán | vivirían | vivan | vivieran | vivan Uds. |

# All verbs: compound tenses

## PERFECT TENSES

### INDICATIVE

| Present Perfect | | Past Perfect | | Future Perfect | | Conditional Perfect | |
|---|---|---|---|---|---|---|---|
| he | hablado | había | hablado | habré | hablado | habría | hablado |
| has | comido | habías | comido | habrás | comido | habrías | comido |
| ha | vivido | había | vivido | habrá | vivido | habría | vivido |
| hemos | | habíamos | | habremos | | habríamos | |
| habéis | | habíais | | habréis | | habríais | |
| han | | habían | | habrán | | habrían | |

### SUBJUNCTIVE

| Present Perfect | | Past Perfect | |
|---|---|---|---|
| haya | hablado | hubiera | hablado |
| hayas | comido | hubieras | comido |
| haya | vivido | hubiera | vivido |
| hayamos | | hubiéramos | |
| hayáis | | hubierais | |
| hayan | | hubieran | |

## PROGRESSIVE TENSES

| | INDICATIVE | | | | SUBJUNCTIVE | |
| --- | --- | --- | --- | --- | --- | --- |
| Present Progressive | Past Progressive | Future Progressive | Conditional Progressive | | Present Progressive | Past Progressive |
| estoy | estaba | estaré | estaría | | esté | estuviera |
| estás | estabas | estarás | estarías | | estés | estuvieras |
| está hablando | estaba hablando | estará hablando | estaría hablando | | esté hablando | estuviera hablando |
| estamos comiendo | estábamos comiendo | estaremos comiendo | estaríamos comiendo | | estemos comiendo | estuviéramos comiendo |
| estáis viviendo | estabais viviendo | estaréis viviendo | estaríais viviendo | | estéis viviendo | estuvierais viviendo |
| están | estaban | estarán | estarían | | estén | estuvieran |

## Irregular verbs

| Infinitive | INDICATIVE | | | | | SUBJUNCTIVE | | IMPERATIVE |
| --- | --- | --- | --- | --- | --- | --- | --- | --- |
| | Present | Imperfect | Preterite | Future | Conditional | Present | Past | |
| **4** caber | **quepo** | cabía | **cupe** | **cabré** | **cabría** | **quepa** | **cupiera** | |
| | cabes | cabías | **cupiste** | **cabrás** | **cabrías** | **quepas** | **cupieras** | cabe tú (no **quepas**) |
| Participles: | cabe | cabía | **cupo** | **cabrá** | **cabría** | **quepa** | **cupiera** | **quepa** Ud. |
| cabiendo | cabemos | cabíamos | **cupimos** | **cabremos** | **cabríamos** | **quepamos** | **cupiéramos** | **quepamos** |
| cabido | cabéis | cabíais | **cupisteis** | **cabréis** | **cabríais** | **quepáis** | **cupierais** | cabed (no **quepáis**) |
| | caben | cabían | **cupieron** | **cabrán** | **cabrían** | **quepan** | **cupieran** | **quepan** Uds. |
| **5** caer(se) | **caigo** | caía | caí | caeré | caería | **caiga** | **cayera** | |
| | caes | caías | **caíste** | caerás | caerías | **caigas** | **cayeras** | cae tú (no **caigas**) |
| Participles: | cae | caía | **cayó** | caerá | caería | **caiga** | **cayera** | **caiga** Ud. |
| **cayendo** | caemos | caíamos | **caímos** | caeremos | caeríamos | **caigamos** | **cayéramos** | **caigamos** |
| **caído** | caéis | caíais | **caísteis** | caeréis | caeríais | **caigáis** | **cayerais** | caed (no **caigáis**) |
| | caen | caían | **cayeron** | caerán | caerían | **caigan** | **cayeran** | **caigan** Uds. |
| **6** conducir | **conduzco** | conducía | **conduje** | conduciré | conduciría | **conduzca** | **condujera** | |
| (c:zc) | conduces | conducías | **condujiste** | conducirás | conducirías | **conduzcas** | **condujeras** | conduce tú (no **conduzcas**) |
| Participles: | conduce | conducía | **condujo** | conducirá | conduciría | **conduzca** | **condujera** | **conduzca** Ud. |
| conduciendo | conducimos | conducíamos | **condujimos** | conduciremos | conduciríamos | **conduzcamos** | **condujéramos** | **conduzcamos** |
| conducido | conducís | conducíais | **condujisteis** | conduciréis | conduciríais | **conduzcáis** | **condujerais** | conducid (no **conduzcáis**) |
| | conducen | conducían | **condujeron** | conducirán | conducirían | **conduzcan** | **condujeran** | **conduzcan** Uds. |

| Infinitive | INDICATIVE Present | Imperfect | Preterite | Future | Conditional | SUBJUNCTIVE Present | Past | IMPERATIVE |
|---|---|---|---|---|---|---|---|---|
| **7** dar | doy | daba | di | daré | daría | dé | diera | |
| Participles: | das | dabas | diste | darás | darías | des | dieras | da tú (no des) |
| dando | da | daba | dio | dará | daría | dé | diera | dé Ud. |
| dado | damos | dábamos | dimos | daremos | daríamos | demos | diéramos | demos |
| | dais | dabais | disteis | daréis | daríais | deis | dierais | dad (no deis) |
| | dan | daban | dieron | darán | darían | den | dieran | den Uds. |
| **8** decir (e:i) | digo | decía | dije | diré | diría | diga | dijera | |
| Participles: | dices | decías | dijiste | dirás | dirías | digas | dijeras | di tú (no digas) |
| diciendo | dice | decía | dijo | dirá | diría | diga | dijera | diga Ud. |
| dicho | decimos | decíamos | dijimos | diremos | diríamos | digamos | dijéramos | digamos |
| | decís | decíais | dijisteis | diréis | diríais | digáis | dijerais | decid (no digáis) |
| | dicen | decían | dijeron | dirán | dirían | digan | dijeran | digan Uds. |
| **9** estar | estoy | estaba | estuve | estaré | estaría | esté | estuviera | |
| Participles: | estás | estabas | estuviste | estarás | estarías | estés | estuvieras | está tú (no estés) |
| estando | está | estaba | estuvo | estará | estaría | esté | estuviera | esté Ud. |
| estado | estamos | estábamos | estuvimos | estaremos | estaríamos | estemos | estuviéramos | estemos |
| | estáis | estabais | estuvisteis | estaréis | estaríais | estéis | estuvierais | estad (no estéis) |
| | están | estaban | estuvieron | estarán | estarían | estén | estuvieran | estén Uds. |
| **10** haber | he | había | hube | habré | habría | haya | hubiera | |
| Participles: | has | habías | hubiste | habrás | habrías | hayas | hubieras | |
| habiendo | ha | había | hubo | habrá | habría | haya | hubiera | |
| habido | hemos | habíamos | hubimos | habremos | habríamos | hayamos | hubiéramos | |
| | habéis | habíais | hubisteis | habréis | habríais | hayáis | hubierais | |
| | han | habían | hubieron | habrán | habrían | hayan | hubieran | |
| **11** hacer | hago | hacía | hice | haré | haría | haga | hiciera | |
| Participles: | haces | hacías | hiciste | harás | harías | hagas | hicieras | haz tú (no hagas) |
| haciendo | hace | hacía | hizo | hará | haría | haga | hiciera | haga Ud. |
| hecho | hacemos | hacíamos | hicimos | haremos | haríamos | hagamos | hiciéramos | hagamos |
| | hacéis | hacíais | hicisteis | haréis | haríais | hagáis | hicierais | haced (no hagáis) |
| | hacen | hacían | hicieron | harán | harían | hagan | hicieran | hagan Uds. |
| **12** ir | voy | iba | fui | iré | iría | vaya | fuera | |
| Participles: | vas | ibas | fuiste | irás | irías | vayas | fueras | ve tú (no vayas) |
| yendo | va | iba | fue | irá | iría | vaya | fuera | vaya Ud. |
| ido | vamos | íbamos | fuimos | iremos | iríamos | vayamos | fuéramos | vamos (no vayamos) |
| | vais | ibais | fuisteis | iréis | iríais | vayáis | fuerais | id (no vayáis) |
| | van | iban | fueron | irán | irían | vayan | fueran | vayan Uds. |
| **13** oír (y) | oigo | oía | oí | oiré | oiría | oiga | oyera | |
| Participles: | oyes | oías | oíste | oirás | oirías | oigas | oyeras | oye tú (no oigas) |
| oyendo | oye | oía | oyó | oirá | oiría | oiga | oyera | oiga Ud. |
| oído | oímos | oíamos | oímos | oiremos | oiríamos | oigamos | oyéramos | oigamos |
| | oís | oíais | oísteis | oiréis | oiríais | oigáis | oyerais | oíd (no oigáis) |
| | oyen | oían | oyeron | oirán | oirían | oigan | oyeran | oigan Uds. |

**14 poder (o:ue)** — Participles: pudiendo, podido

| | Present | Imperfect | Preterite | Future | Conditional | Subj. Present | Subj. Past | Imperative |
|---|---|---|---|---|---|---|---|---|
| yo | puedo | podía | pude | podré | podría | pueda | pudiera | |
| tú | puedes | podías | pudiste | podrás | podrías | puedas | pudieras | puede tú (no puedas) |
| Ud./él/ella | puede | podía | pudo | podrá | podría | pueda | pudiera | pueda Ud. |
| nosotros | podemos | podíamos | pudimos | podremos | podríamos | podamos | pudiéramos | podamos |
| vosotros | podéis | podíais | pudisteis | podréis | podríais | podáis | pudierais | poded (no podáis) |
| Uds./ellos/ellas | pueden | podían | pudieron | podrán | podrían | puedan | pudieran | puedan Uds. |

**15 poner** — Participles: poniendo, puesto

| | Present | Imperfect | Preterite | Future | Conditional | Subj. Present | Subj. Past | Imperative |
|---|---|---|---|---|---|---|---|---|
| yo | pongo | ponía | puse | pondré | pondría | ponga | pusiera | |
| tú | pones | ponías | pusiste | pondrás | pondrías | pongas | pusieras | pon tú (no pongas) |
| Ud./él/ella | pone | ponía | puso | pondrá | pondría | ponga | pusiera | ponga Ud. |
| nosotros | ponemos | poníamos | pusimos | pondremos | pondríamos | pongamos | pusiéramos | pongamos |
| vosotros | ponéis | poníais | pusisteis | pondréis | pondríais | pongáis | pusierais | poned (no pongáis) |
| Uds./ellos/ellas | ponen | ponían | pusieron | pondrán | pondrían | pongan | pusieran | pongan Uds. |

**16 querer (e:ie)** — Participles: queriendo, querido

| | Present | Imperfect | Preterite | Future | Conditional | Subj. Present | Subj. Past | Imperative |
|---|---|---|---|---|---|---|---|---|
| yo | quiero | quería | quise | querré | querría | quiera | quisiera | |
| tú | quieres | querías | quisiste | querrás | querrías | quieras | quisieras | quiere tú (no quieras) |
| Ud./él/ella | quiere | quería | quiso | querrá | querría | quiera | quisiera | quiera Ud. |
| nosotros | queremos | queríamos | quisimos | querremos | querríamos | queramos | quisiéramos | queramos |
| vosotros | queréis | queríais | quisisteis | querréis | querríais | queráis | quisierais | quered (no queráis) |
| Uds./ellos/ellas | quieren | querían | quisieron | querrán | querrían | quieran | quisieran | quieran Uds. |

**17 saber** — Participles: sabiendo, sabido

| | Present | Imperfect | Preterite | Future | Conditional | Subj. Present | Subj. Past | Imperative |
|---|---|---|---|---|---|---|---|---|
| yo | sé | sabía | supe | sabré | sabría | sepa | supiera | |
| tú | sabes | sabías | supiste | sabrás | sabrías | sepas | supieras | sabe tú (no sepas) |
| Ud./él/ella | sabe | sabía | supo | sabrá | sabría | sepa | supiera | sepa Ud. |
| nosotros | sabemos | sabíamos | supimos | sabremos | sabríamos | sepamos | supiéramos | sepamos |
| vosotros | sabéis | sabíais | supisteis | sabréis | sabríais | sepáis | supierais | sabed (no sepáis) |
| Uds./ellos/ellas | saben | sabían | supieron | sabrán | sabrían | sepan | supieran | sepan Uds. |

**18 salir** — Participles: saliendo, salido

| | Present | Imperfect | Preterite | Future | Conditional | Subj. Present | Subj. Past | Imperative |
|---|---|---|---|---|---|---|---|---|
| yo | salgo | salía | salí | saldré | saldría | salga | saliera | |
| tú | sales | salías | saliste | saldrás | saldrías | salgas | salieras | sal tú (no salgas) |
| Ud./él/ella | sale | salía | salió | saldrá | saldría | salga | saliera | salga Ud. |
| nosotros | salimos | salíamos | salimos | saldremos | saldríamos | salgamos | saliéramos | salgamos |
| vosotros | salís | salíais | salisteis | saldréis | saldríais | salgáis | salierais | salid (no salgáis) |
| Uds./ellos/ellas | salen | salían | salieron | saldrán | saldrían | salgan | salieran | salgan Uds. |

**19 ser** — Participles: siendo, sido

| | Present | Imperfect | Preterite | Future | Conditional | Subj. Present | Subj. Past | Imperative |
|---|---|---|---|---|---|---|---|---|
| yo | soy | era | fui | seré | sería | sea | fuera | |
| tú | eres | eras | fuiste | serás | serías | seas | fueras | sé tú (no seas) |
| Ud./él/ella | es | era | fue | será | sería | sea | fuera | sea Ud. |
| nosotros | somos | éramos | fuimos | seremos | seríamos | seamos | fuéramos | seamos |
| vosotros | sois | erais | fuisteis | seréis | seríais | seáis | fuerais | sed (no seáis) |
| Uds./ellos/ellas | son | eran | fueron | serán | serían | sean | fueran | sean Uds. |

**20 tener** — Participles: teniendo, tenido

| | Present | Imperfect | Preterite | Future | Conditional | Subj. Present | Subj. Past | Imperative |
|---|---|---|---|---|---|---|---|---|
| yo | tengo | tenía | tuve | tendré | tendría | tenga | tuviera | |
| tú | tienes | tenías | tuviste | tendrás | tendrías | tengas | tuvieras | ten tú (no tengas) |
| Ud./él/ella | tiene | tenía | tuvo | tendrá | tendría | tenga | tuviera | tenga Ud. |
| nosotros | tenemos | teníamos | tuvimos | tendremos | tendríamos | tengamos | tuviéramos | tengamos |
| vosotros | tenéis | teníais | tuvisteis | tendréis | tendríais | tengáis | tuvierais | tened (no tengáis) |
| Uds./ellos/ellas | tienen | tenían | tuvieron | tendrán | tendrían | tengan | tuvieran | tengan Uds. |

## Table 21–23

| Infinitive | INDICATIVE | | | | | SUBJUNCTIVE | | IMPERATIVE |
|---|---|---|---|---|---|---|---|---|
| | Present | Imperfect | Preterite | Future | Conditional | Present | Past | |
| **21** traer | **traigo** | traía | **traje** | traeré | traería | **traiga** | **trajera** | |
| | traes | traías | **trajiste** | traerás | traerías | **traigas** | **trajeras** | trae tú (no **traigas**) |
| Participles: | trae | traía | **trajo** | traerá | traería | **traiga** | **trajera** | **traiga** Ud. |
| **trayendo** | traemos | traíamos | **trajimos** | traeremos | traeríamos | **traigamos** | **trajéramos** | **traigamos** |
| **traído** | traéis | traíais | **trajisteis** | traeréis | traeríais | **traigáis** | **trajerais** | traed (no **traigáis**) |
| | traen | traían | **trajeron** | traerán | traerían | **traigan** | **trajeran** | **traigan** Uds. |
| **22** venir | **vengo** | venía | **vine** | **vendré** | **vendría** | **venga** | **viniera** | |
| | **vienes** | venías | **viniste** | **vendrás** | **vendrías** | **vengas** | **vinieras** | **ven** tú (no **vengas**) |
| Participles: | **viene** | venía | **vino** | **vendrá** | **vendría** | **venga** | **viniera** | **venga** Ud. |
| **viniendo** | venimos | veníamos | **vinimos** | **vendremos** | **vendríamos** | **vengamos** | **viniéramos** | **vengamos** |
| venido | venís | veníais | **vinisteis** | **vendréis** | **vendríais** | vengáis | **vinierais** | venid (no **vengáis**) |
| | **vienen** | venían | **vinieron** | **vendrán** | **vendrían** | **vengan** | **vinieran** | **vengan** Uds. |
| **23** ver | **veo** | **veía** | **vi** | veré | vería | vea | viera | |
| | ves | **veías** | viste | verás | verías | **veas** | vieras | ve tú (no **veas**) |
| Participles: | ve | **veía** | **vio** | verá | vería | **vea** | viera | **vea** Ud. |
| viendo | vemos | **veíamos** | vimos | veremos | veríamos | **veamos** | viéramos | **veamos** |
| **visto** | **veis** | **veíais** | visteis | veréis | veríais | **veáis** | vierais | ved (no **veáis**) |
| | ven | **veían** | vieron | verán | verían | **vean** | vieran | **vean** Uds. |

## Stem-changing verbs

| Infinitive | INDICATIVE | | | | | SUBJUNCTIVE | | IMPERATIVE |
|---|---|---|---|---|---|---|---|---|
| | Present | Imperfect | Preterite | Future | Conditional | Present | Past | |
| **24** contar (o:ue) | **cuento** | contaba | conté | contaré | contaría | **cuente** | contara | |
| | **cuentas** | contabas | contaste | contarás | contarías | **cuentes** | contaras | **cuenta** tú (no **cuentes**) |
| Participles: | **cuenta** | contaba | contó | contará | contaría | **cuente** | contara | **cuente** Ud. |
| contando | contamos | contábamos | contamos | contaremos | contaríamos | contemos | contáramos | contemos |
| contado | contáis | contabais | contasteis | contaréis | contaríais | contéis | contarais | contad (no contéis) |
| | **cuentan** | contaban | contaron | contarán | contarían | **cuenten** | contaran | **cuenten** Uds. |
| **25** dormir (o:ue) | **duermo** | dormía | dormí | dormiré | dormiría | **duerma** | **durmiera** | |
| | **duermes** | dormías | dormiste | dormirás | dormirías | **duermas** | **durmieras** | **duerme** tú (no **duermas**) |
| Participles: | **duerme** | dormía | **durmió** | dormirá | dormiría | **duerma** | **durmiera** | **duerma** Ud. |
| **durmiendo** | dormimos | dormíamos | dormimos | dormiremos | dormiríamos | **durmamos** | **durmiéramos** | **durmamos** |
| dormido | dormís | dormíais | dormisteis | dormiréis | dormiríais | **durmáis** | **durmierais** | dormid (no **durmáis**) |
| | **duermen** | dormían | **durmieron** | dormirán | dormirían | **duerman** | **durmieran** | **duerman** Uds. |
| **26** empezar (e:ie) (z:c) | **empiezo** | empezaba | **empecé** | empezaré | empezaría | **empiece** | empezara | |
| | **empiezas** | empezabas | empezaste | empezarás | empezarías | **empieces** | empezaras | **empieza** tú (no **empieces**) |
| Participles: | **empieza** | empezaba | empezó | empezará | empezaría | **empiece** | empezara | **empiece** Ud. |
| empezando | empezamos | empezábamos | empezamos | empezaremos | empezaríamos | **empecemos** | empezáramos | **empecemos** |
| empezado | empezáis | empezabais | empezasteis | empezaréis | empezaríais | **empecéis** | empezarais | empezad (no **empecéis**) |
| | **empiezan** | empezaban | empezaron | empezarán | empezarían | **empiecen** | empezaran | **empiecen** Uds. |

| | | INDICATIVE | | | | | SUBJUNCTIVE | | IMPERATIVE |
|---|---|---|---|---|---|---|---|---|---|
| Infinitive | Present | Imperfect | Preterite | Future | Conditional | Present | Past | |

**27** entender (e:ie)

Participles: entendiendo entendido

| | | INDICATIVE | | | | | SUBJUNCTIVE | | IMPERATIVE |
|---|---|---|---|---|---|---|---|---|---|
| | **entiendo** | entendía | entendí | entenderé | entendería | **entienda** | entendiera | |
| | **entiendes** | entendías | entendiste | entenderás | entenderías | **entiendas** | entendieras | **entiende** tú (no **entiendas**) |
| | **entiende** | entendía | entendió | entenderá | entendería | **entienda** | entendiera | **entienda** Ud. |
| | entendemos | entendíamos | entendimos | entenderemos | entenderíamos | entendamos | entendiéramos | entendamos |
| | entendéis | entendíais | entendisteis | entenderéis | entenderíais | entendáis | entendierais | entended (no entendáis) |
| | **entienden** | entendían | entendieron | entenderán | entenderían | **entiendan** | entendieran | **entiendan** Uds. |

**28** jugar (u:ue) (g:gu)

Participles: jugando jugado

| | | INDICATIVE | | | | | SUBJUNCTIVE | | IMPERATIVE |
|---|---|---|---|---|---|---|---|---|---|
| | **juego** | jugaba | **jugué** | jugaré | jugaría | **juegue** | jugara | |
| | **juegas** | jugabas | jugaste | jugarás | jugarías | **juegues** | jugaras | **juega** tú (no **juegues**) |
| | **juega** | jugaba | jugó | jugará | jugaría | **juegue** | jugara | **juegue** Ud. |
| | jugamos | jugábamos | jugamos | jugaremos | jugaríamos | **juguemos** | jugáramos | **juguemos** |
| | jugáis | jugabais | jugasteis | jugaréis | jugaríais | **juguéis** | jugarais | jugad (no **juguéis**) |
| | **juegan** | jugaban | jugaron | jugarán | jugarían | **jueguen** | jugaran | **jueguen** Uds. |

**29** pedir (e:i)

Participles: pidiendo pedido

| | | INDICATIVE | | | | | SUBJUNCTIVE | | IMPERATIVE |
|---|---|---|---|---|---|---|---|---|---|
| | **pido** | pedía | pedí | pediré | pediría | **pida** | **pidiera** | |
| | **pides** | pedías | pediste | pedirás | pedirías | **pidas** | **pidieras** | **pide** tú (no **pidas**) |
| | **pide** | pedía | **pidió** | pedirá | pediría | **pida** | **pidiera** | **pida** Ud. |
| | pedimos | pedíamos | pedimos | pediremos | pediríamos | **pidamos** | **pidiéramos** | **pidamos** |
| | pedís | pedíais | pedisteis | pediréis | pediríais | **pidáis** | **pidierais** | pedid (no **pidáis**) |
| | **piden** | pedían | **pidieron** | pedirán | pedirían | **pidan** | **pidieran** | **pidan** Uds. |

**30** pensar (e:ie)

Participles: pensando pensado

| | | INDICATIVE | | | | | SUBJUNCTIVE | | IMPERATIVE |
|---|---|---|---|---|---|---|---|---|---|
| | **pienso** | pensaba | pensé | pensaré | pensaría | **piense** | pensara | |
| | **piensas** | pensabas | pensaste | pensarás | pensarías | **pienses** | pensaras | **piensa** tú (no **pienses**) |
| | **piensa** | pensaba | pensó | pensará | pensaría | **piense** | pensara | **piense** Ud. |
| | pensamos | pensábamos | pensamos | pensaremos | pensaríamos | pensemos | pensáramos | pensemos |
| | pensáis | pensabais | pensasteis | pensaréis | pensaríais | penséis | pensarais | pensad (no penséis) |
| | **piensan** | pensaban | pensaron | pensarán | pensarían | **piensen** | pensaran | **piensen** Uds. |

**31** reír (e:i)

Participles: riendo reído

| | | INDICATIVE | | | | | SUBJUNCTIVE | | IMPERATIVE |
|---|---|---|---|---|---|---|---|---|---|
| | **río** | reía | reí | reiré | reiría | **ría** | **riera** | |
| | **ríes** | reías | **reíste** | reirás | reirías | **rías** | **rieras** | **ríe** tú (no **rías**) |
| | **ríe** | reía | **rió** | reirá | reiría | **ría** | **riera** | **ría** Ud. |
| | **reímos** | reíamos | **reímos** | reiremos | reiríamos | **riamos** | **riéramos** | **riamos** |
| | reís | reíais | **reísteis** | reiréis | reiríais | **riáis** | **rierais** | reíd (no **riáis**) |
| | **ríen** | reían | **rieron** | reirán | reirían | **rían** | **rieran** | **rían** Uds. |

**32** seguir (e:i) (gu:g)

Participles: siguiendo seguido

| | | INDICATIVE | | | | | SUBJUNCTIVE | | IMPERATIVE |
|---|---|---|---|---|---|---|---|---|---|
| | **sigo** | seguía | seguí | seguiré | seguiría | **siga** | **siguiera** | |
| | **sigues** | seguías | seguiste | seguirás | seguirías | **sigas** | **siguieras** | **sigue** tú (no **sigas**) |
| | **sigue** | seguía | **siguió** | seguirá | seguiría | **siga** | **siguiera** | **siga** Ud. |
| | seguimos | seguíamos | seguimos | seguiremos | seguiríamos | **sigamos** | **siguiéramos** | **sigamos** |
| | seguís | seguíais | seguisteis | seguiréis | seguiríais | **sigáis** | **siguierais** | seguid (no **sigáis**) |
| | **siguen** | seguían | **siguieron** | seguirán | seguirían | **sigan** | **siguieran** | **sigan** Uds. |

**33** sentir (e:ie)

Participles: sintiendo sentido

| | | INDICATIVE | | | | | SUBJUNCTIVE | | IMPERATIVE |
|---|---|---|---|---|---|---|---|---|---|
| | **siento** | sentía | sentí | sentiré | sentiría | **sienta** | **sintiera** | |
| | **sientes** | sentías | sentiste | sentirás | sentirías | **sientas** | **sintieras** | **siente** tú (no **sientas**) |
| | **siente** | sentía | **sintió** | sentirá | sentiría | **sienta** | **sintiera** | **sienta** Ud. |
| | sentimos | sentíamos | sentimos | sentiremos | sentiríamos | **sintamos** | **sintiéramos** | **sintamos** |
| | sentís | sentíais | sentisteis | sentiréis | sentiríais | **sintáis** | **sintierais** | sentid (no **sintáis**) |
| | **sienten** | sentían | **sintieron** | sentirán | sentirían | **sientan** | **sintieran** | **sientan** Uds. |

**34** volver (o:ue)
Participles:
volviendo
**vuelto**

| Infinitive | Present | Imperfect | Preterite | Future | Conditional | Present | Past | IMPERATIVE |
|---|---|---|---|---|---|---|---|---|
| | | | | INDICATIVE | | SUBJUNCTIVE | | |
| | **vuelvo** | volvía | volví | volveré | volvería | **vuelva** | volviera | |
| | **vuelves** | volvías | volviste | volverás | volverías | **vuelvas** | volvieras | **vuelve** tú (no **vuelvas**) |
| | **vuelve** | volvía | volvió | volverá | volvería | **vuelva** | volviera | **vuelva** Ud. |
| | volvemos | volvíamos | volvimos | volveremos | volveríamos | volvamos | volviéramos | volvamos |
| | volvéis | volvíais | volvisteis | volveréis | volveríais | volváis | volvierais | volved (no volváis) |
| | **vuelven** | volvían | volvieron | volverán | volverían | **vuelvan** | volvieran | **vuelvan** Uds. |

# Verbs with spelling changes only

| Infinitive | Present | Imperfect | Preterite | Future | Conditional | Present | Past | IMPERATIVE |
|---|---|---|---|---|---|---|---|---|
| | | | | INDICATIVE | | SUBJUNCTIVE | | |
| **35** conocer (c:zc) | **conozco** | conocía | conocí | conoceré | conocería | **conozca** | conociera | |
| | conoces | conocías | conociste | conocerás | conocerías | **conozcas** | conocieras | conoce tú (no **conozcas**) |
| | conoce | conocía | conoció | conocerá | conocería | **conozca** | conociera | **conozca** Ud. |
| Participles: | conocemos | conocíamos | conocimos | conoceremos | conoceríamos | **conozcamos** | conociéramos | **conozcamos** |
| conociendo | conocéis | conocíais | conocisteis | conoceréis | conoceríais | **conozcáis** | conocierais | conoced (no **conozcáis**) |
| conocido | conocen | conocían | conocieron | conocerán | conocerían | **conozcan** | conocieran | **conozcan** Uds. |
| **36** creer (y) | creo | creía | creí | creeré | creería | crea | **creyera** | |
| | crees | creías | **creíste** | creerás | creerías | creas | **creyeras** | cree tú (no creas) |
| | cree | creía | **creyó** | creerá | creería | crea | **creyera** | crea Ud. |
| Participles: | creemos | creíamos | **creímos** | creeremos | creeríamos | creamos | **creyéramos** | creamos |
| **creyendo** | creéis | creíais | **creísteis** | creeréis | creeríais | creáis | **creyerais** | creed (no creáis) |
| **creído** | creen | creían | **creyeron** | creerán | creerían | crean | **creyeran** | crean Uds. |
| **37** cruzar (z:c) | cruzo | cruzaba | **crucé** | cruzaré | cruzaría | **cruce** | cruzara | |
| | cruzas | cruzabas | cruzaste | cruzarás | cruzarías | **cruces** | cruzaras | cruza tú (no **cruces**) |
| | cruza | cruzaba | cruzó | cruzará | cruzaría | **cruce** | cruzara | **cruce** Ud. |
| Participles: | cruzamos | cruzábamos | cruzamos | cruzaremos | cruzaríamos | **crucemos** | cruzáramos | **crucemos** |
| cruzando | cruzáis | cruzabais | cruzasteis | cruzaréis | cruzaríais | **crucéis** | cruzarais | cruzad (no **crucéis**) |
| cruzado | cruzan | cruzaban | cruzaron | cruzarán | cruzarían | **crucen** | cruzaran | **crucen** Uds. |
| **38** destruir (y) | **destruyo** | destruía | destruí | destruiré | destruiría | **destruya** | **destruyera** | |
| | **destruyes** | destruías | destruiste | destruirás | destruirías | **destruyas** | **destruyeras** | **destruye** tú (no **destruyas**) |
| | **destruye** | destruía | **destruyó** | destruirá | destruiría | **destruya** | **destruyera** | **destruya** Ud. |
| Participles: | destruimos | destruíamos | destruimos | destruiremos | destruiríamos | **destruyamos** | **destruyéramos** | **destruyamos** |
| **destruyendo** | destruís | destruíais | destruisteis | destruiréis | destruiríais | **destruyáis** | **destruyerais** | destruid (no **destruyáis**) |
| destruido | **destruyen** | destruían | **destruyeron** | destruirán | destruirían | **destruyan** | **destruyeran** | **destruyan** Uds. |
| **39** enviar (envío) | **envío** | enviaba | envié | enviaré | enviaría | **envíe** | enviara | |
| | **envías** | enviabas | enviaste | enviarás | enviarías | **envíes** | enviaras | **envía** tú (no **envíes**) |
| | **envía** | enviaba | envió | enviará | enviaría | **envíe** | enviara | **envíe** Ud. |
| Participles: | enviamos | enviábamos | enviamos | enviaremos | enviaríamos | enviemos | enviáramos | enviemos |
| enviando | enviáis | enviabais | enviasteis | enviaréis | enviaríais | enviéis | enviarais | enviad (no enviéis) |
| enviado | **envían** | enviaban | enviaron | enviarán | enviarían | **envíen** | enviaran | **envíen** Uds. |

| Infinitive | INDICATIVE | | | | | SUBJUNCTIVE | | IMPERATIVE |
| --- | --- | --- | --- | --- | --- | --- | --- | --- |
| | Present | Imperfect | Preterite | Future | Conditional | Present | Past | |
| **40** graduarse (gradúo) | **gradúo** | graduaba | gradué | graduaré | graduaría | **gradúe** | graduara | |
| | **gradúas** | graduabas | graduaste | graduarás | graduarías | **gradúes** | graduaras | **gradúa** tú (no **gradúes**) |
| | **gradúa** | graduaba | graduó | graduará | graduaría | **gradúe** | graduara | **gradúe** Ud. |
| Participles: | graduamos | graduábamos | graduamos | graduaremos | graduaríamos | graduemos | graduáramos | graduemos |
| graduando | graduáis | graduabais | graduasteis | graduaréis | graduaríais | graduéis | graduarais | graduad (no graduéis) |
| graduado | **gradúan** | graduaban | graduaron | graduarán | graduarían | **gradúen** | graduaran | **gradúen** Uds. |
| **41** llegar (g:gu) | llego | llegaba | **llegué** | llegaré | llegaría | **llegue** | llegara | |
| | llegas | llegabas | llegaste | llegarás | llegarías | **llegues** | llegaras | llega tú (no **llegues**) |
| | llega | llegaba | llegó | llegará | llegaría | **llegue** | llegara | **llegue** Ud. |
| Participles: | llegamos | llegábamos | llegamos | llegaremos | llegaríamos | **lleguemos** | llegáramos | **lleguemos** |
| llegando | llegáis | llegabais | llegasteis | llegaréis | llegaríais | **lleguéis** | llegarais | llegad (no **lleguéis**) |
| llegado | llegan | llegaban | llegaron | llegarán | llegarían | **lleguen** | llegaran | **lleguen** Uds. |
| **42** proteger (g:j) | **protejo** | protegía | protegí | protegeré | protegería | **proteja** | protegiera | |
| | proteges | protegías | protegiste | protegerás | protegerías | **protejas** | protegieras | protege tú (no **protejas**) |
| | protege | protegía | protegió | protegerá | protegería | **proteja** | protegiera | **proteja** Ud. |
| Participles: | protegemos | protegíamos | protegimos | protegeremos | protegeríamos | **protejamos** | protegiéramos | **protejamos** |
| protegiendo | protegéis | protegíais | protegisteis | protegeréis | protegeríais | **protejáis** | protegierais | proteged (no **protejáis**) |
| protegido | protegen | protegían | protegieron | protegerán | protegerían | **protejan** | protegieran | **protejan** Uds. |
| **43** tocar (c:qu) | toco | tocaba | **toqué** | tocaré | tocaría | **toque** | tocara | |
| | tocas | tocabas | tocaste | tocarás | tocarías | **toques** | tocaras | toca tú (no **toques**) |
| | toca | tocaba | tocó | tocará | tocaría | **toque** | tocara | **toque** Ud. |
| Participles: | tocamos | tocábamos | tocamos | tocaremos | tocaríamos | **toquemos** | tocáramos | **toquemos** |
| tocando | tocáis | tocabais | tocasteis | tocaréis | tocaríais | **toquéis** | tocarais | tocad (no **toquéis**) |
| tocado | tocan | tocaban | tocaron | tocarán | tocarían | **toquen** | tocaran | **toquen** Uds. |

# Guide to Vocabulary

## Contents of the glossary

This glossary contains the words and expressions listed on the **Vocabulario** page found at the end of each lesson in **DESCUBRE** as well as other useful vocabulary. The number following an entry indicates the **DESCUBRE** level and lesson where the word or expression was introduced. Check the **Estructura** sections of each lesson for words and expressions related to those grammar topics.

## Abbreviations used in this glossary

| | | | | | | | |
|---|---|---|---|---|---|---|---|
| *adj.* | adjective | *f.* | feminine | *m.* | masculine | *prep.* | preposition |
| *adv.* | adverb | *fam.* | familiar | *n.* | noun | *pron.* | pronoun |
| *art.* | article | *form.* | formal | *obj.* | object | *ref.* | reflexive |
| *conj.* | conjunction | *indef.* | indefinite | *p.p.* | past participle | *sing.* | singular |
| *def.* | definite | *interj.* | interjection | *pl.* | plural | *sub.* | subject |
| *d.o.* | direct object | *i.o.* | indirect object | *poss.* | possessive | *v.* | verb |

## Note on alphabetization

In current practice, for purposes of alphabetization, **ch** and **ll** are not treated as separate letters, but **ñ** still follows **n**. Therefore, in this glossary you will find that **año**, for example, appears after **anuncio**.

## Spanish-English

### A

**a** *prep.* at; to  1.1
  **a bordo**  aboard  1.1
  **a la derecha**  to the right  1.2
  **a la izquierda**  to the left  1.2
  **a la(s) +** *time*  at + *time*  1.1
  **a nombre de**  in the name of  1.5
  **¿A qué hora...?**  At what time...?  1.1
  **a ver**  let's see  1.2
**abeja** *f.* bee
**abierto/a** *adj.* open  1.5
**abrazo** *m.* hug
**abrigo** *m.* coat  1.6
**abril** *m.* April  1.5
**abrir** *v.* to open  1.3
**abuelo/a** *m., f.* grandfather; grandmother  1.3
**abuelos** *pl.* grandparents  1.3
**aburrido/a** *adj.* bored; boring  1.5
**aburrir** *v.* to bore  1.7
**acabar de (+** *inf.***)** *v.* to have just (*done something*)  1.6
**acampar** *v.* to camp  1.5
**aceite** *m.* oil  1.8
**acordarse (de) (o:ue)** *v.* to remember  1.7
**acostarse (o:ue)** *v.* to go to bed  1.7
**acuático/a** *adj.* aquatic  1.4
**adicional** *adj.* additional
**adiós** *m.* good-bye  1.1
**adjetivo** *m.* adjective
**administración de empresas** *f.* business administration  1.2

**adolescencia** *f.* adolescence  1.9
**¿adónde?** *adv.* where (to)? (*destination*)  1.2
**aduana** *f.* customs  1.5
**aeropuerto** *m.* airport  1.5
**afeitarse** *v.* to shave  1.7
**aficionado/a** *adj.* fan  1.4
**afirmativo/a** *adj.* affirmative
**agencia de viajes** *f.* travel agency  1.5
**agente de viajes** *m., f.* travel agent  1.5
**agosto** *m.* August  1.5
**agradable** *adj.* pleasant
**agua** *f.* water  1.8
  **agua mineral**  mineral water  1.8
**ahora** *adv.* now  1.2
  **ahora mismo**  right now  1.5
**aire** *m.* air  1.5
**ajo** *m.* garlic  1.8
**al** (*contraction of* **a + el**)  1.2
  **al aire libre**  open-air  1.6
  **al lado de**  beside  1.2
**alegre** *adj.* happy; joyful  1.5
**alegría** *f.* happiness  1.9
**alemán, alemana** *adj.* German  1.3
**algo** *pron.* something; anything  1.7
**algodón** *m.* cotton  1.6
**alguien** *pron.* someone; somebody; anyone  1.7
**algún, alguno/a(s)** *adj.* any; some  1.7
**alimento** *m.* food
**alimentación** *f.* diet
**allá** *adv.* over there  1.2
**allí** *adv.* there  1.2
**almacén** *m.* department store  1.6

**almorzar (o:ue)** *v.* to have lunch  1.4
**almuerzo** *m.* lunch  1.8
**alto/a** *adj.* tall  1.3
**amable** *adj.* nice; friendly  1.5
**amarillo/a** *adj.* yellow  1.3
**amigo/a** *m., f.* friend  1.3
**amistad** *f.* friendship  1.9
**amor** *m.* love  1.9
**anaranjado/a** *adj.* orange  1.6
**andar** *v.* **en patineta**  to skateboard  1.4
**aniversario (de bodas)** *m.* (wedding) anniversary  1.9
**anoche** *adv.* last night  1.6
**anteayer** *adv.* the day before yesterday  1.6
**antes** *adv.* before  1.7
  **antes de** *prep.* before  1.7
**antipático/a** *adj.* unpleasant  1.3
**año** *m.* year  1.5
  **año pasado**  last year  1.6
**aparato** *m.* appliance
**apellido** *m.* last name  1.3
**aprender (a +** *inf.***)** *v.* to learn  1.3
**aquel, aquella** *adj.* that  1.6
**aquél, aquélla** *pron.* that  1.6
**aquello** *neuter pron.* that; that thing; that fact  1.6
**aquellos/as** *pl. adj.* those (over there)  1.6
**aquéllos/as** *pl. pron.* those (ones) (over there)  1.6
**aquí** *adv.* here  1.1
  **Aquí está...**  Here it is...  1.5
  **Aquí estamos en...**  Here we are at/in...
**Argentina** *f.* Argentina  1.1
**argentino/a** *adj.* Argentine  1.3

**arqueología** *f.* archaeology 1.2
**arriba** *adv.* up
**arroz** *m.* rice 1.8
**arte** *m.* art 1.2
**artista** *m., f.* artist 1.3
**arveja** *m.* pea 1.8
**asado/a** *adj.* roast 1.8
**ascensor** *m.* elevator 1.5
**asistir (a)** *v.* to attend 1.3
**atún** *m.* tuna 1.8
**aunque** *conj.* although
**autobús** *m.* bus 1.1
**automático/a** *adj.* automatic
**auto(móvil)** *m.* auto(mobile) 1.5
**avenida** *f.* avenue
**avergonzado/a** *adj.*
  embarrassed 1.5
**avión** *m.* airplane 1.5
**¡Ay!** *interj.* Oh!
  **¡Ay, qué dolor!** Oh, what
  pain!
**ayer** *adv.* yesterday 1.6
**azúcar** *m.* sugar 1.8
**azul** *adj.* blue 1.3

### B

**bailar** *v.* to dance 1.2
**bajo/a** *adj.* short (*in height*) 1.3
**bajo control** under control 1.7
**baloncesto** *m.* basketball 1.4
**banana** *f.* banana 1.8
**bandera** *f.* flag
**bañarse** *v.* to bathe;
  to take a bath 1.7
**baño** *m.* bathroom 1.7
**barato/a** *adj.* cheap 1.6
**barco** *m.* boat 1.5
**beber** *v.* to drink 1.3
**bebida** *f.* drink 1.8
**béisbol** *m.* baseball 1.4
**beso** *m.* kiss 1.9
**biblioteca** *f.* library 1.2
**bicicleta** *f.* bicycle 1.4
**bien** *adj., adv.* well 1.1
**billete** *m.* paper money; ticket
**billón** *m.* trillion
**biología** *f.* biology 1.2
**bisabuelo/a** *m.* great-grandfather;
  great-grandmother 1.3
**bistec** *m.* steak 1.8
**bizcocho** *m.* biscuit
**blanco/a** *adj.* white 1.3
**(blue)jeans** *m., pl.* jeans 1.6
**blusa** *f.* blouse 1.6
**boda** *f.* wedding 1.9
**bolsa** *f.* purse, bag 1.6
**bonito/a** *adj.* pretty 1.3
**borrador** *m.* eraser 1.2
**bota** *f.* boot 1.6
**botella** *f.* bottle 1.9
  **botella de vino** bottle of
  wine 1.9
**botones** *m., f. sing* bellhop 1.5
**brindar** *v.* to toast (*drink*) 1.9
**bucear** *v.* to scuba dive 1.4
**bueno** *adv.* well 1.2

**buen, bueno/a** *adj.* good 1.3,
1.6
  **¡Buen viaje!** Have a good
  trip! 1.1
  **Buena idea.** Good idea. 1.4
  **Buenas noches.** Good
  evening.; Good night. 1.1
  **Buenas tardes.** Good
  afternoon. 1.1
  **buenísimo** extremely good
  **¿Bueno?** Hello. (*on telephone*)
  **Buenos días.** Good morning.
  1.1
**bulevar** *m.* boulevard
**buscar** *v.* to look for 1.2

### C

**caballo** *m.* horse 1.5
**cada** *adj.* each 1.6
**café** *m.* café 1.4;
  *adj.* brown 1.6;
  *m.* coffee 1.8
**cafetería** *f.* cafeteria 1.2
**caja** *f.* cash register 1.6
**calcetín (calcetines)** *m.*
  sock(s) 1.6
**calculadora** *f.* calculator 1.2
**caldo** *m.* soup
**calidad** *f.* quality 1.6
**calor** *m.* heat 1.1
**calzar** *v.* to take size... shoes 1.6
**cama** *f.* bed 1.5
**camarero/a** *m., f.* waiter/
  waitress 1.8
**camarón** *m.* shrimp 1.8
**cambiar (de)** *v.* to change 1.9
**cambio** *m.* **de moneda** currency
  exchange
**caminar** *v.* to walk 1.2
**camino** *m.* road
**camión** *m* truck; bus
**camisa** *f.* shirt 1.6
**camiseta** *f.* t-shirt 1.6
**campo** *m.* countryside 1.5
**canadiense** *adj.* Canadian 1.3
**cansado/a** *adj.* tired 1.5
**cantar** *v.* to sing 1.2
**capital** *f.* capital city 1.1
**cara** *f.* face 1.7
**caramelo** *m.* caramel 1.9
**carne** *f.* meat 1.8
  **carne de res** *f.* beef 1.8
**caro/a** *adj.* expensive 1.6
**carta** *f.* letter 1.4; (*playing*)
  card 1.5
**cartera** *f.* wallet 1.6
**casa** *f.* house; home 1.2
**casado/a** *adj.* married 1.9
**casarse (con)** *v.* to get married
  (to) 1.9
**catorce** *n., adj.* fourteen 1.1
**cebolla** *f.* onion 1.8
**celebrar** *v.* to celebrate 1.9
**cena** *f.* dinner 1.8
**cenar** *v.* to have dinner 1.2
**centro** *m.* downtown 1.4

**centro comercial** shopping
  mall 1.6
**cepillarse los dientes/el pelo**
  *v.* to brush one's teeth/one's hair
  1.7
**cerca de** *prep.* near 1.2
**cerdo** *m.* pork 1.8
**cereales** *m., pl.* cereal; grains 1.8
**cero** *m.* zero 1.1
**cerrado/a** *adj.* closed 1.5
**cerrar (e:ie)** *v.* to close 1.4
**cerveza** *f.* beer 1.8
**ceviche** *m.* marinated fish
  dish 1.8
  **ceviche de camarón** *m.*
  lemon-marinated shrimp 1.8
**chaleco** *m.* vest
**champán** *m.* champagne 1.9
**champiñón** *m.* mushroom 1.8
**champú** *m.* shampoo 1.7
**chaqueta** *f.* jacket 1.6
**chau** *fam. interj.* bye 1.1
**chévere** *adj., fam.* terrific
**chico/a** *m., f.* boy; girl 1.1
**chino/a** *adj.* Chinese 1.3
**chocar (con)** *v.* to run into
**chocolate** *m.* chocolate 1.9
**chuleta** *f.* chop (*food*) 1.8
  **chuleta de cerdo** *f.* pork
  chop 1.8
**cibercafé** *m.* cybercafé
**ciclismo** *m.* cycling 1.4
**cien(to)** *n., adj.* one hundred 1.2
**ciencia** *f.* science 1.2
**cinco** *n., adj.* five 1.1
**cincuenta** *n., adj.* fifty 1.2
**cine** *m.* movie theater 1.4
**cinta** *f.* (audio)tape 1.6
**cinturón** *m.* belt 1.6
**cita** *f.* date; appointment 1.9
**ciudad** *f.* city 1.4
**clase** *f.* class 1.2
**cliente/a** *m., f.* customer 1.6
**color** *m.* color 1.3, 1.6
**comenzar (e:ie)** *v.* to begin 1.4
**comer** *v.* to eat 1.3
**comida** *f.* food; meal 1.8
**como** *prep., conj.* like; as 1.8
**¿cómo?** *adv.* what?; how? 1.1
  **¿Cómo es...?** What's...
  like? 1.3
  **¿Cómo está usted?** *form.*
  How are you? 1.1
  **¿Cómo estás?** *fam.* How are
  you? 1.1
  **¿Cómo se llama
  (usted)?** *form.* What's your
  name? 1.1
  **¿Cómo te llamas (tú)?** *fam.*
  What's your name? 1.1
**cómodo/a** *adj.* comfortable 1.5
**compañero/a de clase** *m., f.*
  classmate 1.2
**compañero/a de cuarto** *m., f.*
  roommate 1.2

**compartir** *v.* to share  **1.3**
**completamente** *adv.* completely  **1.5**
**comprar** *v.* to buy  **1.2**
**compras** *f., pl.* purchases  **1.5**
  **ir de compras**  to go shopping  **1.5**
**comprender** *v.* to understand  **1.3**
**comprobar (o:ue)** *v.* to check
**comprometerse (con)** *v.* to get engaged (to)  **1.9**
**computación** *f.* computer science  **1.2**
**computadora** *f.* computer  **1.1**
**comunidad** *f.* community  **1.1**
**con** *prep.* with  **1.2**
  **Con permiso.**  Pardon me.; Excuse me.  **1.1**
**concordar (o:ue)** *v.* to agree
**conducir** *v.* to drive  **1.6**
**conductor(a)** *m., f.* driver  **1.1**
**confirmar** *v.* to confirm  **1.5**
  **confirmar** *v.* **una reservación** *f.* to confirm a reservation  **1.5**
**confundido/a** *adj.* confused  **1.5**
**conmigo** *pron.* with me  **1.4, 1.9**
**conocer** *v.* to know; to be acquainted with  **1.6**
**conocido/a** *adj.; p.p.* known
**conseguir (e:i)** *v.* to get; to obtain  **1.4**
**consejo** *m.* advice
**construir** *v.* to build
**contabilidad** *f.* accounting  **1.2**
**contar (o:ue)** *v.* to count; to tell  **1.4**
**contento/a** *adj.* happy; content  **1.5**
**contestar** *v.* to answer  **1.2**
**contigo** *fam. pron.* with you  **1.9**
**control** *m.* control  **1.7**
**conversación** *f.* conversation  **1.1**
**conversar** *v.* to converse, to chat  **1.2**
**corbata** *f.* tie  **1.6**
**correo electrónico** *m.* e-mail  **1.4**
**correr** *v.* to run  **1.3**
**cortesía** *f.* courtesy
**corto/a** *adj.* short (in length)  **1.6**
**cosa** *f.* thing  **1.1**
**Costa Rica** *f.* Costa Rica  **1.1**
**costar (o:ue)** *f.* to cost  **1.6**
**costarricense** *adj.* Costa Rican  **1.3**
**creer (en)** *v.* to believe (in)  **1.3**
**crema de afeitar** *f.* shaving cream  **1.7**
**cuaderno** *m.* notebook  **1.1**

**¿cuál(es)?** *pron.* which?; which one(s)?  **1.2**
  **¿Cuál es la fecha de hoy?**  What is today's date?  **1.5**
**cuando** *conj.* when  **1.7**
  **¿cuándo?** *adv.* when?  **1.2**
**¿cuánto(s)/a(s)?** *adj.* how much/how many?  **1.1**
  **¿Cuánto cuesta...?**  How much does... cost?  **1.6**
  **¿Cuántos años tienes?**  How old are you?  **1.3**
**cuarenta** *n., adj.* forty  **1.2**
**cuarto** *m.* room  **1.2; 1.7**
  **cuarto de baño** *m.* bathroom  **1.7**
**cuarto/a** *n., adj.* fourth  **1.5**
  **menos cuarto**  quarter to (*time*)
  **y cuarto**  quarter after (*time*)  **1.1**
**cuatro** *n., adj.* four  **1.1**
**cuatrocientos/as** *n., adj.* four hundred  **1.2**
**Cuba** *f.* Cuba  **1.1**
**cubano/a** *adj.* Cuban  **1.3**
**cubiertos** *m., pl.* silverware
**cubierto/a** *p.p.* covered
**cubrir** *v.* to cover
**cultura** *f.* culture  **1.2**
**cuenta** *f.* bill  **1.8**
**cuidado** *m.* care  **1.3**
**cumpleaños** *m., sing.* birthday  **1.9**
**cumplir años** *v.* to have a birthday  **1.9**
**cuñado/a** *m., f.* brother-in-law; sister-in-law  **1.3**
**curso** *m.* course  **1.2**

## D

**dar** *v.* to give  **1.6, 1.9**
  **dar un consejo** *v.* to give advice
**de** *prep.* of; from  **1.1**
  **¿De dónde eres?** *fam.* Where are you from?  **1.1**
  **¿De dónde es usted?** *form.* Where are you from?  **1.1**
  **¿de quién...?**  whose...? *sing.*  **1.1**
  **¿de quiénes...?**  whose...? *pl.*  **1.1**
  **de algodón**  (made) of cotton  **1.6**
  **de buen humor**  in a good mood  **1.5**
  **de compras**  shopping  **1.5**
  **de cuadros**  plaid  **1.6**
  **de excursión**  hiking  **1.4**
  **de hecho**  in fact
  **de ida y vuelta**  roundtrip  **1.5**
  **de la mañana**  in the morning; A.M.  **1.1**

  **de la noche**  in the evening; at night; P.M.  **1.1**
  **de la tarde**  in the afternoon; in the early evening; P.M.  **1.1**
  **de lana**  (made) of wool  **1.6**
  **de lunares**  polka-dotted  **1.6**
  **de mal humor**  in a bad mood  **1.5**
  **de moda**  in fashion  **1.6**
  **De nada.**  You're welcome.  **1.1**
  **de rayas**  striped  **1.6**
  **de repente** *adv.* suddenly  **1.6**
  **de seda**  (made) of silk  **1.6**
**debajo de** *prep.* below; under  **1.2**
**deber (+ *inf.*)** *v.* should; must; ought to  **1.3**
  **Debe ser...**  It must be...  **1.6**
**decidir (+ *inf.*)** *v.* to decide  **1.3**
**décimo/a** *adj.* tenth  **1.5**
**decir (e:i)** *v.* to say; to tell  **1.4, 1.9**
  **decir la respuesta**  to say the answer  **1.4**
  **decir la verdad**  to tell the truth  **1.4**
  **decir mentiras**  to tell lies  **1.4**
**dejar una propina** *v.* to leave a tip  **1.9**
**del** (contraction of **de + el**) of the; from the
**delante de** *prep.* in front of  **1.2**
**delgado/a** *adj.* thin; slender  **1.3**
**delicioso/a** *adj.* delicious  **1.8**
**demás** *adj.* the rest
**demasiado** *adj., adv.* too much  **1.6**
**dependiente/a** *m., f.* clerk  **1.6**
**deporte** *m.* sport  **1.4**
**deportista** *m.* sports person
**deportivo/a** *adj.* sports-related  **1.4**
**derecha** *f.* right  **1.2**
  **a la derecha de**  to the right of  **1.2**
**derecho** *adj.* straight (ahead)
**desayunar** *v.* to have breakfast  **1.2**
**desayuno** *m.* breakfast  **1.8**
**descansar** *v.* to rest  **1.2**
**describir** *v.* to describe  **1.3**
**desde** *prep.* from  **1.6**
**desear** *v.* to wish; to desire  **1.2**
**desordenado/a** *adj.* disorderly  **1.5**
**despedida** *f.* farewell; good-bye
**despedirse (e:i) (de)** *v.* to say good-bye (to)  **1.7**
**despejado/a** *adj.* clear (*weather*)
**despertador** *m.* alarm clock  **1.7**
**despertarse (e:ie)** *v.* to wake up  **1.7**
**después** *adv.* afterwards; then  **1.7**

**después de** *prep.* after 1.7
**detrás de** *prep.* behind 1.2
**día** *m.* day 1.1
   **día de fiesta** holiday 1.9
**diario/a** *adj.* daily 1.7
**diccionario** *m.* dictionary 1.1
**diciembre** *m.* December 1.5
**diecinueve** *n., adj.* nineteen 1.1
**dieciocho** *n., adj.* eighteen 1.1
**dieciséis** *n., adj.* sixteen 1.1
**diecisiete** *n., adj.* seventeen 1.1
**diente** *m.* tooth 1.7
**diez** *n., adj.* ten 1.1
**difícil** *adj.* difficult; hard 1.3
**dinero** *m.* money 1.6
**diseño** *m.* design
**diversión** *f.* fun activity;
   entertainment; recreation 1.4
**divertido/a** *adj.* fun 1.7
**divertirse (e:ie)** *v.* to have
   fun 1.9
**divorciado/a** *adj.* divorced 1.9
**divorciarse (de)** *v.* to get
   divorced (from) 1.9
**divorcio** *m.* divorce 1.9
**doble** *adj.* double
**doce** *n., adj.* twelve 1.1
**doctor(a)** *m., f.* doctor 1.3
**documentos de viaje** *m.,*
   *pl.* travel documents
**domingo** *m.* Sunday 1.2
**don** *m.* Mr.; sir 1.1
**doña** *m.* Mrs.; ma'am 1.1
**donde** *prep.* where
   **¿dónde?** *adv.* where? 1.1
   **¿Dónde está...?** Where
   is...? 1.2
**dormir (o:ue)** *v.* to sleep 1.4
**dormirse (o:ue)** *v.* to go to sleep;
   to fall asleep 1.7
**dos** *n., adj.* two 1.1
   **dos veces** *f.* twice; two
   times 1.6
**doscientos/as** *n., adj.* two
   hundred 1.2
**ducha** *f.* shower 1.7
**ducharse** *v.* to shower; to take a
   shower 1.7
**dueño/a** *m., f.* owner;
   landlord 1.8
**dulces** *m., pl.* sweets; candy 1.9
**durante** *prep.* during 1.7

## E

**e** *conj.* (used instead of *y* before
   words beginning with *i* and *hi*)
   and 1.4
**economía** *f.* economics 1.2
**Ecuador** *m.* Ecuador 1.1
**ecuatoriano/a** *adj.* Ecuadorian
   1.3
**edad** *f.* age 1.9
**(en) efectivo** *m.* cash 1.6
**el** *m., sing., def. art.* the 1.1

**él** *sub. pron.* he 1.1; *pron., obj.*
   *of prep.* him 1.9
**elegante** *adj.* elegant 1.6
**ella** *sub. pron.* she 1.1; *pron.,*
   *obj. of prep.* her 1.9
**ellos/as** *sub. pron.* they 1.1;
   *pron., obj. of prep.* them 1.9
**emocionante** *adj.* exciting
**empezar (e:ie)** *v.* to begin 1.4
**empleado/a** *m., f.* employee 1.5
**en** *prep.* in; on; at 1.2
   **en casa** at home 1.7
   **en línea** inline 1.4
   **en mi nombre** in my name
   **en punto** on the dot; exactly;
     sharp (*time*) 1.1
   **en qué** in what; how 1.2
   **¿En qué puedo servirles?**
     How can I help you? 1.5
**enamorado/a (de)** *adj.* in love
   (with) 1.5
**enamorarse (de)** *v.* to fall in love
   (with) 1.9
**encantado/a** *adj.* delighted;
   pleased to meet you 1.1
**encantar** *v.* to like very much; to
   love (*inanimate objects*) 1.7
**encima de** *prep.* on top of 1.2
**encontrar (o:ue)** *v.* to find 1.4
**enero** *m.* January 1.5
**enojado/a** *adj.* mad; angry 1.5
**enojarse (con)** *v.* to get angry
   (with) 1.7
**ensalada** *f.* salad 1.8
**enseguida** *adv.* right away 1.8
**enseñar** *v.* to teach 1.2
**entender (e:ie)** *v.* to understand
   1.4
**entonces** *adv.* then 1.7
**entre** *prep.* between; among 1.2
**entremeses** *m., pl.* hors
   d'oeuvres; appetizers 1.8
**equipaje** *m.* luggage 1.5
**equipo** *m.* team 1.4
**equivocado/a** *adj.* wrong 1.5
**eres** *fam.* you are 1.1
**es** he/she/it is 1.1
   **Es de...** He/She is from... 1.1
   **Es la una.** It's one o'clock. 1.1
**esa(s)** *f., adj.* that; those 1.6
**ésa(s)** *f., pron.* those (ones) 1.6
**escalar** *v.* to climb 1.4
   **escalar montañas** *v.* to climb
     mountains 1.4
**escoger** *v.* to choose 1.8
**escribir** *v.* to write 1.3
   **escribir un mensaje**
     **electrónico** to write an
     e-mail message 1.4
   **escribir una carta** to write a
     letter 1.4
   **escribir una postal** to write a
     postcard
**escritorio** *m.* desk 1.2
**escuchar** *v.* to listen (to) 1.2

**escuchar la radio** to listen
   to the radio 1.2
**escuchar música** to listen to
   music 1.2
**escuela** *f.* school 1.1
**ese** *m., sing., adj.* that 1.6
**ése** *m., sing., pron.* that
   (one) 1.6
**eso** *neuter pron.* that;
   that thing 1.6
**esos** *m., pl., adj.* those 1.6
**ésos** *m., pl., pron.* those
   (ones) 1.6
**España** *f.* Spain 1.1
**español** *m.* Spanish (language)
   1.2
**español(a)** *adj.* Spanish 1.3
**espárragos** *m., pl.* asparagus
   1.8
**especialización** *f.* major 1.2
**espejo** *m.* mirror 1.7
**esperar (+ *inf.*)** *v.* to wait (for); to
   hope 1.2
**esposo/a** *m., f.* husband; wife;
   spouse 1.3
**esquí (acuático)** *m.* (water)
   skiing 1.4
**esquiar** *v.* to ski 1.4
**está** he/she/it is, you are 1.2
   **Está (muy) despejado.** It's
     (very) clear. (*weather*)
   **Está lloviendo.** It's raining.
     1.5
   **Está nevando.** It's snowing.
     1.5
   **Está (muy) nublado.** It's
     (very) cloudy. (*weather*) 1.5
**esta(s)** *f., adj.* this; these 1.6
   **esta noche** tonight 1.4
**ésta(s)** *f., pron.* this (one); these
   (ones) 1.6
   **Ésta es...** *f.* This is...
     (*introducing someone*) 1.1
**estación** *f.* station; season 1.5
   **estación de autobuses**
     bus station 1.5
   **estación del metro** subway
     station 1.5
   **estación de tren** train
     station 1.5
**estadio** *m.* stadium 1.2
**estado civil** *m.* marital status
   1.9
**Estados Unidos** *m.* (EE.UU.;
   E.U.) United States 1.1
**estadounidense** *adj.* from the
   United States 1.3
**estampado/a** *adj.* print
**estar** *v.* to be 1.2
   **estar aburrido/a** to be
     bored 1.5
   **estar bajo control** to be
     under control 1.7
   **estar de moda** to be in
     fashion 1.6

**estar de vacaciones**  to be on vacation  **1.5**

**estar seguro/a**  to be sure  **1.5**

**No está nada mal.**  It's not bad at all.  **1.5**

**este**  *m., sing., adj.*  this  **1.6**

**éste**  *m., sing., pron.*  this (one)  **1.6**

   **Éste es...**  *m.*  This is... (*introducing someone*)  **1.1**

**estilo**  *m.*  style

**esto**  *neuter pron.*  this; this thing  **1.6**

**estos**  *m., pl., adj.*  these  **1.6**

**éstos**  *m., pl., pron.*  these (ones)  **1.6**

**estudiante**  *m., f.*  student  **1.1, 1.2**

**estudiantil**  *adj.*  student  **1.2**

**estudiar**  *v.*  to study  **1.2**

**estupendo/a**  *adj.*  stupendous  **1.5**

**etapa**  *f.*  stage  **1.9**

**examen**  *m.*  test; exam  **1.2**

**excelente**  *adj.*  excellent  **1.5**

**excursión**  *f.*  hike; tour; excursion  **1.4**

**excursionista**  *m., f.*  hiker

**explicar**  *v.*  to explain  **1.2**

**explorar**  *v.*  to explore

**expresión**  *f.*  expression

## F

**fabuloso/a**  *adj.*  fabulous  **1.5**

**fácil**  *adj.*  easy  **1.3**

**falda**  *f.*  skirt  **1.6**

**faltar**  *v.*  to lack; to need  **1.7**

**familia**  *f.*  family  **1.3**

**fascinar**  *v.*  to fascinate  **1.7**

**favorito/a**  *adj.*  favorite  **1.4**

**febrero**  *m.*  February  **1.5**

**fecha**  *f.*  date  **1.5**

**feliz**  *adj.*  happy  **1.5**

   **¡Feliz cumpleaños!**  Happy birthday!  **1.9**

**¡Felicidades!**  Congratulations!  **1.9**

**¡Felicitaciones!**  Congratulations!  **1.9**

**fenomenal**  *adj.*  great, phenomenal  **1.5**

**feo/a**  *adj.*  ugly  **1.3**

**fiesta**  *f.*  party  **1.9**

**fijo/a**  *adj.*  fixed, set  **1.6**

**fin**  *m.*  end  **1.4**

   **fin de semana**  weekend  **1.4**

**física**  *f.*  physics  **1.2**

**flan (de caramelo)**  *m.*  baked (caramel) custard  **1.9**

**folleto**  *m.*  brochure

**foto(grafía)**  *f.*  photograph  **1.1**

**francés, francesa**  *adj.*  French  **1.3**

**frenos**  *m., pl.*  brakes

**fresco/a**  *adj.*  cool  **1.5**

**frijoles**  *m., pl.*  beans  **1.8**

**frío/a**  *adj.*  cold  **1.5**

**frito/a**  *adj.*  fried  **1.8**

**fruta**  *f.*  fruit  **1.8**

**frutilla**  *f.*  strawberry

**fuera**  *adv.*  outside

**fútbol**  *m.*  soccer  **1.4**

**fútbol americano**  *m.*  football  **1.4**

## G

**gafas (de sol)**  *f., pl.*  (sun)glasses  **1.6**

**gafas (oscuras)**  *f., pl.*  (sun)glasses

**galleta**  *f.*  cookie  **1.9**

**ganar**  *v.*  to win  **1.4**

**ganga**  *f.*  bargain  **1.6**

**gastar**  *v.*  to spend (*money*)  **1.6**

**gemelo/a**  *m., f.*  twin  **1.3**

**gente**  *f.*  people  **1.3**

**geografía**  *f.*  geography  **1.2**

**gimnasio**  *m.*  gymnasium  **1.4**

**golf**  *m.*  golf  **1.4**

**gordo/a**  *adj.*  fat  **1.3**

**gracias**  *f., pl.*  thank you; thanks  **1.1**

   **Gracias por todo.**  Thanks for everything.  **1.9**

   **Gracias una vez más.**  Thanks again.  **1.9**

**graduarse (de/en)**  *v.*  to graduate (from/in)  **1.9**

**gran, grande**  *adj.*  big; large  **1.3**

**grillo**  *m.*  cricket

**gris**  *adj.*  gray  **1.6**

**gritar**  *v.*  to scream  **1.7**

**guantes**  *m., pl.*  gloves  **1.6**

**guapo/a**  *adj.*  handsome; good-looking  **1.3**

**guía**  *m., f.*  guide

**gustar**  *v.*  to be pleasing to; to like  **1.2**

   **Me gustaría...**  I would like...

**gusto**  *m.*  pleasure  **1.1**

   **El gusto es mío.**  The pleasure is mine.  **1.1**

   **Mucho gusto.**  Pleased to meet you.  **1.1**

## H

**habitación**  *f.*  room  **1.5**

   **habitación doble**  double room  **1.5**

   **habitación individual**  single room  **1.5**

**hablar**  *v.*  to talk; to speak  **1.2**

**hacer**  *v.*  to do; to make  **1.4**

   **Hace buen tiempo.**  The weather is good.  **1.5**

   **Hace (mucho) calor.**  It's (very) hot. (*weather*)  **1.5**

   **Hace fresco.**  It's cool. (*weather*)  **1.5**

   **Hace (mucho) frío.**  It's very cold. (*weather*)  **1.5**

   **Hace mal tiempo.**  The weather is bad.  **1.5**

   **Hace (mucho) sol.**  It's (very) sunny. (*weather*)  **1.5**

   **Hace (mucho) viento.**  It's (very) windy. (*weather*)  **1.5**

**hacer juego (con)**  to match (with)  **1.6**

**hacer las maletas**  to pack (one's) suitcases  **1.5**

**hacer (wind)surf**  to (wind)surf  **1.5**

**hacer turismo**  to go sightseeing

**hacer un viaje**  to take a trip  **1.5**

**hacer una excursión**  to go on a hike; to go on a tour

**hambre**  *f.*  hunger  **1.3**

**hamburguesa**  *f.*  hamburger  **1.8**

**hasta**  *prep.*  until  **1.6;**  toward

   **Hasta la vista.**  See you later.  **1.1**

   **Hasta luego.**  See you later.  **1.1**

   **Hasta mañana.**  See you tomorrow.  **1.1**

   **Hasta pronto.**  See you soon.  **1.1**

**hay**  *v.*  there is; there are  **1.1**

   **Hay (mucha) contaminación.**  It's (very) smoggy.

   **Hay (mucha) niebla.**  It's (very) foggy.

   **No hay de qué.**  You're welcome.  **1.1**

**helado/a**  *adj.*  iced  **1.8**

**helado**  *m.*  ice cream  **1.9**

**hermanastro/a**  *m., f.*  stepbrother; stepsister  **1.3**

**hermano/a**  *m., f.*  brother; sister  **1.3**

**hermano/a mayor/menor**  *m., f.*  older/younger brother/sister  **1.3**

**hermanos**  *m., pl.*  siblings (brothers and sisters)  **1.3**

**hermoso/a**  *adj.*  beautiful  **1.6**

**hijastro/a**  *m., f.*  stepson; stepdaughter  **1.3**

**hijo/a**  *m., f.*  son; daughter  **1.3**

   **hijo/a único/a**  *m., f.*  only child  **1.3**

**hijos**  *m., pl.*  children  **1.3**

**historia**  *f.*  history  **1.2**

**hockey**  *m.*  hockey  **1.4**

**hola**  *interj.*  hello; hi  **1.1**

**hombre**  *m.*  man  **1.1**

**hora** *f.* hour **1.1**;  the time
**horario** *m.* schedule **1.2**
**hotel** *m.* hotel **1.5**
**hoy** *adv.* today **1.2**
  **hoy día** *adv.* nowadays
  **Hoy es...** Today is... **1.2**
**huésped** *m., f.* guest **1.5**
**huevo** *m.* egg **1.8**
**humanidades** *f., pl.* humanities **1.2**

### I

**ida** *f.* one way (*travel*)
**idea** *f.* idea **1.4**
**iglesia** *f.* church **1.4**
**igualmente** *adv.* likewise **1.1**
**impermeable** *m.* raincoat **1.6**
**importante** *adj.* important **1.3**
**importar** *v.* to be important to; to matter **1.7**
**increíble** *adj.* incredible **1.5**
**individual** *adj.* private (*room*) **1.5**
**ingeniero/a** *m., f.* engineer **1.3**
**inglés** *m.* English (*language*) **1.2**
**inglés, inglesa** *adj.* English **1.3**
**inodoro** *m.* toilet **1.7**
**inspector(a) de aduanas** *m., f.* customs inspector **1.5**
**inteligente** *adj.* intelligent **1.3**
**intercambiar** *v.* to exchange
**interesante** *adj.* interesting **1.3**
**interesar** *v.* to be interesting to; to interest **1.7**
**invierno** *m.* winter **1.5**
**invitado/a** *m., f.* guest **1.9**
**invitar** *v.* to invite **1.9**
**ir** *v.* to go **1.4**
  **ir a (+ *inf.*)** to be going to *do something* **1.4**
  **ir de compras** to go shopping **1.5**
  **ir de excursión (a las montañas)** to go on a hike (in the mountains) **1.4**
  **ir de pesca** to go fishing
  **ir de vacaciones** to go on vacation **1.5**
  **ir en autobús** to go by bus **1.5**
  **ir en auto(móvil)** to go by car **1.5**
  **ir en avión** to go by plane **1.5**
  **ir en barco** to go by boat **1.5**
  **ir en metro** to go by subway
  **ir en motocicleta** to go by motorcycle **1.5**
  **ir en taxi** to go by taxi **1.5**
  **ir en tren** to go by train
**irse** *v.* to go away; to leave **1.7**

**italiano/a** *adj.* Italian **1.3**
**izquierdo/a** *adj.* left **1.2**
  **a la izquierda de** to the left of **1.2**

### J

**jabón** *m.* soap **1.7**
**jamás** *adv.* never; not ever **1.7**
**jamón** *m.* ham **1.8**
**japonés, japonesa** *adj.* Japanese **1.3**
**joven** *adj. m., f., sing.* (**jóvenes** *pl.*) young **1.3**
**joven** *m., f., sing.* (**jóvenes** *pl.*) youth; young person **1.1**
**jubilarse** *v.* to retire (*from work*) **1.9**
**juego** *m.* game
**jueves** *m., sing.* Thursday **1.2**
**jugador(a)** *m., f.* player **1.4**
**jugar (u:ue)** *v.* to play **1.4**
  **jugar a las cartas** to play cards **1.5**
**jugo** *m.* juice **1.8**
  **jugo de fruta** *m.* fruit juice **1.8**
**julio** *m.* July **1.5**
**junio** *m.* June **1.5**
**juntos/as** *adj.* together **1.9**
**juventud** *f.* youth **1.9**

### L

**la** *f., sing., def. art.* the **1.1**
**la** *f., sing., d.o. pron.* her, it; *form.* you **1.5**
**laboratorio** *m.* laboratory **1.2**
**lana** *f.* wool **1.6**
**langosta** *f.* lobster **1.8**
**lápiz** *m.* pencil **1.1**
**largo/a** *adj.* long **1.6**
**las** *f., pl., def. art.* the **1.1**
**las** *f., pl., d.o. pron.* them; *form.* you **1.5**
**lavabo** *m.* sink **1.7**
**lavarse** *v.* to wash oneself **1.7**
  **lavarse la cara** to wash one's face **1.7**
  **lavarse las manos** to wash one's hands **1.7**
**le** *sing., i.o. pron.* to/for him, her; *form.* you **1.6**
  **Le presento a...** *form.* I would like to introduce you to (name). **1.1**
**lección** *f.* lesson **1.1**
**leche** *f.* milk **1.8**
**lechuga** *f.* lettuce **1.8**
**leer** *v.* to read **1.3**
  **leer correo electrónico** to read e-mail **1.4**
  **leer un periódico** to read a newspaper **1.4**

**leer una revista** to read a magazine **1.4**
**lejos de** *prep.* far from **1.2**
**lengua** *f.* language **1.2**
  **lenguas extranjeras** *f., pl.* foreign languages **1.2**
**lentes (de sol)** (sun)glasses
**lentes de contacto** *m., pl.* contact lenses
**les** *pl., i.o. pron.* to/for them; *form.* you **1.6**
**levantarse** *v.* to get up **1.7**
**libre** *adj.* free **1.4**
**librería** *f.* bookstore **1.2**
**libro** *m.* book **1.2**
**limón** *m.* lemon **1.8**
**limpio/a** *adj.* clean **1.5**
**línea** *f.* line
**listo/a** *adj.* ready; smart **1.5**
**literatura** *f.* literature **1.2**
**llamarse** *v.* to be called; to be named **1.7**
**llave** *f.* key **1.5**
**llegada** *f.* arrival **1.5**
**llegar** *v.* to arrive **1.2**
**llevar** *v.* to carry **1.2**; to wear; to take **1.6**
  **llevarse bien/mal (con)** to get along well/badly (with) **1.9**
**llover (o:ue)** *v.* to rain **1.5**
  **Llueve.** It's raining. **1.5**
**lo** *m., sing., d.o. pron.* him, it; *form.* you **1.5**
  **Lo siento.** I'm sorry. **1.1**
  **Lo siento muchísimo.** I'm so sorry. **1.4**
**loco/a** *adj.* crazy **1.6**
**los** *m., pl., def. art.* the **1.1**
**los** *m., pl., d.o. pron.* them; *form.* you **1.5**
**luego** *adv.* then **1.7**; *adv.* later **1.1**
**lugar** *m.* place **1.4**
**lunares** *m.* polka dots **1.6**
**lunes** *m., sing.* Monday **1.2**

### M

**madrastra** *f.* stepmother **1.3**
**madre** *f.* mother **1.3**
**madurez** *f.* maturity; middle age **1.9**
**magnífico/a** *adj.* magnificent **1.5**
**maíz** *m.* corn **1.8**
**mal, malo/a** *adj.* bad **1.3**
**maleta** *f.* suitcase **1.1**
**mamá** *f.* mom **1.3**
**mano** *f.* hand **1.1**
  **¡Manos arriba!** Hands up!
**mantequilla** *f.* butter **1.8**
**manzana** *f.* apple **1.8**
**mañana** *f.* morning, A.M. **1.1**; tomorrow **1.1**

**mapa** *m.* map 1.2
**maquillaje** *m.* makeup 1.7
**maquillarse** *v.* to put on makeup 1.7
**mar** *m.* sea 1.5
**maravilloso/a** *adj.* marvelous 1.5
**margarina** *f.* margarine 1.8
**mariscos** *m., pl.* shellfish 1.8
**marrón** *adj.* brown 1.6
**martes** *m., sing.* Tuesday 1.2
**marzo** *m.* March 1.5
**más** *pron.* more 1.2
  **más de (+ *number*)** more than 1.8
  **más tarde** later (on) 1.7
  **más... que** more... than 1.8
**matemáticas** *f., pl.* mathematics 1.2
**materia** *f.* course 1.2
**matrimonio** *m.* marriage 1.9
**mayo** *m.* May 1.5
**mayonesa** *f.* mayonnaise 1.8
**mayor** *adj.* older 1.3
  **el/la mayor** *adj.* the eldest 1.8; the oldest
**me** *sing., d.o. pron.* me 1.5; *sing. i.o. pron.* to/for me 1.6
  **Me gusta...** I like... 1.2
  **No me gustan nada.** I don't like them at all. 1.2
  **Me llamo...** My name is... 1.1
  **Me muero por...** I'm dying to (for)...
**mediano/a** *adj.* medium
**medianoche** *f.* midnight 1.1
**medias** *f., pl.* pantyhose, stockings 1.6
**médico/a** *m., f.* doctor 1.3
**medio/a** *adj.* half 1.3
  **medio/a hermano/a** *m., f.* half-brother; half-sister 1.3
  **mediodía** *m.* noon 1.1
  **y media** thirty minutes past the hour (*time*) 1.1
**mejor** *adj.* better 1.8
  **el/la mejor** *adj.* the best 1.8
**melocotón** *m.* peach 1.8
**menor** *adj.* younger 1.3
  **el/la menor** *adj.* the youngest 1.8
**menos** *adv.* less
  **menos cuarto..., menos quince...** quarter to... (*time*) 1.1
  **menos de (+ *number*)** fewer than 1.8
  **menos... que** less... than 1.8
**mensaje electrónico** *m.* e-mail message 1.4
**mentira** *f.* lie 1.4
**menú** *m.* menu 1.8
**mercado** *m.* market 1.6

**mercado al aire libre** *m.* open-air market 1.6
**merendar (e:ie)** *v.* to snack 1.8; to have an afternoon snack
**mes** *m.* month 1.5
**mesa** *f.* table 1.2
**metro** *m.* subway 1.5
**mexicano/a** *adj.* Mexican 1.3
**México** *m.* Mexico 1.1
**mí** *pron., obj. of prep.* me 1.9
**mi(s)** *poss. adj.* my 1.3
**miedo** *m.* fear 1.3
**miércoles** *m., sing.* Wednesday 1.2
**mil** *m.* one thousand 1.2
  **Mil perdones.** I'm so sorry. (*lit. A thousand pardons.*) 1.4
**mil millones** *m.* billion
**millón** *m.* million 1.2
**millones (de)** *m.* millions (of)
**minuto** *m.* minute 1.1
**mirar** *v.* to look (at); to watch 1.2
  **mirar (la) televisión** to watch television 1.2
**mismo/a** *adj.* same 1.3
**mochila** *f.* backpack 1.2
**moda** *f.* fashion 1.6
**módem** *m.* modem
**molestar** *v.* to bother; to annoy 1.7
**montaña** *f.* mountain 1.4
**montar a caballo** *v.* to ride a horse 1.5
**monumento** *m.* monument 1.4
**mora** *f.* blackberry 1.8
**morado/a** *adj.* purple 1.6
**moreno/a** *adj.* brunet(te) 1.3
**morir (o:ue)** *v.* to die 1.8
**mostrar (o:ue)** *v.* to show 1.4
**motocicleta** *f.* motorcycle 1.5
**motor** *m.* motor
**muchacho/a** *m., f.* boy; girl 1.3
**mucho/a** *adj., adv.* a lot of; much 1.2; many 1.3
  **(Muchas) gracias.** Thank you (very much).; Thanks (a lot). 1.1
  **Muchísimas gracias.** Thank you very, very much. 1.9
  **Mucho gusto.** Pleased to meet you. 1.1
**muchísimo** very much 1.2
**muela** *f.* tooth; molar
**muerte** *f.* death 1.9
**mujer** *f.* woman 1.1
  **mujer policía** *f.* female police officer
**multa** *f.* fine
**mundial** *adj.* worldwide
**municipal** *adj.* municipal
**museo** *m.* museum 1.4
**música** *f.* music 1.2

**muy** *adv.* very 1.1
  **Muy amable.** That's very kind of you. 1.5
  **(Muy) bien, gracias.** (Very) well, thanks. 1.1

## N

**nacer** *v.* to be born 1.9
**nacimiento** *m.* birth 1.9
**nacionalidad** *f.* nationality 1.1
**nada** *pron., adv.* nothing 1.1; not anything 1.7
  **nada mal** not bad at all 1.5
**nadar** *v.* to swim 1.4
**nadie** *pron.* no one, nobody, not anyone 1.7
**naranja** *f.* orange 1.8
**natación** *f.* swimming 1.4
**Navidad** *f.* Christmas 1.9
**necesitar (+ *inf.*)** *v.* to need 1.2
**negativo/a** *adj.* negative
**negro/a** *adj.* black 1.3
**nervioso/a** *adj.* nervous 1.5
**nevar (e:ie)** *v.* to snow 1.5
  **Nieva.** It's snowing. 1.5
**ni... ni** neither... nor 1.7
**niebla** *f.* fog
**nieto/a** *m., f.* grandson; granddaughter 1.3
**nieve** *f.* snow
**ningún, ninguno/a(s)** *adj., pron.* no; none; not any 1.7
  **ningún problema** no problem
**niñez** *f.* childhood 1.9
**niño/a** *m., f.* child 1.3
**no** *adv.* no; not 1.1
  **¿no?** right? 1.1
  **No está nada mal.** It's not bad at all. 1.5
  **no estar de acuerdo** to disagree
  **No estoy seguro.** I'm not sure.
  **no hay** there is not; there are not 1.1
  **No hay de qué.** You're welcome. 1.1
  **No hay problema.** No problem. 1.7
  **No me gustan nada.** I don't like them at all. 1.2
  **no muy bien** not very well 1.1
  **No quiero.** I don't want to. 1.4
  **No sé.** I don't know.
  **No se preocupe.** (*form.*) Don't worry. 1.7
  **No te preocupes.** (*fam.*) Don't worry. 1.7
  **no tener razón** to be wrong 1.3

**noche** *f.* night   1.1
**nombre** *m.* name   1.1
**norteamericano/a** *adj.* (North) American   1.3
**nos** *pl., d.o. pron.* us   1.5; *pl., i.o. pron.* to/for us   1.6
   **Nos vemos.** See you.   1.1
**nosotros/as** *sub. pron.* we   1.1; *pron., obj. of prep.* us   1.9
**novecientos/as** *n., adj.* nine hundred   1.2
**noveno/a** *n., adj.* ninth   1.5
**noventa** *n., adj.* ninety   1.2
**noviembre** *m.* November   1.5
**novio/a** *m., f.* boyfriend/ girlfriend   1.3
**nublado/a** *adj.* cloudy   1.5
   **Está (muy) nublado.** It's very cloudy.   1.5
**nuera** *f.* daughter-in-law   1.3
**nuestro(s)/a(s)** *poss. adj.* our   1.3
**nueve** *n., adj.* nine   1.1
**nuevo/a** *adj.* new   1.6
**número** *m.* number   1.1; (shoe) size   1.6
**nunca** *adv.* never; not ever   1.7

## O

**o** *conj.* or   1.7
   **o... o;** either... or   1.7
**océano** *m.* ocean
**ochenta** *n., adj.* eighty   1.2
**ocho** *n., adj.* eight   1.1
**ochocientos/as** *n., adj.* eight hundred   1.2
**octavo/a** *n., adj.* eighth   1.5
**octubre** *m.* October   1.5
**ocupado/a** *adj.* busy   1.5
**odiar** *v.* to hate   1.9
**ofrecer** *v.* to offer   1.6
**oír** *v.* to hear   1.4
   **Oiga./Oigan.** *form., sing./pl.* Listen. (*in conversation*)   1.1
   **Oye.** *fam., sing.* Listen. (*in conversation*)   1.1
**once** *n., adj.* eleven   1.1
**ordenado/a** *adj.* orderly   1.5
**ordinal** *adj.* ordinal (number)
**ortografía** *f.* spelling
**ortográfico/a** *adj.* spelling
**os** *fam., pl., d.o. pron.* you   1.5; *fam., pl., i.o. pron.* to/for you   1.6
**otoño** *m.* autumn   1.5
**otro/a** *adj.* other; another   1.6
   **otra vez** *adv.* again

## P

**padrastro** *m.* stepfather   1.3
**padre** *m.* father   1.3
   **padres** *m., pl.* parents   1.3

**pagar** *v.* to pay   1.6, 1.9
   **pagar la cuenta** to pay the bill   1.9
**país** *m.* country   1.1
**paisaje** *m.* landscape   1.5
**palabra** *f.* word   1.1
**pan** *m.* bread   1.8
   **pan tostado** *m.* toasted bread   1.8
**pantalones** *m., pl.* pants   1.6
   **pantalones cortos** *m., pl.* shorts   1.6
**pantuflas** *f., pl.* slippers   1.7
**papa** *f.* potato   1.8
   **papas fritas** *f., pl.* fried potatoes; French fries   1.8
**papá** *m.* dad   1.3
   **papás** *m., pl.* parents   1.3
**papel** *m.* paper   1.2
**papelera** *f.* wastebasket   1.2
**par** *m.* pair   1.6
   **par de zapatos** *m.* pair of shoes   1.6
**parecer** *v.* to seem   1.6
**pareja** *f.* (married) couple; partner   1.9
**parientes** *m., pl.* relatives   1.3
**parque** *m.* park   1.4
**párrafo** *m.* paragraph
**partido** *m.* game; match (*sports*)   1.4
**pasado/a** *adj.* last; past   1.6
   **pasado** *p.p.* passed
**pasaje** *m.* ticket   1.5
   **pasaje de ida y vuelta** *m.* roundtrip ticket   1.5
**pasajero/a** *m., f.* passenger   1.1
**pasaporte** *m.* passport   1.5
**pasar** *v.* to go through   1.5
   **pasar por la aduana** to go through customs
   **pasar tiempo** to spend time
   **pasarlo bien/mal** to have a good/bad time   1.9
**pasatiempo** *m.* pastime; hobby   1.4
**pasear** *v.* to take a walk; to stroll   1.4
   **pasear en bicicleta** to ride a bicycle   1.4
   **pasear por** to walk around   1.4
**pasta** *f.* **de dientes** toothpaste   1.7
**pastel** *m.* cake; pie   1.9
   **pastel de chocolate** *m.* chocolate cake   1.9
   **pastel de cumpleaños** *m.* birthday cake
**patata** *f.* potato   1.8
   **patatas fritas** *f., pl.* fried potatoes; French fries   1.8
**patinar (en línea)** *v.* to (inline) skate   1.4
**patineta** *f.* skateboard   1.4

**pavo** *m.* turkey   1.8
**pedir (e:i)** *v.* to ask for; to request   1.4; to order (*food*)   1.8
**peinarse** *v.* to comb one's hair   1.7
**película** *f.* movie   1.4
**pelirrojo/a** *adj.* red-haired   1.3
**pelo** *m.* hair   1.7
**pelota** *f.* ball   1.4
**pensar (e:ie)** *v.* to think   1.4
   **pensar (+ inf.)** *v.* to intend to; to plan to (*do something*)   1.4
   **pensar en** *v.* to think about   1.4
**pensión** *f.* boardinghouse
**peor** *adj.* worse   1.8
   **el/la peor** *adj.* the worst   1.8
**pequeño/a** *adj.* small   1.3
**pera** *f.* pear   1.8
**perder (e:ie)** *v.* to lose; to miss   1.4
**Perdón.** Pardon me.; Excuse me.   1.1
**perezoso/a** *adj.* lazy
**perfecto/a** *adj.* perfect   1.5
**periódico** *m.* newspaper   1.4
**periodismo** *m.* journalism   1.2
**periodista** *m., f.* journalist   1.3
**permiso** *m.* permission
**pero** *conj.* but   1.2
**persona** *f.* person   1.3
**pesca** *f.* fishing
**pescado** *m.* fish (*cooked*)   1.8
**pescador(a)** *m., f.* fisherman/ fisherwoman
**pescar** *v.* to fish   1.5
**pimienta** *f.* black pepper   1.8
**piña** *f.* pineapple   1.8
**piscina** *f.* swimming pool   1.4
**piso** *m.* floor (*of a building*)   1.5
**pizarra** *f.* blackboard   1.2
**planes** *m., pl.* plans
**planta baja** *f.* ground floor   1.5
**plato** *m.* dish (*in a meal*)   1.8
   **plato principal** *m.* main dish   1.8
**playa** *f.* beach   1.5
**plaza** *f.* city or town square   1.4
**pluma** *f.* pen   1.2
**pobre** *adj.* poor   1.6
**pobreza** *f.* poverty
**poco/a** *adj.* little; few   1.5
**poder (o:ue)** *v.* to be able to; can   1.4
**pollo** *m.* chicken   1.8
   **pollo asado** *m.* roast chicken   1.8
**ponchar** *v.* to go flat
**poner** *v.* to put; to place   1.4
**ponerse (+ adj.)** *v.* to become (+ adj.)   1.7; to put on   1.7

**por** *prep.* in exchange for; for; by; in; through; around; along; during; because of; on account of; on behalf of; in search of; by way of
  **por avión**  by plane
  **por favor**  please  1.1
  **por la mañana**  in the morning  1.7
  **por la noche**  at night  1.7
  **por la tarde**  in the afternoon  1.7
  **¿por qué?**  why?  1.2
  **por teléfono**  by phone; on the phone
  **por último**  finally  1.7
**porque** *conj.* because  1.2
**posesivo/a** *adj.* possessive  1.3
**postal** *f.* postcard
**postre** *m.* dessert  1.9
**practicar** *v.* to practice  1.2
  **practicar deportes** *m., pl.* to play sports  1.4
**precio (fijo)** *m.* (fixed; set) price  1.6
**preferir (e:ie)** *v.* to prefer  1.4
**pregunta** *f.* question
**preguntar** *v.* to ask (*a question*)  1.2
**preocupado/a (por)** *adj.* worried (about)  1.5
**preocuparse (por)** *v.* to worry (about)  1.7
**preparar** *v.* to prepare  1.2
**preposición** *f.* preposition
**presentación** *f.* introduction
**presentar** *v.* to introduce
  **Le presento a...**  I would like to introduce you to (name).  1.1
  **Te presento a...**  I would like to introduce you to (name). (*fam.*)  1.1
**prestado/a** *adj.* borrowed
**prestar** *v.* to lend; to loan  1.6
**primavera** *f.* spring  1.5
**primer, primero/a** *n., adj.* first  1.5
**primo/a** *m., f.* cousin  1.3
**principal** *adj.* main  1.8
**prisa** *f.* haste  1.3
**probar (o:ue)** *v.* to taste; to try  1.8
**probarse (o:ue)** *v.* to try on  1.7
**problema** *m.* problem  1.1
**profesión** *f.* profession  1.3
**profesor(a)** *m., f.* teacher  1.1,  1.2
**programa** *m.*  1.1
**programador(a)** *m., f.* computer programmer  1.3
**pronombre** *m.* pronoun
**propina** *f.* tip  1.8
**prueba** *f.* test; quiz  1.2

**psicología** *f.* psychology  1.2
**pueblo** *m.* town  1.4
**puerta** *f.* door  1.2
**Puerto Rico** *m.* Puerto Rico  1.1
**puertorriqueño/a** *adj.* Puerto Rican  1.3
**pues** *conj.* well  1.2

**Q**

**que** *conj.* that; which
  **¡Qué...!**  How...!  1.3
  **¡Qué dolor!**  What pain!
  **¡Qué ropa más bonita!**  What pretty clothes!  1.6
  **¡Qué sorpresa!**  What a surprise!
  **¿qué?** *pron.* what?  1.1
  **¿Qué día es hoy?**  What day is it?  1.2
  **¿Qué hay de nuevo?**  What's new?  1.1
  **¿Qué hora es?**  What time is it?  1.1
  **¿Qué les parece?**  What do you (*pl.*) think?
  **¿Qué pasa?**  What's happening?; What's going on?  1.1
  **¿Qué precio tiene?**  What is the price?
  **¿Qué tal...?**  How are you?; How is it going?  1.1; How is/are...?  1.2
  **¿Qué talla lleva/usa?**  What size do you wear? (*form.*)  1.6
  **¿Qué tiempo hace?**  How's the weather?  1.5
  **¿En qué...?**  In which...?  1.2
**quedar** *v.* to be left over; to fit (*clothing*)  1.7
**quedarse** *v.* to stay; to remain  1.7
**querer (e:ie)** *v.* to want; to love  1.4
**queso** *m.* cheese  1.8
**quien(es)** *pron.* who; whom
  **¿Quién es...?**  Who is...?  1.1
  **¿quién(es)?** *pron.* who?; whom?  1.1
**química** *f.* chemistry  1.2
**quince** *n., adj.* fifteen  1.1
  **menos quince**  quarter to (*time*)  1.1
  **y quince**  quarter after (*time*)  1.1
**quinceañera** *f.* young woman celebrating her fifteenth birthday  1.9
**quinientos/as** *n., adj.* five hundred  1.2
**quinto/a** *n., adj.* fifth  1.5
**quitarse** *v.* to take off  1.7
**quizás** *adv.* maybe  1.5

**R**

**radio** *f.* radio (*medium*)  1.2
  **radio** *m.* radio (*set*)  1.2
**ratos libres** *m., pl.* spare (*free*) time  1.4
**raya** *f.* stripe  1.6
**razón** *f.* reason  1.3
**rebaja** *f.* sale  1.6
**recibir** *v.* to receive  1.3
**recién casado/a** *m., f.* newlywed  1.9
**recomendar (e:ie)** *v.* to recommend  1.8
**recordar (o:ue)** *v.* to remember  1.4
**recorrer** *v.* to tour an area
**refresco** *m.* soft drink  1.8
**regalar** *v.* to give (a gift)  1.9
**regalo** *m.* gift  1.6
**regatear** *v.* to bargain  1.6
**regresar** *v.* to return  1.2
**regular** *adj.* so-so; OK  1.1
**reírse (e:i)** *v.* to laugh  1.9
**relaciones** *f., pl.* relationships
**relajarse** *v.* to relax  1.9
**reloj** *m.* clock; watch  1.2
**repetir (e:i)** *v.* to repeat  1.4
**residencia estudiantil** *f.* dormitory  1.2
**respuesta** *f.* answer
**restaurante** *m.* restaurant  1.4
**revista** *f.* magazine  1.4
**rico/a** *adj.* rich  1.6; tasty; delicious  1.8
**riquísimo/a** *adj.* extremely delicious  1.8
**rojo/a** *adj.* red  1.3
**romper (con)** *v.* to break up (with)  1.9
**ropa** *f.* clothing; clothes  1.6
  **ropa interior** *f.* underwear  1.6
**rosado/a** *adj.* pink  1.6
**rubio/a** *adj.* blond(e)  1.3
**ruso/a** *adj.* Russian  1.3
**rutina** *f.* routine  1.7
  **rutina diaria** *f.* daily routine  1.7

**S**

**sábado** *m.* Saturday  1.2
**saber** *v.* to know; to know how  1.6; to taste  1.8
  **saber a**  to taste like  1.8
**sabrosísimo/a** *adj.* extremely delicious  1.8
**sabroso/a** *adj.* tasty; delicious  1.8
**sacar** *v.* to take out
  **sacar fotos**  to take photos  1.5
**sal** *f.* salt  1.8
**salchicha** *f.* sausage  1.8

**salida** *f.* departure; exit **1.5**
**salir** *v.* to leave **1.4**; to go out
  **salir (con)** to go out (with); to date **1.9**
  **salir de** to leave from
  **salir para** to leave for (*a place*)
**salmón** *m.* salmon **1.8**
**saludo** *m.* greeting **1.1**
  **saludos a...** greetings to... **1.1**
**sandalia** *f.* sandal **1.6**
**sandía** *f.* watermelon
**sándwich** *m.* sandwich **1.8**
**se** *ref. pron.* himself, herself, itself; *form.* yourself, themselves, yourselves **1.7**
**secarse** *v.* to dry oneself **1.7**
**sección de (no) fumar** *f.* (non) smoking section **1.8**
**secuencia** *f.* sequence
**sed** *f.* thirst **1.3**
**seda** *f.* silk **1.6**
**seguir (e:i)** *v.* to follow; to continue **1.4**
**según** *prep.* according to
**segundo/a** *n., adj.* second **1.5**
**seguro/a** *adj.* sure; safe **1.5**
**seis** *n., adj.* six **1.1**
**seiscientos/as** *n., adj.* six hundred **1.2**
**semana** *f.* week **1.2**
  **fin** *m.* **de semana** weekend **1.4**
  **semana** *f.* **pasada** last week **1.6**
**semestre** *m.* semester **1.2**
**sentarse (e:ie)** *v.* to sit down **1.7**
**sentir(se) (e:ie)** *v.* to feel **1.7**
**señor (Sr.)** *m.* Mr.; sir **1.1**
**señora (Sra.)** *f.* Mrs.; ma'am **1.1**
**señorita (Srta.)** *f.* Miss **1.1**
**separado/a** *adj.* separated **1.9**
**separarse (de)** *v.* to separate (from) **1.9**
**septiembre** *m.* September **1.5**
**séptimo/a** *adj.* seventh **1.5**
**ser** *v.* to be **1.1**
  **ser aficionado/a (a)** to be a fan (of) **1.4**
**serio/a** *adj.* serious
**servir (e:i)** *v.* to serve **1.8**; to help **1.5**
**sesenta** *n., adj.* sixty **1.2**
**setecientos/as** *n., adj.* seven hundred **1.2**
**setenta** *n., adj.* seventy **1.2**
**sexto/a** *n., adj.* sixth **1.5**
**sí** *adv.* yes **1.1**
**si** *conj.* if **1.4**
**siempre** *adv.* always **1.7**
**siete** *n., adj.* seven **1.1**
**silla** *f.* seat **1.2**
**similar** *adj.* similar

**simpático/a** *adj.* nice; likeable **1.3**
**sin** *prep.* without **1.2**
  **sin duda** without a doubt
  **sin embargo** however
**sino** *conj.* but (rather) **1.7**
**situado/a** *adj., p.p.* located
**sobre** *prep.* on; over **1.2**
**sobrino/a** *m., f.* nephew; niece **1.3**
**sociología** *f.* sociology **1.2**
**sol** *m.* sun **1.4; 1.5**
**soleado/a** *adj.* sunny
**sólo** *adv.* only **1.3**
**solo** *adj.* alone
**soltero/a** *adj.* single **1.9**
**sombrero** *m.* hat **1.6**
**Son las dos.** It's two o'clock. **1.1**
**sonreír (e:i)** *v.* to smile **1.9**
**sopa** *f.* soup **1.8**
**sorprender** *v.* to surprise **1.9**
**sorpresa** *f.* surprise **1.9**
**soy** I am **1.1**
  **Soy yo.** That's me. **1.1**
  **Soy de...** I'm from... **1.1**
**su(s)** *poss. adj.* his, her, its; *form.* your, their **1.3**
**sucio/a** *adj.* dirty **1.5**
**suegro/a** *m., f.* father-in-law; mother-in-law **1.3**
**sueño** *m.* sleep **1.3**
**suerte** *f.* luck **1.3**
**suéter** *m.* sweater **1.6**
**suponer** *v.* to suppose **1.4**
**sustantivo** *m.* noun

## T

**tabla de (wind)surf** *f.* surf board/sailboard **1.5**
**tal vez** *adv.* maybe **1.5**
**talla** *f.* size **1.6**
  **talla grande** *f.* large
**también** *adv.* also; too **1.2; 1.7**
**tampoco** *adv.* neither; not either **1.7**
**tan** *adv.* so **1.5**
  **tan... como** as... as **1.8**
**tanto** *adv.* so much
  **tanto... como** as much... as **1.8**
  **tantos/as... como** as many... as **1.8**
**tarde** *adv.* late **1.7**
**tarde** *f.* afternoon; evening; P.M. **1.1**
**tarea** *f.* homework **1.2**
**tarjeta** *f.* card
  **tarjeta de crédito** *f.* credit card **1.6**
  **tarjeta postal** *f.* postcard
**taxi** *m.* taxi **1.5**
**te** *sing., fam., d.o. pron.* you **1.5**; *sing., fam., i.o. pron.* to/for you **1.6**

**Te presento a...** *fam.* I would like to introduce you to (name). **1.1**
**¿Te gusta(n)...?** Do you like...? **1.2**
**té** *m.* tea **1.8**
  **té helado** *m.* iced tea **1.8**
**televisión** *f.* television **1.2**
**temprano** *adv.* early **1.7**
**tener** *v.* to have **1.3**
  **tener... años** to be... years old **1.3**
  **Tengo... años.** I'm... years old. **1.3**
  **tener (mucho) calor** to be (very) hot **1.3**
  **tener (mucho) cuidado** to be (very) careful **1.3**
  **tener (mucho) frío** to be (very) cold **1.3**
  **tener ganas de (+ *inf.*)** to feel like (*doing something*) **1.3**
  **tener (mucha) hambre** to be (very) hungry **1.3**
  **tener (mucho) miedo (de)** to be (very) afraid (of); to be (very) scared (of) **1.3**
  **tener miedo (de) que** to be afraid that
  **tener planes** to have plans
  **tener (mucha) prisa** to be in a (big) hurry **1.3**
  **tener que (+ *inf.*)** *v.* to have to (*do something*) **1.3**
  **tener razón** to be right **1.3**
  **tener (mucha) sed** to be (very) thirsty **1.3**
  **tener (mucho) sueño** to be (very) sleepy **1.3**
  **tener (mucha) suerte** *f.* to be (very) lucky **1.3**
  **tener tiempo** to have time **1.4**
  **tener una cita** to have a date; to have an appointment **1.9**
**tenis** *m.* tennis **1.4**
**tercer, tercero/a** *n., adj.* third **1.5**
**terminar** *v.* to end; to finish **1.2**
  **terminar de (+ *inf.*)** *v.* to finish (*doing something*) **1.4**
**ti** *pron., obj. of prep., fam.* you **1.9**
**tiempo** *m.* time **1.4**; weather **1.5**
  **tiempo libre** free time
**tienda** *f.* shop; store **1.6**
  **tienda de campaña** tent
**tinto/a** *adj.* red (wine) **1.8**
**tío/a** *m., f.* uncle; aunt **1.3**
**tíos** *m.* aunts and uncles **1.3**
**título** *m.* title
**tiza** *f.* chalk **1.2**
**toalla** *f.* towel **1.7**
**todavía** *adv.* yet; still **1.5**

**todo** *m.* everything  1.5
  **Todo está bajo control.** Everything is under control.  1.7
**todo(s)/a(s)** *adj.* all; whole  1.4
**todos** *m., pl.* all of us; everybody; everyone
**tomar** *v.* to take; to drink  1.2
  **tomar clases** to take classes  1.2
  **tomar el sol** to sunbathe  1.4
  **tomar en cuenta** to take into account
  **tomar fotos** to take photos  1.5
**tomate** *m.* tomato  1.8
**tonto/a** *adj.* silly; foolish  1.3
**tortilla** *f.* tortilla  1.8
  **tortilla de maíz** corn tortilla  1.8
**tostado/a** *adj.* toasted  1.8
**trabajador(a)** *adj.* hard-working  1.3
**trabajar** *v.* to work  1.2
**traducir** *v.* to translate  1.6
**traer** *v.* to bring  1.4
**traje** *m.* suit  1.6
  **traje de baño** *m.* bathing suit  1.6
**tranquilo/a** *adj.* calm
  **Tranquilo.** Relax.  1.7
**trece** *n., adj.* thirteen  1.1
**treinta** *n., adj.* thirty  1.1, 1.2
  **y treinta** thirty minutes past the hour (*time*)  1.1
**tren** *m.* train  1.5
**tres** *n., adj.* three  1.1
**trescientos/as** *n., adj.* three hundred  1.2
**trimestre** *m.* trimester; quarter  1.2
**triste** *adj.* sad  1.5
**tú** *fam. sub. pron.* you  1.1
  **Tú eres...** You are...  1.1
**tu(s)** *fam. poss. adj.* your  1.3
**turismo** *m.* tourism  1.5
**turista** *m., f.* tourist  1.1
**turístico/a** *adj.* touristic

**U**

**Ud.** *form. sing.* you  1.1
**Uds.** *form., pl.* you  1.1
**último/a** *adj.* last
**un, uno/a** *indef. art.* a, an; one  1.1
  **uno/a** *m., f., sing. pron.* one  1.1
  **a la una** at one o'clock  1.1
  **una vez** *adv.* once; one time  1.6
  **una vez más** one more time  1.9
**unos/as** *m., f., pl. indef. art.* some; *pron.* some  1.1

**único/a** *adj.* only  1.3
**universidad** *f.* university; college  1.2
**usar** *v.* to wear; to use  1.6
**usted (Ud.)** *form. sing.* you  1.1
  **ustedes (Uds.)** *form., pl.* you  1.1
**útil** *adj.* useful
**uva** *f.* grape  1.8

**V**

**vacaciones** *f. pl.* vacation  1.5
**vamos** let's go  1.4
**varios/as** *adj., pl.* various; several  1.8
**veces** *f., pl.* times  1.6
**veinte** *n., adj.* twenty  1.1
**veinticinco** *n., adj.* twenty-five  1.1
**veinticuatro** *n., adj.* twenty-four  1.1
**veintidós** *n., adj.* twenty-two  1.1
**veintinueve** *n., adj.* twenty-nine  1.1
**veintiocho** *n., adj.* twenty-eight  1.1
**veintiséis** *n., adj.* twenty-six  1.1
**veintisiete** *n., adj.* twenty-seven  1.1
**veintitrés** *n., adj.* twenty-three  1.1
**veintiún, veintiuno/a** *n., adj.* twenty-one  1.1
**vejez** *f.* old age  1.9
**vendedor(a)** *m., f.* salesperson  1.6
**vender** *v.* to sell  1.6
**venir** *v.* to come  1.3
**ventana** *f.* window  1.2
**ver** *v.* to see  1.4
  **a ver** let's see  1.2
  **ver películas** to see movies  1.4
**verano** *m.* summer  1.5
**verbo** *m.* verb
**verdad** *f.* truth
  **¿verdad?** right?  1.1
**verde** *adj.* green  1.3
**verduras** *f., pl.* vegetables  1.8
**vestido** *m.* dress  1.6
**vestirse (e:i)** *v.* to get dressed  1.7
**vez** *f.* time  1.6
**viajar** *v.* to travel  1.2
**viaje** *m.* trip  1.5
**viajero/a** *m., f.* traveler  1.5
**vida** *f.* life  1.9
**video** *m.* video  1.1
**videojuego** *m.* video game  1.4
**viejo/a** *adj.* old  1.3
**viento** *m.* wind  1.5
**viernes** *m., sing.* Friday  1.2

**vinagre** *m.* vinegar  1.8
**vino** *m.* wine  1.8
  **vino blanco** *m.* white wine  1.8
  **vino tinto** *m.* red wine  1.8
**visitar** *v.* to visit  1.4
  **visitar monumentos** to visit monuments  1.4
**viudo/a** *adj.* widower; widow  1.9
**vivir** *v.* to live  1.3
**vivo/a** *adj.* bright; lively; living
**vóleibol** *m.* volleyball  1.4
**volver (o:ue)** *v.* to return  1.4
**vos** *pron.* you
**vosotros/as** *pron., form., pl.* you  1.1
**vuelta** *f.* return trip
**vuestro(s)/a(s)** *form., poss. adj.* your  1.3

**W**

**walkman** *m.* walkman

**Y**

**y** *conj.* and  1.1
  **y cuarto** quarter after (*time*)  1.1
  **y media** half-past (*time*)  1.1
  **y quince** quarter after (*time*)  1.1
  **y treinta** thirty (minutes past the hour)  1.1
  **¿Y tú?** *fam.* And you?  1.1
  **¿Y usted?** *form.* And you?  1.1
**ya** *adv.* already  1.6
**yerno** *m.* son-in-law  1.3
**yo** *sub. pron.* I  1.1
  **Yo soy...** I'm...  1.1
**yogur** *m.* yogurt  1.8

**Z**

**zanahoria** *f.* carrot  1.8
**zapatos** *m., pl.* shoes
  **zapatos de tenis** tennis shoes, sneakers  1.6

# English-Spanish

## A

a **un, uno/a** *m., f., sing.; indef. art.* 1.1
A.M. **mañana** *f.* 1.1
able: be able to **poder (o:ue)** *v.* 1.4
aboard **a bordo** 1.1
accounting **contabilidad** *f.* 1.2
acquainted: be acquainted with **conocer** *v.* 1.6
additional **adicional** *adj.*
adjective **adjetivo** *m.*
adolescence **adolescencia** *f.* 1.9
advice **consejo** *m.* 1.6
give advice **dar consejos** 1.6
affirmative **afirmativo/a** *adj.*
afraid: be (very) afraid (of) **tener (mucho) miedo (de)** 1.3
be afraid that **tener miedo (de) que**
after **después de** *prep.* 1.7
afternoon **tarde** *f.* 1.1
afterward **después** *adv.* 1.7
again *adv.* **otra vez**
age **edad** *f.* 1.9
agree **concordar (o:ue)** *v.*
airplane **avión** *m.* 1.5
airport **aeropuerto** *m.* 1.5
alarm clock **despertador** *m.* 1.7
all **todo(s)/a(s)** *adj.* 1.4
all of us **todos** 1.1
all over the world **en todo el mundo**
alleviate **aliviar** *v.*
alone **solo/a** *adj.*
already **ya** *adv.* 1.6
also **también** *adv.* 1.2; 1.7
although *conj.* **aunque**
always **siempre** *adv.* 1.7
American (North) **norteamericano/a** *adj.* 1.3
among **entre** *prep.* 1.2
amusement **diversión** *f.*
and **y** 1.1, **e** (before words beginning with *i* or *hi*) 1.4
And you? **¿Y tú?** *fam.* 1.1; **¿Y usted?** *form.* 1.1
angry **enojado/a** *adj.* 1.5
get angry (with) **enojarse** *v.* **(con)** 1.7
anniversary **aniversario** *m.* 1.9
(wedding) anniversary **aniversario** *m.* **(de bodas)** 1.9
annoy **molestar** *v.* 1.7
another **otro/a** *adj.* 1.6
answer **contestar** *v.* 1.2; **respuesta** *f.*
any **algún, alguno/a(s)** *adj.* 1.7
anyone **alguien** *pron.* 1.7
anything **algo** *pron.* 1.7
appear **parecer** *v.*
appetizers **entremeses** *m.,*
pl. 1.8
apple **manzana** *f.* 1.8
appointment **cita** *f.* 1.9
have an appointment **tener** *v.* **una cita** 1.9
April **abril** *m.* 1.5
aquatic **acuático/a** *adj.* 1.4
archaeology **arqueología** *f.* 1.2
Argentina **Argentina** *f.* 1.1
Argentine **argentino/a** *adj.* 1.3
arrival **llegada** *f.* 1.5
arrive **llegar** *v.* 1.2
art **arte** *m.* 1.2
artist **artista** *m., f.* 1.3
as **como** 1.8
as... as **tan... como** 1.8
as many... as **tantos/as... como** 1.8
as much... as **tanto... como** 1.8
ask (a question) **preguntar** *v.* 1.2
ask for **pedir (e:i)** *v.* 1.4
asparagus **espárragos** *m., pl.* 1.8
at **a** *prep.* 1.1; **en** *prep.* 1.2
at + *time* **a la(s)** + *time* 1.1
at home **en casa** 1.7
at night **por la noche** 1.7
At what time...? **¿A qué hora...?** 1.1
attend **asistir (a)** *v.* 1.3
attract **atraer** *v.* 1.4
August **agosto** *m.* 1.5
aunt **tía** *f.* 1.3
aunts and uncles **tíos** *m., pl.* 1.3
automatic **automático/a** *adj.*
automobile **automóvil** *m.* 1.5
autumn **otoño** *m.* 1.5
avenue **avenida** *f.*

## B

backpack **mochila** *f.* 1.2
bad **mal, malo/a** *adj.* 1.3
It's not at all bad. **No está nada mal.** 1.5
bag **bolsa** *f.* 1.6
ball **pelota** *f.* 1.4
banana **banana** *f.* 1.8
bargain **ganga** *f.* 1.6; **regatear** *v.* 1.6
baseball (*game*) **béisbol** *m.* 1.4
basketball (*game*) **baloncesto** *m.* 1.4
bathe **bañarse** *v.* 1.7
bathing suit **traje** *m.* **de baño** 1.6
bathroom **baño** *m.* 1.7; **cuarto de baño** *m.* 1.7
be **ser** *v.* 1.1; **estar** *v.* 1.2
be... years old **tener... años** 1.3
beach **playa** *f.* 1.5
beans **frijoles** *m., pl.* 1.8

beautiful **hermoso/a** *adj.* 1.6
because **porque** *conj.* 1.2
become (+ *adj.*) **ponerse (+ *adj.*)** 1.7; **convertirse (e:ie)** *v.*
bed **cama** *f.* 1.5
go to bed **acostarse (o:ue)** *v.* 1.7
beef **carne de res** *f.* 1.8
before **antes** *adv.* 1.7; **antes de** *prep.* 1.7
begin **comenzar (e:ie)** *v.* 1.4; **empezar (e:ie)** *v.* 1.4
behind **detrás de** *prep.* 1.2
believe (in) **creer** *v.* **(en)** 1.3
bellhop **botones** *m., f. sing.* 1.5
below **debajo de** *prep.* 1.2
belt **cinturón** *m.* 1.6
beside **al lado de** *prep.* 1.2
best **mejor** *adj.*
the best **el/la mejor** *adj.* 1.8
better **mejor** *adj.* 1.8
between **entre** *prep.* 1.2
bicycle **bicicleta** *f.* 1.4
big **gran, grande** *adj.* 1.3
bill **cuenta** *f.* 1.9
billion *m.* **mil millones**
biology **biología** *f.* 1.2
birth **nacimiento** *m.* 1.9
birthday **cumpleaños** *m., sing.* 1.9
have a birthday **cumplir** *v.* **años** 1.9
biscuit **bizcocho** *m.*
black **negro/a** *adj.* 1.3
blackberry **mora** *f.* 1.8
blackboard **pizarra** *f.* 1.2
blond(e) **rubio/a** *adj.* 1.3
blouse **blusa** *f.* 1.6
blue **azul** *adj.* 1.3
boardinghouse **pensión** *f.*
boat **barco** *m.* 1.5
book **libro** *m.* 1.2
bookstore **librería** *f.* 1.2
boot **bota** *f.* 1.6
bore **aburrir** *v.* 1.7
bored **aburrido/a** *adj.* 1.5
be bored **estar** *v.* **aburrido/a** 1.5
boring **aburrido/a** *adj.* 1.5
born: be born **nacer** *v.* 1.9
borrowed **prestado/a** *adj.*
bother **molestar** *v.* 1.7
bottle **botella** *f.* 1.9
bottom **fondo** *m.*
boulevard **bulevar** *m.*
boy **chico** *m.* 1.1; **muchacho** *m.* 1.3
boyfriend **novio** *m.* 1.3
brakes **frenos** *m., pl.*
bread **pan** *m.* 1.8
break up (with) **romper** *v.* **(con)** 1.9
breakfast **desayuno** *m.* 1.2, 1.8
have breakfast **desayunar** *v.* 1.2
bring **traer** *v.* 1.4

brochure **folleto** *m.*
brother **hermano** *m.* 1.3
  brothers and sisters **hermanos**
    *m., pl.* 1.3
brother-in-law **cuñado** *m.* 1.3
brown **café** *adj.* 1.6;
    **marrón** *adj.* 1.6
brunet(te) **moreno/a** *adj.* 1.3
brush **cepillar** *v.* 1.7
  brush one's hair **cepillarse el**
    **pelo** 1.7
  brush one's teeth **cepillarse los**
    **dientes** 1.7
build **construir** *v.* 1.4
bus **autobús** *m.* 1.1
  bus station **estación** *f.* **de**
    **autobuses** 1.5
business administration
    **administración** *f.* **de**
    **empresas** 1.2
busy **ocupado/a** *adj.* 1.5
but **pero** *conj.* 1.2; *(rather)* **sino**
    *conj. (in negative sentences)* 1.7
butter **mantequilla** *f.* 1.8
buy **comprar** *v.* 1.2
by plane **en avión** 1.5
bye **chau** *interj. fam.* 1.1

## C

café **café** *m.* 1.4
cafeteria **cafetería** *f.* 1.2
cake **pastel** *m.* 1.9
  chocolate cake **pastel de**
    **chocolate** *m.* 1.9
calculator **calculadora** *f.* 1.2
call **llamar** *v.*
  call on the phone **llamar por**
    **teléfono**
  be called **llamarse** *v.* 1.7
camp **acampar** *v.* 1.5
can **poder (o:ue)** *v.* 1.4
Canadian **canadiense** *adj.* 1.3
candy **dulces** *m., pl.* 1.9
capital city **capital** *f.* 1.1
car **auto(móvil)** *m.* 1.5
caramel **caramelo** *m.* 1.9
card **tarjeta** *f.;*
    *(playing)* **carta** *f.* 1.5
care **cuidado** *m.* 1.3
careful: be (very) careful **tener** *v.*
    *(mucho)* **cuidado** 1.3
carrot **zanahoria** *f.* 1.8
carry **llevar** *v.* 1.2
cash **(en) efectivo** 1.6
cash register **caja** *f.* 1.6
cashier **cajero/a** *m., f.*
celebrate **celebrar** *v.* 1.9
celebration **celebración** *f.*
  young woman's fifteenth
    birthday celebration
    **quinceañera** *f.* 1.9
cereal **cereales** *m., pl.* 1.8
chalk **tiza** *f.* 1.2
champagne **champán** *m.* 1.9

change **cambiar** *v.* **(de)** 1.9
chat **conversar** *v.* 1.2
chauffeur **conductor(a)** *m., f.* 1.1
cheap **barato/a** *adj.* 1.6
cheese **queso** *m.* 1.8
chemistry **química** *f.* 1.2
chicken **pollo** *m.* 1.8
child **niño/a** *m., f.* 1.3
childhood **niñez** *f.* 1.9
children **hijos** *m., pl.* 1.3
Chinese **chino/a** *adj.* 1.3
chocolate **chocolate** *m.* 1.9
  chocolate cake **pastel** *m.* **de**
    **chocolate** 1.9
choose **escoger** *v.* 1.8
chop *(food)* **chuleta** *f.* 1.8
Christmas **Navidad** *f.* 1.9
church **iglesia** *f.* 1.4
city **ciudad** *f.* 1.4
class **clase** *f.* 1.2
  take classes **tomar clases** 1.2
classmate **compañero/a** *m., f.* **de**
    **clase** 1.2
clean **limpio/a** *adj.* 1.5
clear *(weather)* **despejado/a** *adj.*
  It's (very) clear. *(weather)*
    **Está (muy) despejado.**
clerk **dependiente/a** *m., f.* 1.6
climb **escalar** *v.* 1.4
  climb mountains **escalar**
    **montañas** 1.4
clock **reloj** *m.* 1.2
close **cerrar (e:ie)** *v.* 1.4
closed **cerrado/a** *adj.* 1.5
clothes **ropa** *f.* 1.6
clothing **ropa** *f.* 1.6
cloudy **nublado/a** *adj.* 1.5
  It's (very) cloudy. **Está (muy)**
    **nublado.** 1.5
coat **abrigo** *m.* 1.6
coffee **café** *m.* 1.8
cold **frío** *m.* 1.5;
  be (feel) (very) cold **tener**
    *(mucho)* **frío** 1.3
  It's (very) cold. *(weather)* **Hace**
    *(mucho)* **frío.** 1.5
college **universidad** *f.* 1.2
color **color** *m.* 1.3, 1.6
comb one's hair **peinarse** *v.* 1.7
come **venir** *v.* 1.3
comfortable **cómodo/a** *adj.* 1.5
community **comunidad** *f.* 1.1
comparison **comparación** *f.*
computer **computadora** *f.* 1.1
  computer disc **disco** *m.*
  computer programmer
    **programador(a)** *m., f.* 1.3
  computer science **computación**
    *f.* 1.2
confirm **confirmar** *v.* 1.5
  confirm a reservation **confirmar**
    **una reservación** 1.5
confused **confundido/a** *adj.* 1.5
Congratulations! **¡Felicidades!;**
    **¡Felicitaciones!** *f. pl.* 1.9
contamination **contaminación** *f.*

content **contento/a** *adj.* 1.5
continue **seguir (e:i)** *v.* 1.4
control **control** *m.*
  be under control **estar bajo**
    **control** 1.7
conversation **conversación** *f.* 1.1
converse **conversar** *v.* 1.2
cookie **galleta** *f.* 1.9
cool **fresco/a** *adj.* 1.5
  Be cool. **Tranquilo/a.**
  It's cool. *(weather)* **Hace**
    **fresco.** 1.5
corn **maíz** *m.* 1.8
cost **costar (o:ue)** *v.* 1.6
Costa Rica **Costa Rica** *f.* 1.1
Costa Rican **costarricense** *adj.*
    1.3
cotton **algodón** *f.* 1.6
  (made of) cotton **de**
    **algodón** 1.6
count (on) **contar (o:ue)** *v.*
    **(con)** 1.4
country *(nation)* **país** *m.* 1.1
countryside **campo** *m.* 1.5
couple (married) **pareja** *f.* 1.9
course **curso** *m.* 1.2; **materia** *f.*
    1.2
courtesy **cortesía** *f.*
cousin **primo/a** *m., f.* 1.3
cover **cubrir** *v.*
covered **cubierto** *p.p.*
crazy **loco/a** *adj.* 1.6
create **crear** *v.*
credit **crédito** *m.* 1.6
  credit card **tarjeta** *f.* **de**
    **crédito** 1.6
Cuba **Cuba** *f.* 1.1
Cuban **cubano/a** *adj.* 1.3
culture **cultura** *f.* 1.2
currency exchange **cambio** *m.* **de**
    **moneda**
custard *(baked)* **flan** *m.* 1.9
custom **costumbre** *f.* 1.1
customer **cliente/a** *m., f.* 1.6
customs **aduana** *f.* 1.5
  customs inspector **inspector(a)**
    *m., f.* **de aduanas** 1.5
cycling **ciclismo** *m.* 1.4

## D

dad **papá** *m.* 1.3
daily **diario/a** *adj.* 1.7
  daily routine **rutina** *f.* **diaria**
    1.7
dance **bailar** *v.* 1.2
date *(appointment)* **cita** *f.* 1.9;
    *(calendar)* **fecha** *f.* 1.5;
    *(someone)* **salir** *v.* **con**
    **(alguien)** 1.9
  have a date **tener una**
    **cita** 1.9
daughter **hija** *f.* 1.3
daughter-in-law **nuera** *f.* 1.3
day **día** *m.* 1.1

day before yesterday
**anteayer** *adv.* 1.6
death **muerte** *f.* 1.9
December **diciembre** *m.* 1.5
decide **decidir** *v.* (+ *inf.*) 1.3
delicious **delicioso/a** *adj.* 1.8;
**rico/a** *adj.* 1.8; **sabroso/a**
*adj.* 1.8
delighted **encantado/a** *adj.* 1.1
department store **almacén** *m.* 1.6
departure **salida** *f.* 1.5
describe **describir** *v.* 1.3
design **diseño** *m.*
desire **desear** *v.* 1.2
desk **escritorio** *m.* 1.2
dessert **postre** *m.* 1.9
diary **diario** *m.* 1.1
dictionary **diccionario** *m.* 1.1
die **morir (o:ue)** *v.* 1.8
difficult **difícil** *adj.* 1.3
dinner **cena** *f.* 1.2, 1.8
have dinner **cenar** *v.* 1.2
dirty **ensuciar** *v.;* **sucio/a**
*adj.* 1.5
disagree **no estar de acuerdo**
dish **plato** *m.* 1.8
main dish *m.* **plato principal**
1.8
disk **disco** *m.*
disorderly **desordenado/a**
*adj.* 1.5
dive **bucear** *v.* 1.4
divorce **divorcio** *m.* 1.9
divorced **divorciado/a** *adj.* 1.9
get divorced (from) **divorciarse**
*v.* (de) 1.9
do **hacer** *v.* 1.4
(I) don't want to. **No quiero.**
1.4
doctor **doctor(a)** *m., f.* 1.3;
**médico/a** *m., f.* 1.3
domestic **doméstico/a** *adj.*
domestic appliance
**electrodoméstico** *m.*
door **puerta** *f.* 1.2
dormitory **residencia** *f.*
**estudiantil** 1.2
double **doble** *adj.* 1.5
double room **habitación** *f.*
**doble** 1.5
downtown **centro** *m.* 1.4
draw **dibujar** *v.* 1.2
dress **vestido** *m.* 1.6
get dressed **vestirse (e:i)** *v.*
1.7
drink **beber** *v.* 1.3; **tomar** *v.*
1.2
**bebida** *f.* 1.8
drive **conducir** *v.* 1.6
driver **conductor(a)** *m., f.* 1.1
dry oneself **secarse** *v.* 1.7
during **durante** *prep.* 1.7

each **cada** *adj.* 1.6
eagle **águila** *f.*
early **temprano** *adv.* 1.7
ease **aliviar** *v.*
easy **fácil** *adj.* 1.3
eat **comer** *v.* 1.3
economics **economía** *f.* 1.2
Ecuador **Ecuador** *m.* 1.1
Ecuadorian **ecuatoriano/a**
*adj.* 1.3
effective **eficaz** *adj.*
egg **huevo** *m.* 1.8
eight **ocho** *n., adj.* 1.1
eight hundred **ochocientos/as**
*n., adj.* 1.2
eighteen **dieciocho** *n., adj.* 1.1
eighth **octavo/a** *adj.* 1.5
eighty **ochenta** *n., adj.* 1.2
either... or **o... o** *conj.* 1.7
eldest **el/la mayor** *adj.* 1.8
elegant **elegante** *adj.* 1.6
elevator **ascensor** *m.* 1.5
eleven **once** *n., adj.* 1.1
e-mail **correo** *m.* **electrónico**
1.4
e-mail message **mensaje** *m.*
**electrónico** 1.4
read e-mail **leer** *v.* **el correo**
**electrónico** 1.4
embarrassed **avergonzado/a**
*adj.* 1.5
employee **empleado/a** *m., f.* 1.5
end **fin** *m.* 1.4; **terminar** *v.* 1.2
engaged: get engaged (to)
**comprometerse** *v.* (con) 1.9
engineer **ingeniero/a** *m., f.* 1.3
English (*language*) **inglés** *m.* 1.2;
**inglés, inglesa** *adj.* 1.3
entertainment **diversión** *f.* 1.4
eraser **borrador** *m.* 1.2
establish **establecer** *v.*
evening **tarde** *f.* 1.1
everybody **todos** *m., pl.*
everything **todo** *m.* 1.5
Everything is under control.
**Todo está bajo control.** 1.7
exactly **en punto** 1.1
exam **examen** *m.* 1.2
excellent **excelente** *adj.* 1.5
exciting **emocionante** *adj.*
excursion **excursión** *f.*
excuse **disculpar** *v.*
Excuse me. (*May I?*) **Con**
**permiso.** 1.1; (*I beg*
*your pardon.*) **Perdón.** 1.1
exit **salida** *f.* 1.5
expensive **caro/a** *adj.* 1.6
explain **explicar** *v.* 1.2
explore **explorar** *v.*
expression **expresión** *f.*
extremely delicious **riquísimo/a**
*adj.* 1.8

fabulous **fabuloso/a** *adj.* 1.5
face **cara** *f.* 1.7
fact: in fact **de hecho**
fall (*season*) **otoño** *m.* 1.5
fall: fall asleep **dormirse (o:ue)**
*v.* 1.7
fall in love (with) **enamorarse**
*v.* (de) 1.9
family **familia** *f.* 1.3
fan **aficionado/a** *adj.* 1.4
be a fan (of) **ser aficionado/a**
(a) 1.4
far from **lejos de** *prep.* 1.2
farewell **despedida** *f.* 1.1
fascinate **fascinar** *v.* 1.7
fashion **moda** *f.* 1.6
be in fashion **estar de**
**moda** 1.6
fast **rápido/a** *adj.*
fat **gordo/a** *adj.* 1.3
father **padre** *m.* 1.3
father-in-law **suegro** *m.* 1.3
favorite **favorito/a** *adj.* 1.4
fear **miedo** *m.* 1.3
February **febrero** *m.* 1.5
feel **sentir(se) (e:ie)** *v.* 1.7
feel like (*doing something*)
**tener ganas de** (+ *inf.*) 1.3
few **pocos/as** *adj., pl.*
fewer than **menos de**
(+ *number*) 1.8
field: major field of study
**especialización** *f.*
fifteen *n., adj.* **quince** 1.1
fifteen-year-old girl
**quinceañera** *f.* 1.9
young woman celebrating her
fifteenth birthday
**quinceañera** *f.* 1.9
fifth **quinto/a** *n., adj.* 1.5
fifty **cincuenta** *n., adj.* 1.2
figure (*number*) **cifra** *f.*
finally **por último** 1.7
find **encontrar (o:ue)** *v.* 1.4
find (each other) **encontrar(se)**
*v.*
fine **multa** *f.*
finish **terminar** *v.* 1.2
finish (*doing something*)
**terminar** *v.* **de** (+ *inf.*) 1.4
first **primer, primero/a** *n.,*
*adj.* 1.5
fish (*food*) **pescado** *m.* 1.8
fisherman **pescador** *m.*
fisherwoman **pescadora** *f.*
fishing **pesca** *f.* 1.5
fit (*clothing*) **quedar** *v.* 1.7
five **cinco** *n., adj.* 1.1
five hundred **quinientos/as** *n.,*
*adj.* 1.2
fixed **fijo/a** *adj.* 1.6
flag **bandera** *f.*
flank steak **lomo** *m.* 1.8

floor (*of a building*) **piso** *m.*   1.5
  ground floor **planta** *f.* **baja**   1.5
  top floor **planta** *f.* **alta**
fog **niebla** *f.*
follow **seguir (e:i)** *v.*   1.4
food **comida** *f.*   1.8; **alimento** *m.*
foolish **tonto/a** *adj.*   1.3
football **fútbol** *m.*
  **americano**   1.4
for me **para mí**   1.8
forbid **prohibir** *v.*
foreign languages **lenguas**
  *f. pl.* **extranjeras**   1.2
forty **cuarenta** *n., adj.*   1.2
four **cuatro** *n., adj.*   1.1
four hundred **cuatrocientos/as**
  *n., adj.*   1.2
fourteen **catorce** *n., adj.*   1.1
fourth **cuarto/a** *n., adj.*   1.5
free **libre** *adj.*   1.4
  free time **tiempo libre;**
  **ratos libres**   1.4
French **francés, francesa**
  *adj.*   1.3
French fries **papas** *f., pl.*
  **fritas**   1.8; **patatas** *f., pl.*
  **fritas**   1.8
Friday **viernes** *m., sing.*   1.2
fried **frito/a** *adj.*   1.8
  fried potatoes **papas** *f., pl.*
    **fritas**   1.8; **patatas** *f., pl.*
    **fritas**   1.8
friend **amigo/a** *m., f.*   1.3
friendly **amable** *adj.*   1.5
friendship **amistad** *f.*   1.9
from **de** *prep.*   1.1; **desde**
  *prep.*   1.6
  from the United States
    **estadounidense** *adj.*   1.3
  He/She/It is from… **Es de….**
    1.1
  I'm from… **Soy de…**   1.1
fruit **fruta** *f.*   1.8
  fruit juice **jugo** *m.* **de**
    **fruta**   1.8
fun **divertido/a** *adj.*   1.7
  fun activity **diversión** *f.*   1.4
  have fun **divertirse (e:ie)** *v.*
    1.9
function **funcionar** *v.*

**G**

game **juego** *m.*; (*match*)
  **partido** *m.*   1.4
garlic **ajo** *m.*   1.8
geography **geografía** *f.*   1.2
German **alemán, alemana**
  *adj.*   1.3
get **conseguir (e:i)** *v.*   1.4
  get along well/badly (with)
    **llevarse bien/mal (con)**
    1.9
  get up **levantarse** *v.*   1.7
gift **regalo** *m.*   1.6

girl **chica** *f.*   1.1;
  **muchacha** *f.*   1.3
girlfriend **novia** *f.*   1.3
give **dar** *v.*   1.6,  1.9;
  (*as a gift*) **regalar**   1.9
glasses **gafas** *f., pl.*   1.6
  sunglasses **gafas** *f., pl.*
    **de sol**   1.6
gloves **guantes** *m., pl.*   1.6
go **ir** *v.*   1.4
  go away **irse**   1.7
  go by boat **ir en barco**   1.5
  go by bus **ir en autobús**   1.5
  go by car **ir en auto(móvil)**
    1.5
  go by motorcycle **ir en**
    **motocicleta**   1.5
  go by taxi **ir en taxi**   1.5
  go down **bajar(se)** *v.*
  go on a hike (in the mountains)
    **ir de excursión (a las**
    **montañas)**   1.4
  go out **salir** *v.*   1.9
  go out (with) **salir** *v.* **(con)**
    1.9
  go up **subir** *v.*
  Let's go. **Vamos.**   1.4
  be going to (*do something*) **ir a**
    **(+ *inf.*)**   1.4
golf **golf** *m.*   1.4
good **buen, bueno/a** *adj.*
  1.3, 1.6
  Good afternoon. **Buenas**
    **tardes.**   1.1
  Good evening. **Buenas**
    **noches.**   1.1
  Good idea. **Buena idea.**   1.4
  Good morning. **Buenos**
    **días.**   1.1
  Good night. **Buenas**
    **noches.**   1.1
good-bye **adiós** *m.*   1.1
  say good-bye (to) **despedirse**
    **(e:i) (de)** *v.* 1.7
good-looking **guapo/a** *adj.*   1.3
graduate (from/in) **graduarse** *v.*
  **(de/en)**   1.9
grains **cereales** *m., pl.*   1.8
granddaughter **nieta** *f.*   1.3
grandfather **abuelo** *m.*   1.3
grandmother **abuela** *f.*   1.3
grandparents **abuelos** *m. pl.*   1.3
grandson **nieto** *m.*   1.3
grape **uva** *f.*   1.8
gray **gris** *adj.*   1.6
great **fenomenal** *adj.*   1.5
great-grandfather **bisabuelo** *m.*
  1.3
great-grandmother **bisabuela** *f.*
  1.3
green **verde** *adj.*   1.3
greeting **saludo** *m.*   1.1
  Greetings to… **Saludos a…**
    1.1
  grilled flank steak **lomo** *m.* **a**
    **la plancha**   1.8

ground floor **planta baja** *f.*   1.5
guest (at a house/hotel) **huésped**
  *m., f.*   1.5; (*invited to a func-*
  *tion*) **invitado/a** *m., f.*   1.9
gymnasium **gimnasio** *m.*   1.4

**H**

hair **pelo** *m.*   1.7
half **medio/a** *adj.*   1.3
  half-past… (*time*) …**y**
    **media**   1.1
half-brother **medio hermano**
  1.3
half-sister **media hermana**   1.3
ham **jamón** *m.*   1.8
hamburger **hamburguesa** *f.*   1.8
hand **mano** *f.*   1.1
  Hands up! **¡Manos arriba!**
handsome **guapo/a** *adj.*   1.3
happiness **alegría** *v.*   1.9
happy **alegre** *adj.*   1.5;
  **contento/a** *adj.*   1.5; **feliz**
    *adj.*   1.5
  Happy birthday! **¡Feliz**
    **cumpleaños!**   1.9
hard **difícil** *adj.*   1.3
hard-working **trabajador(a)**
  *adj.*   1.3
haste **prisa** *f.*   1.3
hat **sombrero** *m.*   1.6
hate **odiar** *v.*   1.9
have **tener** *v.*   1.3
  Have a good trip! **¡Buen**
    **viaje!**   1.1
  have time **tener tiempo**   1.4
  have to (*do something*) **tener**
    **que (+ *inf.*)**   1.3; **deber**
    **(+ *inf.*)**
he **él** *sub. pron.*   1.1
hear **oír** *v.*   1.4
heat **calor** *m.*   1.5
Hello. **Hola.**   1.1
help **servir (e:i)** *v.*   1.5
her **su(s)** *poss. adj.*   1.3;
  **la** *f., sing., d.o. pron.*   1.5
  to/for her **le** *f., sing., i.o.*
  *pron.*   1.6
here **aquí** *adv.*   1.1
  Here it is. **Aquí está.**   1.5
  Here we are at/in… **Aquí**
    **estamos en…**
Hi. **Hola.**   1.1
hike **excursión** *f.*   1.4
  go on a hike **hacer una**
    **excursión; ir de**
    **excursión**   1.4
hiker **excursionista** *m., f.*
hiking **de excursión**   1.4
him **lo** *m., sing., d.o. pron.*   1.5
  to/for him **le** *m., sing., i.o.*
  *pron.*   1.6
his **su(s)** *poss. adj.*   1.3
history **historia** *f.*   1.2
hobby **pasatiempo** *m.*   1.4

hockey **hockey** *m.* 1.4
holiday **día** *m.* **de fiesta** 1.9
home **casa** *f.* 1.2
homework **tarea** *f.* 1.2
hope **esperar** *v.* **(+** *inf.***)** 1.2
hors d'oeuvres **entremeses** *m.*,
   *pl.* 1.8
horse **caballo** *m.* 1.5
hot: be *(feel)* (very) hot **tener**
   **(mucho) calor** 1.3
   It's (very) hot **Hace (mucho)**
     **calor** 1.5
hotel **hotel** *m.* 1.5
hour **hora** *f.* 1.1
house **casa** *f.* 1.2
How...! **¡Qué...!** 1.3
   how? **¿cómo?** *adv.* 1.1
   How are you? **¿Qué tal?** 1.1
   How are you? **¿Cómo estás?**
     *fam.* 1.1
   How are you? **¿Cómo está**
     **usted?** *form.* 1.1
   How can I help you? **¿En qué**
     **puedo servirles?** 1.5
   How is it going? **¿Qué tal?** 1.1
   How is/are...? **¿Qué**
     **tal...?** 1.2
   How much/many?
     **¿Cuánto(s)/a(s)?** 1.1
   How much does... cost?
     **¿Cuánto cuesta...?** 1.6
   How old are you? **¿Cuántos**
     **años tienes?** *fam.* 1.3
however **sin embargo**
humanities **humanidades** *f.*, *pl.*
   1.2
hundred **cien, ciento** *n.*, *adj.* 1.2
hunger **hambre** *f.* 1.3
hungry: be (very) hungry **tener** *v.*
   **(mucha) hambre** 1.3
hurry
   be in a (big) hurry **tener** *v.*
     **(mucha) prisa** 1.3
husband **esposo** *m.* 1.3

**I**

I **Yo** *sub. pron.* 1.1
   I am... **Yo soy...** 1.1
ice cream **helado** *m.* 1.9
iced **helado/a** *adj.* 1.8
   iced tea **té** *m.* **helado** 1.8
idea **idea** *f.* 1.4
if **si** *conj.* 1.4
important **importante** *adj.* 1.3
   be important to **importar** *v.*
     1.7
in **en** *prep.* 1.2
   in a bad mood **de mal**
     **humor** 1.5
   in a good mood **de buen**
     **humor** 1.5
in front of **delante de** *prep.* 1.2
   in love (with) **enamorado/a**
     **(de)** 1.5

in the afternoon **de la tarde**
   1.1; **por la tarde** 1.7
in the direction of **para**
   *prep.* 1.1
in the early evening **de la**
   **tarde** 1.1
in the evening **de la noche**
   1.1; **por la tarde** 1.7
in the morning **de la mañana**
   1.1; **por la mañana** 1.7
incredible **increíble** *adj.* 1.5
inside **dentro** *adv.*
intelligent **inteligente** *adj.* 1.3
intend to **pensar** *v.* **(+** *inf.***)** 1.4
interest **interesar** *v.* 1.7
interesting **interesante** *adj.* 1.3
   be interesting to **interesar** *v.* 1.7
introduction **presentación** *f.*
   I would like to introduce you to
     (name). **Le presento a...**
     *form.* 1.1; **Te presento a...**
     *fam.* 1.1
invite **invitar** *v.* 1.9
it **lo/la** *sing.*, *d.o.*, *pron.* 1.5
   It's me. **Soy yo.** 1.1
Italian **italiano/a** *adj.* 1.3
its **su(s)** *poss. adj.* 1.3

**J**

jacket **chaqueta** *f.* 1.6
January **enero** *m.* 1.5
Japanese **japonés, japonesa**
   *adj.* 1.3
jeans **(blue)jeans** *m.*, *pl.* 1.6
jog **correr** *v.*
journalism **periodismo** *m.* 1.2
journalist **periodista** *m.*, *f.* 1.3
joy **alegría** *f.* 1.9
   give joy **dar** *v.* **alegría** 1.9
joyful **alegre** *adj.* 1.5
juice **jugo** *m.* 1.8
July **julio** *m.* 1.5
June **junio** *m.* 1.5
just **apenas** *adv.*
   have just *(done something)*
     **acabar de (+** *inf.***)** 1.6

**K**

key **llave** *f.* 1.5
kind: That's very kind of
   you. **Muy amable.** 1.5
kiss **beso** *m.* 1.9
know **saber** *v.* 1.6;
   **conocer** *v.* 1.6
   know how **saber** *v.* 1.6

**L**

laboratory **laboratorio** *m.* 1.2
lack **faltar** *v.* 1.7
landlord **dueño/a** *m.*, *f.* 1.8
landscape **paisaje** *m.* 1.5

language **lengua** *f.* 1.2
large **grande** *adj.* 1.3;
   *(clothing size)* **talla**
     **grande**
last **pasado/a** *adj.* 1.6;
   **último/a** *adj.*
   last name **apellido** *m.* 1.3
   last night **anoche** *adv.* 1.6
   last week **semana** *f.* **pasada**
     1.6
   last year **año** *m.* **pasado** 1.6
late **tarde** *adv.* 1.7
later (on) **más tarde** 1.7
   See you later. **Hasta la vista.**
     1.1; **Hasta luego.** 1.1
laugh **reírse (e:i)** *v.* 1.9
lazy **perezoso/a** *adj.*
learn **aprender** *v.* **(a +** *inf.***)** 1.3
leave **salir** *v.* 1.4; **irse** *v.* 1.7
   leave a tip **dejar una**
     **propina** 1.9
   leave for *(a place)* **salir para**
   leave from **salir de**
left **izquierdo/a** *adj.* 1.2
   be left over **quedar** *v.* 1.7
   to the left of **a la izquierda**
     **de** 1.2
lemon **limón** *m.* 1.8
lend **prestar** *v.* 1.6
less **menos** *adv.*
   less... than **menos... que** 1.8
   less than **menos de (+** *number*)
     1.8
lesson **lección** *f.* 1.1
let's see **a ver** 1.2
letter **carta** *f.* 1.4
lettuce **lechuga** *f.* 1.8
library **biblioteca** *f.* 1.2
lie **mentira** *f.* 1.4
life **vida** *f.* 1.9
like **como** *prep.* 1.8;
   **gustar** *v.* 1.2
   Do you like...? **¿Te**
     **gusta(n)...?** 1.2
   I don't like them at all. **No me**
     **gustan nada.** 1.2
   I like... **Me gusta(n)...** 1.2
   like very much **encantar** *v.*;
     **fascinar** *v.* 1.7
likeable **simpático/a** *adj.* 1.3
likewise **igualmente** *adv.* 1.1
line **línea** *f.*
listen (to) **escuchar** *v.* 1.2
   Listen! *(command)* **¡Oye!** *fam.*,
     *sing.* 1.1; **¡Oiga/Oigan!**
     *form.*, *sing./pl.* 1.1
   listen to music **escuchar**
     **música** 1.2
   listen (to) the radio **escuchar**
     **la radio** 1.2
literature **literatura** *f.* 1.2
little *(quantity)* **poco/a**
   *adj.* 1.5
live **vivir** *v.* 1.3
loan **prestar** *v.* 1.6
lobster **langosta** *f.* 1.8

long **largo/a** *adj.* 1.6
look (at) **mirar** *v.* 1.2
  look for **buscar** *v.* 1.2
lose **perder (e:ie)** *v.* 1.4
lot of, a **mucho/a** *adj.* 1.2, 1.3
love (*another person*) **querer
(e:ie)** *v.* 1.4; (*inanimate objects*)
**encantar** *v.* 1.7; **amor** *m.*
1.9
  in love **enamorado/a** *adj.* 1.5
luck **suerte** *f.* 1.3
lucky: be (very) lucky **tener
(mucha) suerte** 1.3
luggage **equipaje** *m.* 1.5
lunch **almuerzo** *m.* 1.8
  have lunch **almorzar (o:ue)** *v.*
1.4

## M

ma'am **señora (Sra.)** *f.* 1.1
mad **enojado/a** *adj.* 1.5
magazine **revista** *f.* 1.4
magnificent **magnífico/a**
*adj.* 1.5
main **principal** *adj.* 1.8
major **especialización** *f.* 1.2
make **hacer** *v.* 1.4
makeup **maquillaje** *m.* 1.7
  put on makeup **maquillarse**
*v.* 1.7
man **hombre** *m.* 1.1
many **mucho/a** *adj.* 1.3
map **mapa** *m.* 1.2
March **marzo** *m.* 1.5
margarine **margarina** *f.* 1.8
marinated fish **ceviche** *m.* 1.8
  lemon-marinated shrimp
**ceviche** *m.* **de camarón** 1.8
marital status **estado** *m.*
**civil** 1.9
market **mercado** *m.* 1.6
  open-air market **mercado al
aire libre** 1.6
marriage **matrimonio** *m.* 1.9
married **casado/a** *adj.* 1.9
  get married (to) **casarse** *v.*
**(con)** 1.9
marvelous **maravilloso/a**
*adj.* 1.5
match (*sports*) **partido** *m.* 1.4
  match (with) **hacer** *v.* **juego
(con)** 1.6
mathematics **matemáticas**
*f., pl.* 1.2
matter **importar** *v.* 1.7
maturity **madurez** *f.* 1.9
May **mayo** *m.* 1.5
maybe **tal vez** *adv.* 1.5; **quizás**
*adv.* 1.5
mayonnaise **mayonesa** *f.* 1.8
me **me** *sing., d.o. pron.* 1.5; *mí*
*pron., obj. of prep.* 1.9
  to/for me **me** *sing., i.o.*
*pron.* 1.6

meal **comida** *f.* 1.8
meat **carne** *f.* 1.8
medium **mediano/a** *adj.*
meet (*each other*) **conocer(se)** *v.*
1.8
menu **menú** *m.* 1.8
message **mensaje** *m.*
Mexican **mexicano/a** *adj.* 1.3
Mexico **México** *m.* 1.1
middle age **madurez** *f.* 1.9
midnight **medianoche** *f.* 1.1
milk **leche** *f.* 1.8
million **millón** *m.* 1.2
  million of **millón de** *m.* 1.2
mineral water **agua** *f.*
**mineral** 1.8
minute **minuto** *m.* 1.1
mirror **espejo** *m.* 1.7
Miss **señorita (Srta.)** *f.* 1.1
miss **perder (e:ie)** *v.* 1.4
mistaken **equivocado/a** *adj.*
modem **módem** *m.*
mom **mamá** *f.* 1.3
Monday **lunes** *m., sing.* 1.2
money **dinero** *m.* 1.6
month **mes** *m.* 1.5
monument **monumento** *m.* 1.4
more **más** 1.2
  more... than **más... que** 1.8
  more than **más de
(+ *number*)** 1.8
morning **mañana** *f.* 1.1
mother **madre** *f.* 1.3
mother-in-law **suegra** *f.* 1.3
motor **motor** *m.*
motorcycle **motocicleta** *f.* 1.5
mountain **montaña** *f.* 1.4
movie **película** *f.* 1.4
movie theater **cine** *m.* 1.4
Mr. **señor (Sr.); don** *m.* 1.1
Mrs. **señora (Sra.); doña** *f.* 1.1
much **mucho/a** *adj.* 1.2, 1.3
  very much **muchísimo/a**
*adj.* 1.2
municipal **municipal** *adj. m., f.*
museum **museo** *m.* 1.4
mushroom **champiñón** *m.* 1.8
music **música** *f.* 1.2
must **deber** *v.* **(+ *inf.*)** 1.3
  It must be... **Debe ser...** 1.6
my **mi(s)** *poss. adj.* 1.3

## N

name **nombre** *m.* 1.1
  be named **llamarse** *v.* 1.7
  in the name of **a nombre
de** 1.5
  last name *m.* **apellido**
  My name is... **Me
llamo...** 1.1
nationality **nacionalidad** *f.* 1.1
near **cerca de** *prep.* 1.2
need **faltar** *v.* 1.7; **necesitar** *v.*
**(+ *inf.*)** 1.2

negative **negativo/a** *adj.*
neither **tampoco** *adv.* 1.7
neither... nor **ni... ni** *conj.* 1.7
nephew **sobrino** *m.* 1.3
nervous **nervioso/a** *adj.* 1.5
never **nunca** *adv.* 1.7;
  **jamás** *adv.* 1.7
new **nuevo/a** *adj.* 1.6
newlywed **recién casado/a**
*m., f.* 1.9
newspaper **periódico** *m.* 1.4
next to **al lado de** *prep.* 1.2
nice **simpático/a** *adj.* 1.3;
  **amable** *adj.* 1.5
niece **sobrina** *f.* 1.3
night **noche** *f.* 1.1
nine **nueve** *n., adj.* 1.1
nine hundred
  **novecientos/as** *n., adj.* 1.2
nineteen **diecinueve** *n., adj.* 1.1
ninety **noventa** *n., adj.* 1.2
ninth **noveno/a** *n., adj.* 1.5
no **no** *adv.* 1.1; **ningún,
ninguno/a(s)** *adj.* 1.7
  no one **nadie** *pron.* 1.7
  No problem. **No hay
problema.** 1.7
nobody **nadie** *pron.* 1.7
none **ningún, ninguno/a(s)**
*pron.* 1.7
noon **mediodía** *m.* 1.1
nor **ni** *conj.* 1.7
not **no** 1.1
  not any **ningún, ninguno/a(s)**
*adj.* 1.7
  not anyone **nadie** *pron.* 1.7
  not anything **nada** *pron.* 1.7
  not bad at all **nada mal** 1.5
  not either **tampoco** *adv.* 1.7
  not ever **nunca** *adv.* 1.7;
  **jamás** *adv.* 1.7
  Not very well. **No muy
bien.** 1.1
notebook **cuaderno** *m.* 1.1
nothing **nada** *pron.* 1.1; 1.7
noun **sustantivo** *m.*
November **noviembre** *m.* 1.5
now **ahora** *adv.* 1.2
nowadays **hoy día** *adv.*
number **número** *m.* 1.1

## O

obtain **conseguir (e:i)** *v.* 1.4
o'clock: It's... o'clock. **Son
las...** 1.1
  It's one o'clock. **Es la una.** 1.1
October **octubre** *m.* 1.5
of **de** *prep.* 1.1
offer **ofrecer** *v.* 1.6
Oh! **¡Ay!**
oil **aceite** *m.* 1.8
OK **regular** *adj.* 1.1
  It's okay. **Está bien.**
old **viejo/a** *adj.* 1.3

old age **vejez** *f.* 1.9
older **mayor** *adj.* 1.3
  older brother/sister **hermano/a
  mayor** *m., f.* 1.3
oldest **el/la mayor** *adj.* 1.8
on **en** *prep.* 1.2; **sobre** *prep.* 1.2
  on the dot **en punto** 1.1
  on top of **encima de** 1.2
once **una vez** 1.6
one **un, uno/a** *m., f., sing.
  pron.* 1.1
  one hundred **cien(to)** *n., adj.*
  1.2
  one million **un millón** *m.* 1.2
  one more time **una vez más**
  1.9
  one thousand **mil** *n., adj.* 1.2
  one time **una vez** 1.6
onion **cebolla** *f.* 1.8
only **sólo** *adv.* 1.3; **único/a**
  *adj.* 1.3
  only child **hijo/a único/a**
  *m., f.* 1.3
open **abierto/a** *adj.* 1.5;
  **abrir** *v.* 1.3
open-air **al aire libre** 1.6
or **o** *conj.* 1.7
orange **anaranjado/a** *adj.* 1.6;
  **naranja** *f.* 1.8
order (*food*) **pedir (e:i)** *v.* 1.8
orderly **ordenado/a** *adj.* 1.5
ordinal (*numbers*) **ordinal** *adj.*
other **otro/a** *adj.* 1.6
ought to **deber** *v.* (+ *inf.*) 1.3
our **nuestro(s)/a(s)** *poss. adj.*
  1.3
over **sobre** *prep.* 1.2
over there **allá** *adv.* 1.2
owner **dueño/a** *m., f.* 1.8

## P

P.M. **tarde** *f.* 1.1
pack (one's suitcases) **hacer** *v.* **las
  maletas** 1.5
pair **par** *m.* 1.6
  pair of shoes **par de
  zapatos** *m.* 1.6
pants **pantalones** *m., pl.* 1.6
pantyhose **medias** *f., pl.* 1.6
paper **papel** *m.* 1.2
Pardon me. (*May I?*) **Con
  permiso.** 1.1; (*Excuse me.*)
  Pardon me. **Perdón.** 1.1
parents **padres** *m., pl.* 1.3;
  **papás** *m., pl.* 1.3
park **parque** *m.* 1.4
partner (*one of a married couple*)
  **pareja** *f.* 1.9
party **fiesta** *f.* 1.9
passed **pasado/a** *adj., p.p.*
passenger **pasajero/a** *m., f.* 1.1
passport **pasaporte** *m.* 1.5
past **pasado/a** *adj.* 1.6
pastime **pasatiempo** *m.* 1.4

pay **pagar** *v.* 1.6
  pay the bill **pagar la
  cuenta** 1.9
pea **arveja** *m.* 1.8
peach **melocotón** *m.* 1.8
pear **pera** *f.* 1.8
pen **pluma** *f.* 1.2
pencil **lápiz** *m.* 1.1
people **gente** *f.* 1.3
pepper (*black*) **pimienta** *f.* 1.8
perfect **perfecto/a** *adj.* 1.5
perhaps **quizás** *adv.*; **tal vez** *adv.*
permission **permiso** *m.*
person **persona** *f.* 1.3
phenomenal **fenomenal** *adj.* 1.5
photograph **foto(grafía)** *f.* 1.1
physician **doctor(a)** *m., f.*,
  **médico/a** *m., f.* 1.3
physics **física** *f. sing.* 1.2
pie **pastel** *m.* 1.9
pineapple **piña** *f.* 1.8
pink **rosado/a** *adj.* 1.6
place **lugar** *m.* 1.4; **poner** *v.*
  1.4
plaid **de cuadros** 1.6
plans **planes** *m., pl.*
  have plans **tener planes**
play **jugar (u:ue)** *v.* 1.4; (cards)
  **jugar a (las cartas)** 1.5
  play sports **practicar
  deportes** 1.4
player **jugador(a)** *m., f.* 1.4
pleasant **agradable** *adj.*
please **por favor** 1.1
  Pleased to meet you. **Mucho
  gusto.** 1.1; **Encantado/a.**
  *adj.* 1.1
pleasing: be pleasing to **gustar** *v.*
  1.2, 1.7
pleasure **gusto** *m.* 1.1
  The pleasure is mine. **El gusto
  es mío.** 1.1
polka-dotted **de lunares** 1.6
pool **piscina** *f.* 1.4
poor **pobre** *adj.* 1.6
pork **cerdo** *m.* 1.8
  pork chop **chuleta** *f.* **de
  cerdo** 1.8
possessive **posesivo/a** *adj.* 1.3
postcard **postal** *f.*
potato **papa** *f.* 1.8;
  **patata** *f.* 1.8
practice **practicar** *v.* 1.2
prefer **preferir (e:ie)** *v.* 1.4
prepare **preparar** *v.* 1.2
preposition **preposición** *f.*
pretty **bonito/a** *adj.* 1.3
price **precio** *m.* 1.6
  (fixed, set) price **precio** *m.*
  **fijo** 1.6
print **estampado/a** *adj*
private (*room*) **individual** *adj.*
problem **problema** *m.* 1.1
profession **profesión** *f.* 1.3
professor **profesor(a)** *m., f.*

program **programa** *m.* 1.1
programmer **programador(a)**
  *m., f.* 1.3
pronoun **pronombre** *m.*
psychology **psicología** *f.* 1.2
Puerto Rican **puertorriqueño/a**
  *adj.* 1.3
Puerto Rico **Puerto Rico** *m.* 1.1
pull a tooth **sacar una muela**
purchases **compras** *f., pl.* 1.5
purple **morado/a** *adj.* 1.6
purse **bolsa** *f.* 1.6
put **poner** *v.* 1.4
  put on (*clothing*) **ponerse** *v.* 1.7
  put on makeup **maquillarse** *v.*
  1.7

## Q

quality **calidad** *f.* 1.6
quarter **trimestre** *m.* 1.2
  quarter after (*time*) **y
  cuarto** 1.1; **y quince** 1.1
  quarter to (*time*)
  **menos cuarto** 1.1;
  **menos quince** 1.1
question **pregunta** *f.* 1.2
quiz **prueba** *f.* 1.2

## R

radio (*medium*) **radio** *f.* 1.2
rain **llover (o:ue)** *v.* 1.5
  It's raining. **Llueve.** 1.5; **Está
  lloviendo.** 1.5
raincoat **impermeable** *m.* 1.6
read **leer** *v.* 1.3.
  read e-mail **leer correo
  electrónico** 1.4
  read a magazine **leer una
  revista** 1.4
  read a newspaper **leer un
  periódico** 1.4
ready **listo/a** *adj.* 1.5
receive **recibir** *v.* 1.3
recommend **recomendar (e:ie)** *v.*
  1.8
recreation **diversión** *f.* 1.4
red **rojo/a** *adj.* 1.3
red-haired **pelirrojo/a** *adj.* 1.3
relatives **parientes** *m., pl.* 1.3
relax **relajarse** *v.* 1.9;
  **Tranquilo/a.** 1.7
remain **quedarse** *v.* 1.7
remember **acordarse (o:ue)** *v.*
  **(de)** 1.7; **recordar (o:ue)** *v.*
  1.4
repeat **repetir (e:i)** *v.* 1.4
request **pedir (e:i)** *v.* 1.4
reservation **reservación** *f.* 1.5
rest **descansar** *v.* 1.2
restaurant **restaurante** *m.* 1.4
retire (*from work*) **jubilarse** *v.* 1.9
return **regresar** *v.* 1.2; **volver**

(o:ue) *v.* 1.4
return trip **vuelta** *f.*
rice **arroz** *m.* 1.8
rich **rico/a** *adj.* 1.6
ride: ride a bicycle **pasear** *v.* **en bicicleta** 1.4
ride a horse **montar** *v.* **a caballo** 1.5
right **derecha** *f.* 1.2
be right **tener razón** 1.3
right away **enseguida** *adv.* 1.9
right now **ahora mismo** 1.5
to the right of **a la derecha de** 1.2
right? (*question tag*) **¿no?** 1.1; **¿verdad?** 1.1
road **camino** *m.*
roast **asado/a** *adj.* 1.8
roast chicken **pollo** *m.* **asado** 1.8
rollerblade **patinar en línea** *v.*
room **habitación** *f.* 1.5; **cuarto** *m.* 1.2; 1.7
roommate **compañero/a** *m., f.* **de cuarto** 1.2
roundtrip **de ida y vuelta** 1.5
roundtrip ticket **pasaje** *m.* **de ida y vuelta** 1.5
routine **rutina** *f.* 1.7
run **correr** *v.* 1.3
Russian **ruso/a** *adj.* 1.3

## S

sad **triste** *adj.* 1.5
safe **seguro/a** *adj.* 1.5
sailboard **tabla de windsurf** *f.* 1.5
salad **ensalada** *f.* 1.8
sale **rebaja** *f.* 1.6
salesperson **vendedor(a)** *m., f.* 1.6
salmon **salmón** *m.* 1.8
salt **sal** *f.* 1.8
same **mismo/a** *adj.* 1.3
sandal **sandalia** *f.* 1.6
sandwich **sándwich** *m.* 1.8
Saturday **sábado** *m.* 1.2
sausage **salchicha** *f.* 1.8
say **decir** *v.* 1.4
say (that) **decir (que)** *v.* 1.4, 1.9
say the answer **decir la respuesta** 1.4
scared: be (very) scared (of) **tener (mucho) miedo (de)** 1.3
schedule **horario** *m.* 1.2
school **escuela** *f.* 1.1
science *f.* **ciencia** 1.2
scuba dive **bucear** *v.* 1.4
sea **mar** *m.* 1.5
season **estación** *f.* 1.5
seat **silla** *f.* 1.2
second **segundo/a** *n., adj.* 1.5

see **ver** *v.* 1.4
see movies **ver películas** 1.4
See you. **Nos vemos.** 1.1
See you later. **Hasta la vista.** 1.1; **Hasta luego.** 1.1
See you soon. **Hasta pronto.** 1.1
See you tomorrow. **Hasta mañana.** 1.1
seem **parecer** *v.* 1.6
sell **vender** *v.* 1.6
semester **semestre** *m.* 1.2
separate (from) **separarse** *v.* **(de)** 1.9
separated **separado/a** *adj.* 1.9
September **septiembre** *m.* 1.5
sequence **secuencia** *f.*
serve **servir (e:i)** *v.* 1.8
set (*fixed*) **fijo/a** *adj.* 1.6
seven **siete** *n., adj.* 1.1
seven hundred **setecientos/as** *n., adj.* 1.2
seventeen **diecisiete** *n., adj.* 1.1
seventh **séptimo/a** *n., adj.* 1.5
seventy **setenta** *n., adj.* 1.2
several **varios/as** *adj. pl.* 1.8
shampoo **champú** *m.* 1.7
share **compartir** *v.* 1.3
sharp (*time*) **en punto** 1.1
shave **afeitarse** *v.* 1.7
shaving cream **crema** *f.* **de afeitar** 1.7
she **ella** *sub. pron.* 1.1
shellfish **mariscos** *m., pl.* 1.8
ship **barco** *m.*
shirt **camisa** *f.* 1.6
shoe **zapato** *m.* 1.6
shoe size **número** *m.* 1.6
tennis shoes **zapatos** *m., pl.* **de tenis** 1.6
shop **tienda** *f.* 1.6
shopping: to go shopping **ir de compras** 1.5
shopping mall **centro comercial** *m.* 1.6
short (*in height*) **bajo/a** *adj.* 1.3; (*in length*) **corto/a** *adj.* 1.6
shorts **pantalones cortos** *m., pl.* 1.6
should (*do something*) **deber** *v.* **(+ *inf.*)** 1.3
show **mostrar (o:ue)** *v.* 1.4
shower **ducha** *f.* 1.7; **ducharse** *v.* 1.7
shrimp **camarón** *m.* 1.8
siblings **hermanos/as** *m., f. pl.* 1.3
silk **seda** *f.* 1.6
(made of) silk **de seda** 1.6
silly **tonto/a** *adj.* 1.3
since **desde** *prep.*
sing **cantar** *v.* 1.2
single **soltero/a** *adj.* 1.9
single room **habitación** *f.* **individual** 1.5
sink **lavabo** *m.* 1.7

sir **señor (Sr.)** *m.* 1.1
sister **hermana** *f.* 1.3
sister-in-law **cuñada** *f.* 1.3
sit down **sentarse (e:ie)** *v.* 1.7
six **seis** *n., adj.* 1.1
six hundred **seiscientos/as** *n., adj.* 1.2
sixteen **dieciséis** *n., adj.* 1.1
sixth **sexto/a** *n., adj.* 1.5
sixty **sesenta** *n., adj.* 1.2
size **talla** *f.* 1.6
shoe size **número** *m.* 1.6
skate (in-line) **patinar** *v.* **(en línea)** 1.4
skateboard **andar en patineta** *v.* 1.4
ski **esquiar** *v.* 1.4
skiing **esquí** *m.* 1.4
waterskiing **esquí** *m.* **acuático** 1.4
skirt **falda** *f.* 1.6
sleep **dormir (o:ue)** *v.* 1.4; **sueño** *m.* 1.3
go to sleep **dormirse (o:ue)** *v.* 1.7
sleepy: be (very) sleepy **tener (mucho) sueño** 1.3
slender **delgado/a** *adj.* 1.3
slippers **pantuflas** *f.* 1.7
small **pequeño/a** *adj.* 1.3
smart **listo/a** *adj.* 1.5
smile **sonreír (e:i)** *v.* 1.9
smoggy: It's (very) smoggy. **Hay (mucha) contaminación.**
smoke **fumar** *v.* 1.8
smoking section **sección** *f.* **de fumar** 1.8
nonsmoking section *f.* **sección de no fumar** 1.8
snack **merendar** *v.* 1.8
sneakers **los zapatos de tenis** 1.6
snow **nevar (e:ie)** *v.* 1.5; **nieve** *f.*
snowing: It's snowing. **Nieva.** 1.5; **Está nevando.** 1.5
so **tan** *adv.* 1.5
so much **tanto** *adv.*
so-so **regular** 1.1
soap **jabón** *m.* 1.7
soccer **fútbol** *m.* 1.4
sociology **sociología** *f.* 1.2
sock(s) **calcetín (calcetines)** *m.* 1.6
soft drink **refresco** *m.* 1.8
some **algún, alguno/a(s)** *adj.* 1.7; **unos/as** *pron. m., f. pl.; indef. art.* 1.1
somebody **alguien** *pron.* 1.7
someone **alguien** *pron.* 1.7
something **algo** *pron.* 1.7
son **hijo** *m.* 1.3
son-in-law **yerno** *m.* 1.3
soon **pronto** *adv.*
See you soon. **Hasta pronto.** 1.1
sorry

I'm sorry. **Lo siento.** 1.4
I'm so sorry. **Mil perdones.**
    1.4; **Lo siento
    muchísimo.** 1.4
soup **sopa** *f.* 1.8
Spain **España** *f.* 1.1
Spanish (*language*) **español** *m.*
    1.2; **español(a)** *adj.* 1.3
spare time **ratos libres** 1.4
speak **hablar** *v.* 1.2
spelling **ortografía** *f.*;
    **ortográfico/a** *adj.*
spend (*money*) **gastar** *v.* 1.6
sport **deporte** *m.* 1.4
sports-related **deportivo/a**
    *adj.* 1.4
spouse **esposo/a** *m., f.* 1.3
spring **primavera** *f.* 1.5
square (city or town) **plaza** *f.* 1.4
stadium **estadio** *m.* 1.2
stage **etapa** *f.* 1.9
station **estación** *f.* 1.5
status: marital status **estado** *m.*
    **civil** 1.9
stay **quedarse** *v.* 1.7
steak **bistec** *m.* 1.8
step **etapa** *f.*
stepbrother **hermanastro**
    *m.* 1.3
stepdaughter **hijastra** *f.* 1.3
stepfather **padrastro** *m.* 1.3
stepmother **madrastra** *f.* 1.3
stepsister **hermanastra** *f.* 1.3
stepson **hijastro** *m.* 1.3
still **todavía** *adv.* 1.5
stockings **medias** *f., pl.* 1.6
store **tienda** *f.* 1.6
strawberry **frutilla** *f.*; **fresa** *f.*
stripe **raya** *f.* 1.6
    striped **de rayas** 1.6
stroll **pasear** *v.* 1.4
student **estudiante** *m., f.*
    1.1, 1.2; **estudiantil** *adj.* 1.2
study **estudiar** *v.* 1.2
stupendous **estupendo/a**
    *adj.* 1.5
style **estilo** *m.*
subway **metro** *m.* 1.5
    subway station **estación** *f.*
    **del metro** 1.5
such as **tales como**
suddenly **de repente** *adv.* 1.6
sugar **azúcar** *m.* 1.8
suit **traje** *m.* 1.6
suitcase **maleta** *f.* 1.1
summer **verano** *m.* 1.5
sun **sol** *m.* 1.5
sunbathe **tomar** *v.* **el sol** 1.4
Sunday **domingo** *m.* 1.2
sunglasses **gafas** *f., pl.*
    **de sol** 1.6
sunny: It's (very) sunny. **Hace
    (mucho) sol.** 1.5
suppose **suponer** *v.* 1.4
sure **seguro/a** *adj.* 1.5

be sure **estar seguro/a** 1.5
surfboard **tabla de surf** *f.* 1.5
surprise **sorprender** *v.* 1.9;
    **sorpresa** *f.* 1.9
sweater **suéter** *m.* 1.6
sweets **dulces** *m., pl.* 1.9
swim **nadar** *v.* 1.4
swimming **natación** *f.* 1.4
swimming pool **piscina** *f.* 1.4

## T

table **mesa** *f.* 1.2
take **tomar** *v.* 1.2; **llevar** *v.* 1.6
    take a bath **bañarse** *v.* 1.7
    take (*wear*) a shoe size *v.*
      **calzar** 1.6
    take a shower **ducharse** *v.* 1.7
    take off **quitarse** *v.* 1.7
    take photos **tomar fotos** 1.5;
      **sacar fotos** 1.5
talk *v.* **hablar** 1.2
tall **alto/a** *adj.* 1.3
tape (*audio*) **cinta** *f.*
taste **probar (o:ue)** *v.* 1.8;
    **saber** *v.* 1.8
    taste like **saber a** 1.8
tasty **rico/a** *adj.* 1.8; **sabroso/a**
    *adj.* 1.8
taxi **taxi** *m.* 1.5
tea **té** *m.* 1.8
teach **enseñar** *v.* 1.2
teacher **profesor(a)** *m., f.*
    1.1, 1.2
team **equipo** *m.* 1.4
television **televisión** *f.* 1.2
tell **contar (o:ue)** *v.* 1.4; **decir**
    *v.* 1.4
    tell (that) **decir** *v.* **(que)** 1.4, 1.9
    tell lies **decir mentiras** 1.4
    tell the truth **decir la verdad**
      1.4
ten **diez** *n., adj.* 1.1
tennis **tenis** *m.* 1.4
tennis shoes **zapatos** *m., pl.* **de
    tenis** 1.6
tent **tienda** *f.* **de campaña**
tenth **décimo/a** *n., adj.* 1.5
terrific **chévere** *adj.*
test **prueba** *f.* 1.2; **examen**
    *m.* 1.2
Thank you. **Gracias.** 1.1
    Thank you (very much).
      **(Muchas) gracias.** 1.1
    Thank you very, very much.
      **Muchísimas gracias.** 1.9
    Thanks (a lot). **(Muchas)
      gracias.** 1.1
    Thanks again. (*lit. Thanks one
      more time.*) **Gracias una vez
      más.** 1.9
    Thanks for everything. **Gracias
      por todo.** 1.9
that (one) **ése, ésa, eso** *pron.*
    1.6; **ese, esa** *adj.* 1.6

that (*over there*) **aquél,
    aquélla, aquello** *pron.* 1.6;
    **aquel, aquella** *adj.* 1.6
that's me **soy yo** 1.1
the **el** *m., sing.* **la** *f. sing.,* **los** *m.,
    pl.* **las** *f., pl.*
their **su(s)** *poss. adj.* 1.3
them **los/las** *pl., d.o. pron.* 1.5;
    **ellos/as** *pron., obj. of prep.* 1.9
    to/for them **les** *pl., i.o. pron.*
      1.6
then **después** (*afterward*)
    *adv.* 1.7; **entonces** (*as a
    result*) *adv.* 1.7; **luego** (*next*)
    *adv.* 1.7
there **allí** *adv.* 1.2
    There is/are... **Hay...** 1.1
    There is/are not... **No hay...**
      1.1
these **éstos, éstas** *pron.* 1.6;
    **estos, estas** *adj.* 1.6
they **ellos** *m., pron.* **ellas** *f., pron.*
thin **delgado/a** *adj.* 1.3
thing **cosa** *f.* 1.1
think **pensar (e:ie)** *v.* 1.4;
    (*believe*) **creer** *v.*
    think about **pensar en** *v.* 1.4
third **tercero/a** *n., adj.* 1.5
thirst **sed** *f.* 1.3
thirsty: be (very) thirsty **tener
    (mucha) sed** 1.3
thirteen **trece** *n., adj.* 1.1
thirty **treinta** *n., adj.* 1.1; 1.2
    *thirty minutes past the hour* **y
      treinta; y media** 1.2
this **este, esta** *adj.*; **éste, ésta,
    esto** *pron.* 1.6
    This is... (*introduction*) **Éste/a
      es...** 1.1
those **ésos, ésas** *pron.* 1.6;
    **esos, esas** *adj.* 1.6
those (*over there*) **aquéllos,
    aquéllas** *pron.* 1.6; **aquellos,
    aquellas** *adj.* 1.6
thousand **mil** *n., adj.* 1.6
three **tres** *n., adj.* 1.1
three hundred
    **trescientos/as** *n., adj.* 1.2
Thursday **jueves** *m., sing.* 1.2
thus (*in such a way*) **así** *adj.*
ticket **pasaje** *m.* 1.5
tie **corbata** *f.* 1.6
time **vez** *f.* 1.6; **tiempo** *m.* 1.4
    have a good/bad time **pasarlo
      bien/mal** 1.9
    What time is it? **¿Qué hora
      es?** 1.1
    (At) What time...? **¿A qué
      hora...?** 1.1
times **veces** *f., pl.* 1.6
    two times **dos veces** 1.6
tip **propina** *f.* 1.9
tired **cansado/a** *adj.* 1.5
    be tired **estar cansado/a**
      1.5

to **a** *prep.* 1.1
toast (*drink*) **brindar** *v.* 1.9
toasted **tostado/a** *adj.* 1.8
   toasted bread **pan tostado** *m.* 1.8
today **hoy** *adv.* 1.2
   Today is… **Hoy es…** 1.2
together **juntos/as** *adj.* 1.9
toilet **inodoro** *m.* 1.7
tomato **tomate** *m.* 1.8
tomorrow **mañana** *f.* 1.1
   See you tomorrow. **Hasta mañana.** 1.1
tonight **esta noche** *adv.* 1.4
too **también** *adv.* 1.2; 1.7
   too much **demasiado** *adv.* 1.6
tooth **diente** *m.* 1.7
toothpaste **pasta** *f.* **de dientes** 1.7
tortilla **tortilla** *f.* 1.8
tour **excursión** *f.* 1.4
   tour an area **recorrer** *v.*
tourism **turismo** *m.* 1.5
tourist **turista** *m., f.* 1.1; **turístico/a** *adj.*
towel **toalla** *f.* 1.7
town **pueblo** *m.* 1.4
train **tren** *m.* 1.5
   train station **estación** *f.* **(de) tren** *m.* 1.5
translate **traducir** *v.* 1.6
travel **viajar** *v.* 1.2
travel agent **agente** *m., f.* **de viajes** 1.5
traveler **viajero/a** *m., f.* 1.5
trillion **billón** *m.*
trimester **trimestre** *m.* 1.2
trip **viaje** *m.* 1.5
   take a trip **hacer un viaje** 1.5
truth **verdad** *f.*
try **intentar** *v.;* **probar (o:ue)** *v.* 1.8
   try on **probarse (o:ue)** *v.* 1.7
t-shirt **camiseta** *f.* 1.6
Tuesday **martes** *m., sing.* 1.2
tuna **atún** *m.* 1.8
turkey **pavo** *m.* 1.8
twelve **doce** *n., adj.* 1.1
twenty **veinte** *n., adj.* 1.1
twenty-eight **veintiocho** *n., adj.* 1.1
twenty-five **veinticinco** *n., adj.* 1.1
twenty-four **veinticuatro** *n., adj.* 1.1
twenty-nine **veintinueve** *n., adj.* 1.1
twenty-one **veintiún, veintiuno/a** *n., adj.* 1.1
twenty-seven **veintisiete** *n., adj.* 1.1
twenty-six **veintiséis** *n., adj.* 1.1
twenty-three **veintitrés** *n., adj.* 1.1

twenty-two **veintidós** *n., adj.* 1.1
twice **dos veces** *adv.* 1.6
twin **gemelo/a** *m., f.* 1.3
two **dos** *n., adj.* 1.1
   two hundred **doscientos/as** *n., adj.* 1.2
   two times **dos veces** *adv.* 1.6

## U

ugly **feo/a** *adj.* 1.3
uncle **tío** *m.* 1.3
under **bajo** *adv.* 1.7; **debajo de** *prep.* 1.2
understand **comprender** *v.* 1.3; **entender (e:ie)** *v.* 1.4
underwear **ropa interior** *f.* 1.6
United States **Estados Unidos (EE.UU.)** *m. pl.* 1.1
university **universidad** *f.* 1.2
unmarried **soltero/a** *adj.*
unpleasant **antipático/a** *adj.* 1.3
until **hasta** *prep.* 1.6
us **nos** *pl., d.o. pron.* 1.5
   to/for us **nos** *pl., i.o. pron.* 1.6
use **usar** *v.* 1.6
useful **útil** *adj.*

## V

vacation **vacaciones** *f. pl.* 1.5
   be on vacation **estar de vacaciones** 1.5
   go on vacation **ir de vacaciones** 1.5
various **varios/as** *adj., pl.* 1.8
vegetables **verduras** *pl., f.* 1.8
verb **verbo** *m.*
very **muy** *adv.* 1.1
   very much **muchísimo** *adv.* 1.2
   (Very) well, thank you. **(Muy) bien gracias.** 1.1
video **video** *m.* 1.1
video game **videojuego** *m.* 1.4
vinegar **vinagre** *m.* 1.8
visit **visitar** *v.* 1.4
   visit monuments **visitar monumentos** 1.4
volleyball **vóleibol** *m.* 1.4

## W

wait (for) **esperar** *v.* (+ *inf.*) 1.2
waiter/waitress **camarero/a** *m., f.* 1.8
wake up **despertarse (e:ie)** *v.* 1.7
walk **caminar** *v.* 1.2
   take a walk **pasear** *v.* 1.4
   walk around **pasear por** 1.4

walkman **walkman** *m.*
wallet **cartera** *f.* 1.6
want **querer (e:ie)** *v.* 1.4
wash **lavar** *v.*
   wash one's face/hands **lavarse la cara/las manos** 1.7
   wash oneself **lavarse** *v.* 1.7
wastebasket **papelera** *f.* 1.2
watch **mirar** *v.* 1.2; **reloj** *m.* 1.2
   watch television **mirar (la) televisión** 1.2
water **agua** *f.* 1.8
waterskiing *m.* **esquí acuático** 1.4
we **nosotros(as)** *m., f. sub. pron.* 1.1
wear **llevar** *v.* 1.6; **usar** *v.* 1.6
weather **tiempo** *m.*
   The weather is bad. **Hace mal tiempo.** 1.5
   The weather is good. **Hace buen tiempo.** 1.5
wedding **boda** *f.* 1.9
Wednesday **miércoles** *m., sing.* 1.2
week **semana** *f.* 1.2
weekend **fin** *m.* **de semana** 1.4
well **pues** *adv.* 1.2; **bueno** *adv.* 1.2
   (Very) well, thanks. **(Muy) bien, gracias.** 1.1
   well organized **ordenado/a** *adj.*
what? **¿qué?** *pron.* 1.1
   At what time…? **¿A qué hora…?** 1.1
   What day is it? **¿Qué día es hoy?** 1.2
   What do you guys think? **¿Qué les parece?** 1.9
   What is today's date? **¿Cuál es la fecha de hoy?** 1.5
   What nice clothes! **¡Qué ropa más bonita!** 1.6
   What size do you take? **¿Qué talla lleva (usa)?** 1.6
   What time is it? **¿Qué hora es?** 1.1
   What's going on? **¿Qué pasa?** 1.1
   What's happening? **¿Qué pasa?** 1.1
   What's… like? **¿Cómo es…?** 1.3
   What's new? **¿Qué hay de nuevo?** 1.1
   What's the weather like? **¿Qué tiempo hace?** 1.5
   What's your name? **¿Cómo se llama usted?** *form.* 1.1
   What's your name? **¿Cómo te llamas (tú)?** *fam.* 1.1
when **cuando** *conj.* 1.7
   When? **¿Cuándo?** *adv.* 1.2
where **donde** *prep.*
   where (to)? (*destination*)

¿**adónde?** *adv.* 1.2; (*location*)
¿**dónde?** *adv.* 1.1
Where are you from? ¿**De dónde eres (tú)?** *fam.* 1.1; ¿**De dónde es (usted)?** *form.* 1.1
Where is...? ¿**Dónde está...?** 1.2
which? ¿**cuál?** *pron.* 1.2; ¿**qué?** *adj.* 1.2
In which...? ¿**En qué...?** 1.2
which one(s)? ¿**cuál(es)?** *pron.* 1.2
white **blanco/a** *adj.* 1.3
white wine **vino blanco** 1.8
who? ¿**quién(es)?** *pron.* 1.1
Who is...? ¿**Quién es...?** 1.1
whole **todo/a** *adj.*
whose ¿**de quién(es)?** *pron., adj.* 1.1
why? ¿**por qué?** *adv.* 1.2
widower/widow **viudo/a** *adj.* 1.9
wife **esposa** *f.* 1.3
win **ganar** *v.* 1.4
wind **viento** *m.* 1.5
window **ventana** *f.* 1.2
windy: It's (very) windy. **Hace (mucho) viento.** 1.5
wine **vino** *m.* 1.8
red wine **vino tinto** 1.8
white wine **vino blanco** 1.8
winter **invierno** *m.* 1.5
wish **desear** *v.* 1.2
with **con** *prep.* 1.2
with me **conmigo** 1.4; 1.9
with you **contigo** *fam.* 1.9
without **sin** *prep.* 1.2
woman **mujer** *f.* 1.1
wool **lana** *f.* 1.6
(made of) wool **de lana** 1.6
word **palabra** *f.* 1.1
work **trabajar** *v.* 1.2
worldwide **mundial** *adj.*
worried (about) **preocupado/a (por)** *adj.* 1.5
worry (about) **preocuparse** *v.* **(por)** 1.7
Don't worry. **No se preocupe.** *form.* 1.7; **No te preocupes.** *fam.* 1.7; **Tranquilo.** *adj.*
worse **peor** *adj.* 1.8
worst **el/la peor** *adj.* **lo peor** *n.* 1.8
Would you like to...? ¿**Te gustaría...?** *fam.* 1.4
write **escribir** *v.* 1.3
write a letter/e-mail message **escribir una carta/un mensaje electrónico** 1.4
wrong **equivocado/a** *adj.* 1.5
be wrong **no tener razón** 1.3

## X

x-ray **radiografía** *f.*

## Y

year **año** *m.* 1.5
be... years old **tener... años** 1.3
yellow **amarillo/a** *adj.* 1.3
yes **sí** *interj.* 1.1
yesterday **ayer** *adv.* 1.6
yet **todavía** *adv.* 1.5
yogurt **yogur** *m.* 1.8
you *sub pron.* **tú** *fam. sing.*, **usted (Ud.)** *form. sing.*, **vosotros/as** *fam. pl.*, **ustedes (Uds.)** *form. pl.* 1.1; *d. o. pron.* **te** *fam. sing.*, **lo/la** *form. sing.*, **os** *fam. pl.*, **los/las** *form. pl.* 1.5; *obj. of prep.* **ti** *fam. sing.*, **usted (Ud.)** *form. sing.*, **vosotros/as** *fam. pl.*, **ustedes (Uds.)** *form. pl.* 1.9
(to, for) you *i.o. pron.* **te** *fam. sing.*, **le** *form. sing.*, **os** *fam. pl.*, **les** *form. pl.* 1.6
You are... **Tú eres...** 1.1
You're welcome. **De nada.** 1.1; **No hay de qué.** 1.1
young **joven** *adj., sing.* (**jóvenes** *pl.*) 1.3
young person **joven** *m., f., sing.* (**jóvenes** *pl.*) 1.1
young woman **señorita (Srta.)** *f.*
younger **menor** *adj.* 1.3
younger brother/sister *m., f.* **hermano/a menor** 1.3
youngest **el/la menor** *m., f.* 1.8
your **su(s)** *poss. adj. form.* 1.3; **tu(s)** *poss. adj. fam. sing.* 1.3; **vuestro/a(s)** *poss. adj. form. pl.* 1.3
youth *f.* **juventud** 1.9

## Z

zero **cero** *m.* 1.1

| MATERIAS | ACADEMIC SUBJECTS |
|---|---|
| la administración de empresas | business administration |
| la agronomía | agriculture |
| el alemán | German |
| el álgebra | algebra |
| la antropología | anthropology |
| la arqueología | archaeology |
| la arquitectura | architecture |
| el arte | art |
| la astronomía | astronomy |
| la biología | biology |
| la bioquímica | biochemistry |
| la botánica | botany |
| el cálculo | calculus |
| el chino | Chinese |
| las ciencias políticas | political science |
| la computación | computer science |
| las comunicaciones | communications |
| la contabilidad | accounting |
| la danza | dance |
| el derecho | law |
| la economía | economics |
| la educación | education |
| la educación física | physical education |
| la enfermería | nursing |
| el español | Spanish |
| la filosofía | philosophy |
| la física | physics |
| el francés | French |
| la geografía | geography |
| la geología | geology |
| el griego | Greek |
| el hebreo | Hebrew |
| la historia | history |
| la informática | computer science |
| la ingeniería | engineering |
| el inglés | English |
| el italiano | Italian |
| el japonés | Japanese |
| el latín | Latin |
| las lenguas clásicas | classical languages |
| las lenguas romances | Romance languages |
| la lingüística | linguistics |
| la literatura | literature |
| las matemáticas | mathematics |
| la medicina | medicine |
| el mercadeo/ la mercadotecnia | marketing |
| la música | music |
| los negocios | business |
| el periodismo | journalism |
| el portugués | Portuguese |
| la psicología | psychology |
| la química | chemistry |
| el ruso | Russian |
| los servicios sociales | social services |
| la sociología | sociology |
| el teatro | theater |
| la trigonometría | trigonometry |

| LOS ANIMALES | ANIMALS |
|---|---|
| la abeja | bee |
| la araña | spider |
| la ardilla | squirrel |
| el ave (f.), el pájaro | bird |
| la ballena | whale |
| el burro | donkey |
| la cabra | goat |
| el caimán | alligator |
| el camello | camel |
| la cebra | zebra |
| el ciervo, el venado | deer |
| el cochino, el cerdo, el puerco | pig |
| el cocodrilo | crocodile |
| el conejo | rabbit |
| el coyote | coyote |
| la culebra, la serpiente, la víbora | snake |
| el elefante | elephant |
| la foca | seal |
| la gallina | hen |
| el gallo | rooster |
| el gato | cat |
| el gorila | gorilla |
| el hipopótamo | hippopotamus |
| la hormiga | ant |
| el insecto | insect |
| la jirafa | giraffe |
| el lagarto | lizard |
| el león | lion |
| el lobo | wolf |
| el loro, la cotorra, el papagayo, el perico | parrot |
| la mariposa | butterfly |
| el mono | monkey |
| la mosca | fly |
| el mosquito | mosquito |
| el oso | bear |
| la oveja | sheep |
| el pato | duck |
| el perro | dog |
| el pez | fish |
| la rana | frog |
| el ratón | mouse |
| el rinoceronte | rhinoceros |
| el saltamontes, el chapulín | grasshopper |
| el tiburón | shark |
| el tigre | tiger |
| el toro | bull |
| la tortuga | turtle |
| la vaca | cow |
| el zorro | fox |

## EL CUERPO HUMANO Y LA SALUD

## THE HUMAN BODY AND HEALTH

### El cuerpo humano

### The human body

| | |
|---|---|
| la barba | beard |
| el bigote | mustache |
| la boca | mouth |
| el brazo | arm |
| la cabeza | head |
| la cadera | hip |
| la ceja | eyebrow |
| el cerebro | brain |
| la cintura | waist |
| el codo | elbow |
| el corazón | heart |
| la costilla | rib |
| el cráneo | skull |
| el cuello | neck |
| el dedo | finger |
| el dedo del pie | toe |
| la espalda | back |
| el estómago | stomach |
| la frente | forehead |
| la garganta | throat |
| el hombro | shoulder |
| el hueso | bone |
| el labio | lip |
| la lengua | tongue |
| la mandíbula | jaw |
| la mejilla | cheek |
| el mentón, la barba, la barbilla | chin |
| la muñeca | wrist |
| el músculo | muscle |
| el muslo | thigh |
| las nalgas, el trasero, las asentaderas | buttocks |
| la nariz | nose |
| el nervio | nerve |
| el oído | (inner) ear |
| el ojo | eye |
| el ombligo | navel, belly button |
| la oreja | (outer) ear |
| la pantorrilla | calf |
| el párpado | eyelid |
| el pecho | chest |
| la pestaña | eyelash |
| el pie | foot |
| la piel | skin |
| la pierna | leg |
| el pulgar | thumb |
| el pulmón | lung |
| la rodilla | knee |
| la sangre | blood |
| el talón | heel |
| el tobillo | ankle |
| el tronco | torso, trunk |
| la uña | fingernail |
| la uña del dedo del pie | toenail |
| la vena | vein |

### Los cinco sentidos

### The five senses

| | |
|---|---|
| el gusto | taste |
| el oído | hearing |
| el olfato | smell |
| el tacto | touch |
| la vista | sight |

### La salud

### Health

| | |
|---|---|
| el accidente | accident |
| alérgico/a | allergic |
| el antibiótico | antibiotic |
| la aspirina | aspirin |
| el ataque cardiaco, el ataque al corazón | heart attack |
| el cáncer | cancer |
| la cápsula | capsule |
| la clínica | clinic |
| congestionado/a | congested |
| el consultorio | doctor's office |
| la curita | adhesive bandage |
| el/la dentista | dentist |
| el/la doctor(a), el/la médico/a | doctor |
| el dolor (de cabeza) | (head)ache, pain |
| embarazada | pregnant |
| la enfermedad | illness, disease |
| el/la enfermero/a | nurse |
| enfermo/a | ill, sick |
| la erupción | rash |
| el examen médico | physical exam |
| la farmacia | pharmacy |
| la fiebre | fever |
| la fractura | fracture |
| la gripe | flu |
| la herida | wound |
| el hospital | hospital |
| la infección | infection |
| el insomnio | insomnia |
| la inyección | injection |
| el jarabe | (cough) syrup |
| mareado/a | dizzy, nauseated |
| el medicamento | medication |
| la medicina | medicine |
| las muletas | crutches |
| la operación | operation |
| el/la paciente | patient |
| el/la paramédico/a | paramedic |
| la pastilla, la píldora | pill, tablet |
| los primeros auxilios | first aid |
| la pulmonía | pneumonia |
| los puntos | stitches |
| la quemadura | burn |
| el quirófano | operating room |
| la radiografía | x-ray |
| la receta | prescription |
| el resfriado | cold (illness) |
| la sala de emergencia(s) | emergency room |
| saludable | healthy, healthful |
| sano/a | healthy |
| el seguro médico | medical insurance |
| la silla de ruedas | wheelchair |
| el síntoma | symptom |
| el termómetro | thermometer |
| la tos | cough |
| la transfusión | transfusion |

| la vacuna | vaccination |
|---|---|
| la venda | bandage |
| el virus | virus |

| cortar(se) | to cut (oneself) |
|---|---|
| curar | to cure, to treat |
| desmayar(se) | to faint |
| enfermarse | to get sick |
| enyesar | to put in a cast |
| estornudar | to sneeze |
| guardar cama | to stay in bed |
| hinchar(se) | to swell |
| internar(se) en el hospital | to check into the hospital |
| lastimarse (el pie) | to hurt (one's foot) |
| mejorar(se) | to get better; to improve |
| operar | to operate |
| quemar(se) | to burn |
| respirar (hondo) | to breathe (deeply) |
| romperse (la pierna) | to break (one's leg) |
| sangrar | to bleed |
| sufrir | to suffer |
| tomarle la presión a alguien | to take someone's blood pressure |
| tomarle el pulso a alguien | to take someone's pulse |
| torcerse (el tobillo) | to sprain (one's ankle) |
| vendar | to bandage |

## EXPRESIONES ÚTILES PARA LA CLASE

## USEFUL CLASSROOM EXPRESSIONS

### Palabras útiles
### Useful words

| ausente | absent |
|---|---|
| el departamento | department |
| el dictado | dictation |
| la conversación, las conversaciones | conversation(s) |
| la expresión, las expresiones | expression(s) |
| el examen, los exámenes | test(s), exam(s) |
| la frase | sentence |

| la hoja de actividades | activity sheet |
|---|---|
| el horario de clases | class schedule |
| la oración, las oraciones | sentence(s) |
| el párrafo | paragraph |
| la persona | person |
| presente | present |
| la prueba | test, quiz |
| siguiente | following |
| la tarea | homework |

### Expresiones útiles
### Useful expressions

| Abra(n) su(s) libro(s). | Open your book(s). |
|---|---|
| Cambien de papel. | Change roles. |
| Cierre(n) su(s) libro(s). | Close your book(s). |
| ¿Cómo se dice ___ en español? | How do you say ___ in Spanish? |
| ¿Cómo se escribe ___ en español? | How do you write ___ in Spanish? |
| ¿Comprende(n)? | Do you understand? |
| (No) comprendo. | I (don't) understand. |
| Conteste(n) las preguntas. | Answer the questions. |
| Continúe(n), por favor. | Continue, please. |
| Escriba(n) su nombre. | Write your name. |
| Escuche(n) el audio. | Listen to the audio. |
| Estudie(n) la Lección tres. | Study Lesson three. |
| Haga(n) la actividad (el ejercicio) número cuatro. | Do activity (exercise) number four. |
| Lea(n) la oración en voz alta. | Read the sentence aloud. |
| Levante(n) la mano. | Raise your hand(s). |
| Más despacio, por favor. | Slower, please. |
| No sé. | I don't know. |
| Páse(n)me los exámenes. | Pass me the tests. |
| ¿Qué significa ___? | What does ___ mean? |
| Repita(n), por favor. | Repeat, please. |
| Siénte(n)se, por favor. | Sit down, please. |
| Siga(n) las instrucciones. | Follow the instructions. |
| ¿Tiene(n) alguna pregunta? | Do you have any questions? |
| Vaya(n) a la página dos. | Go to page two. |

## COUNTRIES & NATIONALITIES
## PAÍSES Y NACIONALIDADES

### North America / Norteamérica
| Canada | Canadá | canadiense |
|---|---|---|
| Mexico | México | mexicano/a |
| United States | Estados Unidos | estadounidense |

### Central America / Centroamérica
| Belize | Belice | beliceño/a |
|---|---|---|
| Costa Rica | Costa Rica | costarricense |
| El Salvador | El Salvador | salvadoreño/a |
| Guatemala | Guatemala | guatemalteco/a |
| Honduras | Honduras | hondureño/a |
| Nicaragua | Nicaragua | nicaragüense |
| Panama | Panamá | panameño/a |

| The Caribbean | El Caribe | |
|---|---|---|
| Cuba | **Cuba** | *cubano/a* |
| Dominican Republic | **República Dominicana** | *dominicano/a* |
| Haiti | **Haití** | *haitiano/a* |
| Puerto Rico | **Puerto Rico** | *puertorriqueño/a* |

| South America | Suramérica | |
|---|---|---|
| Argentina | **Argentina** | *argentino/a* |
| Bolivia | **Bolivia** | *boliviano/a* |
| Brazil | **Brasil** | *brasileño/a* |
| Chile | **Chile** | *chileno/a* |
| Colombia | **Colombia** | *colombiano/a* |
| Ecuador | **Ecuador** | *ecuatoriano/a* |
| Paraguay | **Paraguay** | *paraguayo/a* |
| Peru | **Perú** | *peruano/a* |
| Uruguay | **Uruguay** | *uruguayo/a* |
| Venezuela | **Venezuela** | *venezolano/a* |

| Europe | Europa | |
|---|---|---|
| Armenia | **Armenia** | *armenio/a* |
| Austria | **Austria** | *austríaco/a* |
| Belgium | **Bélgica** | *belga* |
| Bosnia | **Bosnia** | *bosnio/a* |
| Bulgaria | **Bulgaria** | *búlgaro/a* |
| Croatia | **Croacia** | *croata* |
| Czech Republic | **República Checa** | *checo/a* |
| Denmark | **Dinamarca** | *danés, danesa* |
| England | **Inglaterra** | *inglés, inglesa* |
| Estonia | **Estonia** | *estonio/a* |
| Finland | **Finlandia** | *finlandés, finlandesa* |
| France | **Francia** | *francés, francesa* |
| Germany | **Alemania** | *alemán, alemana* |
| Great Britain (United Kingdom) | **Gran Bretaña (Reino Unido)** | *británico/a* |
| Greece | **Grecia** | *griego/a* |
| Hungary | **Hungría** | *húngaro/a* |
| Iceland | **Islandia** | *islandés, islandesa* |
| Ireland | **Irlanda** | *irlandés, irlandesa* |
| Italy | **Italia** | *italiano/a* |
| Latvia | **Letonia** | *letón, letona* |
| Lithuania | **Lituania** | *lituano/a* |
| Netherlands (Holland) | **Países Bajos (Holanda)** | *holandés, holandesa* |
| Norway | **Noruega** | *noruego/a* |
| Poland | **Polonia** | *polaco/a* |
| Portugal | **Portugal** | *portugués, portuguesa* |
| Romania | **Rumania** | *rumano/a* |
| Russia | **Rusia** | *ruso/a* |
| Scotland | **Escocia** | *escocés, escocesa* |
| Serbia | **Serbia** | *serbio/a* |
| Slovakia | **Eslovaquia** | *eslovaco/a* |
| Slovenia | **Eslovenia** | *esloveno/a* |
| Spain | **España** | *español(a)* |
| Sweden | **Suecia** | *sueco/a* |
| Switzerland | **Suiza** | *suizo/a* |
| Ukraine | **Ucrania** | *ucraniano/a* |
| Wales | **Gales** | *galés, galesa* |

| Asia | Asia | |
|---|---|---|
| Bangladesh | **Bangladés** | *bangladesí* |
| Cambodia | **Camboya** | *camboyano/a* |
| China | **China** | *chino/a* |
| India | **India** | *indio/a* |
| Indonesia | **Indonesia** | *indonesio/a* |
| Iran | **Irán** | *iraní* |
| Iraq | **Iraq, Irak** | *iraquí* |

| | | |
|---|---|---|
| Israel | **Israel** | *israelí* |
| Japan | **Japón** | *japonés, japonesa* |
| Jordan | **Jordania** | *jordano/a* |
| Korea | **Corea** | *coreano/a* |
| Kuwait | **Kuwait** | *kuwaití* |
| Lebanon | **Líbano** | *libanés, libanesa* |
| Malaysia | **Malasia** | *malasio/a* |
| Pakistan | **Pakistán** | *pakistaní* |
| Russia | **Rusia** | *ruso/a* |
| Saudi Arabia | **Arabia Saudí** | *saudí* |
| Singapore | **Singapur** | *singapurés, singapuresa* |
| Syria | **Siria** | *sirio/a* |
| Taiwan | **Taiwán** | *taiwanés, taiwanesa* |
| Thailand | **Tailandia** | *tailandés, tailandesa* |
| Turkey | **Turquía** | *turco/a* |
| Vietnam | **Vietnam** | *vietnamita* |

### Africa     África

| | | |
|---|---|---|
| Algeria | **Argelia** | *argelino/a* |
| Angola | **Angola** | *angoleño/a* |
| Cameroon | **Camerún** | *camerunés, camerunesa* |
| Congo | **Congo** | *congolés, congolesa* |
| Egypt | **Egipto** | *egipcio/a* |
| Equatorial Guinea | **Guinea Ecuatorial** | *ecuatoguineano/a* |
| Ethiopia | **Etiopía** | *etíope* |
| Ivory Coast | **Costa de Marfil** | *marfileño/a* |
| Kenya | **Kenia, Kenya** | *keniano/a, keniata* |
| Libya | **Libia** | *libio/a* |
| Mali | **Malí** | *maliense* |
| Morocco | **Marruecos** | *marroquí* |
| Mozambique | **Mozambique** | *mozambiqueño/a* |
| Nigeria | **Nigeria** | *nigeriano/a* |
| Rwanda | **Ruanda** | *ruandés, ruandesa* |
| Somalia | **Somalia** | *somalí* |
| South Africa | **Sudáfrica** | *sudafricano/a* |
| Sudan | **Sudán** | *sudanés, sudanesa* |
| Tunisia | **Tunicia, Túnez** | *tunecino/a* |
| Uganda | **Uganda** | *ugandés, ugandesa* |
| Zambia | **Zambia** | *zambiano/a* |
| Zimbabwe | **Zimbabue** | *zimbabuense* |

### Australia and the Pacific     Australia y el Pacífico

| | | |
|---|---|---|
| Australia | **Australia** | *australiano/a* |
| New Zealand | **Nueva Zelanda** | *neozelandés, neozelandesa* |
| Philippines | **Filipinas** | *filipino/a* |

## MONEDAS DE LOS PAÍSES HISPANOS     CURRENCIES OF HISPANIC COUNTRIES

| País / Country | Moneda / Currency |
|---|---|
| **Argentina** | el peso |
| **Bolivia** | el boliviano |
| **Chile** | el peso |
| **Colombia** | el peso |
| **Costa Rica** | el colón |
| **Cuba** | el peso |
| **Ecuador** | el dólar estadounidense |
| **El Salvador** | el dólar estadounidense |
| **España** | el euro |
| **Guatemala** | el quetzal |
| **Guinea Ecuatorial** | el franco |
| **Honduras** | el lempira |
| **México** | el peso |
| **Nicaragua** | el córdoba |
| **Panamá** | el balboa, el dólar estadounidense |
| **Paraguay** | el guaraní |
| **Perú** | el nuevo sol |
| **Puerto Rico** | el dólar estadounidense |
| **República Dominicana** | el peso |
| **Uruguay** | el peso |
| **Venezuela** | el bolívar |

# EXPRESIONES Y REFRANES

# EXPRESSIONS AND SAYINGS

## Expresiones y refranes con partes del cuerpo

## Expressions and sayings with parts of the body

|  |  |
|---|---|
| A cara o cruz | Heads or tails |
| A corazón abierto | Open heart |
| A ojos vistas | Clearly, visibly |
| Al dedillo | Like the back of one's hand |
| ¡Choca/Vengan esos cinco! | Put it there!/Give me five! |
| Codo con codo | Side by side |
| Con las manos en la masa | Red-handed |
| Costar un ojo de la cara | To cost an arm and a leg |
| Darle a la lengua | To chatter/To gab |
| De rodillas | On one's knees |
| Duro de oído | Hard of hearing |
| En cuerpo y alma | In body and soul |
| En la punta de la lengua | On the tip of one's tongue |
| En un abrir y cerrar de ojos | In a blink of the eye |
| Entrar por un oído y salir por otro | In one ear and out the other |
| Estar con el agua al cuello | To be up to one's neck with/in |
| Estar para chuparse los dedos | To be delicious/To be finger-licking good |
| Hablar entre dientes | To mutter/To speak under one's breath |
| Hablar por los codos | To talk a lot/To be a chatterbox |
| Hacer la vista gorda | To turn a blind eye on something |
| Hombro con hombro | Shoulder to shoulder |
| Llorar a lágrima viva | To sob/To cry one's eyes out |
| Metérsele (a alguien) algo entre ceja y ceja | To get an idea in your head |
| No pegar ojo | Not to sleep a wink |
| No tener corazón | Not to have a heart |
| No tener dos dedos de frente | Not to have an ounce of common sense |
| Ojos que no ven, corazón que no siente | Out of sight, out of mind |
| Perder la cabeza | To lose one's head |
| Quedarse con la boca abierta | To be thunderstruck |
| Romper el corazón | To break someone's heart |
| Tener buen/mal corazón | Have a good/bad heart |
| Tener un nudo en la garganta | Have a knot in your throat |
| Tomarse algo a pecho | To take something too seriously |
| Venir como anillo al dedo | To fit like a charm/To suit perfectly |

## Expresiones y refranes con animales

## Expressions and sayings with animals

|  |  |
|---|---|
| A caballo regalado no le mires el diente. | Don't look a gift horse in the mouth. |
| Comer como un cerdo | To eat like a pig |
| Cuando menos se piensa, salta la liebre. | Things happen when you least expect it. |
| Llevarse como el perro y el gato | To fight like cats and dogs |
| Perro ladrador, poco mordedor./Perro que ladra no muerde. | His/her bark is worse than his/her bite. |
| Por la boca muere el pez. | Talking too much can be dangerous. |
| Poner el cascabel al gato | To stick one's neck out |
| Ser una tortuga | To be a slowpoke |

## Expresiones y refranes con alimentos

## Expressions and sayings with food

|  |  |
|---|---|
| Agua que no has de beber, déjala correr. | If you're not interested, don't ruin it for everybody else. |
| Con pan y vino se anda el camino. | Things never seem as bad after a good meal. |
| Contigo pan y cebolla. | You are all I need. |
| Dame pan y dime tonto. | I don't care what you say, as long as I get what I want. |
| Descubrir el pastel | To let the cat out of the bag |
| Dulce como la miel | Sweet as honey |
| Estar como agua para chocolate | To furious/To be at the boiling point |
| Estar en el ajo | To be in the know |
| Estar en la higuera | To have one's head in the clouds |
| Estar más claro que el agua | To be clear as a bell |
| Ganarse el pan | To earn a living/To earn one's daily bread |
| Llamar al pan, pan y al vino, vino. | Not to mince words. |
| No hay miel sin hiel. | Every rose has its thorn./There's always a catch. |
| No sólo de pan vive el hombre. | Man doesn't live by bread alone. |
| Pan con pan, comida de tontos. | Variety is the spice of life. |
| Ser agua pasada | To be water under the bridge |
| Ser más bueno que el pan | To be kindness itself |
| Temblar como un flan | To shake/tremble like a leaf |

## Expresiones y refranes con colores

## Expressions and sayings with colors

|  |  |
|---|---|
| Estar verde | To be inexperienced/wet behind the ears |
| Poner los ojos en blanco | To roll one's eyes |
| Ponerle a alguien un ojo morado | To give someone a black eye |
| Ponerse rojo | To turn red/To blush |
| Ponerse rojo de ira | To turn red with anger |
| Ponerse verde de envidia | To be green with envy |
| Quedarse en blanco | To go blank |
| Verlo todo de color de rosa | To see the world through rose-colored glasses |

| Refranes | Sayings | | |
|---|---|---|---|
| **A buen entendedor, pocas palabras bastan.** | A word to the wise is enough. | **Lo que es moda no incomoda.** | You have to suffer in the name of fashion. |
| **Ande o no ande, caballo grande.** | Bigger is always better. | **Más vale maña que fuerza.** | Brains are better than brawn. |
| **A quien madruga, Dios le ayuda.** | The early bird catches the worm. | **Más vale prevenir que curar.** | Prevention is better than cure. |
| **Cuídate, que te cuidaré.** | Take care of yourself, and then I'll take care of you. | **Más vale solo que mal acompañado.** | Better alone than with people you don't like. |
| **De tal palo tal astilla.** | A chip off the old block. | **Más vale tarde que nunca.** | Better late than never. |
| **Del dicho al hecho hay mucho trecho.** | Easier said than done. | **No es oro todo lo que reluce.** | All that glitters is not gold. |
| **Dime con quién andas y te diré quién eres.** | A man is known by the company he keeps. | **Poderoso caballero es don Dinero.** | Money talks. |
| **El saber no ocupa lugar.** | One never knows too much. | | |

## COMMON FALSE FRIENDS

False friends are Spanish words that look similar to English words but have very different meanings. While recognizing the English relatives of unfamiliar Spanish words you encounter is an important way of constructing meaning, there are some Spanish words whose similarity to English words is deceptive. Here is a list of some of the most common Spanish false friends.

**actualmente** ≠ actually
**actualmente** = nowadays, currently
actually = **de hecho, en realidad, en efecto**

**argumento** ≠ argument
**argumento** = plot
argument = **discusión, pelea**

**armada** ≠ army
**armada** = navy
army = **ejército**

**balde** ≠ bald
**balde** = pail, bucket
bald = **calvo/a**

**batería** ≠ battery
**batería** = drum set
battery = **pila**

**bravo** ≠ brave
**bravo** = wild; fierce
brave = **valiente**

**cándido/a** ≠ candid
**cándido/a** = innocent
candid = **sincero/a**

**carbón** ≠ carbon
**carbón** = coal
carbon = **carbono**

**casual** ≠ casual
**casual** = accidental, chance
casual = **informal, despreocupado/a**

**casualidad** ≠ casualty
**casualidad** = chance, coincidence
casualty = **víctima**

**colegio** ≠ college
**colegio** = school
college = **universidad**

**collar** ≠ collar (of a shirt)
**collar** = necklace
collar = **cuello (de camisa)**

**comprensivo/a** ≠ comprehensive
**comprensivo/a** = understanding
comprehensive = **completo, extensivo**

**constipado** ≠ constipated
**estar constipado/a** = to have a cold
to be constipated = **estar estreñido/a**

**crudo/a** ≠ crude
**crudo/a** = raw, undercooked
crude = **burdo/a, grosero/a**

**divertir** ≠ to divert
**divertirse** = to enjoy oneself
to divert = **desviar**

**educado/a** ≠ educated
**educado/a** = well-mannered
educated = **culto/a, instruido/a**

**embarazada** ≠ embarrassed
**estar embarazada** = to be pregnant
to be embarrassed = **estar avergonzado/a; dar/tener vergüenza**

**eventualmente** ≠ eventually
**eventualmente** = possibly
eventually = **finalmente, al final**

**éxito** ≠ exit
**éxito** = success
exit = **salida**

**físico/a** ≠ physician
**físico/a** = physicist
physician = **médico/a**

**fútbol** ≠ football
**fútbol** = soccer
football = **fútbol americano**

**lectura** ≠ lecture
**lectura** = reading
lecture = **conferencia**

**librería** ≠ library
**librería** = bookstore
library = **biblioteca**

**máscara** ≠ mascara
**máscara** = mask
mascara = **rímel**

**molestar** ≠ to molest
**molestar** = to bother, to annoy
to molest = **abusar**

**oficio** ≠ office
**oficio** = trade, occupation
office = **oficina**

**rato** ≠ rat
**rato** = while, time
rat = **rata**

**realizar** ≠ to realize
**realizar** = to carry out; to fulfill
to realize = **darse cuenta de**

**red** ≠ red
**red** = net
red = **rojo/a**

**revolver** ≠ revolver
**revolver** = to stir, to rummage through
revolver = **revólver**

**sensible** ≠ sensible
**sensible** = sensitive
sensible = **sensato/a, razonable**

**suceso** ≠ success
**suceso** = event
success = **éxito**

**sujeto** ≠ subject (topic)
**sujeto** = fellow; individual
subject = **tema, asunto**

# LOS ALIMENTOS

# FOODS

## Frutas

## Fruits

| | |
|---|---|
| la aceituna | olive |
| el aguacate | avocado |
| el albaricoque, el damasco | apricot |
| la banana, el plátano | banana |
| la cereza | cherry |
| la ciruela | plum |
| el dátil | date |
| la frambuesa | raspberry |
| la fresa, la frutilla | strawberry |
| el higo | fig |
| el limón | lemon; lime |
| el melocotón, el durazno | peach |
| la mandarina | tangerine |
| el mango | mango |
| la manzana | apple |
| la naranja | orange |
| la papaya | papaya |
| la pera | pear |
| la piña | pineapple |
| el pomelo, la toronja | grapefruit |
| la sandía | watermelon |
| las uvas | grapes |

## Vegetales

## Vegetables

| | |
|---|---|
| la alcachofa | artichoke |
| el apio | celery |
| la arveja, el guisante | pea |
| la berenjena | eggplant |
| el brócoli | broccoli |
| la calabaza | squash; pumpkin |
| la cebolla | onion |
| el champiñón, la seta | mushroom |
| la col, el repollo | cabbage |
| la coliflor | cauliflower |
| los espárragos | asparagus |
| las espinacas | spinach |
| los frijoles, las habichuelas | beans |
| las habas | fava beans |
| las judías verdes, los ejotes | string beans, green beans |
| la lechuga | lettuce |
| el maíz, el choclo, el elote | corn |
| la papa, la patata | potato |
| el pepino | cucumber |
| el pimentón | bell pepper |
| el rábano | radish |
| la remolacha | beet |
| el tomate, el jitomate | tomato |
| la zanahoria | carrot |

## El pescado y los mariscos

## Fish and shellfish

| | |
|---|---|
| la almeja | clam |
| el atún | tuna |
| el bacalao | cod |
| el calamar | squid |
| el cangrejo | crab |
| el camarón, la gamba | shrimp |
| la langosta | lobster |
| el langostino | prawn |
| el lenguado | sole; flounder |
| el mejillón | mussel |
| la ostra | oyster |
| el pulpo | octopus |
| el salmón | salmon |
| la sardina | sardine |
| la vieira | scallop |

## La carne

## Meat

| | |
|---|---|
| la albóndiga | meatball |
| el bistec | steak |
| la carne de res | beef |
| el chorizo | hard pork sausage |
| la chuleta de cerdo | pork chop |
| el cordero | lamb |
| los fiambres | cold cuts, food served cold |
| el filete | fillet |
| la hamburguesa | hamburger |
| el hígado | liver |
| el jamón | ham |
| el lechón | suckling pig, roasted pig |
| el pavo | turkey |
| el pollo | chicken |
| el cerdo | pork |
| la salchicha | sausage |
| la ternera | veal |
| el tocino | bacon |

## Otras comidas

## Other foods

| | |
|---|---|
| el ajo | garlic |
| el arroz | rice |
| el azúcar | sugar |
| el batido | milkshake |
| el budín | pudding |
| el cacahuete, el maní | peanut |
| el café | coffee |
| los fideos | noodles, pasta |
| la harina | flour |
| el huevo | egg |
| el jugo, el zumo | juice |
| la leche | milk |
| la mermelada | marmalade, jam |
| la miel | honey |
| el pan | bread |
| el queso | cheese |
| la sal | salt |
| la sopa | soup |
| el té | tea |
| la tortilla | omelet (Spain), tortilla (Mexico) |
| el yogur | yogurt |

## Cómo describir la comida

## Ways to describe food

| | |
|---|---|
| a la plancha, a la parrilla | grilled |
| ácido/a | sour |
| al horno | baked |
| amargo/a | bitter |
| caliente | hot |
| dulce | sweet |
| duro/a | tough |
| frío/a | cold |
| frito/a | fried |
| fuerte | strong, heavy |
| ligero/a | light |
| picante | spicy |
| sabroso/a | tasty |
| salado/a | salty |

## DÍAS FESTIVOS

## HOLIDAYS

### enero
**Año Nuevo (1)**
**Día de los Reyes Magos (6)**
**Día de Martin Luther King, Jr.**

### January
New Year's Day
Three Kings Day (Epiphany)

Martin Luther King, Jr. Day

### febrero
**Día de San Blas (Paraguay) (3)**
**Día de San Valentín, Día de los Enamorados (14)**
**Día de los Presidentes**
**Carnaval**

### February
St. Blas Day (Paraguay)

Valentine's Day

Presidents' Day
Carnival (Mardi Gras)

### marzo
**Día de San Patricio (17)**
**Nacimiento de Benito Juárez (México) (21)**

### March
St. Patrick's Day
Benito Juárez's Birthday (Mexico)

### abril
**Semana Santa**
**Pésaj**
**Pascua**
**Declaración de la Independencia de Venezuela (19)**
**Día de la Tierra (22)**

### April
Holy Week
Passover
Easter
Declaration of Independence of Venezuela
Earth Day

### mayo
**Día del Trabajo (1)**
**Cinco de Mayo (5) (México)**
**Día de las Madres**
**Independencia Patria (Paraguay) (15)**
**Día Conmemorativo**

### May
Labor Day
Cinco de Mayo (May 5th) (Mexico)
Mother's Day
Independence Day (Paraguay)

Memorial Day

### junio
**Día de los Padres**
**Día de la Bandera (14)**
**Día del Indio (Perú) (24)**

### June
Father's Day
Flag Day
Native People's Day (Peru)

### julio
**Día de la Independencia de los Estados Unidos (4)**
**Día de la Independencia de Venezuela (5)**
**Día de la Independencia de la Argentina (9)**
**Día de la Independencia de Colombia (20)**

### July
Independence Day (United States)
Independence Day (Venezuela)
Independence Day (Argentina)
Independence Day (Colombia)

**Nacimiento de Simón Bolívar (24)**
**Día de la Revolución (Cuba) (26)**
**Día de la Independencia del Perú (28)**

Simón Bolívar's Birthday
Revolution Day (Cuba)
Independence Day (Peru)

### agosto
**Día de la Independencia de Bolivia (6)**
**Día de la Independencia del Ecuador (10)**
**Día de San Martín (Argentina) (17)**
**Día de la Independencia del Uruguay (25)**

### August
Independence Day (Bolivia)
Independence Day (Ecuador)
San Martín Day (anniversary of his death) (Argentina)
Independence Day (Uruguay)

### septiembre
**Día del Trabajo (EE. UU.)**
**Día de la Independencia de Costa Rica, El Salvador, Guatemala, Honduras y Nicaragua (15)**
**Día de la Independencia de México (16)**
**Día de la Independencia de Chile (18)**
**Año Nuevo Judío**
**Día de la Virgen de las Mercedes (Perú) (24)**

### September
Labor Day (U.S.)
Independence Day (Costa Rica, El Salvador, Guatemala, Honduras, Nicaragua)
Independence Day (Mexico)
Independence Day (Chile)
Jewish New Year
Day of the Virgin of Mercedes (Peru)

### octubre
**Día de la Raza (12)**
**Noche de Brujas (31)**

### October
Columbus Day
Halloween

### noviembre
**Día de los Muertos (2)**
**Día de los Veteranos (11)**
**Día de la Revolución Mexicana (20)**
**Día de Acción de Gracias**
**Día de la Independencia de Panamá (28)**

### November
All Souls Day
Veterans' Day
Mexican Revolution Day

Thanksgiving
Independence Day (Panama)

### diciembre
**Día de la Virgen (8)**
**Día de la Virgen de Guadalupe (México) (12)**
**Januká**
**Nochebuena (24)**
**Navidad (25)**
**Año Viejo (31)**

### December
Day of the Virgin
Day of the Virgin of Guadalupe (Mexico)

Chanukah
Christmas Eve
Christmas
New Year's Eve

**NOTE:** In Spanish, dates are written with the day first, then the month. Christmas Day is **el 25 de diciembre**. In Latin America and in Europe, abbreviated dates also follow this pattern. Halloween, for example, falls on 31/10. You may also see the numbers in dates separated by periods: 27.4.16. When referring to centuries, roman numerals are always used. The 16th century, therefore, is **el siglo XVI**.

# PESOS Y MEDIDAS

# WEIGHTS AND MEASURES

## Longitud
**El sistema métrico**
Metric system

## Length
**El equivalente estadounidense**
U.S. equivalent

**milímetro = 0,001 metro**
millimeter = 0.001 meter — = 0.039 inch
**centímetro = 0,01 metro**
centimeter = 0.01 meter — = 0.39 inch
**decímetro = 0,1 metro**
decimeter = 0.1 meter — = 3.94 inches
**metro**
meter — = 39.4 inches
**decámetro = 10 metros**
dekameter = 10 meters — = 32.8 feet
**hectómetro = 100 metros**
hectometer = 100 meters — = 328 feet
**kilómetro = 1.000 metros**
kilometer = 1,000 meters — = .62 mile
U.S. system — Metric equivalent
**El sistema estadounidense** — **El equivalente métrico**
inch — = 2.54 centimeters
**pulgada** — **= 2,54 centímetros**
foot = 12 inches — = 30.48 centimeters
**pie = 12 pulgadas** — **= 30,48 centímetros**
yard = 3 feet — = 0.914 meter
**yarda = 3 pies** — **= 0,914 metro**
mile = 5,280 feet — = 1.609 kilometers
**milla = 5.280 pies** — **= 1,609 kilómetros**

## Superficie
**El sistema métrico**
Metric system

## Surface Area
**El equivalente estadounidense**
U.S. equivalent

**metro cuadrado**
square meter — = 10.764 square feet
**área = 100 metros cuadrados**
area = 100 square meters — = 0.025 acre
**hectárea = 100 áreas**
hectare = 100 ares — = 2.471 acres
U.S. system — Metric equivalent
**El sistema estadounidense** — **El equivalente métrico**

**yarda cuadrada = 9 pies cuadrados = 0,836 metros cuadrados**
square yard = 9 square feet = 0.836 square meters
**acre = 4.840 yardas cuadradas = 0,405 hectáreas**
acre = 4,840 square yards = 0.405 hectares

## Capacidad
**El sistema métrico**
Metric system

## Capacity
**El equivalente estadounidense**
U.S. equivalent

**mililitro = 0,001 litro**
milliliter = 0.001 liter — = 0.034 ounces

**centilitro = 0,01 litro**
centiliter = 0.01 liter — = 0.34 ounces
**decilitro = 0,1 litro**
deciliter = 0.1 liter — = 3.4 ounces
**litro**
liter — = 1.06 quarts
**decalitro = 10 litros**
dekaliter = 10 liters — = 2.64 gallons
**hectolitro = 100 litros**
hectoliter = 100 liters — = 26.4 gallons
**kilolitro = 1.000 litros**
kiloliter = 1,000 liters — = 264 gallons
U.S. system — Metric equivalent
**El sistema estadounidense** — **El equivalente métrico**
ounce — = 29.6 milliliters
**onza** — **= 29,6 mililitros**
cup = 8 ounces — = 236 milliliters
**taza = 8 onzas** — **= 236 mililitros**
pint = 2 cups — = 0.47 liters
**pinta = 2 tazas** — **= 0,47 litros**
quart = 2 pints — = 0.95 liters
**cuarto = 2 pintas** — **= 0,95 litros**
gallon = 4 quarts — = 3.79 liters
**galón = 4 cuartos** — **= 3,79 litros**

## Peso
**El sistema métrico**
Metric system

## Weight
**El equivalente estadounidense**
U.S. equivalent

**miligramo = 0,001 gramo**
milligram = 0.001 gram
**gramo**
gram — = 0.035 ounce
**decagramo = 10 gramos**
dekagram = 10 grams — = 0.35 ounces
**hectogramo = 100 gramos**
hectogram = 100 grams — = 3.5 ounces
**kilogramo = 1.000 gramos**
kilogram = 1,000 grams — = 2.2 pounds
**tonelada (métrica) = 1.000 kilogramos**
metric ton = 1,000 kilograms — = 1.1 tons

U.S. system — Metric equivalent
**El sistema estadounidense** — **El equivalente métrico**
ounce — = 28.35 grams
**onza** — **= 28,35 gramos**
pound = 16 ounces — = 0.45 kilograms
**libra = 16 onzas** — **= 0,45 kilogramos**
ton = 2,000 pounds — = 0.9 metric tons
**tonelada = 2.000 libras** — **= 0,9 toneladas métricas**

## Temperatura
**Grados centígrados**
Degrees Celsius
To convert from Celsius to Fahrenheit, multiply by $\frac{9}{5}$ and add 32.

## Temperature
**Grados Fahrenheit**
Degrees Fahrenheit
To convert from Fahrenheit to Celsius, subtract 32 and multiply by $\frac{5}{9}$.

# NÚMEROS

## Números ordinales

| | | |
|---|---|---|
| primer, primero/a | 1º/1ª | |
| segundo/a | 2º/2ª | |
| tercer, tercero/a | 3º/3ª | |
| cuarto/a | 4º/4ª | |
| quinto/a | 5º/5ª | |
| sexto/a | 6º/6ª | |
| séptimo/a | 7º/7ª | |
| octavo/a | 8º/8ª | |
| noveno/a | 9º/9ª | |
| décimo/a | 10º/10ª | |

## Fracciones

| | | |
|---|---|---|
| $\frac{1}{2}$ | un medio, la mitad | |
| $\frac{1}{3}$ | un tercio | |
| $\frac{1}{4}$ | un cuarto | |
| $\frac{1}{5}$ | un quinto | |
| $\frac{1}{6}$ | un sexto | |
| $\frac{1}{7}$ | un séptimo | |
| $\frac{1}{8}$ | un octavo | |
| $\frac{1}{9}$ | un noveno | |
| $\frac{1}{10}$ | un décimo | |
| $\frac{2}{3}$ | dos tercios | |
| $\frac{3}{4}$ | tres cuartos | |
| $\frac{5}{8}$ | cinco octavos | |

## Decimales

| | |
|---|---|
| un décimo | 0,1 |
| un centésimo | 0,01 |
| un milésimo | 0,001 |

# NUMBERS

## Ordinal numbers

| | |
|---|---|
| first | 1st |
| second | 2nd |
| third | 3rd |
| fourth | 4th |
| fifth | 5th |
| sixth | 6th |
| seventh | 7th |
| eighth | 8th |
| ninth | 9th |
| tenth | 10th |

## Fractions

| | |
|---|---|
| one half | |
| one third | |
| one fourth (quarter) | |
| one fifth | |
| one sixth | |
| one seventh | |
| one eighth | |
| one ninth | |
| one tenth | |
| two thirds | |
| three fourths (quarters) | |
| five eighths | |

## Decimals

| | |
|---|---|
| one tenth | 0.1 |
| one hundredth | 0.01 |
| one thousandth | 0.001 |

## OCUPACIONES / OCCUPATIONS

|  |  |
|---------|---------|
| el/la abogado/a | lawyer |
| el actor, la actriz | actor |
| el/la administrador(a) de empresas | business administrator |
| el/la agente de bienes raíces | real estate agent |
| el/la agente de seguros | insurance agent |
| el/la agricultor(a) | farmer |
| el/la arqueólogo/a | archaeologist |
| el/la arquitecto/a | architect |
| el/la artesano/a | artisan |
| el/la auxiliar de vuelo | flight attendant |
| el/la basurero/a | garbage collector |
| el/la bibliotecario/a | librarian |
| el/la bombero/a | firefighter |
| el/la cajero/a | bank teller, cashier |
| el/la camionero/a | truck driver |
| el/la cantinero/a | bartender |
| el/la carnicero/a | butcher |
| el/la carpintero/a | carpenter |
| el/la científico/a | scientist |
| el/la cirujano/a | surgeon |
| el/la cobrador(a) | bill collector |
| el/la cocinero/a | cook, chef |
| el/la comprador(a) | buyer |
| el/la consejero/a | counselor, advisor |
| el/la contador(a) | accountant |
| el/la corredor(a) de bolsa | stockbroker |
| el/la diplomático/a | diplomat |
| el/la diseñador(a) (gráfico/a) | (graphic) designer |
| el/la electricista | electrician |
| el/la empresario/a de pompas fúnebres | funeral director |
| el/la especialista en dietética | dietician |
| el/la fisioterapeuta | physical therapist |
| el/la fotógrafo/a | photographer |
| el/la higienista dental | dental hygienist |
| el hombre/la mujer de negocios | businessperson |
| el/la ingeniero/a en computación | computer engineer |
| el/la intérprete | interpreter |
| el/la juez(a) | judge |
| el/la maestro/a | elementary school teacher |
| el/la marinero/a | sailor |
| el/la obrero/a | manual laborer |
| el/la obrero/a de la construcción | construction worker |
| el/la oficial de prisión | prision guard |
| el/la optometrista | optometrist |
| el/la panadero/a | baker |
| el/la paramédico/a | paramedic |
| el/la peluquero/a | hairdresser |
| el/la piloto | pilot |
| el/la pintor(a) | painter |
| el/la plomero/a | plumber |
| el/la político/a | politician |
| el/la programador(a) | computer programer |
| el/la psicólogo/a | psychologist |
| el/la quiropráctico/a | chiropractor |
| el/la redactor(a) | editor |
| el/la reportero/a | reporter |
| el/la sastre | tailor |
| el/la secretario/a | secretary |
| el/la supervisor(a) | supervisor |
| el/la técnico/a (en computación) | (computer) technician |
| el/la vendedor(a) | sales representative |
| el/la veterinario/a | veterinarian |

# Credits

## Television Credits

**184** By permission of Univision.com.
**220** By permission of Jean Marie Boursicot.
**256** By permission of Sancor Seguros.
**294** By permission of Andres Felipe Roa.
**326** By permission of Javier Ugarte (director).

## Photo and Art Credits

All images © Vista Higher Learning unless otherwise noted. Fotonovela photos provided by Carolina Zapata.

**Cover:** (full pg) © Aurora Open/Getty Images.

**Front Matter (SE): i** © Aurora Open/Getty Images; **xx** (l) © Bettmann/Corbis; (r) © Ann Cecil/Lonely Planet Images/Getty Images; **xxi** (l) © Lawrence Manning/Corbis; (r) © Design Pics Inc./Alamy; **xxii** Carlos Gaudier; **xxiii** (l) © Digital Vision/Getty Images; (r) © andres/Big Stock Photo; **xxiv** © Fotolia IV/Fotolia.com; **xxv** (l) © Goodshoot/Corbis; (r) © Ian Shaw/Alamy; **xxvi** © Shelly Wall/Shutterstock.com; **xxvii** (t) © Colorblind/Corbis; (b) © moodboard/Fotolia.com; **xxviii** (t) © Digital Vision/Getty Images; (b) © Purestock/Getty Images.

**Front Matter (TAE): T1** © Aurora Open/Getty Images; **T8** © Mike Flippo/Shutterstock.com; **T9** (l) © Jordache/Dreamstime.com; (r) © Jose Luis Pelaez Inc/Getty Images; **T24** © SimmiSimons/iStockphoto; **T25** © monkeybusinessimages/Big Stock Photo.

**Lección preliminar: 1** (full pg) © Somos/Media Bakery; **8** The Encounter between Hernando Cortes (1485–1547) and Montezuma II (1466–1520), from 'Le Costume Ancien et Moderne', Volume I, plate 63, by Jules Ferrario, published c.1820s-30s (colour engraving) © Gallo Gallina/Getty Images; **9** © Craig Lovell/Eagle Visions Photography/Alamy; **16** © Images.com/Corbis.

**Lesson Five: 151** (full pg) © Godfer/Fotolia.com; **162** © Gary Cook/Alamy; **163** (t) © AFP/Getty Images; (b) © Mark A. Johnson/Corbis; **167** © iofoto/Fotolia.com; **180** Carlos Gaudier; **181** (tl, tr, m, b) Carlos Gaudier; **182** Carolina Zapata; **186** (tl) © Nanniqui/Dreamstime.com; (tr) José Blanco; (ml) Carlos Gaudier; (mr) © Capricornis Photographic Inc./Shutterstock.com; (b) © Dave G. Houser/Corbis; **187** (tl, bl) Carlos Gaudier; (tr) © Lawrence Manning/Corbis; (br) © PhotoDisc/Getty Images.

**Lesson Six: 189** (full pg) © Asiapix Royalty-Free/Inmagine; **198** (l) © Jose Caballero Digital Press Photos/Newscom; (r) Janet Dracksdorf; **199** (t) © Carlos Alvarez/Getty Images; (bl) © Guiseppe Carace/Getty Images; (br) © Mark Mainz/Getty Images; **201** © Jack Hollingsworth/Corbis; **204** (tl, tm, tr, bl, bm, br) Pascal Pernix; **209** (tl, tr, bl, br) Martín Bernetti; **210** (t, b) Paula Díez; **211** Paula Díez; **216** Paula Díez; **217** Paula Díez; **218** © Chris Schmidt/iStockphoto; **219** Martín Bernetti; **222** (t, mtl, mtr, mb) Pascal Pernix; (b) © PhotoDisk/Getty Images; **223** (tl) © Don Emmert/AFP/Getty Images; (tr, bl) Pascal Pernix; (br) The Kobal Collection at Art Resource.

**Lesson Seven: 225** (full pg) Karen Montoya Betancur; **234** © Stewart Cohen/Blend Images/Corbis; **235** (t) Ali Burafi; (b) Janet Dracksdorf; **237** (l) © Blend Images/Alamy; (r) © Arekmalang/Dreamstime.com; **239** (l) Martín Bernetti; (r) © Ariel Skelley/Corbis; **242** José Blanco; **243** © Monkeybusinessimages/Dreamstime.com; **252–253** © DIDEM HIZAR/Fotolia.com; **254** © Traveler_no1/Dreamstime.com; **255** © Blend Images/Alamy; **258** (t, mtl, mtr) Martín Bernetti; (mbl) © Richard Smith/Corbis; (mbr) © Charles & Josette Lenars/Corbis; (b) © Yann Arthus-Bertrand/Corbis; **259** (tl) Martín Bernetti; (tr) © Mick Roessler/Corbis; (bl) © Jeremy Horner/Corbis; (br) © Marshall Bruce/iStockphoto.